AMERICA'S FORGOTTEN SUFFRAGISTS

Virginia and Francis Minor

NICOLE EVELINA

TWODOT®

ESSEX, CONNECTICUT
HELENA, MONTANA

A · TWODOT® · BOOK

An imprint of Globe Pequot, the trade division of
The Rowman & Littlefield Publishing Group, Inc.
4501 Forbes Blvd., Ste. 200
Lanham, MD 20706
www.rowman.com

Distributed by NATIONAL BOOK NETWORK

British Library Cataloguing in Publication Information available

Library of Congress Cataloging-in-Publication Data

Names: Evelina, Nicole, author.
Title: America's forgotten suffragists : Virginia and Francis Minor / Nicole Evelina.
Description: Essex, Connecticut ; Helena, Montana : TwoDot, [2023] | Includes bibliographical
   references and index.
Identifiers: LCCN 2022036079 (print) | LCCN 2022036080 (ebook) | ISBN 9781493067756
   (Cloth : acid-free paper) | ISBN 9781493067763 (epub)
Subjects: LCSH: Minor, Virginia Louisa, 1824-1894. | Minor, Francis. | Suffragists—United
   States—Biography. | Suffrage—United States.
Classification: LCC JK1898.5 .E94 2023 (print) | LCC JK1898.5 (ebook) | DDC 324.6/
   230973—dc23/eng/20221005
LC record available at https://lccn.loc.gov/2022036079
LC ebook record available at https://lccn.loc.gov/2022036080

♾™ The paper used in this publication meets the minimum requirements of American National
Standard for Information Sciences—Permanence of Paper for Printed Library Materials, ANSI/
NISO Z39.48-1992.

To Notorious RBG and all who have fought to make this quote true,
from Virginia and Francis onward.

Women belong in all places where decisions are being made.
It shouldn't be that women are the exception.
—RUTH BADER GINSBURG

The right of suffrage is as old, as sacred and as universal as the right to life, liberty and the pursuit of happiness. It is indeed the complement and safeguard of these and all civil and political rights to every citizen. . . . So it were mockery to talk of liberty and the pursuit of happiness, until the ballot in the hand of every citizen seals and secures it.
—PARKER PILLSBURY, "THE MORTALITY OF NATIONS," 1867

"Power Shared"

by Sara Knoll Dahmen

You see, women like us, we are not meant to be broken
and we are powerful and full of light and power
and our power is only as strong as the other women around us
and we are not meant to be tethered to men or any others
unless
those we choose for binding are powerful and full of their own light
but it is deeply powerful because it is not arrogant or needy
and is the happy match to our flame.
Only then can we be bound, to someone so strong they can let us fly
and without them we are nothing, for we would be alone
and yet with them we can be more.
We can take risks
and offer ourselves to other (women) who would be as powerful as we are
but are afraid to unleash their light, for fear
of being too bright.
But together we are greater.

Contents

INTRODUCTION

To give a list [of all the men and women who supported us] would
be impossible; for every name would require a eulogy too lengthy. . . .
We will, therefore, record them on the tablets of our memory, with a
hand so firm that they shall standout [sic] brightly till time shall be
no more.
—VIRGINIA MINOR TO SUSAN B. ANTHONY, FEBRUARY 6, 1869

ONE OBITUARY DESCRIBES SUFFRAGIST VIRGINIA MINOR AS WORKING
"hand-in-hand with Miss Susan B. Anthony, Mrs. Lucretia Mott, Mrs.
Julia Ward Howe and Mrs. Elizabeth Cady Stanton,"[1] while a modern
lawyer doesn't hesitate to call Virginia "the most prominent activist in the
early years of the [women's suffrage] movement."[2] Yet most people have
never heard of her or her equally important husband, Francis.

And if they are remembered, it is for their landmark Supreme Court
case, *Minor v. Happersett,* the outcome of which ended hopes for a
constitutional resolution to the question of female suffrage but, like the
Minors, is little known outside of historical and legal circles. This case
also radically altered the balance of power between state and federal
governments, fundamentally changing how American citizens see themselves. Moreover, the negative ruling is cited to this very day as an excuse
for oppressive voting measures, especially against minorities, an excuse
that the Minors, abolitionists and supporters of racial justice, would find
appalling. Nearly 150 years after it was tried, this case is only just beginning to be recognized for its true importance, being placed on a par with
the Dred Scott case for its immediate effects on women's suffrage and its
long-term effects on people of color.[3]

I

While the court case was certainly an important aspect of the Minors' lives, it was not the sum total, or even half, of their contribution to the suffrage movement. Francis was an influential writer, brilliant legal mind, and loving husband who not only empowered and supported his highly educated, freethinking wife, in an era when most women were expected to take their husband's will as gospel, but also made his own mark on the suffrage movement as one of its first and most vocal male allies.

In many ways, Virginia was even more a visionary than her more famous counterparts, founding the nation's first organization solely dedicated to women's suffrage—the Woman Suffrage Association of Missouri—two years before Anthony and Stone started their national organizations. Along with Francis, she was the brains behind the New Departure, a radical theory that the Fourteenth Amendment granted women the right to vote through the use of gender-neutral language. In addition, Virginia was a gifted orator, writer, and brazen activist who wasn't afraid to challenge the law when she felt it was unjust, through tactics such as refusing to pay her taxes, pleading for a condemned woman's life, or traveling cross-country with her better-known peers to stump for women's enfranchisement. She even thumbed her nose at the patriarchy in death, with her funeral wishes and in her will.

However, thanks to more than a century of education focused on a handful of "greats" like Anthony and Stanton, most people associate American women's fight for the ballot with only a few marquee names, while in reality, the women's suffrage movement involved thousands of people, all but a handful of whom have been forgotten.

One of the little-discussed effects of the resurgence in feminism from 2016 on has been an interest in uncovering and telling the stories of women unjustly excluded from the historical record. It is time for Virginia and Francis Minor to be recognized and take their rightful place among the key figures of the suffrage movement. Elevating them to greater visibility will allow future generations to learn from their shared passion that women's rights, which began with suffrage and are still being fought for today, are relevant to all. As women and their male supporters marked one hundred years of being able to influence politics through the vote and continue to fight for an Equal Rights Amendment, the Minors' example and Virginia's assertion that "we must have one law for all American citizens"[4] are more relevant than ever.

A Note on Terminology

Because it has been widely misused in the media and in common speech, much of the terminology around the women's suffrage movement can be confusing. Following are terms frequently used in this book, along with their meaning and an explanation of correct usage.

> **Suffrage.** The right to vote. Comes from the Latin *suffragium*, which can be translated as "vote," "support," or "prayer."[5]

> **Enfranchisement.** Admission of the privileges of a citizen, especially of the right of suffrage.[6] Used in this way from the year 1700. From the Old French *enfranchiss-*, present participle stem of *enfranchir*, "to set or make free."[7]

> **Suffragist versus Suffragette.** Properly speaking, "suffragist" is the correct term for an American woman involved in the suffrage movement. "Suffragette" was first used in 1906[8] and "was a derogatory term for a militant suffragist in England. Suffragist was preferred in the United States, as it denoted a less violent, more lady-like form of protest."[9]

> **Woman Suffrage versus Women's Suffrage.** "Woman" or "woman's" was used in the 1800s and early 1900s to denote all women, just as "man" included all men.[10] Because "women's" is now most commonly used, it is used in this book except for when the correct historical terminology of "woman" or "woman's" is needed in a quote or proper name.

PROLOGUE

The Turning Point

MAY 15, 1866

A deafening boom shattered the tranquility of Minoria, the Minors' country estate on the outskirts of St. Louis, sending songbirds squawking into the air and people rushing to find the source of the commotion. Even as the reverberation faded, the residents' skin crawled, for all recognized the sound: a gunshot—a sound never heard in this loving, peaceful home. It was followed almost immediately by shouts and screams as word passed that Francis Gilmer Minor, Virginia and Francis Minor's only child, was dead at the age of fourteen.

However, this was not the result of a suicide, murder, or even a duel of honor; it was a tragic accident. At the time, neither Francis nor Virginia had any idea what happened, because they were eating dinner while Francis Gilmer was outside shooting birds.[1] But an inquest later revealed the tragic circumstances: "He aimed the [double barrel shot]gun and cracked a cap but it did not go off. He walked around the yard and then commenced to examine his piece with the stock between his legs, and was trying to look into the barrel when the trigger slipped and the discharge of one of the barrels passed through his face causing death in a few minutes after."[2] His parents were told of the tragedy by a servant who had presumably accompanied Francis Gilmer outside.[3] No records indicate whether they had the chance to say farewell before their son died.

Virginia and Francis had been married for nine years when twenty-eight-year-old Virginia gave birth to their first and only child nearly a decade beyond the age at which most women of her time began having children.[4] Francis Gilmer, born February 5, 1852, was a beloved answer to many prayers. Lacking medical records or personal correspondence, one can only speculate, but it is possible the couple had trouble conceiving or that Virginia had suffered miscarriages, though no graves exist for children other than Francis Gilmer.

At the time, such childlessness was uncommon. Generally, women like Virginia—white, upper class, nonimmigrants—had six to nine pregnancies during their childbearing years,[5] though families of fifteen or more were not unheard of. Historian James Volo notes that "childlessness, according to the data, was so low as to be implausible."[6]

Francis and Virginia had been childless for nearly a decade, and now their only child was dead before his life had truly begun. They would not have much time over the coming days for private grief, however, as the closed-casket wake and funeral would take place in the parlor of their home over the next two days.

Because Minoria was five miles outside of the city, coaches were arranged to transport mourners from Fifth and Chestnut to the home beginning at 9:30 a.m.[7] Friends and family who attended those somber events would have seen signs of mourning long before they entered the house. The front door would have been adorned with a wreath of laurel, yew, or boxwood—all long associated with death—or a bow of crepe or ribbon. When they reached the entrance, they found the doorbell clappers and door knockers wrapped in crepe to create a reverential, respectful atmosphere for the family.[8]

Inside, all the clocks were stopped at the time of Francis Gilmer's death, the curtains drawn, and the mirrors, sculptures, and paintings[9] veiled in black—or possibly white since Francis Gilmer was not an adult[10]—creating a hushed, restful feel for those in mourning.[11]

Francis Gilmer's body, having been prepared either by his family or a professional woman known as a "layer-out of the dead,"[12] would have been placed in a coffin in the parlor. Usually, wakes lasted three to four days—in order to give mourners from far away time to arrive, to ensure the deceased was actually dead, and to symbolize the three days Jesus spent in the tomb[13]—but given the summer heat and the nature of Francis Gilmer's untimely death, this somber ritual was shortened to only two days.[14]

As head of the house, Francis, dressed in black and wearing a black or white armband or cockade, was duty-bound to remain outwardly stoic while receiving visitors even as he inwardly grieved. Given how stricken Virginia was, it is natural to wonder whether she was in any shape to accept condolences or if she had to keep herself closeted away with her tears. Neither she nor Francis left any personal journals, and none of the scant extant letters written by them recounts this time, but it is not difficult to imagine their pain as they faced the unimaginable. Both parents would likely have had memento mori made from their son's hair to remember him—such as a ring or watch chain for Francis and earrings, a necklace, or ring for Virginia[15]— though none is publicly extant.

As Episcopalians, the Minors held Francis Gilmer's funeral in their home the day following the wake at 11:00 a.m., according to newspaper accounts.[16]

As the mourners grieved in silence, pallbearers carried the coffin feet first out of the house through the front door[17] and loaded it into the horse-drawn hearse. The family followed, with friends and other mourners bringing up the rear. The procession wound through the streets of St. Louis for approximately four and a half miles, a distance that would have taken about an hour and a half to travel on foot at a reverential pace.

When Bellefontaine Cemetery[18] came into sight, the bell at its chapel began tolling, competing with the wails and sobs of the mourners to tell all passersby of the sad event about to take place. Years later, a cemetery gatekeeper who witnessed the funeral recalled that Virginia was "bereaved."[19] It is far too easy to picture her in flowing black widow's weeds and veil, weeping and relying upon others for support as she trudged the final steps to the grave site, where the minister offered the traditional prayer to commit her only child into the ground forever: "Forasmuch as it hath pleased Almighty God of his great mercy to take unto himself the soul of our dear brother here departed: we therefore commit his body to the ground; earth to earth, ashes to ashes, dust to dust; in sure and certain hope of the Resurrection to eternal life, through our Lord Jesus Christ; who shall change our vile body, that it may be like unto his glorious body, according to the mighty working, whereby he is able to subdue all things to himself."

After a few additional prayers, Francis and Virginia approached the bier to say their final farewell to their son and place flowers on his coffin.

With that, the ceremony was ended, and the Minors were left to their grief, which would publicly last over the next nine months, the mourning period for a child, but privately never cease.[20] Later, the grave-diggers would lower the coffin into the earth and place a small headstone bearing only his name: "Francis G. Minor."

CHAPTER ONE

The Minor Family

EVERY STORY, WHETHER FACT OR FICTION, HAS AN INCITING INCIDENT, a moment in which everything changes so drastically that, afterward, life will never be the same. For the Minors, that moment was the sudden death of their only child, which shook them to their core. For Francis, it was the end of his dreams of his son one day practicing law—an occupation that had practically run in the Minor blood since the founding of the country—and also possibly inheriting his own law firm and the family fortune.

However, for Virginia, the loss was much more than just personal; it was a blow to her very identity in Victorian America. She was not only a mother suffering through the anguish of burying her child but she had also lost her only remaining sense of purpose. Deprived of the invigorating activities she undertook during the Civil War, which will be discussed in detail in chapter 7, raising her son and looking after her household would have been Virginia's sole responsibilities. As described a few years later in *Godey's Lady's Book*, in Victorian society, "the perfection of womanhood . . . [was] the wife and mother, the center of the family, the magnet that draws man to the domestic altar that makes him a civilized being, social Christian. The wife is truly the light of the home."[1] Without motherhood as a purpose, Virginia was lost, and she sank into a deep melancholic malaise.

Fortunately for Virginia and for future generations of women, she did not wallow in grief for long. She found the inner strength to turn this

9

tragedy into triumph and transform "from a wife and bereaved mother to a dedicated activist [in] the following year."[2]

But before diving into the Minors' storied lives as suffragists, activists, and influences on state and national history, an understanding of their family and their early lives is necessary to put this profound change into context.

Tobacco Wealth as Family Foundation

Francis Gilmer Minor's death brought an end to a branch of the sprawling Minor family that dates back to early seventeenth-century America. It was through their ancestors that Virginia and Francis were born into the privilege that allowed them to act and think in ways others of their time could not.

The vast swaths of land their immigrant ancestors had acquired through grants from the Crown and cunning sales were put to good use by the planters of the early eighteenth century. Tobacco, or "tobo" as it was often informally called,[3] had made the Minors very wealthy, placing them in the top 3 percent to 10 percent of Virginia society.[4] They could now import luxury items from Europe such as crystal, wine, china, silver, and fashionable dresses[5] and transport themselves like the gentry of London, with great horses and carriages with attendants.[6] They also built large brick mansions in which dinner became an elaborate ritual of many courses to mimic those of fine English houses.[7] Like English feudal manors, their estates were nearly self-sufficient, with their own carpenters, blacksmiths, tanners, weavers, coopers, and members of other trades.[8] Here, women supervised everything from the household to "the dairy, the smokehouse, the poultry yard and the garden; they cut out all the slaves' clothing and supervised the sewing."[9]

This wealth also brought with it political power that enabled families like the Minors to firmly entrench themselves in law and politics.[10] As historian Timothy H. Breen asserts, "The great planters of Tidewater Virginia enjoy a special place in American history. They included some of the nation's ablest leaders, and without the likes of Washington [to whom Virginia and Francis were distantly related] and Jefferson [a close

Minor family friend], it is hard to see how Americans could have made good their claim to political independence."[11]

However, this power came at a cost. The planters sold their tobacco on consignment by shipping it to English or Scottish merchants, who sold it at the highest price, but the planters also purchased manufactured goods that they desired on credit.[12] Thus the planters became indebted to the merchants, and the planters viewed this as akin to being enslaved to their creditors.[13]

As a result of their financial uncertainty, tobacco became an obsession for the planter class.[14] Major planters could cultivate more than one hundred thousand plants but only if they were very careful, very lucky, and very hardworking; tobacco was one of the most labor-intensive crops grown at the time.[15] Unlike sugar or wheat, tobacco had to be closely tended and, in many cases, it was experience that determined the outcome. One mistake could mean the failure of the whole crop.[16]

This grueling schedule, which affected when men were available for all community activities, including court sessions and militia drills, was one of the reasons why wheat later became more popular. Because it was less demanding, elections, leisure time, and weddings could be reliably scheduled between planting and harvest, when the need for labor was low.[17]

To help ease the burden tobacco had become, many planters began growing other crops such as corn, hemp, flax, silk, cotton, and grapes.[18] By 1765, Virginia planters were quietly discussing ending tobacco cultivation altogether, a drastic step that had already been taken in Maryland.[19] By 1774, wheat was rapidly replacing tobacco as a staple crop.[20] It was easy to ship, kept well over long journeys, sold at prices up to twice that of corn and 50 percent higher than rye, and could be used to make large quantities of bread.[21] In addition, because of tobacco's association with the wealthy political class, it eventually became a symbol of loyalist sentiment, a dangerous association in a land that, as it rapidly headed toward revolution,[22] favored the common man's rights over those of the American "nobility."

As the Revolutionary War dragged into the 1780s, even those stubbornly clinging to tobacco saw the practical wisdom in switching to wheat: soldiers needed to eat.[23] But unlike in previous wars, the soldiers were not located in far-flung areas; they were now fighting in the back-yard of the producers of the wheat and the flour it was milled into.[24] In 1778, one mid-Atlantic miller reported milling more than 7,400 bushels—about half of what he'd purchased from local farmers—for the Continental Army.[25] Flour quickly became "the most valuable 'article of American commerce.'"[26]

The Revolutionary War may have brought about an end to tobacco culture and replaced it with "amber waves of grain" as the symbol of the new independent nation,[27] but it didn't free newly American citizens from their debt to British creditors.

A fledgling country with a debt-ridden economy was the inheritance that John Vivian Minor gained from his father and that he and subse-quent generations had to navigate.

John Minor, son of Garrett and Diane Minor, was a wealthy planter from Spotsylvania County, Virginia,[28] who also served as a captain in the Fairfax County Militia.[29] He was known as an intelligent and well-respected leader who "had a prominent place in the life of colonial Caroline"[30] County, where he married Sarah Carr, daughter of Captain Thomas and Mary Carr,[31] on November 14, 1732. Together, they had eleven children.[32]

As a wedding gift, his father-in-law gave him ownership of Sarah's childhood home, an estate called Topping Castle,[33] on the north bank of the North Anna River in Caroline County.

Three years later, on August 9, 1735, King George II granted twenty-eight-year-old John a Crown Patent for four hundred acres of land, called Gale Hill, in Hanover County, on "the North Fork of the north fork of the James River,"[34] for the sum of forty shillings.[35]

This probably seemed like ideal timing, as Sarah was pregnant with their first child,[36] and they would have been thinking of all the details associated with providing for a new family. The location was surrounded by other Minor family homes,[37] but John chose not to live on Gale Hill, making their home instead at Topping Castle.[38]

John reserved the Gale Hill land for agriculture, for along with the royal gift came the responsibility of "cultivating and improving at least twenty-four of the 400 acres within three years or forfeiting the title. This, in addition to paying 'fee rent' of one shilling per fifty acres or eight shillings a year."[39]

During those three provisional years, tobacco was the main crop of Albemarle County, and it would remain so for another few years. On April 26, 1748, John, a shrewd businessman, bought another four hundred acres of property adjacent to Gale Hill, an area called Waller Grant,[40] from John Waller Jr., who had obtained it on the same date John took possession of Gale Hill, so that by the time he died in 1755, John's children stood to inherit some eight hundred acres.[41]

John Vivian Minor is the last joint ancestor of Virginia and Francis Minor. His sons, John Minor II (the eldest and Virginia's great-grandfather) and Dabney Minor I (the eighth child and Francis's grandfather) are the point at which the family tree splits into two distinct branches.

FRANCIS MINOR'S FAMILY

Little record remains of Francis Minor's father, Dabney Minor II, born July 22, 1779, at Woodlawn, a plantation along the North Anna River in Virginia. He was a lawyer who handled land cases and executed wills,[42] though his tiny, cramped, nearly illegible handwriting better befits a doctor.[43]

He married Lucy Herndon on January 30, 1800.[44] They had nine children, of whom Francis was the second youngest. They lived on a "tract of land purchased from Joseph Alcock's estate"[45] in Orange County, Virginia.[46] The census of 1810 shows Dabney owning ten slaves and five horses,[47] a modest holding for the time neither indicative of poverty nor great wealth, which is in keeping with the fortunes of younger sons of the wealthy. An April 1798 appraisal of his estate valued it at $3,498,[48] or about $84,200 in today's currency.[49]

Francis was only two when his father died after a long, painful illness[50] on March 8, 1822,[51] at the age of forty-two. In an obituary, Dabney was described as "a man of great worth,"[52] which was likely more in reference to his character than his fortune.

His death threw the Minor family into chaos, which will be explored in greater detail in chapter 3, which covers Francis's youth. Dabney provided well for his family. He gave two-thirds of the land on which they lived to his wife, Lucy, and the other third to his daughter, Salley, plus a third of his land in Hanover County to little Francis. This was either split with Christopher Hudson of Albemarle County and Launcelot Minor of Louisa County or held in their ownership until Francis came of age; the will is unclear.[53]

In his will, Dabney also indicated that his estate should be sold, if needed, to fund his children's education and upbringing. "I earnestly desire no expense to be spared to give my children the best education which my estate can afford," he wrote.[54] In an age when most men were concerned with jealously preserving, if not enhancing, their wealth, it is an indication of Dabney's character, both as a man and as a father, that he was willing to do whatever necessary for his children to succeed, even if the family name was slightly diminished in the process.

The Minor family Bible records stop with his generation. Francis and his siblings are not included.

VIRGINIA MINOR'S FAMILY

Virginia Minor's distant relatives were more than bloodlines; they played a pivotal role in the founding of America. Three of her ancestors were members of the commission that sentenced the slaves and white indentured servant rebels in Bacon's Rebellion in 1676 for rising up against the local gentry.[55]

One hundred years later, another of Virginia's relatives—to whom she was related by two lines and eight generations[56]—General George Washington, expanded on Bacon's groundwork, leading the country to independence[57] and becoming the first president of the United States. Throughout her life, Virginia's "Washingtonian blood" was referenced in relation not only to her appearance but also to her independent spirit.[58]

But despite these famous relatives, it was her direct ancestors who most closely shaped Virginia and her revolutionary legacy.

Virginia's father, Warner Washington Minor, was born on November 22, 1792, the eldest child of William and Mildred Gregory Lewis Minor. He was described as a "man of notable presence and personality."[59] Nothing is known of his childhood.

It is likely that he served his country during the War of 1812. A Private Warner W. Minor is listed as fighting for twenty-three and a half days as part of Captain Bentley Brown's Company of the Seventy-Fourth Regiment of the Virginia Militia commanded by Colonel William Trueheart in 1813.[60]

Warner married Maria Timberlake on January 25, 1819. They had seven children, of whom Virginia Louise (or Louisa) was the second daughter and third eldest. Her older siblings were Lewis Madison Timberlake (1828–1874) and Mary Mildred Madison (1821–1843), and her younger sisters were Lucy Ellen (1826–1872), Maria Warner, who was born and died in 1827, and Harriet Ann (1828–1830), plus brother Warner W. (1830–1832).[61]

The children were raised with the help of enslaved people. Even though slavery was beginning to be criticized in Virginia,[62] the Minors owned eleven slaves in 1820[63] and by 1830 had increased their human property to thirty-nine slaves; they also employed nine free Blacks.[64]

Little is known about Warner's life between his marriage and 1825, other than he seems to have lost whatever fortune he had.[65] His plight was not uncommon, however, as 1820 was the beginning of Albemarle's "lean years," which would stretch decades beyond the Civil War.

Many contributing factors made this a tough time for the area. Slavery slowed the efficiency and productivity of a diversified agriculture that had branched out beyond tobacco into wheat and other grains and was quickly becoming the trend in more prosperous parts of the country. On top of that, generations of tobacco farming had worn out the fields, and farmers were facing competition from newly settled, richer lands out west. And in other parts of the country, "the first movement toward urban industrialization was beginning to take place, threatening to leave rural Albemarle behind."[66]

It is unclear where the family was living prior to 1825, when they moved to Charlottesville so Warner could take a job as one of the first "hotelkeepers" at the University of Virginia,[67] employed under Proctor Arthur Spicer Brockenbrugh.[68]

The boardinghouses on campus were called hotels and were separate from the dormitories.[69] The university had six hotels, named

A through F. Warner was in charge of Hotel C.[70] Each was a single story, except for F, which was two. They ranged from thirty-four to fifty feet in size. Each had a basement kitchen and, on the main floor, a large public dining room. Two small rooms made up the private quarters of the hotelkeeper and his family.[71]

Though a supervisory position, a hotelkeeper was not a job people would take if they could help it. "All [of the hotelkeepers] belonged to families that had somehow or another fallen on hard times,"[72] notes Marie Frank. The job was undesirable because it was expensive and thankless. As a hotelkeeper, Warner was responsible for watching over the students in his dormitory and providing their board, furniture, and linen.[73] Yet he was not hired outright. Frank explains:

Visitors rented each of the hotels for $200 per year. In a sense, therefore, the keepers ran their hotels much as independent boarding houses in a village. . . . They had to furnish all the furniture, not only for their own hotels but for the dormitory rooms of the students as well. They contracted for all supplies on their own and hired their own servants or brought their own slaves. They were responsible for feeding the students three times a day, cleaning and making fires in the student rooms, keeping their own building in shape, delivering firewood, water, and ice, and doing their own laundry.[74]

How well a hotelkeeper did financially depended upon the number of students boarded at the hotel.[75] Estimations from 1827 concluded that in order to make a profit, a hotelkeeper had to have at least thirty students. This was nearly impossible for half of the hotelkeepers, as only ninety-eight students boarded that year, so each hotel averaged only sixteen students.[76] The requirement that he supply provisions was a burden to Warner from the beginning. Adding to it was the expectation that he would buy or rent slaves to help oversee the students' needs.[77] He expressed worry that these expenses "would force me to quit this place" in several letters from March 1826 to 1830.[78]

To make money, some keepers kept a bit of the sum they received from the bursar based on the number of students they had.[79] The money was supposed to go toward supplying the students, but holding some back was an easy way to make a little profit.

Those with higher morals used the garden and lot that was a part of their holding to make money, usually by selling produce to one another or to students and faculty.[80] They also performed odd jobs like hauling wood or allowing guests to stay in their hotels during meetings and other events in exchange for a reduction in rent.[81] Warner Minor is on record as having hauled wood for the proctor, as well as for a man named George Long.[82] He also helped someone move house sometime between May 1827 and February 1828, for which he was paid twenty-eight dollars.[83]

Unable to take the strain any longer, Warner finally resigned in the fall of 1828.[84] No further record of his employment currently exists. The next mention of him is his sudden death on March 27, 1830, which left six-year-old Virginia and her siblings without a father, and her mother a widow with three young children.

The loss of the man of the house and provider of income was a severe blow to Virginia's family, but as they would do throughout her life, her fortunes rallied after the tragedy, presenting her with opportunities she otherwise might not have encountered. This once poor daughter of a hotelkeeper would go on to have a privileged education and marry into wealth that would decades later enable her to change the women's suffrage movement irrevocably.

CHAPTER TWO
A Suffragist's Girlhood Reconstructed

WHILE IT OFTEN SEEMED LIKE A PRISON TO HER FATHER, THE SPRAWL-
ing forty-four-acre campus of the University of Virginia—Thomas
Jefferson's "Harvard in Virginia"—probably felt more like a village out
of a fairy tale to young Virginia Minor, who had a certain degree of
freedom to roam the campus while her father toiled and her mother
tended their growing family. Together with the children of other hotelkeepers, with her siblings, or alone, Virginia came to know every inch
of the Academical Village, its surrounding woodland, and most of the
people who called it home.

On any given day, hundreds of uniformed students in suit coats[1] and
their harried professors skittered across the campus, not to mention the
hotelkeepers like her father, janitors, and other free and enslaved workers.
While Virginia's family was relatively small, numbering only nine people, many other campus households averaged more than twenty people.[2]
Slaves alone accounted for between one hundred and two hundred of the
residents,[3] though students were forbidden from "keep[ing] a servant"
while on campus; as such, the students would all be equal.[4] So great
were their numbers that the nonstudent population of the university was
almost equal to that of the students.[5]

With all those people in close quarters, it is little wonder that quiet
was a thing only to be found in the rotunda library on the north end of
campus. Outside, the grating of saws and clinking of hammers on nails
were a constant chorus as joiners, carpenters, masons, and other trades-

men continually made needed repairs or expanded the campus to keep up with an influx of students.[6]

As Virginia wandered past, someone always shouted a friendly hello, pausing while weeding a kitchen garden, whitewashing a wall, or carrying a load to or from the laundry. Mrs. Gray, the proctor's sister, and Mrs. Ward, sister of the proctor's wife—the only female hotelkeepers[7]—were particularly friendly. Virginia also frequently encountered the university's bell ringer Lewis Commodore, a slave owned by Dabney Carr Minor, a descendant of John Minor, the great-grandfather of Francis Minor and Virginia's great-great grandfather.[8]

Though the Academical Village was nearly self-sufficient, there were occasions when Virginia's mother or father took her and her siblings along on the short mile-and-a-half journey into Charlottesville,[9] down Three Notch'd Road (today called Main Street), which connected the town and university.[10] Founded in 1762, Charlottesville wouldn't become a bustling city for another two decades, when railway service began in 1850,[11] but the rural village was a godsend for the university. Here, the air was clearer—not so many hogs, cattle, chickens, and privies making it fetid[12]—and it supplied the university and its residents with goods, such as nails, locks, brown linen, and blankets, and services, such as tailoring.[13]

Besides the hotel in which she lived, the area of the school Virginia would have been most intimately acquainted with was the schoolroom in a dormitory on the East Range. While the rest of the East Range was reserved for outstanding graduate students,[14] this room was set aside for the education of the children of instructors and workers.[15] It was run by Thomas Swann, the son-in-law of Mrs. Ward, the keeper of Hotel D.[16] From him, the students in schoolrooms 16 and 18[17] learned the fundamentals of reading, writing, and arithmetic,[18] the same subjects they would have been taught at home by their families under normal living arrangements. For many of these children, this would have been the sum total of their education; but Virginia was fortunate—especially for a girl—to continue her learning later in life. However, her idyllic world was about to be upended and her education put on hold as her family fought the vagaries of misfortune.

~

Born March 27, 1824, in Caroline County, Virginia was only six years old when her father died suddenly on March 27, 1830, and her cozy campus life came to an end. Now fatherless, and with her mother, Maria Timberlake Minor, distracted by the worries of widowhood and providing for Virginia and her siblings, Virginia faced a situation that required her to mature quickly. The family affairs, which Warner would normally have handled, devolved into disorder, forcing her mother and siblings to depend on male relatives to take them in and care for them as best as possible.[19] John L. Pendleton, a clerk of the Caroline County Court,[20] was appointed guardian ad litem for the children,[21] but beyond that, the historical record is mute regarding the first fifteen years after Warner Washington Minor's death. It is possible the family struggled, just as they had during their years at the university, but as they were related to several other prominent Minors in the state of Virginia, among them wealthy landowners and law professors at the University of Virginia,[22] it is equally possible their relatives furnished a comfortable lifestyle.

Virginia's family was described by a descendant as "a strong, outspoken, liberal-oriented family."[23] Their status as part of the area's elite was cemented in 1839, when William Timberlake, Maria's uncle, petitioned the Court of Caroline County on her behalf to grant her access to the houses and half of the eighty-five and three-quarter acres of land to which she and Warner were heirs through the Timberlake line. They intended to sell the land, which was worth $300 a share or $4 per acre (just over $8,400 in today's currency),[24] and divide the profits, once all creditors were paid among its rightful heirs, to help support her and the children.[25] The land was resurveyed and was sold at public auction on September 13, 1839, as three separate tracts. The one belonging to Maria was sold for $1,301 ($36,187 today).[26] After expenses, she ended up with $1252.90[27] (or just under $35,000 today),[28] a healthy sum with which to raise her children and continue her life.

THE EDUCATION OF A FUTURE ACTIVIST

Virginia appears to have lived a comfortable life from then on, as the Minors are known to have had many slaves, as did most residents of the area. Approximately 635 heads of families owned slaves, with some of the highest numbers (over 100) belonging to Dabney Minor and Thomas Jefferson.[29] There are several Dabney Minors in the Minor family tree. It is likely this reference is to Dabney Carr Minor, who is a distant relation to Francis.

Even if that did not hint at a rise in the Minors' fortunes, Virginia received an education that was usually reserved for only those of means, though the government and the charitable hearts of local wealthy women did make tuition affordable for a select few poor girls.[30]

Several biographical profiles of Virginia state that she "spent a short period at a Charlottesville female academy,"[31] but the name of the school is never mentioned. Source material for schools established around 1820 is very limited[32] and no definitive records as to where Virginia attended school are extant, but it is highly likely she was a student at Edgehill (sometimes spelled Edge Hill) School for Young Ladies in Charlottesville, a small building within sight of Thomas Jefferson's mountain home at Monticello.

Formal female education in Virginia dates back to around 1750, when schools for young ladies were established to teach them subjects such as French, dancing, drawing, and specialized ornamental stitching called fancy work,[33] the skills a wealthy woman needed in order to be a good wife and circulate in high society.

Thanks to the influence of Thomas Jefferson and his family, these schools began to expand and formalize in the late eighteenth and early nineteenth centuries. Jefferson, an avowed lover of education, may have reserved higher education for male students, but he didn't neglect female learning, as seen in this November 1783 letter to his eleven-year-old daughter, Patsy:

> *With respect to the distribution of your time the following is what I should approve.*
>
> *from 8. to 10 o'clock practise music.*
> *from 10. to 1. dance one day and draw another.*

*From 1. to 2. draw on the day you dance, and write a letter the next
day.
From 3. to 4. read French.
From 4. to 5. exercise yourself in music.
From 5. till bedtime, read English, write [i.e., practice penmanship,]
&c.*

*. . . Write also one letter every week. . . . Take care that you never spell
a word wrong.*

*Always before you write a word consider how it is spelt, and, if
you do not remember it, turn to a dictionary. It produces great praise
to a lady to spell well.*[34]

Later in life, Jefferson directed the education of six granddaughters
and talked of creating a "ladies seminary" at Monticello.[35] That never
came to pass, but two of his daughters, Mary and Martha (Patsy), his
grandson, and three great-granddaughters would make this dream a reality at the nearby Edgehill School only two years after his death.[36]

The Edgehill plantation had been part of the Randolph family since
1735, when William Randolph of Tuckahoe was given a land grant of
2,400 acres from King George II. Thomas Mann Randolph Jr. inherited it in 1790 when he married Thomas Jefferson's daughter Martha.[37]
Within thirty years, Randolph found himself in debt and had to sell the
property, which his son, Thomas Jefferson Randolph, purchased on January 2, 1826. He was Thomas Jefferson's favorite grandson and would later
serve as executor to his estate.[38]

Located about five miles east of Charlottesville, along the Chesa-
peake and Ohio Railroad,[39] the Edgehill mansion was situated high on
a hill in a grove of "magnificent old trees" that framed the Piedmont
Valley and had "glorious views" of the Blue Ridge Mountains, and of
Monticello, on a clear day.[40] The house itself was a "modest two-story,
wood frame house with a brick foundation . . . measuring forty-four feet
by eighteen feet. Its value was recorded at $1800" in June 1823.[41] This is
roughly $44,300[42] in today's currency.

Like many homeowners then and now, Randolph wished to expand his residence. However, in order to build the brick mansion he envisioned at the crest of the hill, he had to have the original wood building rolled lower down the hill[43] using large logs.[44] In the process, the slaves rolled it over a group of tulip poplar saplings. But instead of breaking, they lay flat and grew into beautiful trees that the house became known for.[45]

The wood building became the Edgehill School. While it may seem odd today to open a private school on one's property, it was commonplace in the early nineteenth century. According to Olivia Taylor, who has written extensively about Edgehill:

> *In early Virginia days, education of children was most often performed through home or family schools. When there were a number of young people in a family and the house was large, very often neighbors' and friends' children were brought together to be taught by a tutor or governess engaged for this purpose. So it is not uncommon to find a separate "school house" erected for this reason.*[46]

The Edgehill School was founded in 1828 to help pay off some of the debts Col. Thomas Jefferson Randolph (also known as T. J.) inherited from his father and grandfather,[47] as well as to educate his daughters and those of his relatives and friends.[48] The first class consisted of only six girls taught by T. J.'s wife, Mrs. Jane Nicholas Randolph. The students affectionately called T. J. "Grandpa."[49] As the number of students increased, more teachers were hired, and the family advertised to prospective students in the Circular of Edge Hill School, referring to their students as "ladies of attainment and culture."[50] The family also built an addition onto the back of their brick mansion to serve as a dormitory.[51] Students were now allowed to spend summer vacation at the school.[52] With these changes, the family's Edgehill School became "one of the first boarding schools for girls in the State and was the beginning of the famous school which for long held a unique place in Southern life."[53]

Edgehill was arranged into two classes: the primary class and the senior class, with students attending two sessions a year, divided by a summer break. Records for tuition and housing arrangements in the dormitories no longer exist, but one can assume they were similar to those of Charlottesville Female Academy, which had closed in 1829 or 1830. There, tuition for each five-month session "ranged from about $60 to $78 in the first or junior class; and from $65 to $75 in the second or senior class." There were extra charges for music, French, Latin, drawing and painting.[54] In addition, "the charge for fuel, washing, and board was $60 per session [and] each young lady was required to furnish her own bed and bed linen."[55]

Virginia's elder cousin by ten years, Mary Waters Minor, attended Edgehill,[56] so it is reasonable to believe Virginia would have carried on the family legacy there. Mary's daughter,[57] Margaret Randolph Minor Bryan, also was an alumna of the school. Late in life, Margaret recounted that when Edgehill taught proper manners, they meant business. The students dined at a formal table "perfectly arranged with glass and silver," eating food that was "meager, but of good quality."[58]

Margaret recalled her mother telling the following story: "If a pupil should happen to put her elbow, or even the rest of her arm on the table, the dignified head butler would appear beside her with a waiter [a type of tray] on which lay a small bag of nails. He would respectfully lift the offending elbow, place the bag of nails beneath it, and put the elbow back on the bag."[59]

Decorum and social graces were not the only subjects taught at Edgehill. The courses included English, which was described as "the study of history and literature"[60] and was taught by Mrs. Randolph herself; grammar; geography; mathematics (including arithmetic, algebra, geometry, and trigonometry); philosophy; sciences (including chemistry, astronomy, geology, botany, and physiology); and the natural history of Greece, Rome, England, France, Germany, and the United States.

To teach these subjects, the teachers borrowed textbooks from the nearby University of Virginia.[61] It is also possible that some of the University of Virginia professors gave guest instruction at the school,[62] especially given the Minor family's association with the school. So while these girls may not have formally attended the university and been awarded degrees, they were nonetheless benefiting from its educational offerings.

In addition, Edgehill taught music, art, and three languages. Each of these departments awarded prizes and medals to high-achieving students. Music education included everything a woman could need to entertain at parties, whether her talent lay in playing an instrument, singing, or both: vocal training, lessons on various instruments, chorus practice, and theory of music.

No well-rounded society woman's education was complete in the early nineteenth century without some training in art. Edgehill offered classes in drawing, "painting in China," watercolor, and oil painting.[63]

There is no way of knowing which language classes, if any, Virginia took, as the historical record doesn't show her speaking or writing in any language but English. However, if she had taken German, it may have served her well later in life, given St. Louis's large German population and the importance of Germans in the suffrage movement. She could also have chosen French or Latin.

Once their three-year course of education was complete, each student received a diploma, and the four best students were given medals. Those who did not complete the full three years were awarded diploma medals at the end of their studies.[64]

Virginia's Appearance and Comportment

Between graduation and marriage, Virginia lived at home, under the watchful eyes of her mother. Here she learned domestic arts, which she would need as a wife and mistress of a household. She also assisted with rearing her younger siblings, which trained her to be a mother, and she was instructed in the rules of manners and civility, which were highly valued in society.

While out in society but not yet engaged, she would have been chaperoned by her mother, brothers, or an intimate family friend at public events such as theater or dances.[65] She was expected to rebuff any male attention and maintain a polite disinterest in courtship. As the anonymous author of *The Young Lady's Friend* (1837) writes, "The less your mind dwells upon lovers and matrimony, the more agreeable and profitable will be your intercourse with gentlemen. Regard men as intellectual beings who have access to certain sources of knowledge to which you are denied."[66] This last line would likely have raised an eyebrow for Virginia, who believed in intellectual equality and didn't seem to fear "becoming [an] unmarriageable bluestocking,"[67] despite her education and feminist leanings.

Acceptable behavior for a young woman was to reflect "delicacy and refinement" when in the company of young men,[68] but those words could have been used to describe Virginia at any point in her life. By her teenage years she had already engendered a reputation of respectability she would carry with her until death.[69] Family letters describe her as "beautiful, intelligent, known for having 'ladylike manners' and possessing an 'old-fashioned charm.'"[70] She was also called "spirited" and noted for her "talent for organization and management,"[71] which would be vital during the Civil War and during the early years of the suffrage movement in Missouri. Interestingly, Virginia was also known for being a "deeply religious woman,"[72] though she would turn against the clergy of all religions later in life for their opposition to female suffrage.

In *History of Woman Suffrage*, Susan B. Anthony and Elizabeth Cady Stanton affectionately christened Virginia the "dove with the eagle's heart."[73] The *St. Louis Republic*'s glowing obituary paints a portrait of a strong-willed, energetic, yet compassionate woman who championed the rights of all women, not just those of the refined class:

> In every experience, whether joy or sorrow, Mrs. Minor was a faithful and loving wife. Her character presented many phases, and its influence is deeply and extensively felt. To a high order of intelligence she united mental energy and strong will power. She was deeply informed upon a variety of subjects, having in particular, a taste for politics and public affairs. Though of distinguished lineage, Mrs. Minor was in thorough sympathy with the practical workers of life, regarding with particular tenderness her sister women who live by the sweat of their brow.[74]

Only two images of Virginia remain to give us an idea of her appearance. The black-and-white engraving created by John Chester Buttre (based on a photograph by J. A. Scholten and held by the Library of

Congress) is considered her official portrait, but its accuracy is a matter of debate because it may not have been created during her lifetime. Another photograph of Virginia is contained in the book *The Life and Work of Susan B. Anthony: Including Public Addresses, Her Own Letters and Many from Her Contemporaries during Fifty Years, Volume I*,[75] by Ida Husted Harper, which was written and published while Virginia lived.

In both images, which are remarkably similar, she is depicted in middle age, with light, curly chestnut hair[76] parted in the middle and pulled back into a bun. She has a high forehead with the slightest indication of wrinkles, arched eyebrows that lend her an air of surprise, "fiery"[77] oval eyes, and a thin nose over lips that are neither thin nor plump. Her posture is erect and her bearing regal. Her neck is covered by a sheer white scarf tucked into a dark-colored jacket. In the Buttre image, her jacket is embroidered, and she wears an oval pin on her left breast and a rose at her throat. In the one that appears in Harper, the rose, jacket detail, and pin are gone, but one shiny button is visible at the top of the right lapel. She appears to be wearing neither makeup nor jewelry in either image.

The *St. Louis Post-Dispatch* described Virginia as "petite and sweet looking."[78] Her attractiveness in her youth is undoubtable, as upon her death one newspaper described her as having high color in her cheeks or "the Washington blood"[79] in her face. In her youth, she was a beauty, and even at seventy, her face retained a delicacy and refinement that years could not obliterate.[80] Another wrote that she was "noted for her beauty among the beaux of the Old Dominion."[81]

As a Virginian, it is perhaps not surprising that she carried with her the genteel manner for which its women are known. One reporter attending a lecture she gave in West Virginia recorded that Virginia had a "high-bred Southern accent in her voice, and the high-bred Southern grace in her every movement."[82] Jessie Waite of Chicago observed in 1883 that "her manner has all the gentleness and sweetness of the high-born Southern lady. . . . Mrs. Minor spoke in a calm, deliberate manner, with perfect conviction in the truth of her statements and with a winning sweetness of expression that indicated the highest sensibilities of a refined nature."[83]

Virginia's elegance was reflected in her dress as well. Unlike Victoria Woodhull and other dress reformers of the time, who cast off their corsets and bustles in favor of more freeing, comfortable clothing—even sometimes donning men's breeches—Virginia preferred the female fashions of her day. Scholar Donna Monnig suspects this is why she was held in higher regard than her more radical counterparts. "Dressing as a traditional woman thus helped her argument by showing people first hand [*sic*] that she, a perfect lady, was just as capable of conducting public, political affairs the same as any man."[84]

Regardless of the cause, Virginia's intelligence and reputation as a "respectable radical"[85] gave her an advantage over her contemporaries. As later chapters will show, it allowed her to express forward-thinking beliefs, openly protest against taxation without representation, call out elected officials in writing and in speeches, and even break the law without enduring castigation in the press or being portrayed as a sexless shrew as so many other suffrage leaders were. While many suffragists based their rhetoric in vitriol and vinegar, she preferred using honey to get the attention of those in power—beginning with her future husband, Francis Minor.

CHAPTER THREE

Boyhood Tragedy Enables Future Success

What went through Francis Minor's mind as he sat among the semicircle of graduates during the College of New Jersey's (renamed Princeton University in 1896) commencement exercises on September 29, 1841?[1] It is possible he said a prayer that his father, who had died more than two decades prior, was looking down from heaven and would be proud. Like him, Francis was now a lawyer and would carry on the family legacy.

Chances are good he experienced the same nervous excitement tinged with relief that graduates of all time periods feel—and perhaps a little more, for he had been selected to speak just before the valedictorian address and the official conferring of degrees. Francis's speech, "The Ariosto of the North,"[2] "depicted with a skillful hand"[3] the work of Romance poet and novelist Sir Walter Scott, to whom Lord Byron had given the titular honorific.[4]

This was the culmination of a Saturnalia-like[5] week of graduation activities with family, friends, alumni, and community members,[6] including more speeches, parties, and balls than Francis expected to attend in a lifetime.[7] The previous afternoon at the Presbyterian church, Peter McCall Esq., of Philadelphia, an alumnus (1826)[8] and member of the Philadelphia bar,[9] had given a speech before the American Whig and Cliosophic Societies—the former of which Francis was a member—about "the assumed favorable influence of free institutions upon the arts of sculpture, poetry, painting, music and eloquence."[10]

While not overly exciting, it was better than the proslavery speech couched as a commencement address Francis had feared. Though officially the speaker's remarks were meant to "imbue Princeton students with a sense of civic responsibility . . . [and] express and legitimate particular moral, social, and political philosophies intended to guide new graduates in their endeavors beyond campus,"[11] from 1800 through the beginning of the Civil War, speakers often chose to use this platform to air their views about slavery. Despite Princeton being located in the North, from 1838 on, the speaker's views were increasingly proslavery.[12] Francis's were not.

He recalled all too well the stories about what had happened just five years earlier when commencement turned into a particularly nasty event— Theodore S. Wright, Princeton Theological Seminary's first African American graduate and by then an abolitionist and Presbyterian minister, was brutally attacked and forcibly removed from commencement:

> *Following the address, the son of a Southern slaveholder and member of Princeton's junior class followed Wright from the chapel, shouting "Out with the nigger! Out with the nigger!" before grabbing Reverend Wright by the collar and kicking him "in the most ruthless manner." Addressing the incident, Princeton President James Carnahan absolved the college of any responsibility, claiming that the man who beat Wright was not a student nor even a resident of the town. Describing Wright only as a "respectable colored man of New-York," President Carnahan did not note in his letter that Wright had a connection to the neighboring school, or that, like himself, Wright was an ordained Presbyterian minister. The response from college officials echoed the conservative, pro-slavery tone evident in so many Princeton commencement addresses.*[13]

Given this history, Mr. McCall's address with its praise of freedom and free education was particularly striking and was a reminder to twenty-one-year-old Francis that he could live his life as he pleased, even if his abolitionist views didn't match those increasingly voiced at Princeton and in his home state of Virginia.

~

Unlike most of his siblings, Francis Minor,[14] born August 15, 1820, in Albemarle, Virginia, had no memory of his father, who had died of a "protracted and painful illness"[15] when Francis was only two. However, Francis grew up in the knowledge that his father was a good man. He had held a respectable job as an attorney and was described upon his death as a "protector and friend."[16]

What he did recall was the upheaval the death brought to his large family; in addition to caring for ten children—Mary Ann (1801–1833), Ann Meriwether (1803–1872), James Lewis (1805–1826), Dabney (1806), Henry Laurens (1807–1832), Cordelia Lewis (1810–1843), Ellen (1811–1826), Dabney III (1814–1862), John Mercer (1816–1831),[17] and himself—his mother, Lucy Herndon, had a large estate[18] and dozens of slaves to manage in her grief. The Minor family Bible lists slaves (first name, son/daughter of, birthdate) on the front and end papers for the years 1700 through 1823. There are sixty names in total.[19]

Being mistress to a large plantation in the wake of the death of a master was not easy. Lucy now oversaw 1,100 acres, including a large manor house; 600 acres of cultivated land that produced corn, oats, hay, and fodder; as well as extensive forests fed by springs; apple, peach, and other fruit orchards; and livestock, including oxen, horses, cattle, pigs, and sheep.[20] There was the added responsibility of minding the dozens of slaves who worked the fields and served in the house. Even if she had an overseer to help manage them, there was no guarantee they would listen to her or behave as they had when Dabney was alive.[21] As historian Robert Olwell notes, "A 'female master' was a contradiction in terms" because it went against the "patriarchal system that held both slaves and women in check."[22]

No information is available on Lucy Herndon's character or temperament. She may have been a strong, stern woman who shouldered her new burdens with steely resolve. It is worth noting that many Southern women, no matter how genteel, found this resolve within themselves during the Civil War, when they were forced to carry on without their husbands, so it is possible the death of a husband could bring about the same result.

But females such as this were few and far between in the genteel world of early nineteenth-century, upper-class Virginia, where plantation mistresses were used to being obedient to their husbands.[23] Their job was to see to the provision of a "well-ordered table, [and] well cooked, well prepared food,"[24] which meant supervising only house slaves and those who produced domestic goods, such as clothing,[25] and the vast majority of those slaves were women. It is unlikely that Lucy was prepared to manage the entire estate and its human and physical property on her own, a duty she usually relied upon her husband to fulfill. After all, she had not had to issue orders to or confront problems with the male slaves before.[26]

Historian John Hope Franklin notes that it was common for widows to have trouble managing their slaves. "When a husband died and control went to the widow, slaves considered how they might undermine the new regime,"[27] he writes. Some caused trouble—innocent mischief, like sneaking away at night to drink or gamble—or became lax in their duties, but others were physically threatening. Some took advantage of the change in power to run away.[28] When mistresses had misgivings about ordering male slaves to do things, male relatives and friends could step in for a short period,[29] but in the long term, it was her responsibility. The constant threat of uprising[30] "created emotional and psychological strains that brought some women to the edge of a breakdown," especially when they also had young children to care for.[31]

Regardless of what may have happened, Lucy must have managed to eventually earn the respect of her slaves, because upon her death, the plantation was home to more than thirty.

Wealth came to Francis at an early age through death and inheritance. On March 27, 1831, Francis's grandmother, Ann Minor, died and bequeathed her slaves Nelson and his brother Moses to her daughter Sarah Gilmer and divided the others among Sarah's children. Ann also divided the unnamed parts of her property and estate between her "daughters Sarah Elizabeth Anderson, and Sarah Gilmer, and the children of my deceased son Dabney Minor, that is one third to each of my said daughters, & the remaining third to the children of my said son, to them & their heirs forever."[32] The exact size of this third of her land is unknown, but even divided among Francis and his then four living siblings—two would die within the next two years—it guaranteed him a measure of wealth at the tender age of twelve.

On August 12, 1832, just three days shy of his thirteenth birthday, Francis suffered another devastating loss: that of his mother.[33] From her will, he inherited half of the $8,000 earned from the sale of her uncle's slaves, who numbered at least thirty-seven, according to a family receipt book.[34] The other half went to his brother, Dabney III.[35] Woodlawn was divided and the upper part of it was bought by Thomas Estes in 1833, with Francis receiving a significant sum for his share.[36] The lower part of the estate appears to have remained as a residence for the Minors until it was sold in 1845 or 1846.[37]

By the time Francis was eighteen, many of his siblings had passed away, which at least one scholar attributes to cholera.[38] The boy who had begun life with two parents and a large family surrounded by friends, relatives, and slaves was now an orphan with only three of his older siblings left to lean on: his brother, Dabney III, who lived in Holly Springs, Mississippi, and sisters Cordelia, who had married Dr. Samuel Hopson Dabney in 1829;[39] and Ann Meriwether, who married Peter Scales, executor of her mother Lucy Herndon's estate, in 1827.[40]

A LAWYER'S EDUCATION

When Francis was old enough to attend university, he was a wealthy man determined to follow in the footsteps of several generations of ancestors by becoming a lawyer. He attended two of the best law schools in the country, beginning with Princeton, where he was a student from 1838 to 1841, and then studying for a year at the University of Virginia.

During his time at Princeton, Francis was a member of the "old-time Whig Club"—also called the "Plain Dealing Club" and the "American Whig Society" at the time and today known as the American Whig-Cliosophic Society.[41] It is the oldest college literary and debating club in the United States and counts notable figures such as James Madison among its alumni.[42] The purpose of the club was to "develop and sharpen the skills of persuasion, exposition, and cooperation (and conflict) with peers,"[43] skills that certainly helped advance Francis's law career.

Membership in this club was historically said to signify "adherence to ancient principles of British political and religious dissent, principles that later found concrete form in the Revolution and in the founding of the American Republic."[44] This may well have been the beginning of Francis's interest in political advocacy, and he was well-versed in the writings of the Founding Fathers and the ideals that powered the American Revolution, both of which he heavily relied upon in his interpretation of the Constitution to the Supreme Court in 1875.

After graduating in 1841, Francis "was entitled to higher degrees afterward from Princeton, but he never cared for them and never claimed them."[45] This likely refers to the common practice that three years after they earned their bachelor's degrees, if they met certain criteria, students could be eligible for a master of arts degree. Some specialties were automatically eligible, while others might be required to defend a thesis or conduct additional study.[46] Regardless, Francis never claimed his.

Instead, he enrolled in the University of Virginia Law School,[47] where he pursued advanced studies as part of the senior class from 1842 to 1843.[48] Francis studied under Professor Henry St. George Tucker, who was also chairman and head of the faculty[49] and had previously served as a Democratic-Republican member of the US House of Representatives, Virginia state senator, superior court judge in Winchester and Clarksburg, and president of the Virginia Court of Appeals.[50] His classes focused on "the theory and practice of Law, as a profession," and included common and statute law, the principles of equity, and maritime and commercial law.

Each lecture was evaluated based on performance on midterm and final exams. Francis's exam for a course in municipal law still exists in his student file. While it is probable that his answers were typical for any student, two hint at subjects that would soon become important factors in his life once he was married. One answer contrasts Virginia law with that of its English predecessors, including the execution of an adult's estate versus that of an infant[51]—the latter category including married women. Another answer concerns marriage and inheritance law, which shows he may have already been aware of the injustice of the laws he would later defy in his own marriage.[52]

Upon graduation in 1843, Francis was awarded the title bachelor of law and was considered a licensed lawyer in the state of Virginia.[53]

A MAN OF MYSTERY

History is frustratingly devoid of many key details about Francis as a person, such as his appearance. No images of him remain to give us an idea of what the young lawyer may have looked like. The only physical sketch of his appearance comes from late in his life, when he was described as "the mild, gentlemanly-looking man with the silver hair."[54] However, given the many attestations of the love between Virginia and Francis, one can safely assume Virginia thought him handsome.

Francis apparently had at least a moderate southern drawl. An amusing incident recorded in the *St. Louis Republic* on what must have been a slow news day recounts a friendly disagreement between Francis and Judge Samuel Treat on the pronunciation of the word "acoustic." Francis pronounced it "acowstic," "giving the oow sound plumply." The judge asked him to consult a dictionary, preferably Worcester, Walker, or Webster. Thereupon they found Mr. Minor in the right. The article goes on to note that Francis "recognizes Webster as a standard for all English speaking [*sic*] people."[55]

Francis's temperament is also only hinted at in existing sources, but looking at his actions helps fill in the gaps. He had a reputation for having a sober personality, often described as reserved,[56] but was known to be happy and outgoing when he spoke publicly.[57] He took his work as a lawyer very seriously, and was known for his intelligence and ability to craft a clever argument.[58] Francis's writings on women's suffrage and his legal actions with regard to Virginia's rights show he had an open mind and liberal leanings. He was unafraid to air his views in public, even if they were controversial, which hints at self-confidence, though no one ever accused him of vanity.[59] He appears to have been fun-loving as well, laughing and joking with friends at get-togethers and literary salons in St. Louis. After his death, Francis's friends would remember him fondly, indicating he was a kind soul who was loved as much as he gave love, especially where Virginia was concerned.

CHAPTER FOUR

Courtship, Marriage, and Three Years in Holly Springs, Mississippi

VIRGINIA'S EYES SWEPT THE CROWDED BALLROOM, TAKING IN THE FACES of friends, family, and neighbors, all of whom had gathered for a night of fellowship and fun. Or at least that was the official story. Every woman in the room knew the real purpose of such a gathering: to show off their eligible daughters of marriageable age and, God willing, make a match with one of the bachelors present.

Virginia let out a sigh of relief. Though she was now the right age—in her late teens[1]—this was one societal ritual in which she wouldn't have to participate; her family had already decided that she would marry her second cousin, Francis Minor.

She glanced over at him, caught his eye, and he smiled. She had known him nearly her whole life and was pleased with the intelligent, handsome lawyer. She was also relieved that she already knew much about him and didn't have to appraise and evaluate him as she would a stranger. In Francis, she saw someone she could trust, a man of wit and ambition, whom she was growing to love.

All that remained was to finish out their formal courtship and engagement. Then she would become Mrs. Francis Minor.

~

The historical record is mute on whether Francis (or Virginia, for that matter) courted anyone else or had romantic rivals. Based on the cultural traditions of the Tidewater planters, however, it appears a foregone conclusion that Francis and Virginia would marry, given that cousins marrying was common among the upper class, and that their union would unite two branches of the Minor family, thus increasing their power and wealth through shared social, political, and financial interests.[2]

Though it may seem taboo to the modern mind, interfamily marriage was not frowned upon by the nineteenth-century American elite, who viewed themselves as set above others and therefore could only deign to marry within their own class. This sometimes meant looking to their own bloodlines, like their European ancestors had done before them.[3] Exactly how prevalent cousin marriage was is a matter of debate among scholars. Historians Catherine Clinton and Jane Turner Censer believe it occurred in about 10 percent of upper-class marriages,[4] while Bertram Wyatt-Brown argues that it was common among all white southerners, regardless of class, especially in Virginia.[5] He further cites the case of the Jefferson and Lewis families, of which the Minors are a part, noting "there were thirty-five marriages between 1750 and 1810. Seven involved the pairing of cousins—five first-cousins and two second-cousins—twenty percent of the total," which is high even by the measures of countries where the practice is standard.[6]

Virginia and Francis were second cousins—their grandparents, Dabney and John Minor, were brothers.[7] According to Stanford University, because of the generational distance between their shared DNA, "the genetic risk associated with second cousins having children is as small as it would be for two unrelated individuals."[8] However, studies from the *Annals of Human Biology*, the National Center for Biotechnology Information, and the *European Journal of Obstetrics & Gynecology and Reproductive Biology* all note that any degree of cousin marriage can result in infertility,[9] which could be a reason why Virginia and Francis had only one child.

The family unit of the Old South was a far cry from today's nuclear family consisting of parents and children. It also included in-laws, aunts, uncles, nieces, nephews, and cousins. In fact, cousins were considered "intimate" members of the family so much so that they often "lived intermittently with each other, assisted, befriended, and loved each other, and in general played momentous roles in each other's lives. Many cousins spent much of their childhoods in each other's company. . . . Cousins who did not live near each other spent long stretches of time together during extended visits. Their parents encouraged them to correspond, and many did so faithfully throughout their youth and into adulthood."[10]

So it is likely Francis and Virginia grew up aware of each other and may have even been very close. They certainly knew each other's temperaments and personalities, likes and dislikes,[11] which would have provided a measure of relief and promise of stability going into a lifelong commitment.

By the 1830s, marrying for romantic love was a valid choice in society,[12] as the historical model of dominant husband/submissive wife began to fade in favor of "companionate marriage," a "loving partnership governed by affection rather than fear"[13] that was "venerated as the ultimate relationship for fulfilment, stability and happiness."[14]

One of the qualities emphasized for both sexes was a good education, with advocates advising men and women to choose "well-educated and like-minded partners."[15] Women were advised "to question the intellectual worthiness of any future husband: 'Has his education been such as to qualify him to be a pleasing companion to me? Or, if not, can I so far forget my education . . . that he may be so?'"[16] Likewise, men were advised to seek a woman who loves "'to read; she must be able to think, and to have opinion of her very own' . . . advice that suggests an increasing number of early national men valued intelligence in their wives."[17]

This model will be discussed at length in chapter 5, but as their lives together would bear out, this is most certainly the type of marriage to which both Virginia and Francis aspired; in fact, they seemed tailor-made for it. Companionate marriage envisioned "a life based on shared experiences . . . [an] intense sense of mutuality was at the heart of the companionate ideal. His joys became her joys, his cares became her cares, and his sorrows became her sorrows (and vice versa, of course). . . . It was their job, together as a couple, to achieve wedded bliss."[18]

Virginia and Francis's closest relatives would have encouraged their courtship through chaperoned events such as "sallies of wit," tête-à-têtes over tea, dances, concerts, riding, picnics, and "moonlight rambles."[19]

Couples in the early days of courtship were closely watched, but as the relationship progressed, they were given more and more privacy[20] to allow for a measure of sexual expression through petting, which did not violate the maxim forbidding sex before marriage.[21]

Then came the day on which Francis officially asked Virginia to be his wife, a proposal she was free to accept or decline.[22] Unlike today, when a woman is expected to give an answer immediately after being asked, Virginia would have waited until after Francis sought permission from her mother and brother.[23] In many ways, Francis being a blood relation made this process simpler; the family already knew his lineage, social status, financial and job prospects, and ability to provide a stable home for Virginia, all things a woman's guardian had to take into consideration when evaluating her future spouse.[24]

Once the permission was granted and Virginia formally assented to the marriage, the couple entered their engagement period, which could last anywhere from six months to two years, depending on the circumstances. They wrote to close friends and family first, keeping the engagement private for some time. They may have exchanged miniature portraits, as lovers had done for centuries, or perhaps declared their commitment through engagement rings, which were just then becoming popular. These were simple bands with or without stones, but they didn't look anything like the diamond solitaire engagement rings common today; those didn't come into fashion until Tiffany & Co. introduced them in 1886.[25]

The public announcement of their upcoming nuptials set off a series of tasks for the bride-to-be, centered on preparing for her new home. The 1840s were a period of transition for weddings from private, home-based affairs, in which everything was made by the bride's family and the ceremony was small, to the lavish, expensive, and commercial industry brides are familiar with today.[26] In addition to selecting her wedding attire, which likely would have been made by a local dressmaker with an elite clientele, Virginia was responsible for the handwritten wedding invitations and guest list. In between these preparations, Virginia also would have been expected to sew table linens and bedding for her dower chest[27] and make her own intimate apparel, such as petticoats, corset covers, nightgowns, dress sleeves, and handkerchiefs.[28] She would also have to shop for a complete wardrobe for at least a year in dresses—though two years' worth was preferable for underclothes—and her cloak and bonnet for the coming season.[29] Such a trousseau could cost upward of $1,000, or $34,650 in today's currency.[30]

As a bridal or wedding gift, Virginia likely received a leather key basket decorated with her initials and with "stars, diamonds and sheaves of wheat—symbols of love, prosperity, and eternity."[31] This was a traditional gift for a bride in Virginia and North Carolina that symbolized her new role as mistress of a household. Like a chatelaine, it would hold the keys to all the locks in her home—doors, chests, and cupboards—and attested to her supreme authority in management of her home and its contents, from her jewelry to the food in the pantry and cellars.[32]

Meanwhile, Francis would have been in charge of securing a plain gold band for Virginia's wedding ring and booking an officiant for the wedding.[33] The latter responsibility would have been easy for Francis, as the Minor family had been attending Christ Church at least since the time of Doodes Minor, the second generation of Minors in the United States,[34] and they were friends with its rector, Rev. Richard Kidder (R. K.) Meade.[35]

Another thing Francis would have been expected to do while Virginia prepared for the wedding was to secure a suitable home for them. After serious consideration, he decided they would move to Holly Springs, Mississippi, to live with his elder brother, Dabney III, who was a prominent lawyer. This was common practice at the time, as living with family gave the man time to build a business and amass a little capital before buying a home.[36]

The wedding took place on Thursday, August 31, 1843,[37] at the residence of William Wertenbaker Esq., librarian at the University of Virginia,[38] and was witnessed by Lucian Minor,[39] Virginia's second cousin and a prominent professor of law at the College of William and Mary.[40] No records indicate the size of the wedding party or names of other witnesses.

While no descriptions of the wedding remain, one can draw a likely picture using contemporary accounts of other planter weddings. Like all brides who wed after Queen Victoria's 1840 nuptials changed expected bridal attire, Virginia would have worn a white dress made of silk or satin with a fitted bodice and full skirt. Brussels lace was much in fashion for the overdress and long white veil. In imitation of the queen, she would have had a circlet of orange blossoms in her hair.[41] Her shoes would have been white satin or silk slippers decorated with ribbons. She would also have worn white silk stockings and short white kid gloves.[42]

Francis would have been in full formal dress, wearing a frock coat of black, blue, or burgundy and a flower in his collar,[43] a white vest, black pantaloons, and dress boots, with black silk stockings, white kid gloves, and a white cravat.[44]

The wedding took place between 10:00 a.m. and noon[45] in the front parlor of the Wertenbaker estate, with the bridal party arranged in a crescent facing the guests. Opposite of today's custom, Virginia would have stood on Francis's right, with their attendants trailing off on either side.[46] As the Minors were Episcopalian, the ceremony itself would have been brief, taken from the *Book of Common Prayer*. After a short blessing, Francis and Virginia exchanged vows, and Francis placed the gold wedding ring on Virginia's left ring finger. Their vows were solemnized with prayer, followed by scripture readings and possibly Holy Communion, depending on the circumstances.[47] The ceremony ended as it does today, with a kiss between the newly married couple and the proclamation of them as "Mr. and Mrs. Francis Minor."[48]

The wedding reception was always held at the bride's home and would either have been a breakfast that took place just after the wedding[49] or a formal dinner that was held at 8:00 p.m. that night.[50] Either way, after the main meal, the wedding cake—usually a fruit cake with white frosting in a simple single layer—was cut and boxed for the guests to take home with them, rather than eaten at the reception as it is today.[51] Then the couple left for their honeymoon or "bridal tour," a week or two meant to give them time to visit family and friends who couldn't attend the wedding.[52]

When they returned home, Francis and Virginia likely lived for four to six months with her family, which was common for a newly married couple,[53] and prepared for their journey to Holly Springs, Mississippi, which took place sometime before the end of 1843.[54]

NEWLYWEDS IN HOLLY SPRINGS

Sitting next to each other in a cramped stagecoach while it bounced over rutted roads on poor springs wasn't the most leisurely way to travel, but it was the best way to make the most of the two-week, 750-mile journey from Charlottesville to Holly Springs, Mississippi.

Had all the projected railway lines been completed, Virginia and Francis could have taken a train from Harper's Ferry, Virginia, on a leg of the Baltimore and Ohio Railway and switched lines a few times to travel through Kentucky and Tennessee into Mississippi.[55] But at the time, only a portion was serviceable; the rest was still under construction. Besides, they would have had to pick up a carriage in Mississippi anyway, since Holly Springs wasn't yet accessible by rail.[56]

Waiting for them at the other end of the journey was Francis's older brother, Dabney III, who had helped found Holly Springs in 1835 or 1836.[57] The Minor family owned fifty thousand acres of land in the area that they purchased from the Chickasaw Indians[58] as early as 1819, when it was still a territory, but it wasn't until 1835 that the family began to settle in the area in large numbers.[59]

Holly Springs was one of several planned communities across the country meant to bring together people of like interests and relationships.[60] While many others were founded to support a company or to serve as a model of a utopian society,[61] Holly Springs was different. The intent behind its founding was to give the second and third sons of Virginia and Carolina planters a place to live; traditionally, the eldest son inherited the family's wealth and property, the second son went into church ministry, and the third joined the military.[62] Those who did not wish to follow that sequence could start new lives in Holly Springs, just as the Minors were doing.

Francis had many relatives in the area with whom he and Virginia could have lived, but their new home was likely with Dabney and his wife Jane Herndon Minor at the Woodlawn Plantation[63] in the Old Salem neighborhood.[64] According to his grandson, Dabney described the land as "wonderfully rich and beautiful, timbered with oak, hickory, and chestnut, but no pine trees near Holly Springs. The primeval forest resembled an English park for there was no underbrush as it had been kept down by the Indians who burned the grass annually. There was a wealth of wild flowers and all streams were filled with game fish. The late Capt. John McGowan insisted that salmon used to run the streams annually."[65]

Like so many generations before them, Dabney was a prominent lawyer, and Francis likely received his first real-world experience in law in Holly Springs. It was common for relatives to assist new lawyers during the formative years of their careers. "Perhaps the relatively unstructured nature of law practice in the South, where many attorneys simply read law instead of attending formal law schools and professional organizations were few, made patronage and assistance by kin so important."[66]

Unfortunately, most records for the area were lost during the Civil War,[67] so the exact nature of Francis's formative years as a lawyer in Holly Springs may never be known. However, there was no shortage of legal work in the area. At the time, a large number of attorneys invaded the town, eager to profit from the land sales and speculation taking place with the Chickasaws thanks to the 1832 Chickasaw cession (also known as the Treaty of Pontitock Creek), in which the tribe relinquished their native lands in exchange for suitable land west of the Mississippi River.[68] Some speculators bought as much as forty thousand acres of land when it was offered for sale in 1836.[69] As a result, "Holly Springs became a center for law, commerce and agriculture. At one time the county produced more cotton and had more lawyers than any other place in Mississippi."[70]

In addition to his legal work, Francis also appears to have run a school for boys, as an advertisement under his name in the Holly Springs paper, *The Guard*, calls for male boarders at "his school" specifying, "the course will embrace a thorough English and Classical Education [*sic*]. French will be taught if desired for a price of $15,00 [*sic*] for board and tuition."[71] The need for schools in the area was great because of the influx of emigrants from Virginia and the Carolinas, who brought their families with them. By the time Francis and Virginia set down roots, the town already had its first chartered university as well as several single-sex schools for girls and boys. Any of those could have been where Francis taught.[72]

Dabney was heavily involved in politics, so he probably influenced Francis's later political action,[73] though he was a Democrat[74] and Francis a staunch Republican. Virginia and Francis appear to have dipped their toes in advocacy for the first time while in Mississippi. Francis belonged to the Holly Springs Temperance Society and on at least one occasion spoke before the membership, arguing that "a moral and religious constituency" that included temperance was a necessary component of free government. His speech was judged by one reporter as "marked with strong argument, an excellent style and happy delivery."[75]

After three years in Mississippi, Virginia and Francis packed their bags and traveled up the Mississippi River to St. Louis. Their motivation for leaving is not clear, but it is possible that they received an invitation from relatives from the Sunning Hill branch of the family: Patsy Minor and her brother, Andrew Jackson Minor, who lived in St. Louis.[76] After three years practicing in a small town, it would stand to reason that Francis was ready to expand his career and start a new life with Virginia in a bigger city.

CHAPTER FIVE

A New Life in St. Louis

SOMETIME IN AUTUMN 1845 OR SPRING 1846[1] THE MINORS APPROACHED St. Louis on a steamboat gliding up the mighty and, even then, muddy Mississippi River to join a mile-long line[2] of more than 250 other boats waiting to dock at the bustling Laclede's Landing, the United States' second busiest cargo port, just behind New Orleans.[3] These ships, belching smoke and cinders from their tall, black smokestacks, made more than 2,400 trips to St. Louis each year, carrying more than two hundred thousand tons of freight.[4] Despite being a hive of activity, with more than 40 boats loading and unloading at any given time,[5] the landing had no docks or piers. Ship captains parked along the small paved portion of the road so they could lower their landing planks and allow passengers to step on dry land.[6]

As they disembarked from their cabin-class (first-class) accommodations,[7] Virginia and Francis would have been overwhelmed by the activity around them as freight was unloaded and prepared for transport. Dock hands—a combination of Black slaves and employed Irish and German immigrants—carried cords of lumber, copper sheathing, sheet iron, and lead bars as well as massive boxes of coal, hemp, and fur. They also hefted barrels of tobacco, flour, wheat, corn, oats, barley, rye, beans, flaxseed, potatoes, pork, beef, bacon, lard, tallow, butter, beeswax, eggs, feathers, whiskey, coffee, glass, nails, salt, sugar, and tar.[8] Most of it was bound for the tall red brick warehouses that lined the river or was stored in stacks under tarps along Front Street until a dray-pulled wagon could cart it to its final destination.[9] Virginia may even have admired a few cookstoves and brooms headed to the merchant shops just a few streets away.

As they walked into the city, the scent of wood and coal smoke grew stronger as they neared the merchandise district, which was home to hotels, insurance companies, banks, gasworks, railroad offices, and other necessary services, including Francis's future law offices.[10] There were also four major meat and vegetable markets: the original at Market and North Market Streets; the French Market (also called the South Market) at Fourth and South Broadway; Mound Market on the north side near Broadway, Seventh, and Howard; and the newly opened Lucas Market at Twelfth Street between Olive and Chestnut. These were the final destinations of many of the foodstuffs and some of the goods unloaded at the wharves.[11]

A carriage ride through the streets would have shown the Minors that most St. Louis residents were not wealthy like them; rather, they were farmers; trade workers on the river, in the foundries, or in iron and coal mining; employed in service; or small-business craftsmen like blacksmiths, cobblers, coopers, and haberdashers. Cartwrights and wagonmakers were in high demand by those going west, and brickmakers literally helped build the city and its roads.[12] These were the people who lived closest to the river in a disorganized mix of brick and wood rowhouses, decaying colonial structures, shanties, and flounder houses,[13] the latter a unique style of folk architecture in which the sloping triangular roof results in one side of the house being a half or full story higher than the rest.[14] As they moved north and west, they came upon the modest homes of the educated classes—clerks, physicians, lawyers, teachers, and the clergy,[15] the people who would have been their peers were it not for the Minor family money.

On September 17, 1845, Francis purchased a city lot and house between the twelfth and thirteenth blocks of Morgan Street[16] from William Taylor for $381.60 or $13,126 today.[17] This was likely the Minors' first home in St. Louis; the first recorded home address for them dates to 1847 and is listed as being on Morgan west of Fourteenth Street, which is in the same area, but no building number is given.[18]

However, the following year they lived at 368 Morgan, which could be the same location.[19]

This area was a prosperous part of the north end of the city, a dozen blocks away from the river and only five blocks from the city limits.[20] At the time, the wealthy tended to live away from the noise and pollution at the city center, even venturing into the country, as the Minors would later do, in search of peace and fresh air. While none of the Minors' homes remains standing today, if they followed popular style, they were tall, narrow, red brick townhouses with multiple stories, also called terraced houses,[21] examples of which can still be found in downtown St. Louis.

Little is known of their home life during this time, as neither left behind journals or many personal letters, but historian Bonnie Stepenoff notes that "friends in St. Louis regarded [Virginia] as a loving wife and Francis as a devoted husband,"[22] and the *St. Louis Republic* wrote, "For almost half a century Mr. and Mrs. Minor exemplified in a striking manner, the beauty and purity of domestic life."[23] The silence of the historical record could be taken to mean they were intensely private or simply that their records were not preserved.

Regardless, they were members of St. Louis's elite class—they were known to own such luxuries as mahogany furniture, carpets and rugs, a girandole (an ornamental candelabra or lighting fixture like a small chandelier), a feather bed, bathtub, silver cutlery, and a gold watch[24]—and the city had much to offer for those of standing. Members of high society often gathered at the National Hall for balls and debuts.[25] Other annual events included the Franklin Fire Company's supper at the State Tobacco warehouse, the Grand Military and Civic Ball at the concert hall, the Military and Fancy Dress Ball at the Planters' House, and the Grand Fireman's Festival for the benefit of the Tiger Hose Company at the concert hall.[26]

Having been a member of the American Whig Society at Princeton, it is highly likely that Francis was a member of one of St. Louis's many debating clubs, which were mainly composed of young attorneys.[27] Popular clubs included the Jefferson Society and the St. Louis Debating Club, which met every other Saturday at 2:00 p.m.[28] This would not only have been an entertaining diversion for him but an excellent networking opportunity and a way to polish his skills.

Francis's time in the old-time Whig Club at Princeton inspired him to host literary salons throughout his life in St. Louis, where he reunited with some of his Princeton classmates.[29] For example, in December 1869, Francis and Virginia formed the Philo Literary Society at Loomis Hall, located at Ninth and Washington. Francis served as vice president. The goals of the society were "literary improvement and social culture." They took this charge seriously, having as the topic at the inaugural meeting in January the much-debated issue of capital punishment.

Both Francis and Virginia were also prominent members of the Century Club, St. Louis's principal literary organization, where both spoke regularly[30] and would have heard the famous suffragist Miss Thekla M. Bernays give her speech "Diplomatic Women [an Essay Read before the Century Club of St. Louis, Mo.]" in 1883.[31] They were also members of the St. Louis Horticultural Society, where they exhibited cuttings from their pear trees in 1864.[32] Other intellectual pastimes that would have appealed to them included lectures at the St. Louis Lyceum,[33] theater, and music.[34]

Given her later work with the Western Sanitary Commission and St. Louis Ladies Union Aid Society, Virginia may have been a member of one or more of the many charitable organizations that were founded in St. Louis beginning in 1825. The first was the Female Charitable Society, which aimed to "relieve 'distressed females and children and promote industry among the poor,'"[35] the St. Louis Association of Ladies for the Relief of Orphan Children, or the St. Louis Samaritan Society, which "embraced the ladies of the city who associated themselves for the purpose of making up and supplying clothing to those who could not get it in any other way and who were not cared for by any charitable institution."[36] These organizations not only gave purpose beyond keeping house to the lives of wealthy women but also benefited the social needs of a rapidly growing city.

Having been blessed with exceptional educations, the Minors were strong supporters of education. They were both life members and regular donors to the St. Louis Board of Education.[37] They also supported the St. Louis Public School Library, which was founded in 1865.[38] One obituary of Francis states, "He was a man of decided literary ability and a constant patron of the libraries."[39]

As for spiritual pursuits, it is likely that the Minors were members of Christ Church Cathedral, the first Episcopal church west of the Mississippi and the largest in St. Louis.[40] Its original location, founded in 1819 and used until after the Civil War, was a large dance hall.[41] That it bore the same name as their family church back home in Virginia may have been a small comfort in a new town. It is also possible that they later attended Trinity Church on Washington Avenue and Eleventh Streets when it opened on June 6, 1869, as they were known to be members of an offspring of this church later in life.[42]

CHANGING THE MEANING OF MARRIAGE AND WOMEN'S RIGHTS

When Virginia married Francis, she not only promised to "love, honor, and obey" him in all things; she freely gave away her rights under the law. Well, really, she had no choice. That's because American marriage laws were based on the English system of coverture—an antiquated system leftover from America's days as a colony—by which women were "covered" under the law by a man. At birth, a woman's rights were subsumed by her father. Upon marriage they passed into her husband's hands, so during her entire life—unless she became a widow—she had essentially the same rights as a child, a slave, or a person declared mentally unfit. As historian Nancy F. Cott writes,

> *Marriage made women into dependents. . . . The coverture of married women in the Anglo-American common law represented and perpetuated this polarity [that man was independent and woman dependent]. In making a woman a wife, marriage removed from her and transferred to her husband her property and income, the very items that indicated free will. The property cessation both symbolized and operationalized a husband's independence and his wife's (economic) dependence and consequent civic disability. The husband was not seen as expropriating his wife but as getting recompense for supporting, protecting, and representing her: marriage was understood as a reciprocal bargain arising from consent.*[43]

By the late 1840s, some states were beginning to relax marriage laws slightly. By the end of the decade, Missouri women could own property, sue, testify in court, sign deeds, make wills, adopt children, and own slaves.[44] This came about because of an 1849 statute enacted by the Missouri legislature that stated a woman's property—regardless of whether she held it before marriage or acquired it after—could not be used to pay the debts or fines incurred by her husband.[45]

However, there were plenty of loopholes in the law. For example, a husband could get around it by holding his wife's property and disposing of it through common law. He could also apply her property to debts that occurred after marriage or after the property was acquired.[46] This exception wasn't terminated until 1865, but even that new statute left the husband in possession of the land and gave him the right to sue with regard to the title,[47] a right that did not run out until his death.[48] It was not until 1889 that the Missouri Revised Statutes ended coverture completely[49] but even then only for women married in 1889 or after; coverture was still in place for estates "which vested before the statutory provision of 1889 was enacted."[50]

Virginia made no attempt to hide her hatred for this system. In March 1869, she is reported to have addressed the Woman Suffrage Association of Missouri saying, "When a woman marries, her individuality is absorbed by her husband; she bears his name, and when she dies, his name, and not her own, is engraven [sic] on her tombstone. She even enters eternity under a false designation. Although the law gives her the privilege of making a will, yet the law does not allow her to carry it out during the lifetime of her husband."[51]

Virginia was not alone in viewing this tradition as repugnant. There was a growing movement across the country that sought to upend traditional views of love and marriage. These men and women who espoused the idea of companionate marriage believed, "As a freely entered union between equals, marriage set the standard for both personal and political interactions.... Marriage served as a model and metaphor for articulating citizenship and political participation in the young republic."[52]

Companionate marriages were much more like modern ones, based in love and balance of the sexes rather than in the fear and separate spheres for men and women that kept women subservient under the patriarchal coverture system. There was a clear understanding that the marriage would be "egalitarian and emotionally fulfilling,"[53] with the couple's shared intellectual pursuits bringing them together while demonstrating their equality.[54] Women expected their husbands to treat them as equals in conversation and to consult them on domestic matters.[55]

Unfortunately, this system was far from as perfect in practice as it appeared in theory. There could be no true equality while women were still legally subordinate to their husbands.[56] Despite the ideals of a balanced partnership, a woman's place was still in the home,[57] and she was expected to take an active interest in her husband's work, as part of the "mutual cooperation between husband and wife,"[58] even though she was not allowed to have nondomestic or noncharitable pursuits in which he might take an equal interest.

Francis Minor set out to change this and make his marriage as truly equal as he could under the bounds of the law. Prior to Elizabeth Cady Stanton and Susan B. Anthony calling for equal rights for women at the Seneca Falls Convention in 1848, Francis was working to make sure that Virginia had as much gender equality as he could give her in their marriage. On May 18, 1846, not long after they moved to St. Louis, Francis put his real estate investments, along with all his personal property current and future into a trust for Virginia.[59] While it's possible that Francis did this to protect her from the volatile economy of the period and any creditors they had,[60] his future actions point to this being a first step in a carefully crafted strategy to give Virginia more rights than most women of her time were allowed.

In the wording used in the trust, Francis empowered Virginia to

> occupy and enjoy said premises and collect and receive the rents, proceeds and profits thereof to her own use, without impeachment for waste, and free and clear from all management, control or interference on the part of her present or any future husband nor shall any future husband acquire any right as tenant by the courtesy in the property hereby conveyed, and she may through her trustee grant, bargain, sell, mortgage, devise, bequeath or otherwise dispose of the same or any part thereof at her will and pleasure.[61]

She could also "at any time revoke the power of the old and appoint a new trustee"[62] until she was satisfied. This was three years before Missouri law protected a wife's property from her husband's debt, and though it preceded New York marriage property law, it went further in allowing her to sell it at will.[63]

On May 1, 1853, Virginia Minor sold their house in downtown St. Louis (lot 12 on Morgan Street) to Rebecca Hapenny for $3,400[64] and bought ten acres of farmland[65] on the outskirts of St. Louis from Elizabeth Goodfellow for approximately $5,450.[66] They called this land "Minoria."[67] While the exact address of the property is not listed on any documents, the land was most likely located at what is today 5753 Dr. Martin Luther King Drive and 5750 Theodosia, two vacant lots that back up to one another, in the Goodfellow neighborhood of St. Louis.[68]

The fact that Virginia is the one who purchased Minoria is a historic precedent, but it is even more significant because she purchased the property from another woman and then sold her city home to a third woman on May 6. All three were married and were the first married women to buy and sell property among themselves in the state.[69] This was made possible through the use of trusts created specifically for this purpose, which turned the husbands' rights over to a male trustee who acted on behalf of each wife.[70]

Francis also made it possible for Minoria to be inherited by Virginia's designated heirs—who may or may not have been their children, depending who was living upon her death—rather than having the property go automatically to him, as it would have under coverture. Only if all of Virginia's children died before age twenty-one, the age of majority in Missouri at the time, would Francis or his designated heirs inherit upon her death.[71]

This was unthinkable and, to some people, an outrageous amount of freedom to give to any woman, especially one's wife. There were many other prominent men in the St. Louis suffrage movement, but none made similar legal arrangements for their wives.[72] Scholar and attorney Donna Monnig writes, "The power to own let alone sell property greatly empowered women, but the power to leave property to one's descendants, especially at the exclusion of one's husband, extended that power to nearly unprecedented levels. Francis and Virginia's commitment to extinguishing patriarchal power in their marriage, along with the intense women's rights activism they devoted themselves to later in life, indicates a high level of companionship and respect in their marriage."[73]

What Francis essentially did was legally reverse the gender roles in their marriage, giving Virginia the power usually reserved for a husband and essentially taking on himself the role of a married woman. Monnig points out that "even in Louisiana, where civil law allowed married women to own separate property and keep their legal identities, husbands still held administrative power over the property,"[74] a right Francis sacrificed on his wife's behalf.

An interesting quality of their marriage is that neither Minor sought attention for this bit of unique legal maneuvering, despite the prestige it could bring. This might have been because the Minors were humble, but it could also have been because they understood the danger that came with swimming too far outside the current of public acceptability. Monnig notes,

> If the public knew the full extent of the Minors' radicalism it might have proved more of a hindrance than help. . . . Similar marital property arrangements were not unheard of, but they were not commonplace, thus public scrutiny could have brought unwelcome criticism to the Minors and their cause, thus reinforcing their need to remain respectable while pursuing radical causes. Many suffragists and historians would agree that some of the more extreme suffragists who publicly shared their most radical views and feminist beliefs . . . at times did more harm than good for woman's suffrage.[75]

These legal changes were like a test to see how far the law could be stretched. It withstood progressive pressure within the bounds of their marriage on behalf of Virginia's rights as a woman, so later in life they would expand upon it in the public sphere on behalf of all US women.[76]

PESTILENCE AND FIRE

The reason the Minors moved to Minoria is uncertain, but it is possible they fled the city because their only child, Francis Gilmer Minor, had been born the year before and they wanted to protect his health. The infant mortality rate was very high, at 21.7 percent, and St. Louis city was a breeding ground for deadly diseases, including tuberculosis, cholera, typhoid, smallpox, and diphtheria.[77] Children and the elderly were especially susceptible to cholera—in July 1850, a cholera outbreak killed nearly nine hundred people in St. Louis, more than three-quarters of whom were children.[78] This could have been the final straw for Francis; several of his siblings had died of the disease, so it makes sense that he would fear it.[79] In addition, he and Virginia had already lived through 1849, one of the deadliest years in St. Louis history, when 10 percent of the population died of cholera and an unknown number were killed in the Great Fire,[80] an experience they had no desire to repeat.

Leading up to this fateful year, St. Louis's population had exploded beyond anyone's imagination. From a tiny fur-trading post of just under five thousand people in 1830, it had become the country's eighth-largest city with a population of nearly seventy-eight thousand residents by 1850.[81] The city was well known for having poorly maintained dirt roads that were constantly covered in animal excrement, turned into "a mire of mud, manure and puddles" in rain or snow, and produced "ankle deep" dust clouds during the long, hot, and humid summers.[82] On top of that, there was almost no public sanitation system; gutters existed in only a few stone roads.[83] The first 163 miles of sewer wouldn't be complete until 1875,[84] and it wouldn't be until the 1890s that city managers began to plan for projects such as piped water, treated sewer systems, water filtration, and trash collection.[85]

Because of conditions like this, it was normal for any large city to see small disease outbreaks, as St. Louis had in May 1847 when smallpox sickened thirty people.[86] One cholera epidemic had already terrorized the city from summer 1832 through autumn 1833 and killed around two hundred people.[87]

But when St. Louis mayor John M. Krum heard in January 1849 that cholera was killing residents in New Orleans, he began to worry for his town. St. Louis was just a short trip up the Mississippi River from the Big Easy, and thousands of merchants, tourists, and travelers made the journey each year. Any one of them could possibly spread the disease upriver. Hoping to prevent an outbreak, he called for "an increase in public cleanliness, street cleaning, and other actions previously viewed as onerous and oppressive."[88]

He was largely ignored; only a few ponds were drained in an effort to humor him[89]—this despite the fact that the previous month, a steamboat passenger had died of the disease only moments before docking in St. Louis and that St. Louis Hospital had seen its first case of cholera on January 5.[90] The patient died within hours of arriving at the hospital, but his case was not made public, and newcomers to the area were not quarantined.

Over the next several months, newspapers began reporting an uptick in cases, but were also careful not to unduly alarm the public. In April and May, snow melt from the north, late season snowfall, heavy rain, and thunderstorms combined to flood the Missouri and Mississippi Rivers, which, in turn, burst their banks onto the filthy streets, creating a perfect breeding ground for cholera.[91] By early May, cases were increasing rapidly, nearly doubling every two weeks.[92]

In the midst of this public health crisis, another tragedy struck. In river and port towns, steamboat fires and explosions were fairly common since the boats were constructed almost entirely out of wood, but they were always frightening, sometimes deadly, and occasionally they proved disastrous.

On the night of May 17, 1849, the steamer *White Cloud* was moored at the foot of Cherry Street and was seemingly quiet.[93] Accounts vary on exactly what occurred aboard this ship. One[94] has a night watchman encountering a "raggedly dressed Irishman" aboard the ship—he was supposedly looking for a friend—before the same watchman smelled smoke and found the ladies' cabin on fire. Another says a small fire in a mattress earlier in the day rekindled.[95] Historians are split on whether the fire was arson with the intent to collect insurance money on the *White Cloud*, an accident, or the result of mechanical failure in or near the room where the fire started.[96] Whatever the cause, the fire quickly spread out of control and set the whole boat ablaze.

The Missouri Fire Company No. 5[97] and the Liberty Fire Company were first on the scene. They brought in the *Edward Bates* to fight the blaze, but it also caught fire. The crew abandoned ship, and the boat drifted in the current, bumping into at least twenty-two[98] others moored nearby, setting them alight as well. As the wind picked up, it caught the embers and carried them ashore onto the levee, where piles of dried hemp and lumber waited. They caught and ignited nearby barrels of lard and bacon.[99] Engorged by this fuel, the fire became a wall, cutting off the firefighters and spreading until the whole wharf was in flames.

By now, residents as far away as Tenth Street[100] could hear the alarm bells at the landing, and it is possible Virginia and Francis, a mere four blocks farther north, could as well. Their home was safe thanks to the efforts of Central Fire Company No. 1, who was able to stop the fire's northward spread as it broke through the roof of a two-story warehouse south of Green Street.[101] However, Francis would have worried about the fate of his office building, located at 13 Chestnut.[102] It was in the heart of downtown and right in the path of where the fire was headed.[103]

Soon the block between Front and Locust caught fire, its many wooden-frame buildings feeding the flames, which spread south of Walnut, across Second Street at Myrtle, and to Front and Main, endangering residences and draining emergency reservoirs.[104] Residents climbed onto roofs with wet blankets to try to remove sparks and burning embers. Owners and employees of downtown businesses raced to save their inventory and records, and even Town Hall's records were relocated.[105] But for most, Francis included, it was too late; their businesses were destroyed, as were the telegraph office and three newspapers.[106]

In a last desperate attempt to create a firebreak and halt the conflagration's progression, firefighters placed gunpowder from the St. Louis Arsenal in houses at Second and Third and carefully exploded them to bring down the structures without aggravating the fire.[107] In all, the fire raged for ten hours, forcing evacuations as far west as Fourth Street and the merchant area. It completely destroyed the block between Locust and Olive, with fourteen more blocks partially or entirely destroyed. In addition, twenty-three boats, 430 buildings,[108] and 280 businesses were lost, with total estimated damage of between $3.5 million and $6.1 million, or $117.3 million and $204.4 million today.[109] The death toll has never been certain; miraculously, only seven deaths were reported in the media,[110] in addition to that of Fire Captain Thomas Targee, who died creating the firebreak that saved the town.

Cholera Continues Its Devastation

Most of St. Louis lay in ruins, but its citizens didn't have time to grieve their losses. The cholera epidemic rapidly spread, killing one hundred people a week in May.[111] Newly elected mayor James G. Barry knew he had to do something. There was no cure for cholera, and although physicians agreed it was caused by contamination, they were divided over how it was transmitted.[112]

Some believed that cholera spread from vegetables, so the mayor banned the sale of all produce within the city limits and decreed an all-meat diet for St. Louisans.[113] Others connected it to sanitation, so he ordered all citizens to remove harmful debris such as liquid and solid waste from their property. The waste was then picked up and carted away[114] by the city scavenger, who acted much like a modern trash collection service, though less reliable. If they failed to comply, citizens were subject to a $5.00 fine, which was a steep penalty at a time when the average manual worker in Missouri made anywhere from $0.75 to $1.48 a day.[115]

Another theory was that cholera was spread by tainted air, called miasma. Ironically, the "cure" for this was to burn wood, coal, tar, and sulfur fires in the belief that the smoke and fumes would cleanse the air.[116] In reality, all it did was add to the air pollution, recall memories of the Great Fire, and increase the number of home fires for the fire department to put out.

Others were closer to the mark and felt that contaminated water was the cause. The city opened municipal water hydrants so that the poor would have access to clean drinking water.[117] As this idea gained ground in the popular opinion, it morphed into the theory that washing produce in contaminated water could be to blame. The all-meat diet was relaxed, and some fruit and ripe vegetables, such as okra, potatoes, and tomatoes,[118] were allowed to be sold, but washing or even throwing water on the produce was forbidden,[119] as was selling unripe fruits and vegetables.[120]

Most businesses were closed, and entertainment was suspended. Despite these precautions, the seemingly inexorable march of death continued as the heat and humidity of June and July allowed the disease to flourish, striking down 400 to 600 people a week.[121] By June 27, all public school buildings became hospitals.[122] German immigrant Gustavus Wulfing noted in a letter to his family that at the height of the epidemic, 192 people died in twenty-four hours. He lived along a road leading to one of the cemeteries and reported that on many days, more than twenty funerals passed his house.[123] Church bells tolled at funerals and firehouse bells rang when they lost a company member, causing so much noise there were few periods of silence in the day. This so jangled the citizens' nerves that the city suspended both practices until the epidemic was over.[124]

Cemeteries were overburdened, and because bodies were not embalmed prior to the Civil War, the smell from the graveyards permeated the city. People carried scented handkerchiefs to place over their noses and mouths to protect them from any illness that might spread from the smell of decay,[125] and thousands of residents fled the city, especially the wealthy, who could afford summer homes in the country.[126]

Each day as he left for work, Francis kissed Virginia, and they said what could have been their final farewells,[127] as the illness could strike so quickly that one of them might die before evening. This rapid, often disturbing, and painful form of death shattered the Victorian ideal of a "good death" (in which one had time to say goodbye to family and friends and make peace with God before dying quietly at home surrounded by loved ones) and added strain and stress on an already taxed population. The sudden loss of neighbors, social and work acquaintances, and friends was a foretaste of what the Minors would experience in a few short years when their own son, Francis Gilmer, would die a shocking and violent death.

Eventually, the Committee of Public Health was called in to help. It created a quarantine station and hospital on an island in the Mississippi River called Arsenal Island (later nicknamed Quarantine Island) and required all steamboats to stop at this checkpoint before allowing their passengers into St. Louis.[128] This helped tremendously, as did the natural change in temperature as autumn approached. As August's heat waned, so did the number of deaths. By the end of the month, the epidemic was declared over.

St. Louis was by far the hardest-hit city in the nationwide epidemic. No one knows for sure how many people died. The official count is just over 4,500, but historians believe the reality is much higher,[129] with some estimates reaching upward of 6,000.[130] Children were particularly affected, with nearly 2,000 killed.[131] So it is easy to see why the Minors may have feared for the well-being of their much beloved son and heir and spirited him away to grow up in the country, never suspecting that he would still die young, despite their best efforts to protect him.

CHAPTER SIX

Francis Minor's Legal Career

ST. LOUIS CHANGED RAPIDLY IN THE DECADE PRIOR TO THE CIVIL WAR, advancing into a modern city of national importance with a rapidly rising population. By 1850, it was the seventh-largest city in the country, with nearly 75,500 residents.[1] Much of this growth was due to high numbers of German, Irish, and Czech immigrants, with 77 percent of the entire St. Louis adult population being foreign-born by 1860, and only 4 percent of the city's adult population having been born in Missouri.[2]

The state of Virginia was one of the most popular areas of origin for St. Louis emigrants, especially for Germans,[3] making up close to 20 percent of the city's population by 1850.[4] A decade later, Virginia was the third-highest state of origin for emigrants, contributing nearly 54,000 people to the state population.[5] These emigrants came seeking more fertile soil and freedom from the constraints of southern culture, including slavery.[6]

Advances in technology would have changed the way Francis did business, and both Minors moved about the city and beyond. The telegraph came to St. Louis in December 1847, increasing the speed of communication and connecting St. Louis via wire to Louisville, Iowa, Chicago, New Orleans, and the East Coast,[7] enabling companies to conduct more interstate business than ever before. When the railroad arrived in 1853, it made St. Louis the unquestionable business capital of the state[8] and also allowed the city to transition from wood to coal for its power, as the trains were able to import cheap coal from neighboring Illinois.[9] Horse-drawn streetcars began transporting people across the city in 1859,[10] and by 1860, two-thirds of the state's output came from St. Louis, with more than four thousand steamers docking on its banks and loading and unloading more than one million tons of cargo at the city's wharves.[11]

Downtown, where Francis worked, buildings were built taller, up to five stories, and the business district moved farther inland, encroaching on the places the wealthy used to live and shop.[12] This is why many wealthy families, the Minors included, relocated farther west into the country near Thirteenth Street. No matter where he worked, Francis's offices were located either right on the levee or just a few blocks off, near the courthouse, so from his window he could likely see the bustle of activity below, much as the German newspaper *Mississippi Blatter* describes it: "[The levee is] a whirl of activity that appears to be chaotic confusion but that indeed has system and reason. [One can constantly hear] the rumbling of the great haulage wagons, the truly terrifying shrieks of the teamsters, who seem engaged in a perpetual battle of wills with their mules, the demonic puffing of steam boilers, [and see] the thick enveloping dust."[13] Down to the river on the north end of St. Louis, there is "nothing but factories, foundries, nothing small, everything huge; smoky buildings with smudged windows from which machines whir or steam governors shriek, in front of the doors, pieces of machine iron and such, fallen to the earth by their own weight."[14]

Such was the industrialization of St. Louis, now a far cry from its pioneer trading post roots. The city had become a lynchpin in westward expansion and as such secured its place among the powerhouses of the country, leading it to wade into some of the most important social and political debates of the following decades: slavery, women's suffrage, temperance, and race relations. As a crossroads for overland, rail, and river transportation, it was also the perfect place for a young lawyer to build his career.

An Undocumented Career

Francis's life and career have been largely ignored by historians, save for his argument of the famous Supreme Court case that bears his surname. However, overlooking him is a mistake, because understanding his experience and legal mind is key to truly comprehending his role in the suffrage movement and why he and Virginia later had the courage to fight for women's enfranchisement all the way to the top of the judicial branch, succeeding where better-known, more powerful suffragists failed.

Francis was officially registered in the Court of Common Pleas in St. Louis on November 11, 1846,[15] and the criminal court on November 13, 1846,[16] allowing him to try cases in both places. Historians at the Missouri State Archives are still processing St. Louis case files from 1840 to 1861, so solid documentation of the specific cases Francis tried during his early years as an attorney in St. Louis is missing from the historical record.

A January 1848 advertisement shows Francis following the pattern that he established in Holly Springs of giving private lessons to students, perhaps to earn additional income. In the ad, he offers "private instruction to young ladies and others wishing to obtain a more thorough knowledge of history, the fine arts, and the higher branches of English education generally, than can usually be acquired in crowded schools" at their homes "at such hours that may not conflict with his present engagements,"[17] that is, his work as a lawyer and his other interests.

Francis was certainly practicing law then, as his place of business was listed as 13 Chestnut in 1848,[18] where a legal practice owned by attorneys John M. Eager, commissioner of deeds,[19] and Britton A. Hill[20] was located. While no definitive record of employment exists, it is probable that Francis was employed there, as Mr. Eager and Mr. Hill are both listed as references in his ad for private tutoring and Francis's future work is in alignment with the type of law practiced in this firm.

One of the things Mr. Eager worked on was collecting on bounty land warrants from the previous US wars.[21] These warrants for land—millions of acres in New York, Pennsylvania, and Virginia, for Revolutionary War veterans, and Arkansas, Illinois, Michigan, and Missouri, for veterans of the War of 1812—were a reward or incentive for military service and could be collected by the soldier or his heirs. Executing warrants involved tracking down the veterans, obtaining necessary paperwork, having the land surveyed, and ensuring authentic claims were awarded the proper land grant. Because this application process often proved too lengthy and complex for the average person to pursue or even understand, speculators often ended up acquiring the land from its rightful owners.[22] If Francis did similar work, this could explain why the Western Sanitary Commission was so eager to have him work on their war claims during the Civil War; the fundamentals were the same for the lawyer, so his experience would have been valuable.

The office building the firm occupied burned in the Great Fire the following year, but the firm remained operational under the leadership of Hill until 1858,[23] so Francis could have been employed there for up to six years.

Francis is next listed as working in the Office of the Surveyor General for Illinois and Missouri in 1852,[24] where he likely served as either a clerk or a surveyor, experience that would soon lead him to form his own land firm. In either role, he would have reported to M. Lewis Clark, the surveyor general,[25] who held that position through the end of 1853.[26]

In an 1854 newspaper advertisement, Francis is listed as practicing law in an office at the southeast corner of Third and Chestnut Streets. He was said to give particular attention "to the investigation of titles to Real Estate and conveyancing."[27]

On January 6, 1857, Francis hung up his own shingle with John M. Sherrard, a civil engineer and fellow Virginian who moved to St. Louis in 1854,[28] and the firm of Minor & Sherrard was formed at the southeast corner of Third and Chestnut between Main and Second.[29] An ad in the *Richmond Enquirer* describes them as "general land agents for Missouri, Illinois, Iowa and Kansas" who "will attend to the purchase and sale of Lands and Town Lots [sic], the entry and location of Lands, payment of Taxes, effecting Loans, making Collections, and to Land business regularly, in the above States. All business entrusted to the firm will receive the attention of both parties. N.B.—Mr. Minor will continue the practice of his profession heretofore."[30] Another ad for Minor & Sherrard in the same paper appeals to "those interested in Western Lands" on behalf of the office in St. Louis,[31] presumably referring to land in Kansas, while a third lists several downtown St. Louis lots and even two farms with houses in St. Louis County as being for sale.[32]

At first glance, it might seem odd that the firm covered Kansas and Iowa, as they seem out of range for a business based in St. Louis. However, the Missouri Surveyor's office at which Francis was employed worked closely with that of Iowa in 1851 and 1852, especially regarding the highly contested border between the two states.[33] Similarly, Sherrard was previously employed as a clerk by the Surveyor General's Office of Kansas and Nebraska, which would explain the firm's reach into Kansas.[34]

Sherrard appears to have been the real estate salesman of the pair, making a tour of the states the firm represented on a regular basis.[35] Meanwhile, Francis stayed in St. Louis to practice law and handle local matters for their firm. He personally invested in land and for a time was one of four owners of a piece of property on Third Street between Olive and Locust Streets,[36] a deal that was likely part of his work at this firm. He was also given two tracts of land totaling 320 acres in Warsaw, Missouri, in 1857, by the US government.[37]

Unfortunately, their partnership was not to be a long one. On May 31, 1857, Sherrard and Francis dissolved the business arrangement by mutual agreement. Sherrard died just over a year later at the age of twenty-six on June 27, 1858, after a brief illness.[38]

Francis continued on with the business Minor & Sherrard had begun so that no clients were left without representation because of the change.[39] Land he sold during this time included two plots in Prairie Place, just nine miles from the courthouse in St. Louis.[40] On July 28, he advertised in the *Richmond Enquirer* that he was practicing as an attorney in St. Louis, handling "all professional and land business, payment of taxes, collection of rents, accounts, making investments, loan of money &c."[41] A month later, Francis moved to an office in the Gas Company Building on Pine Street between Second and Third,[42] where it appears he was primarily involved in the sale of land, such as 120 acres in Florissant Valley, a village outside of St. Louis.[43]

Only one record exists for an obscure case Francis was part of during this period. It appears to be a follow-up to another unnamed case. On December 13, 1858, the court found that James Castello, sheriff of St. Louis County, had to pay the plaintiffs, or Francis, who represented them, the money they were due.[44] This was not Francis's only run-in with the sheriff, who appears in several St. Louis Circuit cases during his tenure.

In 1859, Francis is listed as having two places of business: 31 and 33 Pine. He may have held multiple jobs simultaneously or quit one to go to work for the other. The property at 31 Pine was home to two related law firms: one owned by Augustus W. Alexander, whose work focused on administration of estates and probate business,[45] and Mastrom D. Lewis, who sold land,[46] as Francis had in the past. In the same building was the firm of Woodson & Bates, formed by Richard Bates, the son of Alexander's former partner Edward Bates, and R. J. Woodson.[47] The Bates family was from Virginia,[48] and there is a reference in Edward Bates's diary on October 12, 1859, to being accompanied by an unidentified "Mr. Minor" when a Dr. James Pollard paid him a visit.[49] Unfortunately, no first name is listed, so it is impossible to say for certain if this was Francis, as there were several Minors in St. Louis at that time, but it does point to a possible connection between the two men.

The other address for Francis that year, 33 Pine, is where the firm of William N. White & Co., U.S. Land Agents,[50] was located. Given Francis's previous work as a land agent, it is not unreasonable to think he may have worked at this firm.

During this period, Francis once again faced the sheriff in the courtroom. The case was for an appointment of receiver—a person who preserves property during litigation—for the case of Sheriff James Castello versus Henry S. Gee and Peter R. Black. On November 22, 1859, Jacob H. Vraland was appointed receiver of the account book, journal, ledger, bills receivable and payable, a cash book, and one note of T. L. Conan for #63,73/100 that were in dispute.[51]

FREEDOM BONDS AND FREEDOM SUITS

Missouri law was peculiar in its treatment of Black people. While allowing slavery, it discouraged settlement by formerly enslaved Blacks, viewing them as "one of the most serious threats to the institution of slavery,"[52] fearing that their presence would encourage slaves to seek their own freedom. Therefore, the Missouri legislature passed a series of laws aimed at keeping tight control over the lives of free Black people. Every free Black male between the age of seven and twenty-one was required to learn a trade, not for their betterment but because idle Black males were seen as both a threat and a burden.[53]

By 1835, under "An act concerning free negroes and mulattoes,"[54] Missouri required all free Blacks to be licensed in order to stay in the state. Free Black people had to have their license on them at all times to prove that they were free. If they could not, they were arrested and had to face the three judges of the Board of County Commissioners, who would decide their fate,[55] which could be anything from being "discharged back into the city, discharged to procure the proper testimony stating that they were free people of color, paying a fine of $10 to $100, or receiving ten to twenty lashes and being exiled from the state, or being enslaved until they worked off the fine, costs and expenses of imprisonment."[56]

From 1843[57] to 1865,[58] lawmakers went one step further, requiring all Black people who had attained the age of majority, been recently freed, or come to St. Louis from another part of the state to appear in court in the hopes of being granted a "free Negro bond."[59] This process involved proving they were employed and would be sponsored by a white person who would sign a security bond for anywhere from $100 to $1,000[60] on their behalf and attest to their character.[61] Wealthy Black people were allowed to put up their own security money,[62] circumventing the need for a white spokesperson, but they were a rarity.

Each judge could decide as he willed. If all went well, the Black person was allowed to live in Missouri on the condition of "good behavior." If the Black person did not live up to the conditions of the bond, he and his security representative would have to pay the security fee to the St. Louis Circuit Court. Nearly 1,500 of these bonds were signed in St. Louis.[63]

These bonds were not only nice to have because they allowed one to live in the state legally—though they did not make one a citizen—but they also rapidly became a requirement. As historian Adam Arenson writes, "As the war approached, though, those rights were increasingly considered null and void, particularly in the South and border states. In response, though not citizenship papers, free negro bonds nevertheless provided security. If they functioned correctly, they could save a free African American from kidnapping or imprisonment."[64]

Demand for these bonds increased after the Dred Scott decision declared that all Blacks, free and enslaved, were "so far inferior that they had no rights which the white man was bound to respect."[65] At the same time, some judges felt this ruling made all previous freedom papers and bonds illegal.[66]

The people most likely to sponsor free Blacks were lawyers[67] and the wealthy, and not only those with abolitionist leanings. In St. Louis, slave traders such as Bernard Lynch and well-known slaveholding families such as the Chouteaus, Carrs, Lucases, and Campbells signed alongside antislavery activists like John Berry Meachum and William Greenleaf Eliot.[68]

That Francis's name appears on two "free Negro" bonds issued in St. Louis not only is a testament to his wealth and influence in the city but is also in keeping with his strongly abolitionist attitude and his employment as a lawyer. He put up $500 each for a "mulatto" named John Carter Brown on April 25, 1861,[69] and a "dark mulatto" named William Gaseway, described as being employed as a "steamboat man," on May 17, 1861.[70]

Many of the people who received freedom bonds went on to sue for their freedom in what became known as St. Louis's Freedom Suits. The Freedom Suits took place from 1812 to 1865 and were based on the same argument that Dred and Harriet Scott used to sue for their own freedom: an 1807 statute from when Missouri was still a territory that was upheld in 1824. Missouri state law said that slaves who had a legal basis could sue their masters for freedom. The most commonly used basis was that the slave had lived for a time in a surrounding state (usually Illinois) where slavery was outlawed before coming to Missouri, though other conditions also applied.

More than three hundred slaves sued in Missouri, but only about a third earned their freedom.[71] Though Francis is not included in the list of defense attorneys, 194 records (63 percent) do not give the attorney's name,[72] so it is possible he may have been involved in them. Even if he was not, as an abolitionist, he would have fully supported them.

LEGAL WORK DURING THE CIVIL WAR

From 1861 onward, most of Francis's cases were focused on collection of debts and special taxes, drawing up contracts or as a trustee in wills and estates. He was also involved in land/real estate cases that involved liens and deeds as well as sales. In addition to working as a claims agent during the Civil War from 1864 to 1877, from 1861 to 1864 he tried twenty cases (seventeen for the plaintiff and three for the defendant) and once acted as a witness in a jurisdiction dispute. Many of his cases would today be tried in small-claims court, but he did try one case where the amount in question was $5,000.

While women could not petition a court in the nineteenth century, they could appear in court with a man speaking for them. In his law practice, Francis occasionally represented female clients, setting the stage for him to represent his own wife before both the Missouri Supreme Court and the US Supreme Court in 1875.

In 1861, Francis represented Emma S. Duncan in the most expensive suit he ever brought before a judge. Ms. Duncan claimed Noah M. and Francis M. Ludlow, who were doing business as Ludlow and Company, owed her $5,000 from a loan she had given them eight years previously. On May 3, 1861, they admitted guilt and agreed to repay the full loan plus 10 percent interest.[73]

In another case that year, Francis represented Mary Ludlow, an orphaned minor from Alabama[74] who was owed $1,060 by Noah M. and Francis M. Ludlow. Tragically, Mary Ludlow died before the case concluded, and in final judgment, given upon her death in 1863, the money owed to her was given to a man named Edward Harris.[75]

Francis also represented Laura Telle, the plaintiff in a September 1864 divorce case. She accused her husband, George Telle, of abandonment and adultery, alleging he deserted her after only two weeks of marriage in December 1862. She said he lived in houses of ill fame and committed adultery with public prostitutes.[76]

Francis served as a judge of election twice, in 1862[77] and in the November 7, 1865, election, both for the Thirty-Third District.[78] While this was a minor position with only token power, it demonstrated his dedication to democracy. Election judges were the presiding officers at polling places and were chosen as representatives of their political party. Their job was to receive the ballots from the voters and deposit them in the ballot box, as well as to monitor the qualifications of the voter and the behavior of the election judges from other political parties.[79] If any disputes regarding election law arose, they judged them, which is where Francis's legal background made him an especially good judge. He would also have been responsible for maintaining peace inside the polling place and alerting the police if the raucousness outside got out of hand.[80] Francis later served on a Vigilance Committee at his polling place in the Sixth Ward during the April 1867 election in St. Louis,[81] presumably to prevent corruption and violence at the polls.

Francis clearly longed to hold a judgeship. He ran for judge of the law commissioner's court, the governing body in county government in Missouri, in November 1863.[82] In this campaign he was supported by fellow Republicans, one of whom wrote anonymously to the *Missouri Daily Democrat* in support of his campaign:

> *In addition to his legal qualifications, there is no more disinterested patriot and lover of freedom in the community. From the beginning of the war he has been the constant and devoted friend of the soldier . . . refusing all consideration for his own and excellent lady's [sic] unremitting labors in their behalf. Other things equal, he has a large claim upon the gratitude of our soldiers, and I doubt not if they generally knew of his disinterested kindness to them, they would gladly give him their votes.*
>
> *As a citizen, Mr. Minor is a most excellent and upright man, and is a lawyer well educated, first rate and reliable and worthy of every trust. Born in a slave state, he is the unflinching advocate of immediate emancipation and the friend of liberty. . . . He is a man of the most liberal and progressive tendencies, and fully in sympathy with his Government . . . giving to it his prayers and hopes, his influence and his means; and believing fully in its final success and triumph over the most unholy and wicked rebellion the world ever knew. It will be a gratification to his many friends to vote for him on the day of election, and it is to be hoped he will be chosen to the responsible office for which he is a candidate.[83]*

Unfortunately, this supporter's wishes were not to be. Francis lost the election to fellow Republican Roderick E. Rombauer,[84] who later went on to become a judge of the circuit court from 1868 to 1871 and judge of the court of appeals, a position he held from 1884 to 1897.[85]

Francis ran a second time for judge of the law commissioner's court in April 1856[86] to fill the unexpired term of Edward Bates, the same man who may have been Francis's previous employer. Francis lost again, this time to the Honorable Charles B. Lord, who held the office for a decade until the court was consolidated into the St. Louis Circuit Court in January 1866.[87]

Similarly, Francis ran as a nominee for judge of the probate court in October 1864 but lost the nomination to John Grether, a former justice of the peace in St. Louis County[88] and councilman for the Eighth Ward.[89]

Two Wrongful Appointments

Two curious scandals, in which Francis did not play an active role, are the only marks on his otherwise pristine legal career. Both involved Francis being illegally appointed to public roles he thought he was holding legally.

The first occurred on December 21, 1861, when Francis was appointed public administrator by the Board of County Commissioners of St. Louis County in response to the previous administrator, P. B. Garesche, vacating his position on December 10, 1861, with less than a year left of his term.[90] This was done under the aegis of "An Act to Make the Office of Public Administrator and Common School Commissioner in Certain Communities Elective," which was approved on March 14, 1859. The Act stated:

> *If any vacancy shall occur in the office of Public Administrator or Common School Commissioner in either of the counties in the act mentioned, to which this is mandatory, by death, resignation, removal from the state, or by any other disqualification, The County Court in the County of which the vacancy shall occur shall make an order to fill such a vacancy, provided such vacancy shall occur more than twelve months before a general election for such offices: if such vacancy shall occur less than twelve months before a general election for such office such vacancy shall be filled by an appointment of the County Court; and the person so appointed to such office shall hold his office until his successor shall be elected and qualified.[91]*

Francis took the oath of this office and offered the bond of $50,000 and two securities as required by law on December 21, the same day it was brought before Judge Ferguson of the probate court. He refused to certify it, offering no reason why. Instead, he claimed the authority to appoint that office and named William J. Romyn to the position.

On December 30, Francis showed Romyn his legal certificate of appointment and proof he had fulfilled all the other requirements of the law. Romyn refused to do the same, so Francis sued him, asking him to prove in court by what authority he claimed to hold this office and for the State of Missouri to rule.

The case came before the St. Louis Circuit Court on January 6, 1862. Romyn's attorneys, Judge James R. Lackland, George W. Cline, and William C. Jamison, argued that the county commissioner's court did not have the authority to appoint Francis but the probate court of St. Louis County did, and the judge had chosen Romyn. They then presented a copy of Romyn's oath, bond, and securities as Exhibit A. George P. Strong argued that the commissioner's court was within its rights.[92]

On February 1, 1862, Judge Samuel M. Breckinridge ruled that Romyn had the right to hold the office.[93]

The second incident occurred when Francis finally realized his dream of being a judge for a handful of days in 1869 and 1870, albeit on a provisional basis. His temporary judgeship was made possible thanks to a Missouri Act of Legislature passed on March 5, 1869, which states: "In the event of the sickness or absence of the Judge of said Court, the Circuit Court of St. Louis County or any Judge thereof in vacation, may appoint for the time being, a Provisional Judge of the said Court, who shall possess the qualifications of a Judge of the Circuit Court, and in the absence, sickness or other incapacity to act, of the Judge of said Court, said Judge shall have all the powers and perform all the duties conferred and imposed by law upon the Judge of said Court."[94]

Francis was first appointed provisional judge on August 30, 1869, when Judge Christian D. Wolff was ill. That day, twenty people— thirteen men and seven women—appeared before Judge Minor. The charges against the men included six counts of assault and battery, two counts of grand larceny, two counts of larceny, one of petty larceny, one count of "open and notorious adultery," and one of selling liquor without a license. The women were charged with four counts of "keeping common Bawdy house," and one count each of "riotously disturbing the peace," larceny, and petty larceny.[95] Their sentences were passed without incident. Judge Wolff resumed his duties the following day, and Francis stepped down.

About a month later, on September 29, 1869, Judge Christian D. Wolff, being again sick, appointed Francis as provisional judge of the court of correction under the authority of St. Louis Circuit Court judge James K. Knight. Judge Wolff returned to work the following day, so Francis stepped down.

On March 2, 1870, when Judge Wolff was again ill, Francis was appointed as provisional judge of the court of criminal correction, again by James K. Knight, who was acting on the authority of his previous appointment. The *Daily Missouri Democrat* wrote that Judge Minor "seemed perfectly at home on the bench, and gave judgement in several cases. One good thing he did, and that was to check the lawyers in their wrangling and bring them square down to the point at issue."[96]

However, one seemingly innocent case that day would come back to haunt him. A woman named Kate Ryan was led before him on the charge of petty larceny. She pleaded guilty and was fined twenty-five dollars but was unable to pay. As a result, she was sent to the St. Louis Workhouse, a debtor's prison that allowed inmates to pay off debt through forced labor.[97]

A few days later, on March 8, she stood before Judge Wilson Primm of the criminal court on a writ of habeas corpus, which alleges unlawful detention or imprisonment and requests that the court determine the legality of the detention. Kate's lawyer, Mr. Seymore Voullaire, argued that because the circuit court was in session that day, Francis's appointment should have been made by that court as a whole, not by the individual judge; therefore, Francis's authority as a provisional judge expired September 30, and he was not legally empowered to sentence Kate. The lawyer then had the audacity to charge that, being once provisionally appointed, Francis regarded himself as a provisional judge of the court at all times.[98]

Francis's attorney, John Lewis, was aghast at the way Kate's lawyer was dragging Francis into a case that wasn't even really about him but rather about whether her imprisonment was lawful, which was the responsibility of Ferdinand Gottschalk, the superintendent of the workhouse,[99] not the judge who fined her. Francis's sentence was the twenty-five-dollar fine, not that she be remanded to the workhouse; that occurred because she was unable to pay the fine. He also noted that Francis, as judge of the criminal court was "not the custodian of the gaol or the records of the court," so Kate's case should have been taken to the circuit court.[100]

Francis, as was his character, kept silent and issued only a single public statement on the matter. It took the form of a brief letter to the editors of the *Daily Missouri Democrat*: "In reply to your local on this subject, and in justice to myself, I wish to say that I have at all times been ready to act as Judge when notified that there was a vacancy, and I requested the deputy clerk so to inform me. I certainly cannot be expected to hang around the courtroom watching for a vacancy."[101]

Privately, Francis assured the court that he had not sought the appointment nor derived any benefit from it. To show his dedication to the law, he wrote out his resignation as a provisional judge for the court. He was convinced to withhold it until Judge Primm gave his decision, which came down on March 18, 1870.

The judge affirmed the facts of the case and that the warrant of conviction was "in due form of law."[102] Kate was discharged from the workhouse on the grounds that Francis's appointment was irregular,[103] and she was committed to the common jail to answer to the charge of petty larceny again. Francis tendered his resignation and never again served as a provisional judge.

WORK AFTER THE CIVIL WAR

Francis's exact location of legal employment from 1866 to 1870 is unclear. In 1866, he is listed as an attorney for R. H. Cowan in a lease transfer for property in city block 587 between his client and Richard Holland.[104] Whatever type of legal work he did during that time earned him $25 a month,[105] according to the *Daily Missouri Democrat*, but his total income was over $1,983 that year.[106]

In 1867, he worked at 305 Olive, a building that housed no less than seven law firms,[107] so he could have worked in any of them or secured his own. The one with most public record is that of Lee and Webster, which was in business from 1867 to 1870, under the ownership of Bradley D. Lee and B. F. Webster.[108]

From 1869 to 1870, Francis worked at 10 North Fourth, Room 19,[109] which was directly across from the courthouse. One of the offices in that building belonged to Benjamin L. Hickman,[110] attorney at law,[111] another possible employer.

In January 1871, Francis was elected a clerk of the Missouri Supreme Court,[112] the only political office he ever held.[113] In this role, he was responsible for receiving and filing petitions, filing paperwork brought in by attorneys, documenting the date filed, writing explanatory notes on the case file, recording it in the docket book, and assigning a case number and court date to the docket book. He also sent out a summons to the person being called into court; recorded any actions, motions, filings, continuances, etc. in the daily record book; issued calls for depositions to be given by those who could not attend the court session; directed the sheriff to assemble two dozen or more white male citizens to be considered for the jury; and entered all status reports and judgments into the book and onto papers filed with the case. On top of this, he took notes, kept the entries in the record books for each day in court, and directed cases back to the circuit court, when needed.[114]

Upon assuming this role, Francis requested permission to move "his office from the room over the Star Clothing store to the small recess between the law library and the Supreme Court room" where "the valuable records of the court, which are stored away in pigeon holes,"[115] would be safer from fire. He apparently never got over the loss of so many records, far less valuable than those of the state supreme court, at his place of employment during the Great Fire. Given Francis's fastidious nature, he likely developed a more sophisticated filing system for them as well.

Records of trials in St. Louis have not been processed past 1872, so it is impossible to say with certainty what cases he was involved in as a clerk and then later in private practice. Francis stepped down from his clerkship in 1873 so that he could present Virginia's case of *Minor v. Happersett* to the Missouri Supreme Court without any conflict of interest.

He did not return to the position after the case moved on to the US Supreme Court; he appears to have gone back into private practice. Francis is listed in the St. Louis directory as working as a lawyer and notary public at 404 Olive in 1874 and at 414 Olive from 1875 to 1877.[116] In July 1876, he advertised for bankruptcy claims in room 19 of the building, and in December was located in room 5,[117] though the nature of his work there is unknown. Upon his death, his practice was lauded as "distinguished and successful."[118]

Francis was a founding member of the Bar Association of St. Louis upon its formation on March 16, 1874,[119] when a group of one hundred lawyers and judges came together at the Old St. Louis Courthouse to formally organize themselves. The pledged duties of this association were "to maintain high standards among practitioners of the law, to be watchful of the fair administration of justice, and to promote social relations among its members."[120]

Such advocacy for their profession was much needed at the time, as it was mired in ethical issues. The Bar Association of Metropolitan St. Louis reports that "standards for admission to the bar were virtually nonexistent, the ethics of some attorneys were questionable, and judgeships were politically determined."[121] Later, Francis's membership was integral in making the St. Louis Bar a major advocate of female suffrage.[122]

Francis was forced to retire from legal practice in 1878 due to problems with his hearing.[123] He came out of retirement only once, to represent Virginia when she sued Mary Ann Finney for repayment of $11,000 resulting from a $6,000 loan made on November 15, 1875, plus subsequent taxes and insurance fees. The case was settled in probate in January 1880, after Ms. Finney's death.[124] Thereafter, Francis's "time was largely devoted to study and to writing," mostly on the issue of female suffrage, as the following chapters will show.[125]

Chapter Seven

The Minors during the Civil War

A BLUISH-GRAY CLOUD OF GUNPOWDER STILL LINGERED AT FARAWAY Fort Sumter in South Carolina, on April 12, 1861, when states began choosing sides in the once unthinkable yet now inevitable Civil War. Missouri, like its eastern counterpart, Kentucky, was a border state with a mixed culture and heritage and would have liked to remain in armed neutrality[1]—a stance in which they did not send men or supplies to either side but would fight any Union or Confederate soldiers who entered the state. Missouri tried to hold that stance for more than two months. But on July 4, President Lincoln rejected the idea that any state could take a neutral stance on the war, declaring neutrality "recognizes no fidelity to the Constitution, no obligation to maintain the Union; and while very many who have favored it are, doubtless, loyal citizens, it is, nevertheless, treason in effect."[2]

Because Missouri had to declare an allegiance, there was now no way of escaping the war unscathed. The outcome of Missouri's decision was significant for many reasons, not the least of which was that if secession occurred, the Confederacy would gain St. Louis, the largest industrial center in rebel territory,[3] which would bring it much-needed resources and manpower. It might seem a foregone conclusion that a state settled by Southerners that was "Southern in culture and heritage"[4] would automatically side with the Confederacy, and indeed that is what pro-secessionist governor Claiborne Fox Jackson expected[5] when he called a state constitutional convention to discuss secession in 1861.[6] But he hadn't counted on the influence of the tens of thousands of German and Irish immigrants[7]—they did not own slaves and were staunchly Unionist—who had recently moved into the state,[8] changing not only its population but its values. When the final vote was taken, the convention delegates shocked the government by voting to stay in the Union.[9]

Despite this official decision, many Missourians were reluctant to dissolve the time-honored tradition of slavery. It was an integral part of the state's past and present, dating back to the 1720 delivery of five hundred slaves to the French southeastern Missouri territory to work in the lead mines.[10] In the Minors' adopted home of St. Louis, the institution was part and parcel with its founding in 1764.[11] When Missouri became a state in 1821, its constitution declared that slaves were the personal property of their owners, who could sell, trade, or free them as they wished, provided there was compensation for the loss and they could swear the slave was mentally stable and would "not become a public charge."[12]

In 1840, just before the Minors relocated to Missouri, the state was home to approximately 58,000 slaves, and by the time the Civil War broke out, about 115,000 slaves lived there.[13] Despite this seemingly impressive number, as of 1860 Missouri ranked fourth on the list of states with the fewest slaves; only one in eight families in the state owned them,[14] with the average family owning 4.7 slaves, as opposed to 12.7 each in the Deep South[15] from which the Minors had just emigrated.

Slavery was not nearly as profitable in St. Louis as in states to the south, thanks to the German and Irish immigrants,[16] who would carry out the same labor at less cost to their employers with no financial risk if they quit.[17] But it was still a common sight. It is estimated there were at least thirty-five offices in St. Louis dedicated to the slave trade,[18] not a stretch of the imagination since St. Louis was a hub for the transportation and sale of slaves into the Deep South.[19] Slave auctions were held on a regular basis at downtown slave markets and even on the steps of the courthouse.[20] Once sold, many of these men, women, and children were separated from their families and taken to plantations in rural Missouri that supplied St. Louis with tobacco, hemp, and limited supplies of cotton,[21] or to ranches where they tended the horses and mules the state was known for, alongside cattle, hogs, and sheep.[22] Others worked the city's docks and ferryboats, in the burgeoning downtown businesses, or were shipped farther south.[23]

St. Louis became inextricably linked to slavery in 1857 with the hearing of the now-famous Dred Scott case at the St. Louis Courthouse, in the very same room where Virginia Minor would later fight for women's suffrage. Scott, a slave owned by US Army surgeon Dr. John Emerson, frequently traveled with his master to military posts in Illinois and the Wisconsin Territory, both of which were free areas. Scott and his wife, Harriet, sued in the St. Louis Circuit Court for their freedom in April 1846 under a Missouri statute that stated anyone who was wrongfully enslaved could sue for freedom and that once slaves were taken to free areas, they were freed even if they returned to Missouri.[24]

While their case appeared legally strong, "Freedom Suits" like the Scotts' were usually not successful; in the preceding two years, only one out of twenty-five resulted in the slave being freed.[25] The first trial ruled in favor of Dr. Emerson on a technicality, but after a long delay, a new trial was granted and the Scotts were freed. However, they were remanded back into slavery when Dr. Emerson took the case to the Missouri Supreme Court, arguing that military law should apply to the case, rather than civil law, because he was ordered by his superiors to go to the free states and had no choice but to take his slaves. On March 22, 1852, the state supreme court found for Dr. Emerson. The following year, the Scotts again sued in the Circuit Court of the United States for the District of Missouri, but that court found in favor of John Sandford, Dr. Emerson's brother-in-law, who now claimed to own the Scotts.[26]

Four years later, in February 1856, the US Supreme Court finally heard *Dred Scott v. Sandford*.[27] Its final decision—a seven-to-two ruling against the Scotts that declared Black people had no claim to freedom or citizenship and that the Missouri Compromise, which admitted Missouri into the Union as a slave state, was illegal—was given on March 6, 1857.[28] It paved the way for the institution of slavery to continue, both in Missouri and throughout the country. While the last slaves were sold in St. Louis three months before the Civil War began,[29] the slave trade continued in Missouri until 1865, when all slaves in the state were emancipated[30] by an ordinance passed on January 11 at the state constitutional convention, a mere three weeks before Congress passed the Thirteenth Amendment.[31]

The Minors must have closely followed the proceedings in the papers with great hope for a favorable outcome for the Scotts, as they firmly opposed slavery. No records exist of them ever owning slaves outside of those kept by their families in childhood, nor did they bring any with them from Mississippi or purchase any once in St. Louis.[32] Unlike many of the leading St. Louis businessmen who quietly supported emancipation,[33] the Minors readily shared their views with friends, business associates, and family. Francis was a member of the Union Emancipation Central Committee, which met at the corner of Third and Locust Streets,[34] and often spoke at their events.[35]

Francis was also a delegate to the 1863 Jacobin Convention and the Missouri State Constitutional Convention in Jefferson City, Missouri, where he was asked to speak.[36] While Jacobinism had been an ideology in the United States since the Revolution,[37] by the 1860s, American Jacobins had morphed into Radical Republicans who strongly allied with the Union,[38] opposed slavery,[39] and viewed the Civil War as a revolution of sorts, analogous to the French Revolution in the principles of *liberté*, *égalité*, and *fraternité*.[40] Like their French counterparts, the moderate members of the party were mostly lawyers and judges,[41] and in Missouri, the cause was especially strong. By early 1863, Radical Republicans functioned under the idea that to be a Jacobin or Radical Republican, one must not only oppose slavery but also embrace "expanded civil and then political rights and equal protection"[42] under the law. Therefore, they felt that new representation in state governments and constitutions were required—changes that, of course, reflected their own views.[43]

To that end, Francis and his fellow delegates, including committee chairman and future US senator B. Gratz Brown, attended the Missouri State Constitutional Convention to present their own Union ticket of candidates for judges of the Missouri Supreme Court: Barton Bates of St. Charles, William Van Ness Bay of St. Louis, and John Debos Sharp Dryden of Marion, Missouri.[44] Opponents called this move the "Missouri Conspiracy" and said it was an attempt to "coerce and compel the Administration at Washington and the Governor and Legislature of Missouri to succumb to their views of policy, under direct and undisguised threats of revolution, in case of refusal . . . [and required the Assembly to] vote for a new Constitutional Convention, threatening all who may refuse to do so to have their names published in every Radical paper in the State, 'that they may be noted, marked and remembered accordingly.'"[45]

These dissenters weren't entirely wrong; the group did call for "a new state government by having primary elections held in October for judges of election, and an independent election held in connection with the regular election in November"[46] for the purposes of "immediate emancipation,"[47] but their intent was not violent nor nearly as revolutionary as the opposing party paints. They simply wanted to use the legal means within their power to accomplish their goals: the end of slavery and the installation of judges who could make that happen.

During his speech, Brown clearly articulated their purpose: "We have come here pledged to do something to rid the State of the terror under which we live. Now let us do it. If we can mandamus [legally intimidate] this corrupt Government out of existence, let us mandamus them into the future world. If we can wipe out of the statute books the obnoxious slave laws, let us wipe them out."[48]

They were successful. All three proposed candidates held seats on the Missouri Supreme Court from 1863 through 1865,[49] and the convention voted for gradual emancipation by July 4, 1870.[50]

Why Francis and Virginia held antislavery views isn't clear, but there are many possible explanations. Their families collectively owned over one hundred slaves as late as the brink of the Civil War,[51] so the Minors certainly grew up around them and may have formed bonds with their closest personal attendants. Louisa H. A. Minor, one of Virginia's distant cousins from Fredericksburg, wrote in her diary of the closeness between her family and their servants,[52] as slaves were often called by their owners,[53] and expressed her belief that they were treated fairly. Making abuse within their natal families even less likely is the evidence of historical letters and records that indicate that most slaves in Albemarle County, Virginia, were very well treated, unlike those in the Deep South.[54]

However, Dabney Minor III, the brother with whom Virginia and Francis lived while in Holly Springs, Mississippi, might have been another story. He owned, bought, and sold[55] slaves frequently and even placed public rewards for runaway slaves during the time the Minors were with him.[56] A resident of Holly Springs for more than a quarter of a century, it is possible he adopted the attitudes of the Deep South regarding a master's treatment of his slaves.

In the "Record of Fugitives," a study of more than two hundred slaves aided by Harriet Tubman through the Underground Railroad in 1855 and 1856, the most commonly cited reason for running away was physical abuse.[57] Pulitzer Prize–winning historian Eric Foner notes, "The fugitives who arrived in New York told stories replete with accounts of frequent whippings and other brutality; their words of complaint included 'great violence,' 'badly treated,' 'ruff times,' 'hard master,' 'very severe,' 'a very cruel man,' and 'much fault to find with their treatment.'"[58] So if Dabney was abusive, Francis and Virginia could have soured on the institution during their time with him.

Even if this wasn't the case, they may have been against the institution on religious or moral grounds. The Minor family was Episcopalian, and a division of that church had a strong abolitionist contingent.[59] While living in Virginia, they were close to Bishop William Meade and his son, R. K. Meade, both of whom were against slavery and had freed their own slaves.[60] The bishop helped found the Albemarle Colonization Society, which campaigned for the removal of African slaves to Africa.[61] His son, R. K., who was the officiant at Virginia and Francis's wedding, was an active member as well, so either could have influenced the young couple.

The relocation of free Blacks also was a popular initiative in St. Louis by the time the Minors moved there and was carried out by the Missouri Colonization Society, with particular success from 1850 to 1855.[62] In their new home, the Minors would have come into regular contact with both slaves and free Blacks. In 1840, about a third of Missouri's freed Black people lived in St. Louis. By 1850, more than half called the city home,[63] and by 1860, 97 percent of St. Louis's Black population was free.[64] More than a thousand of these freed Black citizens were prosperous heirs of old money, business owners such as barbers, steamboat stewards, saloon or boardinghouse owners, and farmers[65]—part of what came to be known as

St. Louis's "Colored Aristocracy."[66] These men and women owned large homes, fine carriages, and luxury goods, such as pianos, and they traveled across the country just as their white counterparts did.[67]

Seeing so many former slaves prospering may have been enough to reverse any proslavery mindsets the Minors learned in their youth, such as family friend and former president Thomas Jefferson's belief that slaves were "incapable as children of taking care of themselves."[68] However, the social mixing of Blacks (freed or slaves) and whites was strictly regulated by Missouri law, regardless of their wealth. For example, whites ten or older could not attend any social events/balls with Blacks.[69] "Colored" organizations, churches, and schools[70] had to be separate from their white counterparts, even when engaging in the same civic or philanthropic activity. This means the Minors would have had little social contact with Black people, at least until the atrocities of war brought them together against a common enemy.

UNION SUPPORTERS FROM A CONFEDERATE FAMILY

While it may never be known for certain why Virginia and Francis supported emancipation, this choice and their decision to side with the Union placed them in opposition with their family back home, who continued to support slavery and fought on the side of the Confederacy. There is no evidence of their male siblings who were alive at the start of the Civil War, Dabney Minor III (Francis's brother) and Lewis Madison Minor (Virginia's brother), fighting on the front lines, though it was not uncommon for the upper classes to find ways around military service.

However, the feelings of her family were made crystal clear in a letter from William Waters Minor to Prof. John B. Minor, Francis's great uncle, on February 16, 1861: "In times like these, when the 'irrepressible conflict' of *black* Republicanism is at our very doors, it does appear to me that all the calls of patriotism & friendship & kindred too, should unite us, John, & all true Virginians against the aggression of our Northern enemies, who have defrauded us of our property, our equal rights under the Constitution, & who we are preparing (so far as we can see) to coerce us to submit to them as our superiors, unless we speedily humble ourselves to their unjust & unrighteous demands."[71]

A. L. Holladay, a distant relative, fought at the Battle of Spotsylvania and was taken prisoner in Fort Delaware.[72] Francis's second cousin once removed, Minor Meriwether—with whom he would become close later in life and who affectionately called him "Uncle Frank"[73]—was antislavery in his views, though he served in the Confederate Army as an engineer officer.[74] Meriwether even freed his slave, Henry, but the young man refused to leave his service, even going to war with him.[75]

In contrast, Meriwether's wife, Elizabeth Avery—who would later fight alongside Virginia in St. Louis on the issue of women's suffrage—was a virulent white supremacist,[76] though she admits in her memoir, "My dear husband who fought for years in the Confederate army, seemed to feel no bitterness in his heart, not even in the years immediately following Lee's surrender. Were he living now . . . he would probably be as kindly and as just in his estimate of a northern, as of a southern, soldier."[77] Despite this, Elizabeth goes on to recount that her husband was one of the counselors and lieutenants of Ku Klux Klan founder and Supreme Grand Wizard General Nathan Bedford Street.[78]

It is also unclear how direct Minor relations in Virginia fared during the war. However, one can draw logical inferences from what was taking place in the countryside around them. While Albemarle County was relatively untouched given that no major battles took place on its soil,[79] the people still had to deal with looting soldiers. Francis's side of the Minor family sold Woodlawn in 1845 or 1846 and moved to Mississippi,[80] and Gale Hill did not suffer damage, but Virginia's family home could have been in danger, given that the family lived in close proximity to former president Jefferson's home of Monticello, which was at the time owned by New Yorker Uriah Phillips Levy and seized by the Confederate Army in 1862.[81]

When the Union Army marched on Charlottesville on March 3, 1865, John B. Minor, Francis's great uncle, served as a Confederate guard and an attendant at the military hospital in Louisa Court House at the University of Virginia (UVA). It was because of his influence that Major General George A. Custer and General Philip H. Sheridan not only changed their plans to burn the venerable institution—as they had done to the University of Alabama, which was modeled on UVA, only a few weeks before—but also posted guards to protect it.[82]

The rest of Charlottesville was not as fortunate. Union troops burned Charlottesville Manufacturing Co. because they made Confederate uniforms, and with empty haversacks and bellies, the troops scoured the countryside for food. Many local estates were vandalized, including Sunnyside and Wyndhurst, home of UVA's rector Thomas Preston.[83]

Louisa H. A. Minor recorded in her diary that she was forced to feed, cook for, and give up her bed to the troops of General Ewell, in addition to entertaining him in her parlor when his troops marched through the area in June 1862.[84] Later, in March 1865, when federal troops invaded Albemarle County, Louisa had her property confiscated by the Union army.[85] She recalls in her diary for Sunday, March 5: "This was a day of terror! The enemy were coming in all day long. Searched Mama and E's rooms, broke [the] safe and carried off the guns and other arms in the house. Stole most of Daddy's clothes . . . broke into the desk, carried off bonds and other papers of balance. . . . Stole the bag of playthings (a box of Dominos) and made their exit."[86]

The following day she wrote of the relief of watching "the Yankees depart" and praying that "we might never behold them again!"[87]

A Divided State and City

Those concerns, however, were thousands of miles from Virginia and Francis's daily lives. While their relatives took to the battlefields, the Minors waited to see which way the fate of their adopted home state would fall. Missouri was unique in that it was both a slave state and a border state that, while technically declared Union, had many citizens who actually supported the Confederacy.[88] It was important to the future of the war because it was the most populated state west of the Mississippi, the nation's third-highest producer of corn and pork, and a main producer of grain and livestock as well as iron and lead.[89]

St. Louis was a key strategic city, as it controlled the mouth of the Ohio River, the Missouri River,[90] and a major section of the Mississippi River,[91] as well as the hub of the most extensive railroad west of the

Mississippi, with eight hundred miles of tracks snaking out in every direction.[92] It was also home to the federal subtreasury, which held $400,000 in cash,[93] the equivalent of about $11.6 million in today's currency.[94]

But perhaps more importantly, the St. Louis Arsenal supplied thousands of troops out west with arms, ammunition, artillery,[95] and basic equipment such as haversacks, canteens, and bedrolls.[96] The men stationed there assembled weapons and manufactured cannonballs and bullets, including the dreaded Minie ball[97] that wounded and killed so many on the battlefield. It is estimated the arsenal could equip as many as fifty thousand men.[98] In 1861, its inventory was said to be the "largest store of weapons west of the Mississippi River,"[99] including "sixty thousand muskets, ninety thousand pounds of powder, one-and-a-half million cartridges, forty cannon, and equipment for the manufacture of arms."[100] As a result, whoever controlled the St. Louis Arsenal and its large cache of weapons controlled Missouri.[101]

Situated in the southern part of the city on bluffs overlooking the Mississippi River, it was also an important strategic site. From the ramparts, soldiers could see anyone approaching for miles around, while at ground level the meeting of the river and stone formed a natural port that could be used to transport goods and men as well as house a small navy for defense.[102] In addition, the arsenal had its own railroad, so controlling it meant controlling everything that was delivered to and shipped from this location.[103] Despite all this, the arsenal was guarded by only forty Union soldiers, so it was viewed as an easy target.[104]

For a while, St. Louis was home to two opposing armies, each of whom had their eyes set on the arsenal. As one St. Louisan later wrote of the standoff over this valuable asset, "Men of the same race, the same nation, the same State, the same city, hot with passion, stood face to face."[105] On April 20, the stalemate broke when the Confederate Army took control of the much smaller Liberty Arsenal in Clay County, Missouri. They took 1,500 rifles and muskets, a few cannons, and a significant amount of powder and ammunition.[106] On May 6, 1861, Confederates amassed at Lindell Grove, in a place they nicknamed Camp Jackson, as part of a plot to divert the stolen Confederate weapons to the St. Louis Arsenal so that Governor Jackson, a Southern sympathizer, could seize control.

But fortune was not with Camp Jackson. Union captain Nathaniel Lyon found out about the plot and had most of the arsenal's weaponry quietly moved to safety in nearby Alton, Illinois,[107] leaving the men at the arsenal—forty guards, supplemented by 493 federal troops[108] and a volunteer army of nearly 10,000[109]—with only seven thousand muskets to defend it.[110] On May 10, Captain Lyon sent several thousand soldiers[111] to surround the encampment and arrest the far smaller, 600-person Confederate army.

As they were led through the streets to the arsenal to be imprisoned, the crowd that had gathered, some out of curiosity but many to help defend the Confederates with "rifles, shotguns, and pistols,"[112] quickly turned into a mob. Alternating cheering, spitting on, and cursing at the prisoners[113] and "bitterly taunt[ing and] strik[ing] with their fists, the captors of their relatives and friends,"[114] members of the crowd hurled rocks and shots were fired. Officially, no one knows which side started the shooting, though one witness blamed the undisciplined volunteer soldiers who "were unable to stand motionless and in silence when attacked by stones and guns"—leaving twenty-eight people dead, including soldiers and innocent men, women, and children as young as twelve,[115] and another seventy-five wounded.[116]

This is widely considered to be the first battle of the Civil War in St. Louis,[117] but rather than serving as a warning, it only heightened tensions between Northern and Southern sympathizers.[118] Within the city itself, people holed up, waiting to see what would happen. "As soon as it was dark, from fear of riot, the saloons and restaurants were closed and their doors were bolted and barred. The windows of many private houses were also shut and securely fastened. The theaters and all places of public amusement were empty. The police were on the alert but were taxed to the utmost to nip in the bud any show of disorder,"[119] reported one citizen.

The two sides clashed in minor skirmishes across the city in May and June, increasing local panic and killing at least another dozen soldiers and thirty civilians, including a few women and children.[120] Seeing something had to be done, the federal government stepped in to ring the city in fortifications, soldiers began staffing up Jefferson and Benton Barracks,[121] and armored gunboats were launched from Carondelet, eight miles south of St. Louis.[122] Between this fortification of the state's largest city and Union/Missouri State Guard victories at the battles of Booneville, Lexington, and Carthage during the summer of 1861, the Union increased its power,[123] making it clear the Confederates would have to look elsewhere to gain ground in Missouri.

Four months into the war, by the humid dog days of August 1861, the northern half of the state was firmly backing the Union, while the southern counties threatened secession.[124] Fearing its own civil war, Missouri's Union soldiers sought to rein in the Southerners. They forced the Confederate-sympathizing government from the safety of the capital in Jefferson City into the rural southwest corner of the state. Incensed and seeking to eradicate the Union opposition, the displaced politicians rallied the Missouri State Guard and called in favors across the state line in Arkansas to form their own Confederate battalion. The two regiments met at Wilson's Creek, near Springfield, in a bloody battle involving more than sixteen thousand troops—more than eleven thousand on the Confederate side and only a little over five thousand on the Union side[125]—on August 10.[126] The battle lasted only about six hours, but it was deadly—one in ten were killed or wounded.[127] The exhausted Union Army eventually retreated to Springfield[128] and ceded control of the southwestern part of the state to the Confederates.[129]

THE ST. LOUIS LADIES UNION AID SOCIETY

The resulting casualties of the Battle of Wilson's Creek, numbering over two thousand and evenly split among both sides,[130] quickly overwhelmed field hospitals and facilities in neighboring Springfield. This required the wounded to be transported more than one hundred miles via wagon, a five- to six-day journey[131] over bumpy, rocky terrain and poorly constructed roads, to the last stop on the southwestern branch of the St. Louis Railroad[132] in Rolla. There, the less seriously injured Union soldiers were left to recuperate.[133] Emergency cases faced another one hundred miles to St. Louis via freight cars, a journey that could take upwards of another five to six days,[134] ample time for an injured person to fall victim to infection or die.[135]

However, even once they reached St. Louis, many wounded soldiers were unable to find help. St. Louis's only military hospital, known as the New House of Refuge, had opened just four days before the Battle of Wilson's Creek but was not yet staffed or stocked with provisions. Still, it was a place to house the wounded, who numbered nearly one thousand in St. Louis alone,[136] and it quickly filled. The other local hospitals, St. Louis Hospital, run by the Sisters of Charity, and City General Hospital did what they could with those sent to their doors.[137] Despite this, many had to wait weeks for treatment, still dressed in the same, bloody, dirt- and sweat-encrusted uniforms in which they fell in the field.[138]

In response to the growing local unrest and nearing violence, General Samuel Curtis and a group of seven[139] concerned St. Louis women, Virginia Minor among them,[140] met at the home of Mrs. F. Holy[141] to form the Ladies Union Aid Society of St. Louis (LUAS) on July 26, 1861. Within days, their numbers more than tripled. A St. Louis resident described the group of twenty-five original volunteers as being "made up of the best and most efficient women of the city. Social distinctions were for the time being obliterated. The hearts of the rich and the poor were for a time united by the common danger and by a common love of country. Anyone who could do some useful service to suffering soldiers was welcomed by all."[142]

The LUAS was one of many such benevolent groups run by Northern middle-class women as an act of patriotism and philanthropy.[143] Fueled by changing economic forces, which gave them more leisure time, and the ideals of the Second Great Awakening, which proposed among other things that people should wholeheartedly work for God's kingdom and not just rely on grace to save them,[144] Protestant women began forming charitable organizations as early as 1785 in Orange County, Virginia, where the Minors were from.[145] The Unitarian movement had a similar effect on St. Louis by the 1830s.[146] These groups taught women business and financial skills and gave them, at least in some states, legal autonomy as members of incorporated groups they didn't have as individuals but would desperately need to run busy, complex centers of healing during the Civil War.[147] By the time the fighting ceased, more than seven thousand aid societies existed in the North and Midwest,[148] some segregated but others that cared for Black and white soldiers.[149]

Led by Mrs. Anna Landing Wendell Clapp and Mrs. Joseph Crawshaw,[150] the mission of the LUAS was to provide what aid they could to the Union wounded,[151] starting with what they could scavenge from their own homes.[152] The women donated material intended for their own clothing, "scraped lint, knit socks, made under-garments, furnished beds for the sick in the hospitals, and secured aid and employment for the wives of soldiers."[153]

Having exhausted their own resources, the LUAS made their first public appeal for clothing and food on September 16.[154] By October 4, the group moved its headquarters to City General Hospital,[155] which was located downtown at the corner of Fifth and Chestnut,[156] and began their formal work. Volunteers rolled bandages day and night, prepared food and clothing for wounded soldiers and refugees,[157] and made hospital calls as needed,[158] tending to soldiers dropped off each night by the newly created rail ambulances that ran the Pacific Railroad each day.[159] This nonstop schedule for caring for more than twenty thousand soldiers[160] and thousands of refugees[161] during a bitterly cold winter[162] killed at least two members, Margaret Breckenridge and Mary Palmer, who died from exhaustion directly related to their volunteer work.[163] Others, such as Adaline Couzins, mother of famed St. Louis suffragist Phoebe Couzins,[164] served as nurses on the front lines of Missouri's battles, enduring gunshots, frostbite, and disease for their troubles.[165]

At the same time, Rev. William Greenleaf Eliot, pastor of the Unitarian Church of the Messiah, was formulating his own plan. With the help of Jessie Benton Fremont, wife of General John Fremont, the departmental commander, and Dorothea Dix, army superintendent of women nurses, they formed the Western Sanitary Commission, which was charged with equipping, overseeing, and staffing military hospitals in order to provide adequate care and provisions while the soldiers recovered.[166]

The LUAS soon became the main auxiliary of the Western Sanitary Commission.[167] Together, the two organizations hired medical staff and gathered the equipment and supplies needed to open the New House of Refuge as a functioning hospital. Fearing even worse battles to come, they also prepared St. Louis to handle an influx of nearly two thousand wounded soldiers at any one time, in addition to the thousand convalescing nearby at Benton Barracks.[168] A railroad line dedicated to transporting the wounded from battle sites across the state was set up,[169] and the US Sanitary Commission set aside a dozen ships to transport the wounded to St. Louis on the river and to function as floating hospitals.[170]

They would soon need all of these resources, as Missouri was still deeply divided into two armies and two governments. The secessionist government was led by former governor Jackson, and the Union government was helmed by Hamilton Rowan Gamble, who was appointed provisional governor after Jackson was removed from office in July.[171] Missouri seceded from the Union on October 28, 1861, and was accepted as the thirteenth Confederate state on November 5.[172] Many scholars consider this more of a symbolic gesture than a legally binding move since the members of the Missouri General Assembly voted to pass the Neosho ordinance, and even Jackson, who signed it, had no real power or authority in the state.[173] Gamble's provisional government was thought to be the official governing body.[174] In addition, questions remain as to whether Jackson's government had the quorum necessary to make its action legal.[175]

Nonetheless, a series of high-casualty battles followed over the next six months, sending large numbers of wounded into St. Louis from the battles of Fort Donelson, Tennessee; Pea Ridge, in northwest Arkansas; and Shiloh, Tennessee. These people were rushed to the military hospital at Jefferson Barracks[176] and nearly overwhelmed it, even with the progress made to date. Professor Galusha Anderson of the University of Chicago, who lived in St. Louis during the Civil War, paints the gruesome picture after the Battle of Shiloh: "On that field of carnage, 1,735 Union soldiers were killed outright, and 7,882 were wounded. The latter were sent to St. Louis by boat-loads. They were carried on stretchers up through our streets to the hospitals. The businessmen, merchants, clerks, manufacturers, bankers and artisans of various crafts helped bear along these ghastly burdens. Young men, the flower of the north-western states had been maimed, crippled, shot to pieces in defense of the Union."[177]

Even after turning many other facilities—churches, schools, prisons, and office space—into hospitals, St. Louis's ability to care for this massive influx of wounded wasn't enough. Workers from the LUAS and other volunteers had to transform two large halls into hospitals, bringing St. Louis's capacity to six thousand patients at fifteen hospitals.[178] By January 1862, these cumulative improvements made St. Louis the center of military medicine for the state as well as the entire Mississippi River Valley.[179] The LUAS was open around the clock through the fall of 1862 and winter 1863, so great was the need for bandage rolling and preparation of other supplies.[180] Though originally intended only to aid Union soldiers, as the war progressed, the LUAS saw the need for aid on both sides and in 1863 amended their charter to include "all 'who suffer at the cause of the Union, and also sick and wounded prisoners of war.'"[181]

Knowing disease ran rampant among the wounded and in refugee camps—it is estimated that twice as many men died of diseases like cholera, typhus, typhoid fever, malaria, and dysentery[182] during the Civil War than were killed on the battlefield[183]—the LUAS workers took special precautions to prevent widespread illness. They triaged cases, treating less serious wounds in camp and regimental hospitals, and sent stabilized soldiers to recover in camps outside the city.[184] They also set up special quarantined areas for measles and smallpox victims.[185]

Already actively involved in the state Republican Party, both Francis and Virginia rushed to aid the Union cause, he as a war claims agent and she as a founding member of the LUAS.[186] Francis must have supported Virginia's work with the LUAS, because societal mores required a husband's or father's approval for any work a woman pursued outside the home. Here again Francis proved progressive, as a number of men were known to have refused to allow their wives and daughters to provide aid during the war.[187]

Unlike many of the other LUAS members whose residences were in downtown St. Louis, Virginia lived in the rural suburbs on ten acres of farmland, roughly six miles from downtown. While this may not seem like an insurmountable distance to modern minds, it would have taken her more than an hour to travel to City Hospital by horse with or without a buggy,[188] which limited her to daytime activities; she was also too far away to be on call for late-night hospital emergencies or even to attend the society's evening meetings.[189] On top of that, at various times, martial law prohibited travel between the city and the country without prior approval, even during daylight hours.[190]

Nighttime travel during the Civil War was even more dangerous. In addition to lack of light outside the city proper and unreliable roads, guerrilla activity was common in northwest St. Louis County, so citizens were advised to stay off the roads after dark. In an example that literally hit close to home, the Six-Mile House Tavern on St. Charles Road, only a mile from where the Minors lived, was broken into on the night of July 26–27, 1864. A group of Southern rebels stole a horse, money, food, and various other items to support their military activities.[191]

The following day, the Fortieth and Forty-First Missouri Volunteers were mustered at nearby Benton Barracks to "protect the populace from the Confederate soldiers who 'have been sent or permitted to come among [the citizens of St. Louis] to recruit, rob, plunder, and murder, as best they can, in violation of the laws of war and of humanity.'"[192]

By the end of September, the guerrilla activity in St. Louis had progressed to the point that "all citizens exempt from military service, but 'capable of defending their homes' [were] asked to organize under the direction of the major." More than five thousand men responded[193]—though Francis's name does not appear in extant records—and were organized under Col. B. Gratz Brown under the name Militia Exempts or the "Old Guard," as they came to be affectionately known.[194]

Distance and nighttime danger notwithstanding, Virginia was still one of the most consistently participative and enthusiastic members of the LUAS, which had about forty-five active members and countless others who volunteered as time and circumstances allowed.[195] Virginia organized society meetings aimed at soliciting help from the public[196] and, being well known and liked in the community, used her natural charm and Francis's social and political connections to help raise money.[197] This excerpt from an April 12, 1864, letter from Virginia on behalf of the Floral and Horticultural Department of the Mississippi Valley Sanitary Fair is one example of her fundraising correspondence: "I beg leave to call your attention to the enclosed circular, and to ask what you will contribute in plants, in pots, bouquets or fruit, to be sent in your own name at the time of the Fair, or money enclosed to me now. I have made a list of all in this Township, which I shall return to the Department with the amount of each person's contribution opposite his or her name. So far, I have not a single refusal; those who had no fruit or flowers, sent money."[198]

Even though it kept her from some activities, Virginia's country estate proved to be a unique and valuable asset for the LUAS. Though they had access to a commissary, most of the food and drink the soldiers were served came from donations.[199] Virginia provided the hospitals and refugee camps with daily supplies of milk and cheese from her dairy,[200] chickens from her farm,[201] and vegetables and canned goods from her gardens,[202] and she encouraged her neighbors to do the same.[203] It is said that when she heard of an outbreak of scurvy among the soldiers, Virginia combed the countryside in her buggy[204] for fruit and personally delivered cherry preserves she made with her own hands with fruit from her orchards.

Though her location made trips to the downtown hospitals an infrequent occurrence, Benton Barracks, which doubled as a convalescent hospital and central location for assembling more than nineteen thousand troops[205] from the nearby states of Ohio, Indiana, Illinois, and Iowa,[206] was only three miles north of her estate,[207] at the intersection of Natural Bridge and Grand Avenue. Virginia made regular visits to the soldiers, whose injuries and illnesses often took weeks or months to heal,[208] offering conversation and comfort to those recuperating from their wounds and reading to those with nothing but time to kill.[209] She could have also brought them supplies of clean clothing, spectacles, cologne, paper, envelopes, stamps, wine, and books, all of which were in high demand.[210] Chaplains often were not present at the hospitals, so many of the volunteers also doubled as missionaries, praying with the sick and dying, even though the LUAS was not affiliated with any one religion.[211] Virginia could have also helped staff the kitchen, which served more than nineteen thousand meals in a six-month period[212] or even the special diet kitchen, for those with unusual, physician-approved dietary needs,[213] which served around twenty-four thousand meals in the same period.[214]

Another possible duty was overseeing the soldiers' wives who were employed to cut and sew hospital garments.[215] These women, who had no other source of employment, would pick up raw materials on a Thursday, sew them together over the next week, and bring them back the following Thursday. The LUAS volunteers checked the garments for quality and paid the wives[216] about three or four dollars a week for their work.[217] Women who didn't know how or could not sew due to poor eyesight or arthritis worked rolling bandages at a rate of twenty-five cents per one hundred yards of bandage.[218]

Virginia's antislavery views would have been welcome at Benton Barracks, which housed approximately three hundred to four hundred Black soldiers[219] as well as freemen and runaway slaves, many of whom chose to join the Colored Infantry that mustered there[220] beginning in 1863.[221] With her own strong education and connections to the University of Virginia, it is possible that Virginia may have taught at the schools run by the Christian Commission at the barracks to help former slaves learn to read and spell[222] or otherwise aided the Black women and children who found refuge behind the fortified walls,[223] at least until the Colored Union Aid Society of St. Louis took over the care of Black residents in 1864.[224]

It is also likely that Virginia was a member of the Ladies National Union League of St. Louis, which was formed in May 1863[225] as a chapter of the Woman's Loyal National League. The national organization of around five thousand members,[226] started by Susan B. Anthony and Elizabeth Cady Stanton, and its local chapters shared the same main goals as the all-male Loyal Leagues: to support the Union war effort and fight to end slavery. But the women's organization also had an additional purpose, one that would covertly continue the woman's suffrage movement during the war: "to educate women on their political rights and obligations."[227] In the year of the Woman's Loyal National League's existence—Susan B. Anthony shut it down toward the end of 1864—their biggest accomplishment was to collect more than four hundred thousand signatures, of which Virginia's likely was one,[228] in favor of universal suffrage for all. On January 29, 1866, Massachusetts senator Charles Sumner presented this petition to the Senate chamber, making it the first national petition that mentions women's suffrage.[229]

ENROLLING OFFICER AND WAR CLAIMS AGENT

In the initial haze of patriotism and fervor, the Civil War did not lack for willing fighting men. According to the Department of the Army, "in the first enthusiasm in the North which followed the President's first two calls for Militia and Volunteers, states frequently organized more units than their quota."[230] But as the war dragged on and devastation hit close to home in battles and guerrilla conflict, men became more reluctant to sign up. They didn't want to risk their lives and leave their wives, families, and property behind with the strong likelihood they would never lay eyes upon them again.

By 1862, the South instituted a draft and Missouri and Iowa were threatening their citizens with conscription.[231] The following year, Congress passed the Civil War Military Draft Act,[232] also known as the Enrollment Act, which required all men between the ages of twenty and forty-five to enroll for Union service,[233] with the proviso that married men could not be drafted until all available single men had been.[234] Exemptions were also made for the mentally or physically impaired, who were thought incapable of fighting; widows' only sons, who would carry on the family line; sons of ill parents who might need caregiving; and widowers with dependent children who would become orphans in the event of the father's death.[235]

Despite being only forty-one at the time of the draft, no records indicate that Francis ever saw battle in the military. He is, however, known to have been appointed an enrolling officer for the Thirty-Third District in St. Louis for the Enrolled Missouri Militia. He was appointed by Col. Lewis Merrill[236] and reported to William R. Fenn, superintendent for enrollment.[237] This role was developed as part of a special order issued by Missouri governor Hamilton Rowan Gamble on July 22, 1862, in response to a strong organized movement of violent guerrilla bands across the state who robbed and murdered innocent citizens.[238] This militia was charged with "punish[ing] all such crimes and ... destroy[ing] such bands."[239] Outside of this unusual activity, the militia was meant to be a part-time position, only called upon and paid in emergency circumstances but otherwise conducting local patrols and guard duty.[240]

Enrollment officers were, as their title implies, charged with "enroll[ing] all citizens subject to military duty." This involved filling out paperwork for each male citizen who presented as required under the law, even those who claimed exemption. Determination of the validity of the exemption was left to the Board of Enrollment. Enrollment officers were required to weekly submit reports to the Board of Enrollment and were paid three dollars a day for their service.[241]

Instead of picking up a rifle, Francis picked up a pen and served as a US claims agent while still practicing law. In this role, he represented the legal rights of soldiers and their widows and orphans,[242] as well as helped soldiers of the Missouri State Militia collect their bounties.[243] Over the course of the Civil War, only Tennessee and Virginia would see more Civil War battles than Missouri did,[244] and by the end, more than twenty-seven thousand men on both sides would be dead,[245] so Francis had plenty of people to fight for. Wounded or ill soldiers often filed claims for back pay or payment for the use of their own horses, wagons, and resources,[246] while widows and orphans usually sought access to the deceased's pension. Because of its large number of battles and casualties, Missouri ended the war with the highest claims of any state.[247]

Claims agents—some like Francis, with previous experience as notaries or lawyers, and others as former soldiers—acted as intermediaries between the applicant and large government pension firms. Their job was to listen to the claim, and if it appeared valid, help the person gather the necessary evidence—such as military, birth, or marriage records and affidavits[248]—and shepherd the paperwork through the labyrinthine administration of the US Pension Bureau.[249] While the job may have been noble and claims were filed free of charge, agents were awarded a portion of the fee in successful cases, a minimum of ten dollars,[250] in addition to any expenses paid by their client,[251] which could include a commission of up to 33 percent.[252]

War claims became big business as the fighting dragged on. In November 1861, only two St. Louis offices advertised such services in the *Daily Missouri Democrat*, but by 1865, that number had more than quadrupled as claims offices readily advertised their services.[253] In fact, by

1898, more than sixty thousand attorneys represented veterans nation-wide, with the most ambitious, George E. Lemon, handling 125,000 claims at once.[254]

All claims agents in Missouri had to swear to and sign the same oath, attesting to their civilian status and Union patriotism, in addition to promising to follow the law of country and state in the presence of the clerk of the St. Louis County Court and a second witness. Francis signed the oath on October 26, 1863,[255] and officially began his work as a claims agent on January 1, 1864, while supporting the Western Sanitary Commission. He explains how he later came to work for the government:

An act of the Legislature of Missouri, approved 13 February 1864, provided for the appointment of a special agent, to forward and prosecute the claims of orphans of deceased soldiers, and for the soldiers of Missouri in the service of the United States. . . . The act also provided for the appointment of county agents, in the several counties of the state, and on the 7th of March 1864, the county court of St. Louis County appointed the writer, agent for St. Louis County. I had previously been appointed to act as such agent, by the Western Sanitary Commission.[256]

In his state role, Francis's superior was German-born Albert Sigel, colonel of the Fifth Missouri Cavalry and state claims agent for Missouri, for whom he worked from 1864 to 1877.[257] During that time, Francis filled nine large volumes of claims, working with claimants from his law office, and juggling thousands of records. In the letter mentioned above, he explains the nature of his record keeping, which was vital to the successful completion of his job: "I kept record of all the claims prepared by me for the state agent; took his receipt for the same, and when paid, I also took the receipt for the party. Also kept a record of claims rejected."[258]

He also used these books to document his own thoughts and progress notes about each case, as well as keep a record of related correspondence such as letters and a few newspaper clippings with relevance to his cases.

He placed reference charts in their pages to aid him when rules changed and wrote notes to himself about what to do in certain complicated situations. For example, in 1864, he noted that when the mother and father of a deceased soldier were still both living, only the mother could lawfully claim the pension.[259]

Moreover, he pasted into the front and endpapers of each book relevant documents such as letters, advertisements, and newspaper articles pertaining to his work, making the books a kind of scrapbook of his war work. In the back of volume 4, he compiled an emotional collection of wartime poetry by Lord Byron and Theodore O'Hara as well as other patriotic verses[260]—works that are as close to seeing into his undocumented mental and emotional state as possible given currently available documentation—sober reminders of the dead for whom he labored and among whom he could so easily have been counted.

From the business cards Francis kept in these books, one can trace his office relocations during the war: 29 Pine Street; 25 Olive Street; 10 North Fourth Street, Room 19 (March 1, 1867, January 2, 1868); 45 Olive Street (November 1865, June–November 1866); and finally, 305 Olive Street.[261]

Francis's records were much more scrupulous than many, and his effort paid off. In the years following the war, Missouri was struck with a major corruption scandal involving unpaid and fraudulent claims,[262] as well as charges of agents speculating with the state's claims. In the matter of the unpaid claims, it appears that some of the agents did not follow through correctly on their duties, but did the minimum required of them to file the claim and then never followed up unless specifically asked to do so. According to G. C. Bingham, adjutant-general of Missouri, "There appears to have been done for them only what was required when an individual soldier filed his own claim and compelled action upon it, or an attorney did so for him."[263]

There were also cases of outright "mass fraud,"[264] in which "aided by a few agents in different parts of the state, organizations which were until that time unheard of in the records of this office were hunted up or improvised and pay rolls for them made out, in some cases by employees of the State. . . . These certificates were issued to certain agents and sold, many of them, to innocent purchasers, and the money pocketed by those in the fraud."[265]

In addition, the Arrears Act of 1879, which granted soldiers a lump-sum payment for newly uncovered war-related disabilities equal to what they would have received if they'd filed a claim during the war, made the claims system especially vulnerable to fraud.[266]

Because of his honesty and detailed records, Francis was not implicated, for as the adjutant-general noted after an extensive audit of claims records in Missouri, "nearly every valid claim is proved by the entries upon the original pay rolls . . . [and] contains in the voucher filed in 1874 either the proof of its justness or reason for its rejection."[267]

COMMENDED FOR LOYAL CITIZENSHIP

During and after the war, both Virginia and Francis were commended for their services. In 1862, the Fifth Street Hospital publicly acknowledged Virginia's generosity with the goods from her estate in the *Daily Missouri Democrat*.[268] After the war was over, James Yeatman, president of the Western Sanitary Commission, thanked the Minors for their efforts[269] by letter, enclosing a generous check for Virginia's work. She promptly returned the check, saying she served out of love for her fellow man, not for money.[270] The letter itself has been lost, but the sentiments are said to have been similar to those expressed in this October 7, 1863, note from Mr. Yeatman to Francis:

I am directed by our board to return to you their thanks on behalf of the soldiers in the hospitals for your long-continued remembrance of them, and for the daily supply of fresh fruits, vegetables and milk, which you have furnished for the sick now more than two years. . . . What you have done has been in the most quiet and unobtrusive way. The sick soldier has no more constant, uniform and untiring friend, and it is with pleasure that I convey the thanks of the board, both to yourself and wife [sic], who has been as indefatigable at home in preparing canned fruits and other delicacies for the sick soldiers in the field, as you have been in providing for those in the hospitals.[271]

Though neither had seen combat, Francis and Virginia emerged from their wartime roles forever changed. The memory of the widows, orphans, and wounded and dead soldiers whose claims he processed would forever haunt Francis's mind, eventually moving him to donate his claims books to the Missouri Historical Society, explaining, "It occurred to me that in the years to come, it would prove of interest to the descendants of the original parties, and possibly, to the general public."[272]

Virginia found in her wartime activities an unexpected sense of purpose and civic pride she was loath to relinquish when the battlefields fell silent. The result was a restless spirit, a need to be and do[273] that would eventually find its outlet in fighting for the rights of all women in her state and, later, the entire country.

CHAPTER EIGHT

The Birth of the Women's
Suffrage Movement in Missouri

VIRGINIA RATTLED AROUND THE ROOMS AND GARDENS OF MINORIA IN the months after Francis Gilmer's death, pacing in her black mourning gown from one place to another and back again, getting in the way of the servants as they tried to go about their work and annoying them when she tried to help. Just when she would settle into a task, her eye fell upon something that reminded her of her son—a sock forgotten in a corner, a trinket carelessly discarded on a shelf, or even a place in the hall that held a particular memory—and she would be off again in her grief.

She was out of sorts, and it wasn't just because she was in mourning. She was restless and needed something to do. What she wouldn't give to have her wartime work to distract her from her pain; but even the women who had stayed together once the war was over to help the sick and needy[1] were drifting apart, back to their prewar lives as wives and mothers.

And perhaps had she not so enjoyed her LUAS activities and had Francis Gilmer not passed away, she would still be content. But she wasn't. Isolated in her country estate with Francis working downtown and her LUAS friends increasingly distant—their organization had officially disbanded on March 8, 1867[2]—she was at sea with no purpose to guide her life.

However, she increasingly had the thought that she couldn't be alone in what she was feeling. Many women had lost husbands, children, and other relatives to the war, and now back in their traditional domestic lives, they were adrift. On top of that, though slaves had been freed and were now considered equal citizens under the law, thanks to the Thirteenth and Fourteenth Amendments of the Constitution, and there was talk about them being enfranchised soon, there had been no serious conversation about women, who had provided so much service during the war, receiving the vote as a reward or expression of gratitude from the government.

More than anything else, that stuck in Virginia's craw. With each passing day it was looking increasingly like if women wanted the vote, they would have to campaign for it. In the Northeast, women were speaking up and taking action in favor of enfranchisement. On May 10, 1866, Elizabeth Cady Stanton chaired the first National Woman's Rights Convention since the Civil War. Their main order of business was making official Susan B. Anthony's brainchild, the American Equal Rights Association (AERA), which advocated for both abolition and female suffrage through their "goal of pursuing universal enfranchisement without distinction of race or sex."[3] The AERA spent the next three years petitioning Congress for a Sixteenth Amendment "to both assert the principle of national citizenship suffrage and explicitly to bar disenfranchisement by sex."[4]

Anthony was shrewd enough to realize women would have a harder time than Black men would in getting the vote, if for no other reason than the Black vote could be politically beneficial to Republicans, who therefore favored it. They believed the former slaves were likely to support the Republican party that freed them, whereas women had no such loyalty and would vote as their minds and hearts moved them,[5] so their enfranchisement didn't particularly benefit either party.

On top of that, some of their previous abolitionist allies were turning against them. The loudest of these was Wendell Phillips, who believed it "was the negro's hour"[6] and "women were not ready for the ballot. They were too concerned with fashion . . . and needed to learn to turn their heads to more important matters before the ballot could do them any good."[7] The tension between the two organizations would continue to simmer until it finally came to a head in 1868, forcing the suffragists to split from the abolitionists and, ultimately, the women's suffrage movement to fracture into two distinct organizations.

While Susan B. Anthony and Elizabeth Cady Stanton were firing up the East Coast, some of the western territories were considering making women's suffrage a requirement of statehood. This was done not out of a sense of justice but purely for political purposes. Lawmakers in Wyoming wanted to give the territory some positive publicity and they hoped that by dangling the lure of women's suffrage in front of potential emigrants, more women would come to the area and vote for the party that gave them the right to vote—the Democrats.[8] Politics aside, women were desperately needed on the frontier. There were six adult men in the Wyoming Territory for every adult woman, and very few children,[9] so if the territory was to survive, let alone thrive, it needed female citizens.

Even in Kansas, the unlikely bulwark of Midwest women's suffrage, things were heating up. In 1867, the state put two unusual referenda on their ballot: one for "Negro" suffrage and the other for women's suffrage.[10] Momentum was strong until tensions between the Black and the women's suffrage groups exploded over Anthony inviting George Francis Train into the fold. Despite being a supporter of female suffrage and a defender of the Union during the war, Train was also lukewarm, if not hostile, to the idea of abolition.[11] Knowing this, abolitionists sided with the anti-suffrage supporters, and their collective power was enough to kill both measures on the ballot—for the time being.[12]

However, just across the border, Missouri was a different story. Virginia's home state had been strangely silent on the issue. But did its women have to be? Virginia mulled the idea over in her mind. She had been contemplating the necessity of women's suffrage since the war ended.[13] She and her fellow females may not have set foot on the battlefield, but neither had her husband, and that did not make him any less entitled to vote. In addition, she and other volunteers had toiled in their own way, witnessing firsthand the aftereffects of war, from the physical deformation and suffering to the mental scarring and spiritual destitution that remained long after the battles were won or lost. They were just as entitled to the full rights of citizens as former slaves were. There was no logical reason why both groups shouldn't be allowed to vote.[14]

So much rested on the final language of the Fourteenth Amendment, which was being used as a political ping-pong by lawmakers as they debated how granting former slaves (who used to be counted as only three-fifths a person) and women the right to vote would affect their representation numbers in the House.[15] As a compromise, they added the word "male" to the amendment three times, marking the first time ever that the Constitution distinguished between men and women[16] and outraging suffragists across the nation.

But it didn't have to remain that way. Women had just as much right to the vote as Black men did. If no one else in Missouri would say it out loud, Virginia would. And anyone who felt the same was welcome to join her.

THE POST-CIVIL WAR SUFFRAGE DEBATE

The first time Congress ever debated women's constitutional rights was in 1835 in response to women's antislavery petitions. At that time, lawmakers declared that "women inherently and traditionally lacked equal citizenship, that the framers did not intend for women to possess the right to petition, and that women were 'madly shooting out of their proper sphere'"[17] by getting involved in politics at all. This is why the Seneca Falls Convention in 1848 and the early agitation of Susan B. Anthony, Elizabeth Cady Stanton, and others was so groundbreaking. During the late 1840s and 1850s, these East Coast elite toured the western territories and states speaking about women's rights and trying to get suffrage and rights provisions into the legislatures and constitutional conventions.[18] But their work was largely grassroots and uncoordinated; they didn't have, or even desire, a national organization to lead them, had no leadership or organizational experience, and thus had a very difficult time getting the attention of lawmakers.[19]

By the time the Civil War came to an end, women were in a much different place than when it started. Not only were they experienced in work outside the home but that work had given them confidence to throw off their previous submissive attitudes, and it exposed them to methods of leadership, organization, and communication[20] they hadn't previously experienced. Top advocates like Anthony, Stanton, and Lucy Stone began organizing conventions, speeches, articles, and pamphlets geared toward publicizing the idea that "the emancipation of slaves had brought the question of enlarging the electorate to the foreground, and that women might also be given the vote."[21]

Thanks to these efforts, the first congressional discussions over women's suffrage after the Civil War occurred as part of the Reconstruction debates. Lawmakers, however, were not interested in the suffragists' arguments. They had plenty of reasons to believe that women should not vote. First, "if women are entitled to the rights of the franchise, they would correspondingly come under the obligation to bear arms,"[22] which several senators pointed out was a non sequitur because service in the army was not a precondition to suffrage. Second, women being exposed to the "angry and turbulent strifes [sic]"[23] of the polling place would harm their virtue and demoralize them.[24] Pro-suffrage lawmakers responded that if this was the case, it meant polling places and the men who frequented them needed to be reformed, not that women needed to be barred from them.[25] Once these arguments were rebuked, anti-suffrage leaders pointed out that giving women the vote had simply never been done[26]— to which examples from Hungary, Germany, France, and Moravia were given to dispute this "fact."[27]

Finally, Congress concluded that "women could not be enfranchised because in the United States and all civilized political communities 'man assumed the direction of government and war, woman of the domestic and family affairs.' Maintaining women's roles in the domestic sphere was so essential to women's identity and national identity that 'it [was] necessary that she should be separate from the exercise of suffrage.'"[28] Furthermore, the idea of women being given the ability to vote posed a threat "not just to the state but to the powers and privileges of men as a sex,"[29] to male identity, as well as to the whole patriarchal system, and the marital system of coverture it enabled.[30]

At the same time, state opinions on the issue of women's suffrage varied as much as those of their populace. Just as it had on the issue of slavery, Missouri equivocated. On one hand, it had the potential to show itself as a cosmopolitan state of the future transformed by the Civil War. On the other, it feared taking the liberal ideas of freedom that were rife in the aftermath of the war too far and alienating those who believed that not even freed slaves should have the right to vote, much less women.[31] In its largest and most rapidly growing city—between 1860 and 1870, St. Louis's population exploded from 160,000 to well over 300,000[32]— it had a diverse population and political atmosphere rife for change,[33] but yet the tendency to fall back on traditional ways usually won out.

However, Missouri had one strong pro-suffrage voice in the Senate: B. Gratz Brown. He was one of the loudest voices disputing the arguments against women's suffrage mentioned above. On December 12, 1866, during debate in the Senate of the United States on the issue of female suffrage in the District of Columbia, he expressed his pro-suffrage stance in no uncertain terms to the president:

I have to say then, sir, here on the floor of the American Senate, I stand for universal suffrage, and as a matter of fundamental principle do not recognize the right of society to limit it on any ground of race, color, or sex. I will go further, and say that I recognize the right of franchise as being intrinsically a natural right; and I do not believe that society is authorized to impose any limitation upon it that does not spring out of the necessities of the social state itself. . . . That the rights of women, however, are intrinsically the same with those of men, may not be consistently denied; and that all the advance of modern civilization has been toward according them greater equality of condition is attested by the current history of every nation within its pale. . . . Mr. President, I have listened in vain for the argument on which is predicated the assertion that sex alone affords a rightful ground for exclusion from the rights of franchise. I do not find anything to justify that view, even in the position of those who contend that franchise is a mere political privilege and not founded in any right, for that would apply to men equally as to women, and does not touch the question of relative rights. The position would still remain to be established why the franchise should be given to the one and not to the other. It would remain still to present grounds of principle on which that right as such may be denied to her and not denied to him. I have heard reasons of policy, reasons of sentiment, reasons of precedent advanced to justify this exclusion; but in all frankness, and with no disrespect intended, I must say that those which have been presented during this debate seem to me trivial, illogical, and contradictory of one another.[34]

Despite Brown's stirring speech, the amendment to strike out the word "male" in the Suffrage Bill for the District of Columbia was defeated nine to thirty-seven.[35]

VIRGINIA MINOR TAKES THE LEAD

When Virginia read Senator Brown's speech in the paper, she knew she had found a powerful ally—at least for now, as he would later turn coat on the issue.[36] She decided to thank him on behalf of the women of Missouri. In early 1867, she wrote him a letter and asked several of her former LUAS members and friends if they would sign it. Many did, including St. Louis suffragist Rebecca Hazard, who would go on to found the Missouri Woman Suffrage Association with Virginia.[37] This letter was given to Senator Brown when he returned home to Missouri, but nothing is recorded of his reaction.[38]

Virginia followed this up by sending a petition for women's suffrage to the Missouri legislature on her own behalf, becoming the first person in the state to do so.[39] Then in March, when an amendment to Missouri's constitution that included the word "male" came up for a vote, she drafted a petition to the Missouri General Assembly asking for the word to be struck from the bill. The petition stated in part, "We believe that all persons who are subject to the law, and taxed to support the government have a voice in the selection of those who are to govern and legislate them. . . . We therefore pray that an amendment may be proposed striking out the word 'male' and extending to women the right of suffrage."[40] Virginia collected 355 signatures, which were published in the newspaper to document them,[41] but the legislature voted down her request 89 to 5.

However, this show of support by so many women, along with Francis's "enthusiastic endorsement"[42] gave Virginia the courage to take her pro-suffrage stance public—in a big way.[43] She and Francis sold Minoria and moved back downtown to 1010 Pine to be closer to their friends and the center of action in St. Louis.[44] On May 8, 1867, Virginia met with at least six other women in the Director's Room[45] of the Mercantile Library and officially formed the Woman Suffrage Association of Missouri (WSAM). Its purpose was to "secure the ballot for women upon terms of equality with men." This single focus made it the first organization of its kind in the country, and some scholars claim it was the first in the world.[46]

The group elected Virginia as president. Other officers included Penelope Allan, vice president; Rebecca Hazard, corresponding secretary; Lucretia Hall, recording secretary; and Anna Banker, treasurer. Additional members of the group included Adaline and Phoebe Couzins, who were the wife and daughter of the police chief of St. Louis. Along with Virginia and Francis, this mother-daughter duo "were among the most intellectually adventurous of the Radical Republican community in St. Louis."[47]

The WSAM spent its first meeting adopting five primary resolutions:[48]

1. *Whereas, The subject of universal suffrage is now attracting the attention of the leading minds of this nation, causing the revision of constitutions, both of the General and State Governments; and*
2. *Whereas, We believe that the true idea of a Republic is achieved only where the elective franchise is impartially bestowed; and*
3. *Whereas, Women are subject to taxation, and are made amenable to the laws; and therefore*
4. *Resolved, That we will make all suitable exertions to obtain such an amendment to our State constitution as shall confer the right of suffrage on women.*
5. *Resolved, That for this purpose we will organize ourselves into an Association, to be called the Woman's Rights Association of Missouri.*

Rebecca Hazard recalled the formation of the organization years later to Susan B. Anthony:

Meeting an old friend and neighbor not long after, the talk turned upon negro suffrage. I expressed myself in favor of that measure, and

timidly added, "And go farther—I think women also should vote."
She grasped my hand cordially, saying, "And so do I!" This was Mrs.
Virginia L. Minor. We had each cherished this opinion, supposing that
no other woman in the community held it; and this we afterwards
found to have been the experience of many others. This was in 1866.
. . . But as yet no effort had been made toward an organization. The
first step in that direction was in May, 1867, by Mrs. Lucretia P.
Hall and her sister, Miss Penelope Allen, daughters of Mrs. Beverly
Allen, and nieces of General Pope, in the parlors of Mrs. Anna L.
Clapp, the president of the Union Aid Society during the war. Mrs.
Hall, Mrs. Clapp and myself called a public meeting on May 8, when
the Woman Suffrage Society of Missouri was organized.[49]

Meetings were scheduled for the first and third Saturdays of each month.[50] Eventually the membership grew too large for the Mercantile Library and meetings were moved to the Pickwick Theatre[51] and changed to take place during the week. Aware that meeting during the day would prevent working women from joining the organization, Virginia insisted the WSAM hold evening meetings so all could attend. The organization also spawned a separate committee that held meetings for the women with jobs to advocate for their rights, including equal pay. This committee, which had at least thirty members,[52] met regularly until the local Working Women's Protective Union[53] was formed in April 1869.[54]

Virginia believed that developing local women into speakers and advocates was the best thing she could do for the community, so the WSAM spoke frequently to local groups.[55] Unlike other suffragists who focused on women like themselves—white, wealthy, and with a lengthy American pedigree[56]—Virginia and Francis especially targeted German immigrant women,[57] who were generally opposed to slavery[58] and temperance[59] and were suspicious of the rich American women who ran the movement.[60] That they would be a difficult group to sway in favor of suffrage because of its ties to temperance all the way into the 1910s[61] makes these early efforts all the more laudable.

The timing of the foundation of the WSAM might not have been just good fortune; at the same time, the neighboring state of Kansas was considering its own suffrage amendment, which Virginia would have been aware of. As a result, national suffrage leaders made St. Louis a prime stop on their lecture tours, drawing well-known women like Anthony and Stanton to the city on their way west.[62] Anthony, especially, spoke several times in St. Louis,[63] where the presence of a local suffrage organization could not have escaped her notice.

This is likely how the Minors became acquainted with Anthony. By January 22, 1868, Francis was penning letters to her newspaper,[64] *The Revolution*, asking for the WSAM to be recorded as part of the national movement and addressing the readers in Missouri, explaining why he believed women's desire to vote was "just and right":

> *Taxation and Representation should go hand in hand. This is the very corner-stone of our government. . . . The man who believes in that declaration, cannot justly deny to women the right of suffrage. They are citizens, they are tax-payers; they bear the burdens of government—why should they be denied the rights of citizens? We boast about liberty and equality before the law, when the truth is, our government is controlled by one-half only of the population. The others have no more voice in the making of their laws, or the selection of their rulers, than the criminals who are in our penitentiaries; nay, in one respect, their condition is not as good as that of the felon, for he may be pardoned and restored to a right which woman can never obtain. And this, not because she has committed any crime, or violated any law, but simply because she is, what God made her—a woman! . . . Give her a chance—give her the opportunity of proving whether these objections are well founded or not. Her influence for good is great . . . and my firm belief is, that that influence would be greatly enhanced and extended by the exercise of this new right. It would be felt at the ballot-box and in the halls of legislation. Better men, as a general rule, would be elected to office, and society in all its ramifications, would feel and rejoice at the change.[65]*

Less than a month later, the WSAM petitioned the Missouri legislature again "praying that the right of suffrage be extended to the female sex."[66] It was accompanied by the following cover letter, signed by Virginia and the other WSAM officers[67] on behalf of all members:

> *To the General Assembly of the State of Missouri:*
> GENTLEMEN: *The undersigned women of Missouri, believing that all citizens who are taxed for the support of the government and subject to its laws, should have a voice in the making of those laws, and the selection of their rulers; that, as the possession of the ballot ennobles and elevates the character of man, so, in like manner, it would ennoble and elevate that of woman by giving her a direct and personal interest in the affairs of government; and further, believing that the spirit of the age, as well as every consideration of justice and equity, requires that the ballot should be extended to our sex, do unite in praying that an amendment to the constitution may be proposed, striking out the word "male" and extending to women the right of suffrage.*[68]

When this letter was later reproduced in *The Revolution*, Francis appended this note:

> *These papers will serve to show that the idea has taken root in other States beyond the Mississippi besides Kansas; and may also be somewhat of a guide to others, who may desire to accomplish the same purpose elsewhere. A work of such magnitude requires, of course, time for development; but the leaven is working. The fountains of the great deep of public thought have been broken up. The errors and prejudices of six thousand years are yielding to the sunlight of truth. In spite of pulpits and politicians, the great idea is making its way to the hearts of the people; and woman may rejoice in believing that the dawn of her deliverance, so long hoped for and prayed for, is at last approaching.*[69]

Despite these very public and enthusiastic efforts, initially few people outside the movement took the WSAM seriously.[70] When they ran stories on the group's meetings or advocacy, newspapers spent more time commenting on the member's looks and comportment—the recording secretary had a "clear sweet voice," the corresponding secretary was "daintily habited in black," and the treasurer was "swathed in purple"[71]—than the issues they were debating. And the legislature paid them even less mind; their petition for amendment was roundly defeated.

Fueled by such opposition, Virginia kept thinking of ways to expand the movement and Missouri's presence in it. A letter she wrote to Stanton on May 4, 1868, shows her mind at work:

> *Dear Friend: Our gentlemen friends urge us to memorialize Congress on the question of Suffrage in the District [of Columbia]. Well knowing how a single petition is suffocated, would it not be well for all the states to unite, and be presented at the same time? . . . It seems to me that one state should not go it alone, if all the state organizations were notified to send in their lists immediately to whoever you think will be most likely to do justice to the cause, we could make quite a formidable display combined.[72]*

The WSAM spent the last several months of 1868 trying to find a delegate to attend the National Woman's Suffrage Convention scheduled to be held in Washington the following year. Virginia was nominated by the membership for that role, but felt it would be "impossible for me to go without great and serious inconvenience."[73] Instead, the group recommended that rather than being unrepresented, they send one of their male allies to the convention if no female could be convinced to attend.

They also gathered six hundred signatures on petitions to Sen. Samuel Pomeroy of Kansas, a leading congressional supporter of women's suffrage.[74] Upon receiving them, he wrote a letter thanking the women and saying, "I am so glad you have decided to move upon this subject. The hour has now arrived for securing all American citizens equality of rights, and of all their rights. The American type of Republicanism is nothing short of this."[75]

Change came to the WSAM at the first meeting of 1869, held on January 16, when men were admitted as members for the first time. The only stipulation was that they had to sign the organization's constitution. Admitted that day were "two or three" men, most likely Francis, William Greenleaf Eliot, and James Yeatman.[76] All three men later served as vice presidents of the organization, and Francis often ran meetings in Virginia's absence.[77]

Virginia had to miss that meeting but sent a letter to be read. Because their prior decision to send a male delegate to the convention was

> *so extremely unpopular among our friends, and by our enemies imputed to want of earnestness in our work, with the approval of the officers of the association, there being no time for a more general consultation, I determined to represent you in person to the best of my ability, which action I hope may meet with your approval. I further desire to say that, in my opinion, it is not only right, but highly important that our German ladies should be represented in the delegation to Jefferson City, and I therefore propose the following named ladies be added to the list of delegates, earnestly hoping they will accept the appointment: Mrs. Fiala, Mrs. Finkelnberg, Mrs. [unreadable,] Mrs. Rumbold and Miss Kehr.*[78]

Satisfied that Virginia had agreed to represent them, the members elected Mrs. Col. John S. Phelps as a delegate to the convention to accompany their president.[79]

While extensive travel was not possible for, or desirable to, many WSAM members, they were much keener to attend events closer to home. On February 2, a "large delegation"[80] of women traveled to Jefferson City by train to present lawmakers with yet another memorial—this one with over two thousand signatures[81]—in favor of women's suffrage.

On the train, the delegates decided to take an impromptu poll of their fellow passengers and add signatures to their petition. Virginia later told the *Daily Missouri Republican* that she was "quite amused" by the reactions of the travelers. "Some would immediately glance towards our feet, expecting, no doubt, to see the much-dreaded *pants*. Others would scan us with a puzzled look, as if doubting their own eyes or ears at seeing a real specimen of the 'genus homo' woman's rights before them attired in crinoline and presenting a respectable appearance."[82] She went on to describe that with a handful of exceptions, people were courteous and even encouraging of the women and their legal endeavors.[83]

They were shrewd enough to make the details of their visit public,[84] so when they descended the train at the station, they were met by Lieutenant Governor Edwin Obed Standard and the Speaker of the House John C. Orrick, as well as "two or three inquisitive news reporters" and a crowd of well-wishers.[85] As neither House was in session, the women were given leave to use the House building, and over the next two days, many members, both male and female, addressed the lawmakers. Among these were Mrs. J. G. Phelps of Springfield, Dr. Ada Greunan of St. Louis, and Miss Phoebe Couzins, who would go on to become a famous orator.[86]

Reaction to this display was mixed. Liberal leaders who shared their views cheered the women and welcomed them with open arms, while others listened politely. The governor went so far as to sign one of their petitions,[87] as did between seventy and eighty senators and representatives,[88] but no real action resulted. The Senate referred it to the Committee on Constitutional Amendments by a vote of twenty-two to four. In the House, the first vote tabled it by a vote of fifty-nine to forty-three, a second was defeated by sixty-two to forty-two, and the third and final vote was fifty-one to forty-five.[89]

Virginia reported that there was only one "individual from whom we received disrespectful and insulting treatment. He called our attention to the fact that his remarks were but a foretaste of what we should receive, if we entered the political arena."[90] However, this attitude was likely more widespread than Virginia was willing to acknowledge or admit. After the WSAM had departed, "one house member told a reporter that the women had 'unsexed themselves by coming here with their demands.'"[91]

But the action cemented the WSAM as a force to be reckoned with in the eyes of national suffrage leaders. *The Revolution* reported Virginia declaring only days after the event: "It will not be feminine to say, yet I fear I must say, the women of Missouri have stormed their capitol, and if it is not yet taken, the outworks are in our hands, and I believe with a few more well-directed blows the victory will be ours."[92]

CHAPTER NINE

Suffrage and the New Departure

As THE CRISP WINDS OF FALL DEEPENED INTO THE BITING GRIP OF WIN-
ter 1869, the scents of woodsmoke and coal were not the only things
carried on the wind across America—change had come along with them.
Just a few months earlier, Congress passed and two-thirds of the states
ratified the Fourteenth Amendment to the Constitution. This was the
second of three amendments that sought to expand the rights of former
slaves. While the Thirteenth Amendment freed them, the Fourteenth
granted citizenship to them and all persons born or naturalized in the
United States and guaranteed all citizens "equal protection of the laws."

Now Congress was debating yet another amendment, one that if
passed, would give these former slaves the right to vote. It stated, "The
right of citizens of the United States to vote shall not be denied or
abridged by the United States or by any state on account of race, color,
or previous condition of servitude." It was likely to face little presidential
opposition, given the country was in the "lame duck" period between
the presidencies of the wildly controversial Andrew Johnson and the
incumbent Ulysses S. Grant. The suffragists were split over its passage;
all wanted to see the Black men get the franchise, but some, Virginia
included, were offended that it did not include women.[1] St. Louis suffragists took to the streets, and "certain 'loyal women' of St. Louis, headed
by Mrs. Virginia Minor and Mrs. Rebecca Hazard . . . went to a Republican newspaper office and protested" against the exclusion of women.[2]

Inside their new home at 900 Pine, Virginia and Francis spent many
nights by the fire discussing how these new laws could be leveraged to

help the women's suffrage movement. One evening, Virginia tremulously voiced a radical idea to Francis: women already had the right to vote under the Fourteenth Amendment.

Intrigued, Francis went to his study and retrieved a copy of the Constitution and its Amendments, reading, "All persons born or naturalized in the United States and subject to the jurisdiction thereof, are citizens of the United States and of the State wherein they reside. No State shall make or enforce any law which shall abridge the privileges or immunities of citizens of the United States; nor shall any State deprive any person of life, liberty, or property, without due process of law; nor deny to any person within its jurisdiction the equal protection of the laws."

He could see his wife's line of thinking. By using the gender-neutral term "citizens" instead of "men" or "males," the amendment could be interpreted to open the door to women's suffrage without the need for an additional amendment. His lawyer's mind immediately started forming a case. It would not be an easy or simple argument to make, and it would require a whole new way of looking at the Constitution, especially the division between national rights and states' rights, but it could be done.

With the snow falling outside, over the next several weeks, they worked together to lay out the four key points to their argument in concepts they hoped everyone could understand, with legal citations to support each point:

1. The Constitution was the authority of the land, but the will of the people is what sustains the government. The people are the source of all political power and therefore expect their government to protect their natural and legal rights. The Preamble of the Constitution bears this out by clearly stating it is the people, not the government, who are establishing the Constitution.

2. While in the past people viewed the federal government as the enemy of individual rights granted by the states, in the aftermath of the Civil War and the passage of the Fourteenth Amendment, that had changed. The federal government was now the protector of citizen's rights against the radical actions of the states (like

secession). National citizenship was proven supreme over state citizenship by the first section of the Fourteenth Amendment. Evidence of this also could be found in provisions of Article I and the supremacy clause of Article IV of the Constitution.

3. The Thirteenth, Fourteenth, and Fifteenth Amendments put those who had been historically deprived of rights, namely, women and slaves, on equal footing as national citizens.

4. The right to vote was one of the basic "privileges and immunities" of American citizenship as written in the Constitution. The Fourteenth Amendment declared citizenship to be a national concern granted through federal power. The 1823 case of *Corfield v. Coryell*[3] found that the right to vote was protected under Article IV. In addition, the pending Fifteenth Amendment would give the federal government rather than the states the ability to grant or deny suffrage. Therefore, when taken together, the two amendments meant that all national citizens were automatically given the right to vote.[4]

The suffragists should have no problem with this progressive interpretation of the Constitution because they were used to challenging the intent of the framers from their days advocating for abolition; they believed it needed to be a living document that could be interpreted to meet the needs of the time.[5] But would lawmakers and average citizens be so accommodating?

If they were going to take a stand, now was the time. The public was more open to change in the last decade due to the idea of evolution posited in Charles Darwin's *On the Origin of Species*. After all, if beings could evolve, why not ideas and interpretations?

And as a lawyer, Francis understood that the law was changing too. Judges, politicians, and common people alike used to view property, contract, and tort law as set in stone, but now, thanks to the efforts of prewar abolitionists like Frederick Douglass and Alvan Stewart, people were beginning to see that it could change, as could views of the Constitution.[6] In attempting to rebuild the country after the Civil War, lawmakers were faced with new interpretations of the Constitution as expressed in the Thirteenth, Fourteenth, and pending Fifteenth Amendments. Doggedly sticking to the argument that "the framers' intentions should control the political system" no longer made sense.[7]

What he and Virginia were posing would be a powerful test case. Yes, the ideal situation would be that they would change the law, but the more likely outcome was that they would only be able to show how wide the gulf was between the principles the law claimed to uphold—equality for all—and the actual experience of that law in action by citizens.[8]

By the time spring thawed the ground and flowers bloomed in the gardens, the only thing left was to find the perfect forum to announce their revolutionary ideas.

A FRACTURED NATIONAL SUFFRAGE MOVEMENT

By 1869, the unity of the AERA was crumbling. In embracing the controversial figure of George Train and opposing the Fifteenth Amendment, Stanton and Anthony had alienated more moderate members of the organization, like Lucy Stone and her husband, Henry Blackwell. Add to this Train's known dislike for Black people and Stanton and Anthony's increasingly racist, xenophobic, classist, and anti-male rhetoric[9]—Stanton's "catchphrase of the season was 'aristocracy of sex'"[10]—and a split was inevitable.

On May 12, 1869, the AERA held its annual anniversary conference in New York. After Stanton spoke, abolitionist Stephen S. Foster stood up and accused them of no longer being fit to run the organization, saying they "had dragged the AERA away from its mission by their attacks on black suffrage, the Republican Party, and the Fifteenth Amendment."[11] Frederick Douglass then stood and made his case that because of the threat of the Ku Klux Klan and other anti-Black organizations, which included former slaveholders, it was more important at the moment that Black men be granted the right to vote, as it was a form of protection.[12] Women, he argued, were already protected by their husbands and could influence their vote; therefore they could wait.[13]

Anthony challenged him, stating women getting the vote would not "change anything in respect to the nature of our sexes. . . . It will change one thing very much, and that is the dependent condition of woman. It will place her where she can earn her own bread, so that she may go out into the world an equal competitor in the struggle for life."[14]

Lucy Stone and Frances Ellen Watkins Harper each attempted to play the role of peacemaker, insisting that women could support the Fifteenth Amendment *and* support a separate one for women's suffrage. Stone stated, "Mrs. Stanton will, of course, advocate the precedence for her sex, and Mr. Douglass will strive for the first position for his, and both are perhaps right. . . . We are lost if we turn away from the middle principle and argue for one class."[15]

However, these efforts were in vain. The AERA was fractured beyond repair.

Three days later, Stanton and Anthony formed the National Woman's Suffrage Association (NWSA) for the AERA members who agreed with them in opposing the Fifteenth Amendment and wanted to continue to pursue a national referendum to win the vote. The organization reluctantly allowed male members but insisted that only women govern it. Over time, their members proved to be more radical, showing "some of the most extreme manifestations of the feminist spirit in the nineteenth century."[16]

In November, Lucy Stone formed the American Woman Suffrage Association (AWSA). The main differences between this group and the NWSA were that they allowed men to take a large role in governing the organization, were dedicated to a state-by-state strategy of winning the vote by changing state constitutions, and supported the Fifteenth Amendment. They also drew a more conservative membership than the NWSA.[17]

This suffrage "civil war"[18] was particularly hard on local chapters of the now-defunct AERA—among them the WSAM—which were forced to pick a side. Virginia herself was torn because she felt that continually petitioning the Missouri legislature to amend its state constitution was worthwhile, but she also believed in the potential and power of a federal amendment. She did not want to force the women of her organization to choose. To that end, Francis introduced a resolution "declaring that each member of the society should be free to join the National body of his or her choice, and that the Missouri Association, as a society, should not become auxiliary to either the 'National' or the 'American.' The good faith of the association was thus pledged to respect the feelings and wishes of each member," and the resolution was unanimously adopted.[19] This neutrality held until 1871 when the group became an auxiliary of the AWSA. That is when Virginia stepped down as president, wishing to remain loyal to the NWSA and Anthony. Francis and other members did the same.

Despite the chapter's neutrality, Anthony and Stanton remained close to Virginia and the WSAM, visiting St. Louis often. In February 1869, Stanton was in St. Louis as part of the suffrage movement's first lengthy Midwest speaking tour—it also included Milwaukee, Madison, Toledo, and other cities[20]—and the Minors were her host, giving her accommodations and taking her on a tour of the city's parks, gardens,[21] and new plank board, brick, and cobblestone streets of the city that covered the old dirt ones.[22]

Anthony, too, kept in touch, encouraging Missouri women to keep petitioning: "Let her then petition—petition constantly. Let her petition Washington, Jefferson City, every state capital, persistently and unremittingly, for this great right to the ballot."[23]

And petition she did. In May 1869, as president of the WSAM, Virginia addressed the State Convention of Publishers and Editors in St. Louis, asking them to use their influence over the minds of the people of the state to support female suffrage:

> Over all [sic] you wield a powerful influence, either for good or evil. We ask you to wield this influence for our good, for the elevation of our sex. . . . When you carry the musket in defence [sic] of the state, we are taxed to buy that musket, we are taxed to support your government in every yard of ribbon we buy, the very income we derive from that instrument of death, the needle or sewing machine, is taxed to support your government; we are required to swear allegiance to your government; we are amenable to the law of treason; condemnation and assessment know no sex. If we are citizens, this is just, the burdens of the government should fall equally on all. . . . If we are citizens (which no one denies) then are we entitled to all our privileges and

immunities in every States, and the State should not restrict us; for we hold these privileges and immunities under the paramount authority of the Federal government and its courts are bound to maintain and enforce them; the constitutional laws of the State to the contrary not-withstanding. . . . We are here to appeal to your justice: to ask you to alter this constitution of Missouri, place the women of the state where your God intended they should be, by your side, your equals in intellect, your ever reliable and faithful allies in the battle of life. Do this, and you will find that while a bountiful nature has with lavish abundance supplied to your State the richest mineral wealth, your elevated women will be your richest, your greatest treasure, for "her price will be above rubies."[24]

This speech contains the first tentative public expression of the ideas put forth in the theory she and Francis created: that women were forced to pay taxes—the same ones that voting men paid—without being able to pick their representatives, that by the privileges and immunities clause, women should have the same rights as citizens as men, and that national law trumped state law. It is as if this was her practice speech for a more important one to follow.

It is highly likely that Virginia and Francis discussed their Fourteenth Amendment theory with Stanton and Anthony, given that both immediately embraced it after it was made public. And it was these two powerful women who gave them the biggest possible platform to share their bold ideas with the nation.

THE ST. LOUIS CONVENTION
AND A LIFE-CHANGING RESOLUTION

On October 6, 1869, the NWSA held its first convention in St. Louis. Their choice of location was probably in part due to the Minors' influence, but St. Louis was also at the center of a national debate about moving the country's capital. As the country continually expanded westward, lawmakers began to discuss locating the capital in a more centralized location, ideally somewhere on the banks of the Mississippi. This was because it would make it easier for the government to flee to well-developed suburbs, if needed under threat or occupation,[25] and also to respond to a crisis in any direction without having to travel clear across the country. In addition, Washington, DC, was a muddy, flooded, stinking mess since it was located on a tidal plain.[26]

Originally, four cities were put into contention for the new national capital: Cincinnati, Chicago, Memphis, and St. Louis. Cincinnati was ruled out because its surrounding hills, while picturesque, would make it difficult to lay out the myriad buildings and structures needed by the government; Chicago fell out of favor because of the extremes of its weather; and Memphis was struck from the list for not only being too far south but also for still holding secessionist political leanings. St. Louis quickly became the top candidate, with its strong history of commerce and manufacturing, central location, and beautiful scenery overlooking the Mississippi.[27]

From 1866 to 1870, Congress debated the possibility quite seriously. Legend has it that seventy-four congressmen voted to move the capital to St. Louis.[28] But the opposition was strong, arguing instead for federal appropriations to improve Washington, DC. Eventually, President Grant requested that these appropriations be passed, ending the relocation debate on March 3, 1871.[29]

But for now, St. Louis was in the spotlight, and the NWSA decided it was the ideal place to hold its conference, which was the first event of its kind in the state. Members met at the Mercantile Library Hall at 10:00 a.m.[30] Virginia, as president of the local organization, called the meeting to order and led the attendees in prayer: "O Thou, who in times past didst send Deborah to lead the arms of Israel, grant that the women of this our day may be so panophed [sic] in the armor of Justice and Truth, that they may contend successfully against oppression and wrong wherever they may be found."[31]

She went on to give the opening address, in which she famously declared,

I believe that the Constitution of the United States gives me every right and privilege to which every other citizen is entitled; for while the Constitution gives the States the right to regulate suffrage, it

nowhere gives them power to prevent it. The power to regulate is one thing, the power to prevent is an entirely different thing. Thus the State can say where, when, and what citizens may exercise the right of suffrage. . . . This question of woman's right to the ballot has never yet been raised in any quarter. It has yet to be tested whether a free, moral, intelligent woman, highly cultivated, every dollar of whose income and property are taxed equally with that of all men, shall be placed by our laws on a level with the savage. . . . Now, I ask you, can a woman or negro vote in Missouri? You have placed us on the same level. Yet, by such question you hold us responsible for the unstatesmanlike piece of patchwork which you call the Constitution of Missouri! Women of the State, let us no longer submit to occupy so degraded a position! Disguise it as you may, the disfranchised class is ever a degraded class. Let us lend all our energies to have the stigma removed from us. Failing before the Legislatures, we must then turn to the Supreme Court of our land and ask it to decide what are our rights as citizens, or, at least, not doing that, give us the privilege of the Indian, and exempt us from the burden of taxation to support so unjust a Government.[32]

Later in the day, the Minors stood to propose their history-making resolutions:

Whereas. In the adjustment of the question of suffrage now before the people of this country for settlement, it is of the highest importance that the organic law of the land should be so framed and construed as to work injustice to none, but secure as far as possible perfect political equality among all classes of citizens: and

Whereas, All persons born or naturalized in the United States, and subject to the jurisdiction thereof, are citizens of the United States, and of the state wherein they reside; be it

Resolved, 1. That the immunities and privileges of American citizenship, however defined, are national in character and paramount to all state authority.

2. That while the Constitution of the United States leaves the qualifications of electors to the several states, it nowhere gives them the right to deprive any citizen of the elective franchise which possessed by any other citizen—to regulate, not including the right to prohibit the franchise.

3. That, as the Constitution of the United States expressly declares that "no state shall make or enforce any laws that shall abridge the privileges or immunities of citizens of the United States." Those provisions of the several state constitutions that exclude women from the franchise on account of sex, are violative alike of the spirit and letter of the Federal Constitution.

4. That, as the subject of naturalization is expressly withheld from the states, and as the states clearly would have no right to deprive of the franchise naturalized citizens, among whom women are expressly included, still more clearly have they no right to deprive native-born women citizens of this right.

5. That justice and equity can only be attained by having the same laws for men and women alike.

6. That having full faith and confidence in the truth and justice of these principles, we will never cease to urge the claims of women to a participation in the affairs of government equal with men.[33]

These resolutions were the only thing on attendees' lips at dinner that night, and for the rest of the convention. This was something new and exciting. No one had ever distinguished between the regulation and prohibition of suffrage before.[34] Not only that, the Minors were going against the sage advice of Joseph Story in his famous *Commentaries of the Constitution of the United States* (1833), where he wrote the Constitution "is to have fixed, uniform, permanent construction. It should be, so far at least as human infirmity will allow, not dependent upon the passions or parties of particular times, but the same yesterday, to-day, and forever."[35] By proposing a new interpretation, the Minors were saying the Constitution was a living document that should change with the times. And they were developing one of the first legal strategies to challenge the long-held belief that women had absolutely no place in politics.[36]

Anthony called their arguments the "first ray of encouragement"[37] that the suffrage movement had seen in quite some time. Stanton made sure they were published in *The Revolution* on October 21, 1869, along with detailed coverage of the convention. She even printed an extra ten thousand copies and made sure each member of Congress received one.[38]

Just over a week after the convention, Francis wrote a stirring note to readers of *The Revolution*, noting that while he was thankful the convention was a success, he felt some additional points needed to be made about the resolutions he and Virginia proposed:

> *These resolutions place the cause of equal rights far in advance of any position heretofore taken.*
>
> *Now, for the first time, the views and purposes of our organization assume a fixed purpose and definite end. We no longer beat the air—no longer assume merely the attitude of petitioners. We claim a right, based upon citizenship. These resolutions will stand the test of legal criticism—and I write now to ask, if a case can not be made at your coming election. If this were done, in no other way could our cause be more widely, and at the same time definitely brought before the public. . . . The question would be thoroughly discussed by thousands, who now give it no thought—and by the time it reached the court of final resort, the popular verdict would be in accord with the judgment that is sure to be rendered.*[39]

In referring to "your coming election," Francis meant the New York State election, which took place on November 2, 1869. He was essentially asking that the subject of women's suffrage be brought into the political debates, where it would undoubtedly be covered by the press and thus spread to citizens across the country. He was also covertly calling on women to go out and exercise the right to vote the Fourteenth Amendment gave them.

The convention and this letter marked Francis's first public association with the NWSA. While men like Frederick Douglass and George Francis Train supported Anthony and Stanton in the abolition and early suffrage movements, Francis was one of the first men, if not *the* first, to take an unofficial leadership position within the NWSA through his role in the development of and advocacy for this new legal position.[40] Because of the visibility of his later Supreme Court case, Hoff and Whites credit him with providing a masculine face for the NWSA,[41] which is especially noteworthy given how the group was so averse to male leadership.

CONTROVERSY OVER THE NEW DEPARTURE

The Minors' resolutions quickly became known as the New Departure because they were so different from any other theories or tactics used by women's suffrage advocates to date. However, they not only changed the movement but they changed how the law was interpreted, which has repercussions even today.[42] UCLA professor of constitutional law Adam Winkler notes that "historians, lawyers, and political scientists have yet to recognize the New Departure activists as early players in one of the most significant transformations in American judicial practice."[43]

Because of their willingness to reinterpret the Constitution, the Minors were pioneers of what is today known as Living Constitutionalism, the idea that rather than being immutable, the Constitution should be reinterpreted according to the needs of the times. Winkler notes, "Traditional historical thought attributes the first living constitutionalism to Woodrow Wilson and Louis D. Brandeis in the early twentieth century," but scholars are now beginning to see it actually began to emerge much sooner, at the end of the nineteenth century. Winkler credits "women suffragists as important innovators at the forefront of modern constitutional thought."[44] As Justice Oliver Wendell Holmes Jr., the Minors' contemporary, said in *Missouri v. Holland*, it "must be considered in light of our whole experience and not merely in that of what was said a hundred years ago."[45] If it was not, it would lose its meaning and become only a relic of the past.

That average citizens like Francis and Virginia dared to interpret the law on their own without the help of lawmakers and judges was about as heretical as was the idea that laypeople could read the Bible without the aid of a priest in the Middle Ages. Previously, constitutional interpretation was the sacred domain of the elected, who held themselves above the ordinary American. By offering their own ideas, the Minors "claimed the emancipatory power of written texts and asserted the authority of individuals rather than heretical institutions to read and interpret those texts correctly,"[46] opening up the opportunity for any citizen to challenge the law.

This must have been a truly frightening prospect for lawmakers, most of whom held firm that the only way to change the Constitution was through the formal amendment process. "The Framers set up various institutions and defined their relative powers, creating a regime of rights from which the judiciary was not free to stray. Once instituted, the regime could be changed only through formal procedures for textual amendment, themselves a product of the Framers and binding on future generations."[47] In their eyes, with the formality of this process broken, as the Minors were saying it should be, a multitude of lawsuits could arise from others straying from traditional interpretations, imperiling the legal profession, the court system, and law itself.

In addition, the Minors were daring to say that the framers used gender-neutral language—"persons," "inhabitants," "citizens" instead of "men"—purposefully so that they would be understood as meaning everyone, male and female,[48] offering a legal foundation for universal suffrage. This was a boon not only for white women but also for Black women, who, even with the passage of the Fifteenth Amendment, would have been torn between identifying by race or gender regarding their rights.[49]

Opponents believed the framers said what they meant and meant what they said. They did not mention women because they believed that "women had no role to play in government."[50] To try casting new interpretations on their venerable words was patriotic blasphemy. Even judges did not do that; they merely interpreted what the law said, not what they wanted it to be.

Another point on which the New Departure varied from tradition was by making national citizenship superior to state citizenship. David M. Dismore, archivist for the Feminist Majority Foundation, notes, "Historically, states had conferred voting rights, with various restrictions, such as age, length of residency, property requirements–and sex. In no state had all citizens had an automatic right to vote, so US citizenship and suffrage have never been identical. Therefore, women and other groups could be denied a right to vote by their states, unless the Constitution specifically said otherwise."[51]

But the Minors were arguing that the national government wasn't the big, scary behemoth threatening to plunge the country from the heights of democracy into the cesspool of monarchy, as many of the Founders had feared. Over the last century, experience had proved the American Experiment solid, even in the aftermath of a Civil War. Therefore, it was time for its citizens to let go of the old way of thinking, that the states were their benevolent guardians, and realize that, as the Civil War had shown, states had the potential to be more like abusive parents—limiting their rights and dragging them into potentially dangerous situations. In addition, every state had different laws, so one child had some rights another did not, which did not jibe with the American ideal of equality. That was why they needed the protection of their rights as national citizens; those were governed by the Constitution and couldn't be taken away on a whim. With regard to the franchise, it was a right inextricably entwined with citizenship, no matter one's color or gender, and according to the Constitution, the states could not change that.

ADOPTION AND ACTION

Despite its controversy, or perhaps because of it, the NWSA quickly adopted the Minors' strategies as official policy from 1868 to 1875.[52]

On December 30, 1869, Francis wrote another letter to *The Revolution*, asking them to republish the resolutions adopted at the St. Louis convention and stating that he and Virginia planned to "make a test case in her instance at our next election; take it through the courts of Missouri, and thence to the Supreme Court of the United States at Washington."[53] This is the first time the Minors explicitly stated how they were going to put their resolutions into practice: by attempting to vote and using the right they believed the Constitution gave to Virginia.

One of the reasons the New Departure was so popular is that it gave women a choice of how to react. They could take the theory privately to the courts or, if they were more action-oriented, take to the streets and vote.[54] It was the first strategy in the movement's history that catered to both conservative and radical mindsets. "As they embraced the language of the law to advocate the expansion of citizenship rights, these individuals presented themselves not as rebels but as patriots, as reformers who revered the law and ought to extern its beneficence rather than as revolutionaries seeking to overthrow,"[55] write Ray and Richards. This is an important point, emphasizing the nonviolent nature of the women's suffrage movement; change would come, but only through the peaceful exercise of their rights and by following the laws as set forth.

On January 10, 1870, Stanton testified before the Senate Committee on Privileges and Elections in favor of Senate Resolution 12 that would keep states from denying anyone the right to vote "on account of sex."[56] She used the New Departure as the basis for her argument:

> Permit me to say, that with the Hon. Charles Sumner, we believe that our Constitution, fairly interpreted, already secures the humblest individual all the rights, privileges and immunities of American citizens. . . . It was said that the great truths set forth in the prolonged debates of thirty years on the individual rights of the black man, culminating in the Fourteenth and Fifteenth Amendments of the Constitution, had no significance for women. Hence, we ask that this anomalous class of beings, not recognized by the powers as either "persons" or "citizens" may now be defined and their rights declared in the Constitution. . . . Universal manhood suffrage makes all men sovereigns, all women slaves—the most odious form of aristocracy the world has yet seen.[57]

The following year, the NWSA changed their female-only governing rules in order to keep up with the AWSA, which was attracting some of the most famous male names in the country. They elected Theodore Tilton their first male president. He wrote a seventeen-page letter to Charles Sumner titled "The Title Deed to Woman's Franchise,"[58] regarding the Constitution and its Fourteenth Amendment. In it he stated that the use of "persons" to include women was "too self-evident to have been ever questioned in any court,"[59] gave a thorough legal argument in support of the New Departure, and silently rolled his eyes at arguments about the framers' intent, stating that "with or without intent, a law stands as it is written."[60] These words are sometimes attributed to Elizabeth Cady Stanton, so he may have consulted her before writing.

That same year, on January 11, Tilton's married lover, Victoria Wood-hull, an upstart newcomer to the NSWA who had declared herself a candidate for the US presidency in 1870,[61] presented her memorial before the House Judiciary Committee. She was the first woman to ever speak before a congressional committee on the issue of women's suffrage,[62] and her argument, crafted together with Senator Benjamin Butler, was based on the Minors' New Departure. Woodhull's memorial stated:

> *That since the adoption of the Fifteenth Article of Amendments to the Constitution, neither the state of New York nor any other state, nor any territory, has passed any law to abridge the right of any citizen of the United States to vote, as established by said article, neither on account of sex or otherwise.*
>
> *That, nevertheless, the right to vote is denied to women citizens of the United States by the operation of Election Laws in the several states and territories, which laws were enacted prior to the adoption of the said Fifteenth Article, and which are inconsistent with the Constitution as amended, and, therefore, are void and of no effect; but which being still enforced by the said states and territories, render the Constitution inoperative as regards the right of women citizens to vote.*
>
> *And whereas, Article Six, Section Two, declares "That this Constitution, and the laws of the United States which shall be made in pursuance thereof, and all treaties made or which shall be made under the authority of the United States, shall be the supreme law of the land; and all judges in every state shall be bound thereby, anything in the Constitution and Laws of any state to the contrary notwithstanding."*
>
> *And whereas, no distinction between citizens is made in the Constitution of the United States on account of sex, but the Fourteenth Article of Amendments to it provides that "no state shall make or enforce any law which shall abridge the privileges and immunities of citizens of the United States," "nor deny to any person within its jurisdiction the equal protection of the laws."*
>
> *And whereas, the continuance of the enforcement of said local election laws, denying and abridging the Right of Citizens to Vote on account of sex, is a grievance to your memorialist and to various*

other persons, citizens of the United States, being women—There-
fore your memorialist would most respectfully petition your Honor-
able Bodies to make such laws as in the wisdom of Congress shall be
necessary and proper for carrying into execution the right vested by
the Constitution in the citizens of the United States to vote, without
regard to sex.[63]

While these high-profile efforts were taking place, ordinary women across the nation were taking to the polls to do as Francis suggested: exercise the right the Fourteenth Amendment had already given them. But voting was not the simple, private affair of today; it was a very public, very radical act.

Ballots were rarely secret until the 1888 election, when America began using the "Australian Ballot," along with the first mass-marketed, automated polling system: the Myers Automatic Booth. "Our forebears considered casting a 'secret ballot' cowardly, underhanded, and despicable," wrote Harvard professor Jill Lepore.[64]

Therefore, most polling places were set up in a specific way. A voting window separated the election officials from the voters. This required voters to step up onto a platform in full view of everyone else in the room to cast their vote.[65] Voters either placed their ballots— which were cut out of the newspaper or handed to them by candidates or their volunteers[66]—in ballot boxes or glass globes labeled by party or candidate, or they handed their ballot to the official, who put it in the corresponding box, which was within sight but out of reach of the voter.[67] Ballots were only recognized as votes once they were in the hands of election judges. Some places used colored tickets for voting or, as in St. Louis, wrote the number next to the person's name in the registration book on the ticket, which made it easy to see how someone had voted.[68] A few states, such as Missouri, Minnesota, and Kentucky,[69] allowed verbal voting, whereby a vote was stated publicly and recorded, allowing for no secrecy whatsoever.[70]

In order to vote, women were literally entering the male sphere, as voting took place in the county courthouse in the large towns or in shoe, furniture, or general stores; homes; fire stations; warehouses; barbershops;

livery stables; and even taverns[71]—places no respectable woman would ordinarily go. These polling places were often rowdy and violent. Party agents translated platforms for the masses and were known to employ deception, bribery, and manipulation to get votes for their candidate. Physical intimidation was also common.[72]

On top of that, parties often provided free drinks, especially at saloons, to voters as an inducement to vote, and candidates showed gratitude for voter support by supplying alcohol, which often led to fisticuffs and all-out brawls; newspapers regularly reported violence on election days.[73] Almost ninety people were killed at the polls across America from 1828 to 1861.[74] It is little wonder why some men believed it would be dangerous to a woman's virtue for her to enter a polling place or why Northwestern University professor Angela Ray considers attempting to vote "the most physically confrontational suffrage activism prior to the parades, pickets, and hunger strikes of the twentieth century."[75]

Decades of petitioning the government, both before and after the Civil War, had come to naught; it was now "time for women to assail registry offices, polling places, and courtrooms, insisting on their right as citizens to participate in their own governance."[76] In the first five years of the New Departure, "at least seven hundred women that we know of voted or attempted to vote in local, state, and federal elections" in thirteen states and territories,[77] including over 170 in New Jersey in 1868; an unknown number of Black women in South Carolina in 1870; 40 women in Massachusetts in 1870, where they had the vote as early as 1776 and were determined to have it again; and 70 in Washington, DC, in 1871.[78] That same year, in Hammonton, New Jersey, 15 women voted.[79] It is estimated that "some one-hundred-fifty members of the National Woman's Suffrage Association . . . engaged in a widespread campaign of mild civil disobedience during the elections of 1872"[80] alone.

Every one of these brave women had to first register as a voter in her state. Like Virginia, most were refused at that point by the local registrar. In 1871, a judge of elections in Hammonton, New Jersey, refused to allow a group of women to vote—including his own wife.[81] Most kept to the letter of the law, but those who looked the other way were "censured or convicted of error, as institutional authority closed ranks."[82] Historian

Ray cites several such examples: "In Charleston, South Carolina, Kit Green and Stephen Shepard, managers of election, were convicted of 'neglect of duty and violation of the law.' Peter Hill, alderman in Detroit, Michigan, was 'discountenanc[ed]' by the Detroit Board of City Canvassers. Beverly W. Jones, Edwin T. Marsh, and William B. Hall inspectors of election in Rochester, New York, were convicted and fined for receiving the votes of [Susan B.] Anthony and other women."[83]

But that didn't stop the suffragists from trying. A few lucky women voted successfully. Marilla Ricker, a rich widow from New Hampshire, "became the first woman of the era to successfully register to vote in March 1870; on Election Day, however, her ballot voting the straight Republican ticket was refused."[84] Despite this, she was allowed to vote in March 1871 without incident.[85] Elizabeth Avery of Memphis, Tennessee, wife of Francis's second cousin once removed, Minor Meriwether, detailed her experience of voting in the South in 1871 in her journal. She successfully voted, accompanied to the polls by three colonels who had fought on the Confederate side.[86]

Those who were not so lucky and were turned away reacted in different ways. Some left quietly but complained to family and friends and wrote about their experiences in *The Revolution* or other feminist journals. Some, like Angelina and Sarah Grimké, from Hyde Park, Massachusetts,[87] had brought their own ballot boxes along with them and symbolically deposited their ballots there,[88] thumbing their noses at the men who barred them from the real boxes. Others were well educated and had either studied law—formally or on their own—or had fathers or husbands who were lawyers,[89] so they were more than ready to debate the finer points of law with those who would refuse them their rights. Many read from the national or state constitutions to support their cause.[90] In 1873, in Glastonbury, Connecticut, Rosella E. Buckingham was turned away at the polls but left joyful, calling it a "glorious day." She added, "I must say, that happy as I have been in social assemblies, never at parties, balls, festivals, theaters, concerts, or at Church on Christmas Eve, have I ever known the exalted pleasure that I enjoyed at the polls yesterday."[91]

For safety and to get around one of the most common arguments against women's suffrage—that it would destroy the family—many women took their family members with them when they attempted to register. Husbands and wives, like Francis and Virginia, "sisters and sisters-in-law, nieces and aunts, and mothers and daughters went to the polls together."[92] On November 7, 1871, Victoria Woodhull and her sister, Tennessee "Tennie" Claflin, led a group of women in a parade to their polling place,[93] and a year later, Anthony and three of her sisters voted in Rochester, New York.[94] In 1871, in Washington, DC, a group of more than seventy women showed up at their local registrar's office together with their husbands and other allies.[95]

However, it was not only the wealthy white women of the suffrage movement who went to the polls. Once the Fifteenth Amendment passed on February 3, 1870, some Black women interpreted the passage "the right of citizens of the United States to vote shall not be denied or abridged by the United States or by any State on account of race, color, or previous condition of servitude" to mean that they could vote.[96] Sojourner Truth attempted to vote in Battle Creek, Michigan, in 1872, but did not succeed in casting a ballot.[97] There were even Black election officials in South Carolina who encouraged Black women to vote in 1870.[98] Later that year, five women in the same city were able to vote successfully with the help of two Black judges of election.[99]

Most men were not so supportive; in fact, they were threatened. They went so far as to try to make the gender-neutral term "voter" a masculine term. As early as 1868, newspapers across the country, including the *New York World*[100] and *Cincinnati Daily Enquirer*[101] refused to dignify women as "voters," instead calling them by the diminutive "votresses." When women were forced to put their votes on or under the ballot box because election officials refused to officially take them,[102] men mocked them as "playing vote,"[103] as though they were children mimicking adult behaviors rather than exercising their rights as American citizens. In 1871, when the WSAM petitioned the House Committee on the Judiciary for a women's suffrage amendment, they argued "that without the vote, women were stamped, 'an inferior class,' an inequity that fostered 'feebleness and dependence,'"[104] putting them literally in the very position the pejorative language of men and their laws confined them to metaphorically.

Women were asking to be recognized legally that they were more than the infants and lunatics the law of coverture would have them be; they were asking to be given the same rights as former slaves, convicts, and immigrants, to be recognized as people with equal rights. And to do this, they had to beg "besotted, debauched white male citizens, legal voters, soaked in whiskey, simmered in tobacco, and parboiled in every shameless vice and sin, to recognize them also as human, and graciously accord to them the rights of intelligent beings!"[105]

Despite these fiery protests, not all women were excited about the prospect of action based on the New Departure. Some simply were not brave enough to buck convention. "It took a bold woman to participate in such public, and traditionally male acts. Such actions not only challenged the law, but had to be carried out amid imposing environments surrounded by men," writes Donna Monnig.[106]

Others were too conservative in their views, seeing women who would protest or vote as traitors to their sex and "semi-women, mental hermaphrodites."[107] Adherents to the idea of "True Womanhood," believed a woman's life was made up of "four cardinal virtues: piety, purity, submissiveness and domesticity. Put them all together and they spelled mother, daughter, sister, wife-woman,"[108] the proper roles for women in society, which did not include going to the polls.

In 1850, the *Ladies Wreath*, a monthly women's magazine, held an essay contest on the topic, "How May an American Woman Best Show Her Patriotism?"[109] The winner, novelist Susan Estes, who wrote under the pen name Miss Elizabeth Wetherell, wrote that voting was *not* one of the ways, "because their doing so would only bring, in public affairs, a vast increase of confusion and expense without in the smallest degree affecting the result. And at home . . . if we were to go a step further and admit the children to a share in our deliberations, they would rise up as one man through the country and vote their mothers at home."[110]

Regardless of this opposition, by the time the presidential election of 1872 neared—the first since the Minors gave voice to the New Departure—thousands of women across the country were ready to vote on November 6. A few would vote for Victoria Woodhull, fellow suffragist and first woman to ever run for president in the United States—Victoria planned to cast her own vote on Election Day but could not because she ended up in jail—but many others would support the incumbent Republican Ulysses S. Grant, and still others the Democratic/Liberal-Republican Horace Greeley.[111] But no matter who they voted for, the women of the United States knew it was going to be a historic day, thanks to Minor and Anthony—they just could not know how historic and where their bold actions would lead.

CHAPTER TEN

Minor v. Happersett

ON OCTOBER 15, 1872, VIRGINIA DONNED HER WHITE SILK GLOVES, straightened her hat, and took Francis's proffered arm as they stepped out onto the front porch of their upper-middle-class home at 2652 Olive in downtown St. Louis and into the brisk autumn air. The office of the Board of Election, located at 2004 Market Street[1] was just over half a mile from their home, so they decided to walk.

Virginia took a deep breath, trying to quell her nerves. She was merely doing what hundreds of women had done before her—asserting her right to vote as a US citizen. But in the back of her mind, she knew this could be so much more. She and Francis had already decided what they would do if the registrar denied her the chance to vote for a second term for President Grant.[2] It was in God's hands now.

When they reached the Board of Election office and stated their purpose—Virginia was there to register as a voter in the city of St. Louis in the Thirteenth District and Sixth Ward—they were shown into a small office, where a man sat behind a desk. He introduced himself as Reese Happersett, the election registrar. He listened politely as Virginia explained that she was invoking her right under the Fourteenth Amendment of the Constitution and Missouri law to register so that she could vote in the upcoming presidential election.

Mr. Happersett sat back, considering her words for a long moment before telling her he could not acquiesce to her request, because the Missouri constitution forbade it since she was "not a 'male' citizen but a woman!"[3] Under the Constitution of Missouri, Article II, Section 18, only "male citizens" of the United States were entitled or permitted to vote.[4]

Virginia respectfully disagreed, and the two exchanged arguments for a short time, with Francis interjecting when needed. Finally, she smoothed her skirt and rose, bidding Mr. Happersett good-day. She had no desire to make a scene as other suffragists had.

Outside on the building steps, Francis squeezed her hand. This was not the best-case scenario, but it was still an outcome they could work with. Acting as Virginia's representative—married women would not be able to sue in Missouri courts without a man until 1889—he would begin right away on a lawsuit against Mr. Happersett for $10,000 in damages in the St. Louis County Circuit Court.[5] They would test the mettle of the law and see just how far it would bend.

THE MINORS' PETITION

Francis immediately started drafting a brief to the court, bringing the ideas that he and Virginia had been discussing for the last four years together with the legal arguments that supported them, crafting as solid a case as possible. Unlike their friend, Anthony, who was arrested for attempting to vote on November 6 and charged with a criminal act, Virginia's case was a civil suit; in this way, the fact that Happersett had blocked Virginia from action at the polls was a blessing.[6]

In bringing their case before the courts, they were charting new waters; very few, if any, other women who were turned away at the polls fought back through legal action. Part of this was likely due to laws that kept women from bringing suit on their own[7] and to women's general lack of knowledge of the law and judicial system. There was also the matter of the time and money such an action, which could—and did—drag out for years, would cost.[8]

In many ways, the Minors were the perfect people to fight this battle, despite being less well known outside of Missouri than other suffragists were. Virginia "was respectably married and had the full support of her husband, an attorney, to press the matter in the courts. . . . No scurrilous past undermined her credibility," as it had for Victoria Woodhull. "She embodied the virtues of the wife and mother. Tragically, she had lost her only son at a young age,"[9] which endeared her to the public and lent sympathy to her cause.

Legally, Virginia needed a man to represent her, and Francis was willing to do anything to take her cause as far as it would go, regardless of the consequences. As a lawyer, he had to understand that he could lose everything—his job, his reputation, perhaps even his license—if their case failed. "The fact that he willingly put his reputation and practice on the line further reinforces his commitment to his wife and the cause of women's rights,"[10] writes Monnig. But in his heart, Francis was "a woman's rights man"[11] and wanted to show through his actions, not just his writing and background support, that men had a role to play in the women's suffrage movement too.[12]

Francis is believed to be the sole author of all of the briefs involved in the Minors' three court cases, rather than the other lawyers on his team. Legal scholars have noted that similarities between these and others he wrote are enough to at least make this plausible, if not provide proof.[13] This would make sense, given that he and Virginia were the creators of the theory they were now defending; they knew it and its legal intricacies better than anyone.

Francis filed their petition on November 9, 1872.[14] In short, their argument was that "women are citizens; citizens participate in self-government; the mechanism for self-government is the franchise; [therefore] women can and should vote."[15] But the petition itself was much more complex. After establishing that Virginia "was a native-born, free white citizen of the United States, and of the State of Missouri, and on the day last mentioned she was over the age of twenty-one years . . . for more than twenty years had been and is a tax-paying, law-abiding citizen of the county and State aforesaid," the petition laid out the facts of the case, including where and when Mrs. Minor attempted to register and why. It continued with the following points:

1. As a US citizen, she "was then and there entitled to all the privileges and immunities of citizenship, chief among which is the

elective franchise, and as such, was entitled to be registered, in order to exercise said privilege: yet . . . she was deprived of her right to vote."

2. The state Constitution and registration law of Missouri are therefore "in conflict with, and repugnant to the Constitution of the United States, which is paramount to State authority" and that they are especially in conflict with the section of Article I that forbids Bills of Attainder; sections of Article IV that entitle all citizens in a state to "all privileges and immunities of citizens in the several States" and "guarantee to every State a republican form of government"; and Article VI, which places the US Constitution as "the Supreme law of the land" above all state constitutions and laws.

3. By denying her right to vote, Mr. Happersett and the State of Missouri were also guilty of defying several amendments to the Constitution, including Article V, which said no one would be "deprived of life, liberty, or property without due process of law"; Article IX, which states "certain rights . . . shall not be construed to deny or disparage others retained by the people"; and Article XIV, which states that all citizens are protected from laws that seek to "abridge the privileges or immunities of citizens of the United States. Nor shall any State deprive any person of life, liberty, or property, without due process of law; nor deny to any person within its jurisdiction, the equal protection of the laws."

In citing these specific examples, Virginia and Francis argued that voting was a "privilege" of citizenship that gave each person the right "to participate in his or her government." If anyone would seek to deny or limit that right, they would have to show where in the Constitution such activity was allowed, and if they could not, the Missouri constitution and state law would have to submit to the national Constitution.[16]

The Minors felt that the situation women found themselves in, being unable to exercise a constitutionally enabled right, resulted from a "widespread misunderstanding of the characteristics of state and federal citizenship."[17] They argued that each citizen of the United States had rights afforded to them by the federal government as well as by the state in which they reside.[18] But rather than being in competition with one another, these rights worked together so that the states did not need to restrict federal rights. To them, the "federal state [w]as the protector and guarantor of national citizenship rights."[19] At the same time, the states "had the power to regulate—but not prohibit—the rights guaranteed to national citizens by the Constitution. . . . For the Minors, citizenship could not be partial, and any exclusions from federal citizenship rights had to be made explicit in federal law."[20]

While twenty-first-century minds tend to regard suffrage as a right of national citizenship conferred upon one's eighteenth birthday, in the nineteenth century, citizenship and suffrage were not necessarily linked.[21] There was considerable tension between federal and state powers rooted in the country's break with Britain and founding as an independent nation. Even the Founding Fathers debated the issue of whether Congress should have the power to negate state laws, at the Constitutional Convention. James Madison said yes, for he "'considered the negative . . . essential' to prevent the states from 'pursu[ing] their particular interests in opposition to the general interest' and to keep them from encroaching on national authority as they had under the Articles of Confederation."[22] Agreeing, James Wilson thought it "better to prevent the passage of an improper law, than to declare it void when passed."[23]

However, some foresaw that this national power could cripple the states. Hugh Williamson opposed "giving a power that might restrain the States from regulating their internal police,"[24] while John Dickinson worried that it was "impossible to draw a line between the cases proper & improper for the exercise of the negative."[25] He saw the situation as a Gordian Knot in which either the states or national government would be harmed at some point: "[We] must take our choice of two things—either subject the States to the danger of being injured by the power of the Natl. Govt. or the latter to the danger of being injured by that of the States."[26]

The Convention was split over the issue, but ended up leaving it out by a vote of six to five,[27] leading to confusion until after the Civil War, when the Reconstruction Amendments began to provide some direction about "exactly what it meant to be a citizen of the United States ... what rights citizenship conveyed, or whether they applied equally to all."[28]

In the end, the Minors were essentially saying Madison, Wilson, and the others who sided with them were correct, even though the language explicitly stating so was left out of the Constitution. Francis wrote that "the vast majority of voters easily conclude that their right to vote for every office is derived from the State, when in truth, the States have no jurisdiction whatever over the Federal right of suffrage.... Their authority is confined to the control of Federal elections, and even this is subject to the superior power of Congress."[29]

Moreover, the Minors argued that the Enforcement Acts,[30] three bills passed by Congress in 1870 and 1871 that protected former slaves' rights to not be harassed, to vote, and to receive equal protection under the law[31] applied to Virginia, for as a woman, she was an enslaved party under the Thirteenth and Fourteenth Amendments.[32]

Many people—the courts included—thought they were reaching too far afield by saying that women should be included under the Thirteenth Amendment's language regarding slavery, but when the law of coverture is examined, it is not difficult to see their line of thinking. Historian Catherine Allgor explains:

> At birth, a female baby was covered by her father's identity, and then, when she married, by her husband's.... Because they did not legally exist, married women could not vote, make contracts, or be sued. They could not own or work in business. Married women could not own land or any other property, not even the clothes on their backs, and upon the death of her husband, a woman's legal agency would transfer to her nearest male relative.... In the same way that while men exerted total control over black bodies—up to and sometimes including death—so they owned their wives.... He owned her labor and could even lease her to work for someone else, taking her wages. He had absolute ownership of his wife's children. If he chose, he could take custody of children after a divorce and could refuse to allow his former wife to ever see them again; and he could seize her property from other

*heirs upon her death. . . . A husband also had absolute right to sexual
access to his wife, regardless of her wishes. Within marriage, a woman's consent was implied, so under the law, all sex-related activity,
including rape, was legitimate. And of course, a husband could legally
beat his wife, or ask that she be remanded to prison or an asylum. . . .
When it came to their rights as specifically women and wives, legally
the only difference between a slave and a married woman was that
a husband could not sell his wife nor could he prostitute her out, and
even these distinctions were sometimes shaky.*[33]

HAPPERSETT'S DEFENSE

There are two sides to every story, and Reese Happersett wasn't buying
a word of the Minors' argument. When he learned of the lawsuit, the
registrar asked the court to appoint a lawyer for him, claiming he couldn't
afford his own attorney. Justice Stremmel turned down the request, and
Happersett was forced to find his own counsel.[34] He hired Smith P. Galt,
a Civil War veteran and attorney best known for his work defending the
St. Louis Railways.[35]

The Minors' petition was presented to the court as a written statement
on January 2, 1873. Galt objected to the Minors' version of the events,
filed a demurrer, legalese for an objection to the petition, and appealed
to have the case heard during the general term of the circuit court.[36] He
argued the Minors failed to "state sufficient facts to constitute a cause of
action for the following reasons: Because said Virginia L. Minor had no
legal right to vote at the general election; Because said Virginia L. Minor
had no right to be registered for voting by said defendant; Because it was
the duty of the defendant to refuse to place the said Virginia L. Minor's
name upon the list of registered voters."[37]

Furthermore, Galt argued that Mr. Happersett was simply doing his
job as a registrar. "As a representative of the government he was bound to
uphold the law. Confronted with a woman insisting that he do just that,
he found it necessary to make an interpretation."[38]

In the end, both parties claimed their actions were defended by either
the Constitution of the United States (Minor) or the Constitution of
the State of Missouri (Happersett). The case came down to a conflict

between the two documents,[39] an interesting parallel to the Minors' arguments about state versus national citizenship.

The St. Louis Circuit Court Case

Happersett's demurrer was upheld, and arguments were heard in writing by Judge Horatio M. Jones[40] on February 3, 1873, without a trial or jury.

In addition to Francis, two other attorneys represented the Minors. One of them, John B. Henderson, was the author of the Thirteenth Amendment and the principal agitator for the Fifteenth Amendment, which granted former slaves the right to vote.[41] His very presence was a strong reminder to the court of what was at stake and on what constitutional grounds the Minors presented their case.

The other attorney was John M. Krum, the former mayor of the cities of St. Louis, Missouri, and Alton, Illinois,[42] whom Francis had met in 1861 when they faced off in a courtroom battle.[43] Mr. Krum was also a well-known supporter of female suffrage, having said publicly two years prior, "How has it that only one-half of our adult population have the privilege of the ballot? . . . I shall not stop to refute what is implied against our countrywomen by the restricted and unjust ballot system now in practice. This restriction, in my humble judgement, is fundamentally wrong."[44]

Judge Jones read the arguments of both parties. The Minors' brief was similar in logic to their original petition. Their petition also contained new arguments that showed not only how their thinking had evolved, but also the thoroughness with which they scoured the law for any and all arguments that would help their case:

1. By keeping women from exercising all of their rights, they are "degraded in the estimation of [their] fellow men and reduce[d] below the level of those who constitute the great body of people of which the government is composed. It moreover inflicts a penalty which, by the laws of this state, is part of the punishment inflicted for a felony, and which follows conviction for such a crime."[45] So although women committed no crime and were neither tried nor convicted of one, they were forced to endure its punishment—exclusion from the voting populace.[46]

2. Denying women the right to vote was a violation of the right of free speech. "We claim . . . that the right to vote or express one's wish at the polls, is embraced in the spirit, if not the letter, of the First Amendment."

3. Missouri laws violated the Thirteenth Amendment, because women without the vote were placed in a position of involuntary servitude. "Although a citizen, Mrs. Minor had never been able to consent to the laws, but her property was taken and she was taxed to pay the men who denied her this privilege of suffrage."[47]

4. They also invoked natural law, moral principles that are independent of the laws of any state or nation: "Suffrage is never conferred by the government upon a citizen. He holds it by higher title . . . the origin and source of the individual himself."[48]

Having considered both these arguments and those made in the demurrer of Mr. Happersett, Judge Jones ruled against the Minors without comment beyond his decision and affirmation of their legal right to appeal.[49]

Perhaps unsurprisingly, local newspapers took great joy in mocking the case and its defendants. The *Missouri Republican* ran two of the first stories on the Minors' lawsuit on November 10, 1872. "Interesting Suffrage Case" was the kind of neutral journalism one would expect, recounting the facts of the case and reproducing their petition in full.[50] That duty complete, they also printed "Mrs. Minor Not Allowed to Vote,"[51] a sexist article that does everything the author can to make sport of the case.

After some off-color puns about Mr. and Mrs. Minor being "joined according to law," which may be a sexual reference but is also a backhanded compliment about the legality of their marriage, the author makes much of the notations in the petition that Virginia is white and over the age of twenty-one. While both items were included because they were legally expected in a brief like this, the author twists them into "evidence" that the Minors are racist: "the thought that the plaintiff by the obtrusion of the hateful word 'white' strikes a sad and mortifying blow at our colored native born free citizens of the United States over the age of twenty-one years. Is Diana to be be [*sic*] left shivering in the cold without *her* rights . . . being protected? Perish the idea!"[52] By comparing Virginia to the goddess Diana, the author also inserts a subtle accusation of classism by putting the white, wealthy plaintiff on a pedestal above mere mortals in the minds of readers.

He then turns to her age, making a childish pun about her surname and then joking "that it might be difficult at elections to bring out the full feminine vote if it were necessary for applicants at registration to acknowledge that they had arrived at manhood's age," joking that many women would rather remain disenfranchised than reveal their age in public to a man.

The article ends with a disingenuous statement that the author wrote the article "by no means with the view of criticizing her course unkindly," despite clear evidence to the contrary, and does her the compliment of admitting "she is a woman of culture, of strong convictions, and has doubtless entered this suit, not for the purpose of making money, but for testing a knotty and very interesting question, in which Mrs. MINOR *may* prove a major."[53]

Unfortunately, this article seems to have set a precedent, for other papers across the country followed suit in gleefully reveling in puns on the Minors' name. The Mississippi paper *American Citizen*, published one such joke: "Mrs. Virginia Minor . . . must unquestionably be nonsuited; for, however ambiguous the word 'citizen' may be under the Fifteenth Amendment, the law is very explicit in withholding the right of suffrage from minors." Monnig notes that this double entendre "is a classic reminder that nineteenth-century law regarded women as having no more rights or mental capacity than children."[54]

Some publications did more than joke, accusing the Minors of being unscrupulous. The *Buffalo Morning Express* stopped just short of accusing the Minors of being publicity seekers: "There is nothing more gratifying to some people than notoriety, and Mrs. Minor doubtless has accomplished all she desired in filing this bill. She gets her name into Court, and thence into the papers, and thereby secures a vast amount of advertising at little or no expense. In making this notice, we contribute our proportion of the gratuitous glorification of the strong-minded Mrs. Minor. We hope, however, that her success in this line will not induce others of her sex to embark in similar business."[55]

St. Louis's own paper, the *St. Louis Times*, went one step further by saying the Minors were only seeking attention with their suit: "Mrs. Minor is a lady of the highest respectability, and belongs to a class of reformers who would not stoop to any such action [attempting to vote] for the sake of creating a sensation,"[56] subtly linking Virginia to such scorned upstarts in the movement as Victoria Woodhull, who admittedly sought publicity in everything she did. This association could do nothing but damage Virginia's reputation because by the time the article was printed (October 16, 1872), Woodhull was persona non grata in the NWSA and hated by many across the country for her antics.

HEARING BEFORE THE MISSOURI SUPREME COURT

It was amid this black cloud of public opinion that the Minors advanced their case to the Missouri Supreme Court on appeal. This was a big step, not only legally but personally, for the Minors. Francis's first action was to resign from his position[57] as a clerk for the Supreme Court so as not to present any conflict of interest. This meant not only a loss of income, which the Minors could afford, but the loss of an important, and by all indications, enjoyable, position that provided Francis with many connections. His willingness to give all of this up was yet another sign of his commitment to their cause and belief in the rightness of their argument.

On May 7, 1873, the Missouri Supreme Court heard the Minors' case in their chambers on the second floor, west side of the south wing of the Old Courthouse.[58] The room in which the proceedings took place was Circuit Court 5, which is today the park library, Old Courthouse room 212.[59] This was the very same place where the famous Dred Scott case was held, uniting two minorities, a slave and a woman, in a quest for freedom as US citizens under the law.

The Minors presented the same argument they had given before the circuit court, but the State of Missouri, "reassured by an earlier ruling that states could refuse to license women lawyers [*Bradwell v Illinois*], did not even bother to contest the case."[60]

Bradwell v. Illinois originated with the suit of Mrs. Myra Bradwell, who sued for her right to practice law in the state of Illinois.[61] The Illinois Supreme Court found against her, so like the Minors, she took her case to the US Supreme Court. It was heard six months earlier than the Minors' case was, and the findings struck down the argument that the privileges and immunities clause protected an individual from the actions of state law. The decision of Justice Samuel Freeman Miller stated, "The protection designed by that clause, as has been repeatedly held, has no application to a citizen of the State whose laws are complained of." Justice Joseph P. Bradley agreed, writing about the same clause regarding the right to practice law (and vis-à-vis the Minor case the right to vote): "It certainly cannot be affirmed, as an historical fact, that this has ever been established as one of the fundamental privileges and immunities of the sex. On the contrary, the civil law, as well as nature herself, has always recognized a wide difference in the respective spheres and destinies of man and woman."

As it turned out, the State of Missouri was right to not worry over its defense. The Missouri Supreme Court—Ephraim Brevard Ewing, Henry M. Vories, Washington Adams, and J. A. Sherwood (Chief Justice David Wagner was absent)[62]—found against the Minors. Judge Vories wrote the opinion of the court, citing two main arguments. The first was that Virginia's right to vote was not protected by the wording of the Fourteenth Amendment, which was intended only to protect former slaves from "unfriendly legislation in which they could take no party, that unless these people had the right to vote and thus protect themselves against oppression. . . . It was not intended that females or persons under the age of twenty one years should have the right of suffrage conferred on them."[63]

Second, "the right to restrict the right of suffrage to the male inhabitants by a state is clearly recognized. . . . I think the circuit court committed no error in sustaining the demurrer to the petition. Judge Wagoner being absent, the other judges concurring the judgement of the circuit court is affirmed."[64]

In summarizing the findings of this case for publication, Missouri Supreme Court reporter Truman Post wrote, "There is no conflict between the Constitution of the State and the registration laws, restricting the right of voting to male citizens, and the Fourteenth Amendment to the Constitution of the United States."[65]

With this ruling, the Minors were again facing a disappointment, but one rife with opportunity. They now had the legal power to do something no one else in the country—not even their friend Anthony, with her dramatic court case—had been able to accomplish: take their case for female suffrage before the US Supreme Court. There they would argue for woman's equality under the law. The court would either side with them, recognizing American women had the right to vote, or rule against them, in which case they would still make history.

CHAPTER ELEVEN

A Woman Challenging the Nation's Highest Court

ON FEBRUARY 9, 1875,[1] FRANCIS MINOR ROSE FROM HIS SEAT BEHIND the counsel table, straightened his black suit, and faced the bench, behind which the black-robed justices sat: Chief Justice Morrison Waite in the center, the others trailing off on each side by seniority.[2] He took a deep breath. This was the pinnacle of any lawyer's career: to argue a case before the Supreme Court of the United States. It was something not even his venerable forebears had achieved; he hoped they were proud. Instead of representing a stranger or a faceless corporation, as most lawyers in his position were, his client was not only his wife but also all of the women of the United States whom she represented[3] and, in some ways, the US Constitution itself. Although his cocounsels Henderson and Krum signed the brief, he would be the only one giving oral arguments,[4] and there was no opposing counsel.[5]

Chief Justice Waite had only been in office for a little over a year, but his court already proved itself to be conservative, preferring to react "to changes proposed in dissenting opinions or the theories of lawyers and legal scholars."[6] Rather than being proactive in leading change, "it tended to see itself as the keeper of tradition."[7] This meant Francis had his work cut out for him if he was going to convince these judges to take such a revolutionary step as endorsing women's suffrage. Having argued this case twice before, he was well prepared, but he also planned to reemphasize a few elements he hoped would appeal to the traditional side of the court and help them see his argument as not really new at all but rather as a clarification of what the Founding Fathers always intended for the nation.

As soon as the Chief Justice recognized him by name, Francis began. "Mr. Chief Justice and may it please the Court. . . ."[8]

Francis's argument was "elaborate . . . partially based on what he deemed true political views, and partially resting on legal and constitutional grounds."[9] In addition to the three foundational arguments covered in the previous chapter, the Minors elaborated on two other points that were part of their briefs all along but now had taken on new urgency and deserved greater explanation. The first was that the right of suffrage was a "privilege" of citizenship because it was the very right that enabled a "citizen to participate in his or her government."[10] The other was that if the Constitution of the United States didn't deny women the right to vote, no other legal document or court decision could.

To argue the first point, Francis invoked the Thirteenth and Fourteenth Amendments, applying George W. Julian's January 16, 1866, remarks before the House of Representatives on the issue of Black suffrage to the issue of female suffrage: "Sir, without the ballot no man is really free, because if he enjoys freedom it is by the permission of those who govern, and not in virtue of his own recognized" right of suffrage. "By the right of suffrage I mean the right to a share in the governing power."[11]

Francis argued that because women were subject to the system of coverture—by which their rights and property were governed by their nearest male relative—they essentially had the same rights as slaves. Coverture made women into a special class of citizens who were not capable of understanding or acting on the same level of legal and political duty as men were. While over the years the strictness of these laws had loosened, women were still not seen as on par with men when it came to matters of government. Even though the Thirteenth Amendment freed the slaves, it did not free Black women (or any women) from the subjugation of coverture, the oppression of unpaid domestic labor, and the dominance of their husbands.[12]

In Francis's argument, women were people just like anyone else and should be treated with the same rights as other citizens. Hence, as the

Black man was now protected under the Thirteenth, Fourteenth, and Fifteenth Amendments, so should women be. Instead, they were held as a lower class of citizen, branded with a "badge of servitude"[13] that made them equivalent with slaves with regard to not being able to exercise their rights. Francis cited the following example as but one proof of his point:

> *Take one illustration, evidenced by a recent decision of the Supreme Court of Missouri,* in Clark vs. The National Bank of the State of Missouri, *47 Mo. Rep., 1. We use our own words, but we state it correctly; that a married woman can not [sic], by the law of Missouri, own a dollar's worth of personal property, except by the consent of another! It makes no difference that that other is her husband. This, it is true, is a State law, a matter exclusively of State legislation; but we mention it to show how utterly helpless and powerless her condition is without the ballot.*[14]

Comparing a wealthy white woman with her lack of personal identity and rights under the law to a slave was certainly a novel argument. However, some scholars feel the Minors' case would have been stronger if they had clearly voiced the case for Black women in their argument. After all, Black women, unlike Virginia, had been slaves and still were under the very laws Francis was arguing against. Ray and Richards write, "It is not clear whether women of color were routinely embraced under the term woman as it was used by the Minors. Grammatically and logically they were, but culturally and contextually this reading is less certain. To the extent that the Minors' arguments represented Virginia Minor as an emblem of womanhood, her personal characteristics as a white taxpayer were elided with those of the symbolic woman citizen."[15]

As a result, in a way, they undermined their own argument, which was already the weakest plank in their defense.

Yet this comparison was minor when held next to the larger question of citizenship. The debate over women's status as citizens had been raging since the Revolution, when Americans made the transition from subjects of the British crown to citizens of their own nation. While the word "citizen" is written in the Constitution nearly a dozen times, the word is not defined in it, and there was no unified national understanding of what it meant until after the Civil War.[16] Scholars point out that "even though women were not specifically mentioned in the Constitution, it was understood that they were members of a dependent class and, by nature, lacked the capacity to exercise full citizenship. . . . The Founders defined a special role for women as 'republican mothers,' whose contributions were not to fight or vote but to care for the home and raise future citizens."[17] Because they were hidden away in the domestic realm, citizenship was considered antithetical to what it meant to be female.[18]

For the most part, women went along with this idea until the turn of the century, when they began to see flaws in this argument thanks to the writings of outspoken critics like Lydia Maria Child, Sarah Josepha Hale, Elizabeth Ellet, and Caroline Dall.[19] These female writers reimagined the women's history they had been fed up to this point—penned almost exclusively by men—and questioned the traditional ideals of "domestic citizenship," especially with regard to women's economic dependence on men and their inability to own property in their own right.[20]

Child, in particular, noted the contradiction inherent in the rules of society for women. It was considered "unfeminine to think, unladylike to work" and to have an interest in politics,[21] but yet "as American citizens we profess to believe that every human being has a right to a voice in the laws by which he is governed; and if we do not believe this, our professions of freedom are hollow brass."[22] Unlike many of her contemporaries, Child went on to assert that both women and Black men should have the right to vote and that society would be better for it.[23]

She was writing in a world where "the right to vote [had become] the emblem of American citizenship, if not in law . . . then in common usage and understanding," as Foner points out. "Noah Webster's *American Dictionary of the English Language* noted that in the United States, but not in Europe, the word 'citizen' had, by the 1820s, become synonymous with the right to vote. Of course, Webster was writing about men; white women were certainly citizens although denied the suffrage . . . [and] legally, despite Webster's dictionary, access to the ballot box was a privilege or 'franchise,' not a right."[24]

These legal technicalities did not stop early women's citizenship activists like Sarah and Angelina Grimké and Margaret Fuller from publicly challenging popular notions of the inequality of the sexes in the 1830s and 1840s.[25] On February 21, 1838, in a speech before a special committee of the Massachusetts House of Representatives, Angelina Grimké pointedly called out past interpretations of women's proper roles in society as oppressive by asking, "Are we bereft of citizenship because we are the mothers, wives, and daughters of a mighty people? Have women *no* country?"[26] Abolitionists like the Grimkés, many of whom were women, expressed a belief that suffrage was "the heart and soul of their freedom" and a crucial part of "the rights of an American citizen," both for the slave and themselves.[27]

By the 1850s, women began to understand that citizenship was only being denied to them because of their gender. Stanton thundered before the New York Legislature in 1854 that women "have every qualification required by the Constitution, necessary to the legal voter, but the one of sex." To illustrate her point, she went on to note that women "have governed nations, led armies, filled the professor's chair, taught philosophy and mathematics to the savans [*sic*] of our age, piloted ships across the sea, [yet] are denied the most sacred rights of citizens because, forsooth, we came not into this republic crowned with the dignity of manhood!"[28]

These demands to be legally classified as full citizens turned into heated debates in which women argued for universal rights, by which they meant "the ability to participate equally with men in the political, economic, and intellectual life of the nation."[29] Meanwhile, others attempted to draw women back into the purely domestic roles of wife and mother by painting this life as emblematic of the American patriotic ideal.[30] This debate grew in intensity alongside the budding women's suffrage movement and seemed poised to create change until the Civil War brought all extraneous political activities to a halt.

The debate once again picked up steam with the passage and ratification of the Fourteenth Amendment in the mid- and late 1860s. In 1865, Rep. John Bingham, a member of the Joint Committee on Reconstruction,[31] proposed an amendment that would allow the passage of "all laws necessary and proper to secure all persons . . . equal protection in their rights to life, liberty, and property . . . absolute equality under the law of all persons."[32] He was one of the few people at the time who believed that the states should be held to the privileges and immunities clause and that his idea would "remedy this defect in the Constitution," by "arm[ing] the Congress of the United States . . . with the power to enforce the bill of rights,"[33] making states accountable for "any action that deprived citizens of essential rights."[34] This idea and its broad wording was the basis of the first section of the Fourteenth Amendment, which the Minors invoked in their lawsuit, and is the reason for its gender-neutral language, ambiguity that is said to have "charmed" Bingham[35]—except, apparently, when it came to women being included in the definition of "all persons."

In 1871, when Victoria Woodhull spoke before the Senate Judiciary Committee on the subject of women's enfranchisement, Representative Bingham reminded her before she even started speaking, "Madam, you are no citizen." When she asked him what she was, he replied, "You are a woman."[36] Women would not be declared citizens independent of their husbands in the United States until September 22, 1922, with the passage of the Cable Act. While Representative Bingham's universal language would on the surface seem to include women, he really meant "the male citizens, for that is the meaning of the term 'the people' as used in the Constitution."[37]

Admittedly, he did hold a personal definition of citizenship that was slightly different from what the Fourteenth Amendment actually said, one he would have to continually defend throughout his life—that women, while being citizens and having basic civil rights, were not entitled to all the same rights as male citizens,[38] which is what he meant when speaking with Woodhull. In this way of thinking, he and many others drew a distinction between political citizenship, which involved actions like voting, serving on a jury, or running for office,[39] and private citizenship, which covered the civil rights of all US citizens. He later clarified that if being a citizen was equivalent to having actionable political rights, "your wives and mothers and daughters . . . are not to be considered invested with the rights of citizenship."[40]

An oft-used extension of this very argument—that if women were considered political citizens, children would have to be as well—came up during Francis's argument before the Supreme Court. Justice Stephen Johnson Field asked Francis if children were citizens, to which Francis agreed.[41] The *New York Times* reported the subsequent exchange:

> Justice Field: "So you hold that citizenship confers the right to vote?"
> Minor answered, "Yes, sir."
> Field then asked, "Have children the right to vote?"
> Minor again answered, "Yes, sir."[42]

Francis did not give an explanation for his seemingly baffling and illogical answer, even when the justices prodded him for more. While it is possible this was a result of his hearing loss or a nervous slip of the tongue Francis did not desire to admit to, lest he seem to contradict himself, historian Bonnie Stepenoff believes Francis said no more because he knew that if he had answered in the negative, it would affirm the government's right to "restrict voting rights on the basis of age and immaturity for children. [Because of their legal status under coverture,] this could be extrapolated to argue the same for women, too."[43]

The fact of the matter was that by omitting any reference to gender, the beginning of the Fourteenth Amendment and all of the Fifteenth Amendment left the door open for states to grant women the right to vote, which some territories had already done.[44] However, the majority were entrenched in their old mindset and ways, leaving women, as Anthony noted, "the only human beings outside of state prisons and lunatic asylums adjudged incompetent" to vote.[45]

The second element of the Minors' argument that received increased attention at the Supreme Court trial was the historical veracity of female enfranchisement according to the founders of the country and framers of the Constitution. By harkening back to this foundational document of the United States, Virginia and Francis sought to bolster their claim that women were already qualified to vote under its rules, as well as to show a traditional court that if the framer's intentions were taken into consideration, no new interpretation was needed to uphold this idea.[46]

They began by examining the origin of the word "citizen":

Before the colonists asserted their independence they were politically bound to the sovereign of Great Britain, by what is termed in English law, "allegiance"; and those from whom this allegiance was due were termed "subjects." But when these "bands," as they are termed in the Declaration of Independence, were dissolved, the political relation became changed, and . . . the term citizen was substituted for that of "subject." But this was not a mere change of name; the men who framed the Constitution of the United States had all been subjects of the English king, and they well knew the radical change wrought by the revolution.

In the new political sovereignty thus created, the feudal idea of dependence gave way to that of independence, and the people became their own sovereigns or rulers in the government of their own creation. Of this body politic, represented by the Constitution of the United States, all persons born or naturalized therein and subject to the jurisdiction thereof, are members, without distinction as to political rights or privileges.[47]

To support this argument, the Minors cited statements by the men who framed and/or ratified the constitution. Quoting James Madison in the "Note to His Speech on the Right of Suffrage," they stated that any attempt to deny suffrage to women "violates the vital principle of free government, that those who are to be bound by laws, ought to have a voice in making them."[48] In addition, they echoed the sentiments of Luther Martin, a delegate to the Constitutional Convention of 1787 and an early advocate for equal suffrage for all citizens of the United States. He believed that as part of a democracy, "when . . . individuals enter into government, they have each a right to an equal voice in its first formation, and afterward have each a right to an equal vote in every matter which relates to their government."[49]

Finally, Francis asked, "If this be so, why was not the question sooner raised? We answer, at that very time, and for nearly twenty years afterward, women did vote, unquestioned and undisputed, in one of the

States [New Jersey]. The men who framed the Constitution were then living—some of them in this very State; yet we hear no mention of its being unconstitutional, no objection made to it whatever."[50]

Women's participation in politics in New Jersey is an anomaly in US history. In 1702, a female business owner was one of the signatories on the document that gave control of the colony to Queen Anne of Great Britain. That did not sway the queen to give her female subjects greater rights, however. The next election law written under the governance of the queen "included a reference to 'the Division for which he shall vote;'"[51] that single word was enough to keep women from having the ballot for nearly three-quarters of a century.[52] Not all smaller locations seemed to be aware that women lacked the ballot, however. While only "freeholders voted for the state assembly, householders voted in township elections and candidates actively curried the favor of the 'lower class' at least as early as 1772."[53]

The women of New Jersey were enfranchised in 1776 according to the state constitution without the public giving it a second thought.[54] New Jersey law defined voters as adult inhabitants "worth fifty pounds" who resided in the state for a year, regardless of sex or race. As married women's property ownership was limited by the law of coverture, in reality only single women (including widows) could vote.[55] This concession was the result of political wrangling between the Patriots, Federalists, and Republicans from 1789 to 1807; each party courted them for their votes and women happily cast their ballots.[56] However, this "right" was "debated and purposefully written" into state law for the specific purpose of political gain by lawmakers and therefore never resulted in a change in women's legal status or a popular call for an extension of other female rights.[57]

Even though they had been given the franchise by political parties hoping to gain their support at the polls, the unmarried women of New Jersey voted as they saw fit. They represented the entire continuum of political thought, and many voted their hearts, even if their fathers, brothers, or other male relatives disagreed with them.[58] Although married women were excluded, women still had sufficient numbers to make an impact. Contemporary pamphleteer William Griffith estimated that "of widows and spinsters above twenty one, there can not [sic], I imagine, be fewer than 10,000."[59]

Women's enthusiastic embrace of the ballot pleased the Federalists to no end. On July 4, 1793, Elias Boudinot, a close friend of Alexander Hamilton, declared, "The rights of women are no longer strange sounds to an American ear, and I devoutly hope the day is not far distant when we shall find them dignifying in a distinguishing code, the jurisprudence of several states of the Union."[60]

But such optimism was not to pan out. By the end of the decade, Federalists were not so keen on female voters anymore, as they began to suspect their votes helped the Republicans more than their own party, and the tide of cultural opinion started to view political activity as firmly rooted in the domain of men. Thus they began to call for a revision to the state constitution that would disenfranchise women "and bring it more in tune with the federal constitution."[61]

By 1804, the state had a third party, formed of disgruntled moderate Republicans who siphoned away enough votes from the two major parties as to prove a threat.[62] By the fall 1807 election, the Republicans still hadn't reunited, and they feared losing the all-important 1808 presidential election. The scapegoats became the traditional Federalist voters: single women and Blacks, who now had to lose the rights they had held for nearly two decades in the name of political expediency.[63]

Lewis Condict of Morris, New Jersey, a moderate Republican and the chairman of the election law committee defended taking away suffrage from women, "arguing that the authors of the constitution could not have intended to enfranchise women, blacks, and aliens and that the corruption which prevailed in state elections necessitated the disfranchisement of these groups"[64]—very similar logic to that used by Chief Justice Waite in his decision on the Minor trial. The law was supported by both parties and easily passed. It would be another 113 years before women in New Jersey would vote again.[65]

In his final argument, Francis cited several court cases that he believed upheld his view of the dual nature of citizenship and that national citizenship superseded that of the state, especially with regard to a person's rights as a citizen. They were from his current home state of Missouri (*Cummings v. The State of Missouri* and *Blair v. Ridgley*), South Carolina (*Talbut v. Jansen*), Maryland (*Murray v. McCarty*), Nevada (*Davies v. McKeeby*), and Tennessee (*The State v. Staten*).[66] He then reiterated the constitutional evidence laid out in his previous trials,[67] ending with the sweeping words: "Finally—Such is the nature of this privilege—so individual—so purely personal is its character, that its indefinite extension detracts not in the slightest degree from those who already enjoy it, and by an affirmation of the plaintiff's claim all womanhood would be elevated into that condition of self-respect that perfect freedom alone can give."[68]

THE SUPREME COURT'S DECISION

Virginia and Francis had done all they could; all that remained was to wait for the court to issue their decision. It is said that Virginia "had much confidence and hope of success in the trial,"[69] even going so far as to write to Susan B. Anthony in 1874,[70] "As to my right as a citizen to vote under the constitution, I have never had a doubt, and my expectations of success have been confirmed by a recent decision of the Supreme Court itself, from which I quote: 'The negro having, by the Fourteenth Amendment, been declared to be a citizen of the United States, is thus made a voter in every State of the Union.' . . . I therefore make my appeal to this tribunal, in all confidence, with this decision in my hand, where in they declare that citizenship carries with it the right to vote."[71]

Still, she was not one to turn a blind eye to what was happening around her. Women were losing cases left and right in lower courts—including Myra Bradwell's 1873 attempt to be admitted to the Illinois bar[72] and Anthony's own trial on the charge of voting illegally[73]—so she had to have known her chances of victory were slim.[74] Both Bradwell and another case that same year, commonly known as the Slaughterhouse Cases,[75] invoked the privileges and immunities clause of the Constitution, and both were struck down under the rationale that enforcing the clause was "the province of state law," not federal. As UCLA constitutional law professor Adam Winkler notes, "This set a negative cultural tone for both the Anthony and Minor trials."[76] More alarmingly, it also effectively negated the Minors' argument that national citizenship superseded that of the state, which left the Minors with really only one leg to stand on: their assertion that suffrage was a right of citizenship.[77]

Bookmakers certainly wouldn't be expecting Chief Justice Waite's court to issue a favorable ruling. The past several years had proven this court was slow to react to the Reconstruction Amendments or offer a liberal interpretation of the Fourteenth Amendment.[78] Rather than look forward and create new rights for a new country, "the Waite Court tended to look backward for its cues . . . and was hesitant to expand its own authority. . . . It [had a] tendency to indulge in excessively formalistic or hyperformalistic reading of a statute."[79] The justices were used to seeing the states as protectors of the rights of their citizens, entities that had supreme authority and viewed the federal government as a threat and whose reach into everyday life should be limited.[80]

Waite, too, seemed unsure of himself and hesitant to use his full authority, perhaps because he knew he was woefully underqualified for the position, especially compared to those who had held the chief justiceship previously. His predecessors had all been former presidential cabinet members. The highest public office Waite had held was as a commissioner on the US delegation that settled Alabama's claims against Great Britain that it supplied Confederate privateers during the Civil War. His legal experience was in corporate finance and railroads.[81]

He was also well aware that he was not President Grant's first choice to replace Chief Justice Salmon P. Chase. As Waite biographer Paul Kens recounts, it took eight months to fill the position. The process was "at times such a fiasco that one member of Congress sarcastically suggested a bill to abolish the chief justiceship 'so as to spare the president the mortification of further appointments.'"[82] Waite was actually the seventh man to be asked, the others either turning down the offer or being eliminated for some scandal in their past. Waite was not well liked, with newspapers across the country decrying his lack of legal experience at the national level and his fellow justices calling him "mediocre," "a man of fair but not great abilities" and of "limited legal acumen."[83] Yet his confirmation took only two days and was unanimous.[84]

In some ways Waite appeared to be an ideal chief justice for this case, given that he was known to be favorable toward women's rights and education. He was said to believe that "if a woman does a man's work and does it as well as he can, she ought to have a man's pay."[85] In his advanced years, he even employed a female physician and was one of only three justices in favor of admitting women as members of the Supreme Court bar.[86]

However, that attitude was nowhere in evidence on March 9, 1875, when the Waite court unanimously decided the Minors' case. Rather than quote the court's lengthy opinion in its entirety, it is enough to take a few of the most salient points and explore their impact.

The decision began, just like the Minors' brief had, by addressing the question of citizenship, both nationally and in the state of Missouri. Unlike Representative Bingham, Waite decreed,

> *There is no doubt that women may be citizens. They are persons, and by the Fourteenth Amendment "all persons born or naturalized in the United States and subject to the jurisdiction thereof" are expressly declared to be "citizens of the United States and of the State wherein they reside." But, in our opinion, it did not need this amendment to give them that position. . . . Citizen is now more commonly employed, however, and as it has been better suited to the description of one living under a republican government, it was adopted by nearly all of the States upon their separation from Great Britain, and was afterwards adopted in the Articles of Confederation and in the Constitution of the United States. When used in this sense it is understood as conveying the idea of membership of a nation, and nothing more.*[87]

It was a big step for women to finally formally be declared citizens of the United States in no uncertain terms by the Supreme Court, but the court's limited definition of a citizen left much to be desired, namely, the automatic conveyance of basic rights, especially that of suffrage. "Theirs was a citizenship without substance," writes attorney Jennifer K. Brown,[88] a designation with no real meaning and conferring little to no agency. Waite clearly drew a definitive line between men and the rest of the population, writing, "Women and children are, as we have seen, 'persons.' They are counted in the enumeration upon which the apportionment is to be made, but if they were necessarily voters because of their citizenship unless clearly excluded, why inflict the penalty for the exclusion of males alone? Clearly, no such form of words would have been selected to express the idea here indicated if suffrage was the absolute right of all citizens."[89]

This flew in the face of the Minors' assertion that "there can be no half-way citizenship." Once again, women were asked to be satisfied with being "members of a political community,"[90] along with children, making them a special class of citizens, even as the Chief Justice claimed that being male or female didn't really matter:

> *Sex has never been made one of the elements of citizenship in the United States. In this respect men have never had an advantage over women. The same laws precisely apply to both. The Fourteenth Amendment did not affect the citizenship of women any more than it did of men. In this particular, therefore, the rights of Mrs. Minor do not depend upon the amendment. She has always been a citizen from her birth, and entitled to all the privileges and immunities of citizenship. The amendment prohibited the State, of which she is a citizen, from abridging any of her privileges and immunities as a citizen of the United States; but it did not confer citizenship upon her. That she had before its adoption.*[91]

Because women were considered a special class of citizens—placing them below white men just as the Dred Scott case did with Black men—it meant that only a constitutional amendment could override the court's decision. Just as "it took the Thirteenth Amendment to abolish the special category of slavehood for African-Americans by granting them citizenship . . . it finally took the Nineteenth Amendment to abolish in part the special category of citizenship for women by granting them the right to vote,"[92] historian Joan Hoff writes in an analysis of the case.

Waite also clearly articulated that it was the states that defined which of their citizens could vote, not the federal government:

> *The Constitution of the United States does not confer the right of suffrage upon any one. . . . The Constitution does not define the privi-*

leges and immunities of its citizens. For that definition we must look elsewhere. In this case we need not determine what they are, but only whether suffrage is necessarily one of them. . . . The United States has no voters in the States of its own creation. The elective officers of the United States are all elected directly or indirectly by State voters. . . . The power of the State in this particular is certainly supreme until Congress acts.[93]

Monnig notes that this part of the decision was more about a squabble between "Northern Republicans and Southern Democrats. As Hoff points out, it fell to the Supreme Court to take on the role of 'referee' in the struggle,"[94] and they came down on the side of the South, the traditionalists, and the narrowest interpretation of the Fourteenth Amendment possible, saying it "did not add to the privileges and immunities of a citizen. It simply furnished an additional guarantee for the protection of such as he already had. No new voters were necessarily made by it."

In addition, Waite waved away the Minors' assertion that the founders of the United States intended by inference that women should be voters, writing,

It cannot for a moment be doubted that if it had been intended to make all citizens of the United States voters, the framers of the Constitution would not have left it to implication. So important a change in the condition of citizenship as it actually existed, if intended, would have been expressly declared. . . . Women were excluded from suffrage in nearly all the States by the express provision of their constitutions and laws. If that had been equivalent to a bill of attainder, certainly its abrogation [the annulment of a right] would not have been left to implication. . . . So also of the amendment which declares that no person shall be deprived of life, liberty, or property without due process of law, adopted as it was as early as 1791. If suffrage was intended to be included within its obligation, language better adapted to express that intent would most certainly have been employed.[95]

These words show that Waite was not only unmoved by the argument that one should read between the lines of the Constitution to find women included but that he believed "that it was 'too late' to claim the right of suffrage by implication; the Founders had been men who weighed their words carefully. Nearly a hundred years of failure to claim inclusion by implication made a difference,"[96] writes historian Linda Kerber. Just as most crimes have a statute of limitations, so too, according to the court, did questioning the Founders' intent, and the deadline had passed.

Furthermore, the Minors' use of the example of New Jersey to bolster their case was absurd in the court's collective mind. Waite made the point that the state was an outlier. "No new State has ever been admitted to the Union which has conferred the right of suffrage upon women, and this has never been considered a valid objection to her admission [to the Union]."[97] Lying between the lines was the message that because of this, not all citizens were voters.

Waite closed his argument by effectively giving the Supreme Court an excuse to ignore the question of women's suffrage in perpetuity. One can almost picture him, like Pontius Pilate, washing his hands of the whole matter, with the excuse that it was the state lawmakers' job to change laws deemed unfair; the court was merely the interpreter and arbiter of those laws:

> If the law is wrong, it ought to be changed; but the power for that is not with us. The arguments addressed to us bearing upon such a view of the subject may perhaps be sufficient to induce those having the power, to make the alteration, but they ought not to be permitted to influence our judgment in determining the present rights of the parties now litigating before us. No argument as to woman's need of suffrage can be considered. We can only act upon her rights as they exist. It is not for us to look at the hardship of withholding. Our duty is at an end if we find it is within the power of a State to withhold.[98]

That was an end to it, as Waite saw it. Because the Supreme Court did not make new laws or reinterpret the Constitution, unless or until the states changed their laws or a constitutional amendment was passed, there was nothing more the court could—or would—do.[99]

A SMALL VINDICATION

Women's suffrage advocates were not about to take the Waite ruling, or any others that infringed upon a person's right to vote, quietly. At the NWSA Convention in 1875, the organization's president, Matilda Joslyn Gage, took the Supreme Court to task by arguing that the federal government had already created eight classes of voters by its laws: "The black man, the amnestied man, the naturalized man, the foreigner honorably discharged from the Union army, voters for the lower house of Congress, voters for Presidential electors, [and] pardoned civil and military criminals."[100] Therefore, they, not state governments, had the authority to determine who got to vote. Her speech, like so many others, fell upon deaf ears.

Nine years later, though, the Minors received a small vindication in the ruling of the Supreme Court case *Yarbrough, Ex Parte 110 U.S. 651.* This 1884 case was based in the conviction of Jasper Yarbrough and several other members of the Ku Klux Klan for assaulting Berry Saunders, a Black man, to keep him from voting in a congressional election.[101] It is the only Supreme Court case to address the question of whether voting was part of the privileges and immunities cited in the Constitution, which was ignored by the Waite court's ruling in the Minor case. The court, still headed by Waite, unanimously reversed its previous opinion, ruling, "It is not true, therefore, that the electors for members of Congress owe their right to vote to the State law, in any sense which makes this the exercise of the right to depend exclusively on the law of the State."[102] In essence, the court admitted that the power to regulate voting did lie in the hands of the federal government after all. Hoff explains the importance of this ruling:

> Later decisions interpreted this to mean that voting for a national official was therefore, a privilege and immunity of national citizenship. . . . While the Yarbrough decision did not technically overrule the position taken by the Minor court, by any logical determination it was overruled sub silentio. Yet the Court argued unconvincingly that Yarbrough could be distinguished from Minor because private actions

of intimidation were involved, not state qualifications for voting, and because somehow the requirements by states that electors be male was a lawful state qualification for voting and not an abridgement of the rights of females to vote. The crucial, if questionable, distinction that the Courts made between Yarbrough *and* Minor *was based in part on the difference between the right of a state to set qualifications for voting and the actual abridgment of a citizen's right to vote. A sex qualification was by implication not an abridgement.*[103]

As could be expected, Francis was overjoyed at this verdict, crowing in his pamphlet "Citizenship and Suffrage," that the court had changed its views and agreed with him that the right of federal suffrage does exist based upon the Constitution of the United States.[104]

While this ruling did not change the voting status of women in the United States, it was a heartwarming—albeit too little, too late—victory for the Minors that proved their argument sound. Had this ruling legally erased the *Minor* ruling from the record books, American history may have turned out very differently. However, because it did not, years of discrimination against women and people of color were sanctioned by the court.

CHAPTER TWELVE

The Lasting Impact of the
Minor Case on Voting Rights

Though not a "household name" to most Americans—like *Brown v. Board of Education* or *Roe v. Wade*, for example—*Minor v. Happersett* still influences the daily lives of Americans, especially marginalized people, even as it is "dismissed almost offhand" and "flies under the radar"[1] of the attention of most people, even those in legal circles.

When J. L. Central, a contemporary of Virginia's and supporter of female suffrage, heard the court's ruling, he cried, "The court tells us in its opinion in this case, that 'there cannot be a nation without a people'—but it seems there may be a nation without voters!"[2] As the years went by, this statement proved to be prescient, as the courts went on to cite Waite's ruling, primarily on issues surrounding the Fourteenth Amendment, in several cases that led to voter suppression, an issue the United States is dealing with even well into the twenty-first century.

Minor v. Happersett was a landmark case not only for its handling of women's suffrage but perhaps even more so because of what it said about who is a citizen, what the privileges and immunities of citizenship do and do not include, and the distinctions between political and civil rights. All of these are part of the Reconstruction Amendments—especially the Fourteenth—and are "central to the functioning of a democratic republic and have far-reaching legal implications."[3] Most importantly, the power the *Minor* decision gave to the states to enforce voting laws is still being abused today.

Historian Lisa Tetrault notes that the *Minor* decision was also "denial of black civil rights." Between 1873 and 1875, Northern white people lost a lot of "their will to protect African Americans," which meant they "were less and less willing to sanction the logic of the New Departure."[4] As a result, almost immediately, the Supreme Court began turning the states' rights part of the *Minor* decision against Black voters. As one political science professor laments, "It was judges, alas, that had the task of giving meaning to the Fourteenth Amendment, and the meaning they have given it has changed it drastically."[5]

In one of the earliest cases, just a few months after the *Minor* verdict, in *United States v. Reese*, "the Supreme Court validated the states' right to use poll taxes to keep black citizens from voting."[6] On the surface, this case was similar to that of the Minors' only in that it was a Black man whose vote was refused by the local registrar because he failed to pay a poll tax.[7] Under Waite's leadership, the court gave just as narrow an interpretation of the Fifteenth Amendment as it had for the Minors under the Fourteenth. It ruled that "it is only when the wrongful refusal at such an election is because of race, color, or previous condition of servitude, that Congress can interfere, and provide for its punishment."[8] Because the plaintiff's vote was denied due to a poll tax and not due to his race and because suffrage was a state issue, the court claimed it could not intervene.

The same year, in *U.S. v. Cruikshank*, the Waite court cited its finding in *Minor* that the "Constitution of the United States has not conferred the right of suffrage upon any one," and from *Reese* that "the right of suffrage is not a necessary attribute of national citizenship."[9] Therefore, states were within their Fourteenth and Fifteenth Amendment rights to discriminate against Black voters.[10] As a result, states began regularly instituting poll taxes, literacy tests, and other means to keep Black men from voting, measures that eventually paved the way for the rise of the Ku Klux Klan and normalization of the Jim Crow laws.

In 1896, the justification behind the *Minor* case was extended beyond voting rights for the first time by the Supreme Court to legalize segregation in *Plessy v. Ferguson*.[11] The plaintiff, Homer Adolph Plessy,[12] a mixed-race man from Louisiana who could easily pass for white, made the mistake of sitting in the white section of an East Louisiana Railway train. He was later asked by the conductor to change seats into the area reserved for nonwhite passengers. Plessy refused and was eventually forcibly ejected from the train and arrested for "having criminally violated an act of the general assembly of the state" which required "Negros" to sit in a separate section of the train. Plessy argued that his Thirteenth and Fourteenth Amendment rights had been violated,[13] but the court felt otherwise, writing,

> *That it does not conflict with the Thirteenth Amendment, which abol-*
> *ished slavery and involuntary servitude, except as a punishment for*
> *crime, is too clear for argument . . . refusing accommodations to colored*
> *people, cannot be justly regarded as imposing any badge of slavery*
> *or servitude upon the applicant. . . . The object of the [Fourteenth]*
> *Amendment was undoubtedly to enforce the absolute equality of the*
> *two races before the law, but, in the nature of things, it could not have*
> *been intended to abolish distinctions based upon color, or to enforce*
> *social, as distinguished from political, equality, or a commingling of*
> *the two races upon terms unsatisfactory to either. Laws permitting,*
> *and even requiring, their separation, in places where they are liable*
> *to be brought into contact, do not necessarily imply the inferiority of*
> *either race to the other, and have been generally, if not universally,*
> *recognized as within the competency of the state legislatures. . . . We*
> *consider the underlying fallacy of [Plessy's] argument to consist in the*
> *assumption that the enforced separation of the two races stamps the*
> *colored race with a badge of inferiority. If this be so, it is not by reason*
> *of anything found in the act, but solely because the colored race chooses*
> *to put that construction upon it.*[14]

With these words, the "separate but equal" laws that had begun to crop up in Southern states over the previous decade were affirmed as legal, and any outrage felt by Black people as a result was deemed to be their own fault. In ruling that Fourteenth Amendment privileges only applied to political and civil rights, not social ones,[15] the court allowed white state governments to discriminate against Black citizens for the next seventy years, until the civil rights movement finally broke their stranglehold.

In 1901, Kate M. Gordon of Louisiana and Laura Clay of Kentucky, both members of the National American Woman's Suffrage Association (NAWSA) board, betrayed everything the Minors stood and fought for by attempting to use the decision in the *Minor* case to give white women the vote while excluding their sisters of color.[16] Clay was convinced that bringing southern white women on board with female suffrage was the key to eventually winning the vote nationwide, but they would never be able to do so if Black women were enfranchised as well.[17] Gordon and Clay argued that because "the court found that the Fourteenth Amendment had not created any new voters, only gave extra protection to the rights and immunities already possessed," it could not apply to Black women because they never had the right to vote. Sadly, NAWSA leaders such as Anthony and Carrie Chapman Catt agreed, teaching chapters across the South how to use this argument to win over southern white women[18] and ushering the suffrage movement into an era of open discrimination against Black women.

Once women won the vote in 1920, one would think the ramifications and citation of the *Minor* case would come to an end—and many argue that it did. However, the Nineteenth Amendment did not really nullify it, only the part that upheld discrimination against women voting in the United States. In reality, the Nineteenth Amendment didn't cover all women, only white women. For Black women in the Jim Crow South, the same bullying, threats of violence and sabotaging of electoral practices, all used to deny Black men their voting rights after ratification of the Fifteenth Amendment (1870), were now turned on them.[19] Native American women and men would wait another four years to be able to vote after Congress passed the Indian Citizenship Act in 1924, finally—and ironically—recognizing them as citizens.[20] Even then, biased and corrupt polling practices kept them from voting in certain states until 1957.[21] Asian American women couldn't vote until 1952, when federal policy changed to allow them to become citizens. It was not until the Voting Rights Act of 1965 that the federal government finally stepped in to enforce universal enfranchisement.[22]

In response to the gains won by the Nineteenth Amendment, judges and lawmakers began to apply it in new ways, namely, with regard to voting in US territories. A series of cases in 1901, which came to be known as the Insular Cases, limited the rights of citizens in territories of the United States. The cases began with *Downes v. Bidwell*, which cited *Minor* as justification that the Constitution did not necessarily apply to territories[23] and "political rights were incidental to national belonging."[24]

That did not sit well with the women of Puerto Rico, who became American citizens in 1917 when the United States acquired the island from Spain.[25] Turning the court's citation against them, they created their own New Departure, modeled on the Minors' original, and attempted to vote under the Nineteenth Amendment. On March 24, 1924, Mariana Morales Bernard and Milagros Benet de Mewton, both residents of San Juan, Puerto Rico, took on the role of Virginia Minor and attempted to register to vote in a national US election. They were rejected and, like the Minors, their case made it all the way to the Puerto Rican Supreme Court, where Chief Justice Emilio Del Toro ruled that "the right of suffrage is not a personal and fundamental right and, therefore, that the amendment as framed is not in force in Porto Rico [*sic*]."[26] This decision was backed up by the argument that while the Nineteenth Amendment included women in Hawaii, it did not cover the territories of the Philippines or Puerto Rico,[27] because as territories rather than states, they did not have the power to ratify or reject it. Literate Puerto Rican women were finally given the right to vote in US elections in 1929, and in 1935 the right was extended to all women in the territory.[28]

It wasn't until the late 1960s that the Supreme Court stopped relying on the *Minor* ruling to justify its decisions related to enfranchisement and upheld "voting to be a fundamental right for the purposes of the Equal Protection Clause of the Fourteenth Amendment."[29] *Minor v. Happersett* was cited no fewer than nine times during the 1962 hearings before the Subcommittee on Constitutional Rights of the Committee on the Judiciary, in which literacy tests and voting requirements were debated.[30] The Voting Rights Act of 1965 finally made literacy tests illegal and attempted to end other forms of voter discrimination,[31] and poll taxes were declared illegal in 1966 by *Harper v. Virginia Board of Elections*.[32]

Minor v. Happersett was also used in 1965 by a Senate committee when debating amendments to the Voting Rights Act of 1965. This Act included a "freezing principle" created by Judge John Minor Wisdom, the great-great-grandson of one of Virginia Minor's cousins[33] and a member of the US Fifth Circuit Court of Appeals. It "expressly prohibit[ed] the implementation of any 'test or device' as a prerequisite to voter registration that was discriminatorily motivated or generated a discriminatory effect,"[34] which the Minors would have been in full agreement with. The committee, however, disagreed and cited *Minor* as part of their argument that "the franchise is essentially a matter of state concern."[35]

Even in 2022, American citizens, especially those of color, are still fighting against interpretations of *Minor* and the Fourteenth Amendment. It is ironic that an amendment that "was designed to protect, and should be read to protect, far more than has ever been alleged"[36] allows voter ID laws and other restrictions, such as purging of voter rolls and gerrymandering. In addition, "Felon disenfranchisement laws, residency requirements, and a citizenship test continue to limit the number of adults eligible to vote," writes Richard Briffault, professor of law at Columbia Law School.

All of these suppression tactics are held to be legal because the Fourteenth Amendment and the Waite court decision that gave the states the right to regulate voting are still in place.[37] Moreover, the 2013 Supreme Court decision to overturn Section 4(b) of the Voting Rights Act, which "triggered careful review of voting changes in political jurisdictions with a history of racial discrimination in voting before they could take effect," allowed laws and practices that discriminate on the basis of race and language to flourish.[38]

One example of these tactics is voter ID laws—which began in 2006 and are currently in place in thirty-four states.[39] They are directly tied to proving one's residency, which may not be difficult for Americans who drive or have a state-issued ID, but they place undue burden upon the poor, elderly, disabled, and others who cannot easily obtain such identification.[40] They are also unfair to "millions of commuters, migrant workers, and second home owners [who] are subject to local taxation, law enforcement, and land use regulation, and depend on locally provided public services in communities where they spend considerable time on a regular basis but are unable to vote"[41] on laws that affect them. Just as women's suffrage leaders fought a state-by-state battle for the vote, the League of Women Voters[42] and other advocacy groups, such as the American Civil Liberties Union and the National Association for the Advancement of Colored People, are suing states across the country in the hopes of seeing these requirements overturned.[43]

The League of Women voters also supports passage of the Voting Rights Advancement Act of 2019 (HR 4), which would bring the Voting Rights Act of 1965 up-to-date and require states to obtain "preapproval from the Department of Justice or the US District Court for the District of Columbia before making legal changes that would affect voting rights."[44] This bill would limit the effects of the *Minor* ruling by giving the federal government greater sway over what at least some states[45] can and cannot do regarding voting practices.

In addition to lingering restrictions from the Waite court's interpretation of *Minor*, nowhere in the Constitution are all citizens given the right to vote; laws about suffrage are all written in the negative—that is, they restrict rather than grant the right.[46] Legal scholar Garrett Epps explains:

> The "right to vote" is mentioned five times [in the Constitution]— and yet the Court has brushed it aside as a privilege that states may observe at their convenience. Even an overwhelming majority of Congress—which is given the power to enforce the right in no fewer than four different places in the Constitution—cannot protect this right more strongly than the Court feels appropriate. . . . The right to vote of citizens of the United States remains a kind of stepchild in the family of American rights.[47]

Therefore, one proposed solution to oppressive tactics is a "Right-to-Vote" constitutional amendment granting the right to vote to all citizens. Nonpartisan groups such as Fair Vote, political journals like *Democracy*, and several US Congress members argue such an amendment would

> help resolve most of these cases in favor of voters. It would not make every limitation unconstitutional—it is the essential nature of voting, for instance, that there be a date certain by which votes must be

cast in order to be counted—but it would ensure that these limitations are judged under the standard known as "strict scrutiny," meaning that governments would have to show that the restrictions were carefully designed to address a compelling interest of the state. We would come to find that many familiar aspects of our current voting system would not meet this standard and access to the ballot could be extended to millions who are now actively or effectively disenfranchised.[48]

It would also, in effect, totally negate the *Minor* ruling and bring nearly 150 years of misuse of that ruling to an end.

In addition, women are still fighting to pass the Equal Rights Amendment (ERA), to the Constitution. First put forth by suffragist leader Alice Paul in 1923,[49] the ERA would enshrine in the US Constitution a guarantee of equal rights for all citizens regardless of sex.[50] According to the official website in support of the Equal Rights Amendment, "For the first time, sex would be considered a suspect classification, as race, religion, and national origin currently are. Governmental actions that treat males or females differently as a class would be subject to strict judicial scrutiny and would have to meet the highest level of justification—a necessary relation to a compelling state interest—to be upheld as constitutional."[51]

While many people believe that the Fourteenth Amendment's words that neither the United States nor any of its states shall "deny to any person within its jurisdiction the equal protection of the laws" negates the need for an ERA, this is a misreading of the text. As Virginia Kase, CEO of the League of Women Voters of the United States and former Stanford Law School dean, pointed out in 2019, the United States is "the only industrialized democracy with a Bill of Rights in the world that doesn't have a gender rights provision in the constitution."[52] Even the closest reading of the Constitution will not turn up an example of where women's rights are mentioned as equal to men other than in their right to vote under the Nineteenth Amendment. "In other respects," the late Supreme Court justice Ruth Bader Ginsburg wrote, "Our fundamental instrument of government was thought an empty cupboard for sex equality claims."[53]

In fact, the equal protection clause has only been used to apply to sex discrimination since 1971 and "it has never been interpreted to grant equal rights on the basis of sex in the uniform and inclusive way that the ERA would."[54] That is because since the 1950s, the Supreme Court has held laws pertaining to gender to a lower standard than those pertaining to race; they imposed "strict scrutiny" on racial matters and only "heightened" or "intermediate" scrutiny on laws pertaining to gender and sex. Baer explains that "heightened" means "minimal scrutiny;" "intermediate" means "some reasonable relationship must be shown between the statute and a legitimate governmental purpose;" and "strict" means the law must be "necessary . . . to the accomplishment of [the state's] purpose or to the safeguarding of its interest."[55]

In ruling after ruling, they showed that they did not view the Fourteenth Amendment as providing equal protection because men and women were different[56]—women could have children, were less physically strong, and menstruated—all of which somehow made them inferior[57] in the eyes of lawmakers and judges, dooming them to remain in a separate class, just as the Waite court said they were a century before. But like the Minors, Ginsburg spent years trying to persuade the courts that the Fourteenth Amendment's equal protection clause applied not just to race but to gender as well.[58] She said in an interview with National Public Radio, "The words of the Fourteenth Amendment's equal protection clause—'nor shall any state deny to any person the equal protection of the laws.' Well that word, 'any person,' covers women as well as men."[59]

The courts didn't listen, however, even going so far as to undo the legal equality guarantees women could have achieved.[60] "By depriving women of the right to challenge disadvantages built on preferences for men—even those made possible by the near-complete exclusion of women by law or policy—the court largely reduced the Equal Protection Clause to a minimalist intervention against some explicitly discriminatory articulations termed 'facial,'"[61] or surface as opposed to in depth, thus dismissing them as less important or worthy of attention.

Even taken in conjunction with additional legislation such as the Equal Pay Act, the Pregnancy Discrimination Act, and Titles VII and IX of the 1964 Civil Rights Act, the equal protection clause of the

Fourteenth Amendment still does not add up to women having the same equal rights as men under US law.[62] Ginsburg predicted in 1979 that "until the US Constitution is amended to explicitly state that 'equality of rights cannot be denied or abridged on account of sex,' the political and judicial victories women have achieved with over two centuries are vulnerable to erosion or reversal at any time—now or in the future,"[63]—and her words are equally relevant decades later.

As Ginsburg noted, legal equality of the sexes could be accomplished with a constitutional amendment, but "history strongly suggests the task will remain on a legislative backburner absent the stimulus explicit constitutional commitment would supply."[64] In order to pass such an amendment, Congress would have to undo the *Minor* decision because it made women a special class of citizens under the Fourteenth Amendment, a classification that is in opposition to the ERA.[65] Ginsburg suggested that doing so would not only erase outdated laws and rulings like *Minor* but would also alleviate "the uneasiness judges feel in the gray zone between interpretation and alteration of the Constitution."[66]

A proposed alternative is to not waste time fighting for the old, flawed ERA but rather to propose a New Equality Amendment[67] that better reflects the diversity and complexity of the modern world. Catharine A. MacKinnon, feminist law professor at Michigan and Harvard Law Schools, and Kimberlé W. Crenshaw, law professor at UCLA and Columbia Law School specializing in civil rights, suggest a three-part amendment beginning with these words: "Women in all their diversity shall have equal rights in the United States and every place subject to its jurisdiction."[68] They note that this would negate the previously touted power of the states, as there is no action required of the states. They would no longer have the power to deny equality but would rather be held responsible if they failed to prevent violations of these equal rights or hinder/fail to allow legal claims to be brought against them.

Should this positive language not be enough, they follow it by mirroring the "negative" language of the 1972 wording of the ERA as well as the Nineteenth Amendment in order to provide specific instruction to the Supreme Court about what is meant by equality and inequality, in order to avoid the legal quagmire of opinion and interpretation the country has experienced in the past.[69]

The third section requires states to take all the legal measures necessary to take legislative and other steps to prevent or make up for past inequality and to abolish old laws that would allow for such discrimination,[70] such as the oft-cited Waite court interpretation of the Fourteenth Amendment.

Finally, they propose a fourth section that prevents the second section from being used against the first or third sections, as has been done with previous amendments.[71] To date, this amendment has not been presented to any legislative body but serves as a blueprint for lawyers and lawmakers for what a successful change to the Constitution might entail.

While these fights to finally put an end to the destructive interpretations of *Minor v. Happersett* and the Fourteenth Amendment continue, modern citizens can take comfort in the words of Anthony after the *Minor* ruling: "Although defeated at every point, woman's claim as a citizen of the United States to the Federal franchise is placed upon record in the highest court of the Nation, and there it will remain forever."[72] As the following pages will illustrate, the Minors continued to fight for what they believed in, and so will those fighting for an ERA.

CHAPTER THIRTEEN

Down, but Not Out

VIRGINIA SLUMPED IN HER CHAIR WHEN SHE HEARD THE SUPREME Court's ruling. That was it, then: years of hard work and advocacy only for the door to be once again slammed in their faces. And this time it appeared to be locked as well. The court's opinion wasn't a complete surprise, nor did it "greatly stun"[1] her, as the papers would later claim, but it certainly was a disappointment.

"Time to start again," she said to herself.

That night she scribbled a letter to Susan B. Anthony, who was likely having the same thoughts as she: What next? The suffragists in the NWSA certainly weren't about to give up. They simply needed to change tack. It was time to strategize their next move.

THE VERDICT AND THE NATIONAL SUFFRAGE MOVEMENT

As Anthony later said, "Women did not expect to get justice from a court composed of men, acting under men-made [*sic*] laws, for men."[2] Regardless of their expectations, it was still a huge setback to all who supported female suffrage. With the bang of a gavel, the Supreme Court effectively ended women's hope for a legal solution to their cause. It essentially cut off the key strategy of the NWSA and forced them to abandon the New Departure. They were left with only one way forward: swallow their pride and take up the tactics already espoused by their rival, the AWSA. They would have to pursue a state-by-state approach[3] to changing the law until eventually the whole country followed suit.

While this was galling for members of the NWSA, it wasn't necessarily the devastating blow that previous historians have made it out to be. The forced change in tactics unified the movement under a single approach, and while the two groups did not reunify as the National American Woman Suffrage Association until 1890, this was the first baby step toward bringing them back together. "Minor refocused the mobilization already underway to enact a suffrage amendment that would admit women to the 'constitutional community,'" writes attorney Jennifer K. Brown. "Suffrage went beyond 'asking to have certain wrongs redressed.' Now the American woman 'demanded that the Constitutions—State and National—be so amended as to give her a voice in the laws, a choice in the rulers, and protection in the exercise of her rights as a citizen of the United States.'"[4]

The focus on the states and reemphasis of their power over their voters also enabled some of the Western territories who had already granted their women suffrage, like Wyoming, to enter the Union as states with equal suffrage. The same was true for Colorado in 1893 and Idaho and Utah in 1896.

Also, though the Minors' court case failed in its stated goal, it gave great publicity to the cause of women's suffrage. It was historic because no one else ever had—or ever would—raise the issue of a woman's right to vote at that level of the US legal system. Historian Norma Basch writes that *Minor v. Happersett* was

> *a turning point in the role of gender in the Constitution. The historical dimensions of* Minor *are mis construed [sic] from the start if we conceive of it only as relegating women to second-class citizenship; women were second class citizens both before and after the decision. The case's importance lies in the fact that it drew the inferiority of women's status out of the groves of common-law assumptions and state provisions and thrust it into the maelstrom of constitutional conflict. The demands for woman suffrage did not die when the decision was rendered; they acquired a contentious national life.*[5]

Because of this, historian Allison Sneider called it "one of the single most important Supreme Court rulings of the nineteenth century."[6] The case also "established public grounds upon which women could claim to be legitimate participants in the political sphere and could act accordingly,"[7] ushering in a whole new era in female activism and advocacy.

THE CURIOUS CASE OF ANNA HALLENSCHEID

On December 1, 1875, eight months after the Supreme Court ruled against her, a distressing article in the newspaper caught Virginia's eye. An elderly German-speaking woman named Anna Hallenscheid of Herman, Missouri, a town approximately 80 miles west of St. Louis, was due to hang for murder in just over two weeks and it looked like no one was going to come to her aid. The article lamented,

> But little effort will be made on the part of the friends of Mrs. Anna Hallenscheid to save her neck from the sentence of the law on the 17th of December. She and her husband . . . have but little sympathy in their own neighborhood and Judge Saey, before whom the case was tried in Gasconade County . . . was here yesterday, and says it was certainly one of the most brutal murders he ever heard of, and earnestly participated in by her with no apparent compulsion on the part of her husband. Her age and sex are the only points wherein she can depend upon Governor Hardin for relief, even provided anyone makes an appliation [sic].[8]

The condemned woman and her husband, Henry, had been convicted of murder in the first degree on November 12, 1875, for killing their son-in-law, Christian Alband, an event one reporter called "the most terrible crime ever committed in our community."[9] According to their confessions in court, Christian and their daughter, Wilhelmina, were living with the couple, and Henry and Christian fought constantly.[10] On the night of July 16, the two men got into a heated argument "about prohibiting Wilhelmina . . . from wearing a particular dress,"[11] during which the two women held Christian's hands while Henry[12] beat "him in and upon the head and face with a club or some other blunt instrument, and . . . [threw] him out of the garret-window [sic] of [their] dwelling-house down upon hard ground and rocks by all said means inflicting several mortal wounds."[13] Henry then loaded the body into a wheelbarrow, stripped it of all clothing but a shirt, dumped it in a gulley, and covered it with a thin layer of dirt and brush. Eight days later it was dug up by dogs.[14] All three were arrested and convicted and Wilhelmina died in jail not long after while serving her sentence on the charge of second-degree murder.[15]

Virginia, by her own admission,[16] did not know Anna, and whether or not she knew the gruesome details of the case is unclear. Virginia would have had to have read about the trial in the Herman newspapers—the *Advertiser-Courier* covered the trial in English, while the *Hermanner Volksblatt* did so in German—or conducted her own research, as the St. Louis paper contained no additional information. But she was determined to be the one to come to the prisoner's aid. She couldn't stand to see injustices inflicted wrongly on women; regardless of their guilt or innocence, no woman deserved to be abused at the hands of prison authorities. That was why she and forty-nine others had signed a petition to the St. Louis County Court asking for proper treatment of female prisoners in its new jail in June 1869[17] and why she would speak up now.

On December 3, 1875, Virginia wrote to Missouri governor Charles H. Hardin, asking him to spare Anna's life. She had "no desire to shield her from any just punishment"[18] but asked him to consider her circumstances under the law. In this letter, Virginia's own education, experience with the law, and Francis's influence as an attorney come together to demonstrate her astute legal acumen:

> *Being a married woman, she is as you well know, placed by the law under coverture of her husband, and under obligation of obedience to him; so much so, that if through constraint of his will, she commits unlawful acts, she shall be excused, and whatever of a criminal nature the wife does in the presence of her husband, is presumed to be compelled by him. I am well aware that to this rule, of coercion by the presence of the husband, murder and some other offenses are exceptions; but how are ignorant women to know anything about the four legal exceptions, to the one unvarying law of marital obedience. Though legally without excuse for her obedience in this instance, how*

could she distinguish the technicalities of the law? . . . While she is in reality subjected to the severest penalties which the law can inflict, it is impossible to estimate the influence which this dual condition may have had over her actions; and while this constitutes no legal justification for the crime, it forms the basis upon which I appeal to you to commute her punishment to imprisonment for life, and spare the state the disgrace of what would be, if she is hanged, a legal murder.[19]

In Virginia's mind, then, this elderly woman could not have known that legally she would be held responsible for her crimes, even if she was acting out of obedience to or fear of her husband. It was this system of coverture, which Virginia so despised, that forced Anna into this situation; yes, she should be punished for her crime but not at the price of her life, especially when she could not control the system that entrapped her. If a woman has no legal existence or rights under the law, where was the justice in trying, convicting, and killing her under that same law?[20]

Virginia's letter, along with three others that were written on Anna's behalf,[21] had their intended effect, because on the scheduled day of execution, the governor commuted her sentence. She was moved to the state penitentiary[22] in "Jefferson City where he gave her in charge of the warden of our state prison in which she [was to be] confined for the remainder of her natural term of life."[23] Her husband, however, was not so lucky; he was hanged before a crowd of four thousand people and killed instantly.[24]

SUFFRAGE BECOMES PATRIOTIC
In the wake of the *Minor* trial, the leaders of the two factions of the women's suffrage movement began to see their fight for the vote as part of their patriotic duty to their country—as American as red, white, and blue flags and fireworks on the Fourth of July. And what better time to demand their rights as citizens and call for constitutional change than the centennial of the nation's founding? At the seventh annual meeting of the AWSA, Lucy Stone, the group's founder, spoke out, comparing the experience of the colonialists during the reign of George III to the experience of women under the current laws:

If it was wrong for George III to govern the colonies a hundred years ago without their consent, it is just as wrong now to govern women without their consent; that if taxation without representation was tyranny then it is tyranny now, and no less tyranny because it is done to women than if it were done to men; that the usurpation of the rights of women is as high-handed a crime as was the usurpation of the rights of the colonists by the British Parliament, and will be so regarded a hundred years hence.[25]

Stone said that women should not attend the official national celebration in Philadelphia at Independence Hall on July 4, 1876; by staying away, she believed that women would be denying the government the respect that it denied them daily and imitating the deeds of their brave ancestors toward the colonial government.[26] She instructed women to

Shut their doors and darken their windows on that day, and let a few of the most matronly women dress themselves in black and stand at the corners of the streets where the largest procession is to pass, bearing banners inscribed, "We are governed without our consent; we are taxed without representation." The Declaration of Independence belonged to men. Let them have their masculine celebration and masculine glory all to themselves, and let the women, wherever they can get a church, go there and hold solemn service and toll the bell. It will give us a chance for moral protest such as we shall never have again, for before another hundred years it must surely be that the growth of public sentiment will sweep away all distinctions based solely on sex.[27]

Always the more demonstrative group, the NWSA decided boycotting the event wasn't enough, especially when their request to be a part of the official festivities was denied. They had asked nicely, assuring Gen. Joseph Hawley, president of the US Centennial Commission, they would not make trouble. "We do not ask to read our declaration, only to present it to the President of the United States, that it may become an historical part of the proceedings,"[28] they said.

However, Hawley could not grant their request. He wrote, "I understand the full significance of your very slight request. If granted, it would be the event of the day—the topic of discussion to the exclusion of all others. I am sorry to refuse so slight a demand; we cannot grant it."[29]

Outraged, Stanton and Lucretia Mott decided to follow Stone's advice and boycott the ceremony,[30] but Anthony and Matilda Joslyn Gage had other ideas. Together, Anthony, Stanton, and Gage drafted a Woman's Declaration of Rights, along with a formal protest document, which was signed by more than twenty-five women's suffrage leaders, including Virginia Minor.[31]

The document lists nine Articles of Impeachment, alleging treason of the US government toward its female citizens, beginning with the charge of "the introduction of the word 'male' into all the State constitutions, denying to woman the right of suffrage, and thereby making sex a crime."[32] The list also included unjust imprisonment, a demand to be able to serve on juries, taxation without representation, being held as "a perpetual minor" under the law, having no rights as a person, being held to her husband's will under coverture, not being allowed the right of self-government, and denial of the franchise.[33]

On July 4, "one of the most oppressive days of that terribly heated season,"[34] Stanton, Gage, Sara Andrews Spencer, Lillie Devereux Blake, and Couzins went to Independence Square, where "they determined to seize upon the moment when the reading of the Declaration of Independence closed, to proclaim to the world the tyranny and injustice of the nation toward one-half its people."[35] Using their platform passes, which were really meant only to allow them to observe the event from the audience,[36] they stormed the stage and presented the stunned chairman, Sen. Thomas Ferry, with the documents they had written.[37]

But they did not stop there. As they left the stage, they flung printed copies of their documents into the crowd, which were grabbed up by the men assembled there, some standing on chairs to get the ladies' attention.[38] Anthony then mounted the bandstand in front of Independence Hall and proceeded to read a four-page speech, which quickly drew the attention of the crowd away from the official program, just has Hawley had feared. Anthony began, "We cannot forget, even in this glad hour, that while all men of every race, and clime and condition, have been invested with the full rights of citizenship, under our hospitable flag, all women still suffer the degradation of disenfranchisement."[39] Anthony went on to enumerate the grievances contained in their declaration and petition so that those who weren't lucky enough to have snatched a copy from the air would know what all the fuss was about. After several minutes, she ended with the powerful statement, "We ask our rulers, at this hour, no special favors, no special privileges, no special legislation. We ask justice, we ask equality, we ask that all the civil and political rights that belong to citizens of the United States, be guaranteed to us and our daughters forever."[40]

TAX RESISTANCE AND REVOLTS

Even though Virginia hadn't been there to witness Anthony's stunt at the centennial celebration, the *Washington Post* reported years later that "this dramatic presentation demonstrated that the movement had entered a new phase, kicked off by Virginia Minor" and her court case.[41]

It was indeed a new era for the suffrage movement, and Virginia was certainly not done leading it. As she knew well from her experience with abolition and temperance, for a movement to succeed, it had to remain visible, relevant, and on the lips of those both for and against it. In order to do that, women would have to continue their public protests and petitions and sway others to their point of view.[42]

One of Virginia's first moves after the court cases were over and she had more free time to focus on the suffrage movement again was to remind women that they were still being taxed without the ability to have a say in their government. On June 8, 1876, Virginia wrote an open letter to the Board of Freeholders in St. Louis, reprimanding them for

> utterly ignor[ing] the fact that a large proportion of the tax payers of the city are utterly disfranchised. . . . I have now before me the names of (53) fifty three women, joint owners of property . . . and also the names of 934 women who are sole owners. But far more numerous and important is the great body of women tax-payers, who own only a small amount of property not included in these figures, to whom every

cent levied by your Assessor may be bread out of their mouths and that of their children. Yet these women are by law deprived of the birth-right of every American citizen—representation before taxation.

I, therefore, pray you as an act of justice, and in conformity with the principles on which this government is founded, to exempt from city taxation the property of all women, as long as they are disfran-chised. Article 10, section 6, of the Constitution allows you to exempt the homes of the dead, and women are, in law, equally dead and voiceless, as helpless to defend their homes as they.[43]

This was not a new theory. Women had been using taxes as a form of revolt as early as the 1850s. One of the first known cases is that of Dr. Harriet K. Hunt of Boston, which dates to 1852, when she began an annual protest "against being compelled to pay taxes while not rec-ognized in the government."[44] That year, she wrote a letter to "Frederick W. Tracy, Treasurer, and the Assessors, and other Authorities of the city of Boston, and the Citizens generally," in which she "beg[ged] leave to protest against the injustice and inequality of levying taxes upon women, and at the same time refusing them any voice or vote in the imposition and expenditure of the same." She went on to cite that women in Boston were not offered the same educational opportunities as men on the high school, college, or professional level.[45]

The following September, at the Woman's Rights Convention in New York, she reflected on the incident that had motivated her to make such a bold move:

In October, 1851, I went to pay my taxes in Boston. Going into the Assessor's office, I saw a tall, thin, weak, stupid-looking Irish boy. It was near election time, and I looked at him scrutinizingly. He held in his hand a document, which, I found on inquiry, was one of natural-ization; and this hopeful son of Erin was made a citizen of the United States, and he could have a voice in determining the destinies of this mighty nation, while thousands of intellectual women, daughters of the soil, no matter how intelligent, how respectable, or what amount of taxes they paid, were forced to be dumb!

Now, I am glad to pay my taxes, am glad that my profession enables me to pay them; but I would like very much to have a voice in directing what is to be done with the money I pay. I meditated on what I had seen, and, in 1852, when paying my taxes, I took to the Treasurer's office my protest.[46]

That same year, Stanton and Stone called for action from women at the third National Woman's Rights Convention in Syracuse, New York. Though she could not be present, Stanton sent a letter that emphasized the power of tax resistance while recognizing the repercussions those who resisted would experience:

Should not all women, living in States where woman has a right to hold property, refuse to pay taxes, so long as she is unrepresented in the government of that State? Such a movement, if simultaneous, would no doubt produce a great deal of confusion, litigation and suffering, on the part of woman; but shall we fear to suffer for the maintenance of the same glorious principles, for which our fore fathers [sic] fought, and bled, and died. Shall we deny the faith of the old revolutionary heroes . . . by declaring in action, that taxation without representation is just? Ah! no; like the English Dissenters, and high-souled Quakers, of our own land, let us suffer our property to be seized and sold? But let us never pay another tax, until our existence as citizens, our civil and political rights, be fully recognized.[47]

Immediately following, Stone addressed the convention:

[I] urge upon woman, the duty of resisting taxation, so long as she is not represented. It may involve the loss of friends, as it surely will that of property. But let them all go: friends, house, garden-spot, all. The principle at issue requires the sacrifice. Resist; let the case be tried in the courts; be your own lawyers; base your cause on the admitted self-evident truth, that "taxation and representation are inseparable." One such resistance, by the agitation that would grow out of it, will do more to set this question right, than all the Conventions in the

world. . . . Sisters, the right of suffrage will be secured to us, when we
ourselves are willing to incur the odium, and loss of property, which
resistance to this outrage on our rights will surely bring with it.[48]

Stone practiced what she advocated. In 1858, she returned her tax bill
to the tax collector of Orange, New Jersey, without payment.[49] As a result,
her mortgage was foreclosed upon and a sale was held at which some
of her household goods were auctioned.[50] She was lucky to only lose
replaceable items; other women lost far more: their homes, land, and even
livestock.[51] Some women, like Lydia Sayer Hasbrouck of Orange County,
New York, were forced into manual labor "such as digging tree stumps or
'spreading sand and gravel'"[52] on the roads to pay off what they owed.[53]

In the 1860s and 1870s, two of the most prominent tax resisters were
Julia and Abby Smith, wealthy septuagenarian sisters from Glastonbury,
Connecticut. They had been battling rising anger toward local tax officials
for unfair and discriminatory practices since 1868, but after attending an
AWSA convention in October 1873, they refused to pay their November
1873 tax installment. Over the next two years, their refusal to pay cost
them seven cows and eleven acres of meadow land, which they believed
was sold for less than 10 percent of what it was worth. They sued the tax
collector for auctioning their land and selling all their furniture, cows, and
hay. Though the court found in their favor, the sisters had to endure years
of appeals and delays, during which time they lost more cows and bank
stock. Their fight ended when Abby died in July 1878 and Julia married
a year later, her husband paying her back taxes against her will.[54]

Although these women connected the issues of suffrage and taxation
to some extent, very few focused on the power of the correlation on a
mass scale; tax revolts were not official tactics of either suffrage organization[55]—not, that is, until the Minors got involved. In 1868, Francis wrote
to *The Revolution* stating plainly that if women paid taxes, they should
have the right to vote. The next year, at the woman's suffrage convention
in St. Louis, Virginia took her plea to the public, demanding that if the
government refused to grant women full citizenship and all the rights
and privileges that came with it, women should be exempt "from the
burden of taxation to support so unjust a Government."[56]

As a follow-up, Virginia wrote to the St. Louis city assessor, Robert J. Rombauer, demanding to know how much property tax the city obtained from women.[57] The assessor responded on January 30, 1869, with an indirect answer: "In reply to your request to report to your association the amount of property listed in the city of St. Louis in the name of ladies, permit me to state that the property in question is represented by over 2,000 tax-paying ladies, and assessed at the value of $14,490,199,"[58] which is equivalent to just over $276 million today.[59]

That seemingly simple statement carried a strong assessment of potential political, social, and economic influence. Though their numbers were relatively small in a city of approximately 310,000 people[60]— the property-owning women represented only 0.6 percent of the population—they held nearly $15 million in assets, all of which was taxed at a rate of fifty cents per $100 in 1869.[61] If they withheld that $75,000 ($1.4 million today)[62] in taxes, they could deal a severe economic blow to both the city and the state. With this threat hanging over them, surely lawmakers would have to listen to their demands.

History of Woman Suffrage recounts the public reaction when this information was disclosed:

> *This exhibit has opened the eyes of a good many people. "Two thousand on 'em," exclaimed a male friend of mine, "and over fourteen millions of property! Whew! What business have these women with so much money?" Well, they have it, and now they ask us, "Shall 2,000 men, not worth a dollar, just because they wear pantaloons go to the polls and vote taxes on us, while we are excluded from the ballot-box for no other reason than sex?" What shall we say to them? They ask us if the American Revolution did not turn on this hinge, No taxation without representation. Who can answer?*[63]

Across the country, while men debated other forms of taxation, like tariffs, the Civil War income tax, and alcohol and tobacco taxes,[64] the upper- and middle-class (mostly) white women[65] who paid taxes looked ahead to the centennial of the Boston Tea Party, adopted as their role models their Revolutionary counterparts, and took up the chant "No taxation without representation."[66]

By 1873, antitax leagues were being founded across the country in cities such as San Francisco,[67] Cincinnati,[68] Boston,[69] Pittsburgh,[70] and Chicago, where a group of women met with Gage downtown at State and Madison to form their own league,[71] and even in the small town of St. Joseph, Missouri,[72] about 55 miles north of Kansas City, Missouri, and 290 miles west of St. Louis.

Virginia didn't sit idly by while her case was winding its way through the court system. In March 1874, she presented a memorial on women's suffrage to the Missouri legislature. It stated:

> *Believing that only those who enjoy the privileges of a government should be burdened with its supports, and that it is manifestly unjust to deprive one-half of the adult citizens of the State of the franchise, and at the same time require them to pay a full half of the expenses of the government, we do most respectfully pray your honorable body that an amendment to the Constitution may be proposed exempting from taxation all property, real or personal, owned by women in this State [sic]—in one county of which alone women own and are taxed on over $20,000,000 worth of property, and if 'taxation without representation was tyranny' in 1774, we are utterly unable to see why it is not equally so in 1874.*[73]

News of Virginia's memorial spread quickly across the country, as an article, originally printed in St. Louis, that praised Virginia as "a leading spirit in the woman's movement" and cited her status as a "femme covert [and as such unable to] . . . own the money wherein to pay taxes thereon"[74] was reprinted in the *New York Herald* and then in papers in Virginia, Illinois, South Carolina, Pennsylvania, Vermont, and Ohio.[75]

Once her court case made it onto the docket of the Supreme Court in 1874, Virginia had to give her full attention to it,[76] but the NWSA stepped in where she left off. They went so far as to make tax resistance and revolt a main topic at their national conventions in 1874 and 1875,[77] which kept the subject in the papers and energized women to action.

When the court case was over and the furor caused by her 1876 open letter to the Board of Freeholders had died down, Virginia seems to have continued her protest quietly until 1879. Tax records for this time are scant, so there is no record that Virginia ever lost property, was fined, or was punished in any way for her actions. On August 26, she wrote to David Powers, president of the Board of Assessors in St. Louis, reiterating her reason for continuing to withhold her taxes:

> *I honestly believe and conscientiously make an oath that I have not one dollar's worth of property subject to taxation. The principle on which this Government rests is representation before taxation. My property is denied representation, and therefore cannot be taxable. The law which you quote as applicable to me in your notice to make my tax return is in direct conflict with the thirteenth section of the Bill of Rights of the Constitution of the State, which declares, "No person shall be deprived of life, liberty, or property without due process of law." And that surely cannot be "due process of law" wherein one of the parties only is law-maker, judge, jury and executioner, and the other stands silent, denied the power either of assent or dissent, a condition of "involuntary slavery" so clearly prohibited in the thirty-first section of the same article, as well as in the Constitution of the United States, that no legislation or judicial prejudice can ignore it. I trust you will believe it is from no disrespect to you that I continue to refuse to become a party to this injustice by making a return of property to your honorable body, as clearly the duties of a citizen can only be expected where rights and privileges are equally accorded.*[78]

This protest, like those before it, was reprinted from coast to coast. The *Cincinnati Daily Star* applauded her bravery in this brief September 1879 article: "Mrs. Virginia L. Minor, of St. Louis, refuses to pay her taxes, and when the collector threatens to sue, she plants her feet firmly on the Constitution of the United States and tells him to fire away."[79] Likewise, the *New Northwest*, of Portland, Oregon, supported her wholeheartedly, writing,

It is impossible for men to be so blind as not to see the justice and sound sense of the following letter.... The above is a sensible way of avoiding taxation without representation. But she will find it impracticable, as did the Smith sisters, of Glastonbury, Conn. The tax-gatherers care nothing for law or justice. However, every effort at resistance causes discussion, and discussion can only result in the triumph of political equality. Let women generally oppose the one-sided laws as the Smith sisters and Virginia L. Minor are doing, and it will be but a short time until their demands meet the justice they deserve.[80]

However, not everyone thought withholding taxes was a practical solution. The *Richmond Democrat* out of Ray County, Missouri, was one of the fiercest critics, expressing what was likely the opinion of most men in the nation at the time. They hyperbolically claimed that Virginia believed her property was tax-exempt

because she is not allowed by the laws to vote and wear pantaloons, and society don't [sic] sanction her chewing tobacco and swearing around like a man.... The fact is, Mrs. Minor has a husband to do the voting for the family, and if she cannot get him to vote as she wishes, she had better give up the representation business and attend strictly to her domestic affairs. The world will think more of her if she will remain in her own legitimate sphere. The husband is the legitimate head and protector of the family, and a woman unsexes herself when she attempts to assume his duties.[81]

While many women's history and legal scholars praise the women who engaged in this form of peaceful protest, others believe the reasoning behind it was not sound. Scholars have since pointed out that depending on where a woman lived, tax revolts were incompatible with what the Minors advocated in the New Departure, which urged women to exercise the right to vote given to them by the Fourteenth Amendment. The problem was that some states, such as Massachusetts, Delaware, Pennsylvania, and Georgia, mandated payment of poll taxes as a qualification for voting. That meant that if women showed up to register or cast their ballot and refused to pay the tax, they were being legally refused, which invalidated the principles behind the New Departure.[82] In addition, as time passed, legal analysts began to argue that because the Waite court decided "that there was no link between citizenship and voting (that voting was not a right of citizenship), then there was no link between taxation and representation (that voting was not a requirement for taxation.).["83] Therefore, the logic behind tax protests was inherently flawed.

Despite all of Virginia's efforts to get lawmakers to understand and accept her logic and the press and publicity her tax revolts received, she is almost entirely left out of the major studies of tax revolts to date, both in books and articles dedicated to the subject as well as those on the suffrage movement. In fact, although Tutt acknowledges, "Only a handful of other tax resisters appear in the records of the movement" and "[u]ndoubtedly there were others,"[84] even she relegates Virginia to a footnote,[85] which is the only mention of her in relation to the subject that is not from her lifetime. The notable exceptions are *History of Woman Suffrage*, for which researchers have much to thank for the remaining records, and historical newspaper coverage. Virginia's role in the national tax rebellion movement, and its glaring omission from works to date, are areas that deserve further study by modern scholars of the law and women's history.

Protesting the "Social Evil Law"

By the end of the Civil War, St. Louis was home to thousands of prostitutes who were attracted to the city during the war because it was the headquarters of the Department of the Missouri, a command center for the army, which meant there was no shortage of soldiers who were missing their wives/girlfriends and looking for female companionship. Some of these women were native to the city, but most were women and young girls who had fled to St. Louis from war-torn areas in need of protection, food, shelter, employment, and money,[86] all of which prostitution could provide in a city full of soldiers.

These houses of ill repute ranged from the brothels, dance halls, saloons, and gaming dens of Almond Street to the Varieties Theater, where while respectable patrons were watching a ballet or opera from the floor level or mezzanine, prostitutes and their clients were engaging in another type of entertainment on the third tier, which was reserved for this purpose.[87] A St. Louis newspaper reported in 1866, "Everyone who knows anything about the city is aware of the fact that a very large proportion of the upper stories on Fourth Street from Chesnut [sic] to Locust are occupied by gamblers, while women of bad repute monopolize whole blocks in the very heart of the city."[88]

In the years following the war, the vagrancy laws under which prostitution fell allowed police to arrest any women "they suspected of lewd behavior"[89] without a warrant or evidence. This meant that any woman who found herself alone in the wrong neighborhood, who was "a working-class woman living alone in a boardinghouse or walking to or from work after sunset" was subject to arrest, as was any woman working in a saloon, dram shop, or beerhouse.[90]

When ever-increasing penalties under the law didn't work to curb the city's vice problem, St. Louis leaders decided to try a novel approach. From July 5, 1870, to the spring of 1874, prostitution was legal in the city of St. Louis—the only city in the country at the time to have such an ordinance.[91] Called the "social evil law" by most residents and then the media, it was based on laws in European cities where brothels were registered with and licensed by the state. Each brothel owner or madam had to pay "$10 per month for hospital dues . . . and $1 each week for examination fees; each prostitute, courtezan [sic] or lewd woman shall pay the sum of $1.50 per week as hospital dues."[92] Those fees were to be used to maintain the health of the prostitutes, who were registered with the police and regularly examined by doctors for venereal disease. The fees also maintained a special hospital, for women infected with venereal disease, and a "house of industry," where prostitutes could learn domestic skills that would give them alternative employment opportunities.[93]

Lawmakers and law enforcement officials hoped these actions would slow the spread of disease, reduce crime, and protect neighbors from depreciation by designating specific areas where brothels were allowed to operate.[94] The law's most ardent supporters were its author, Mr. William Currie, a member of the Board of Health; several former Police Board of Commissioners members, including Ferdinand Meyers;[95] St. Louis Chief of Police James McDonough; and Mayor Joseph Brown.[96] It may seem obvious that such figures of authority would be eager for their new law to improve the city; what was not widely known is that its backers stood to benefit from it.

While the public at large met the law with indifference,[97] its administration proved to be more difficult in practice than it had seemed on legal paper. "The police were overwhelmed with applications for change of residence, which grew from 821 in 1871 to 5,662 in 1872,"[98] resulting from both brothels moving to the legally designated areas and residents moving out so as not to be associated with them.[99] In addition, only six doctors were assigned to collect fees from and tend to the health of more than 1,200 registered prostitutes.[100] Because they couldn't keep up, they often issued clean bills of health without actually examining the women,[101] thus countermanding both the letter and spirit of the law and endangering public health.

Suffragists raged against the fee system built into the law, which they viewed as the very taxes they were protesting against paying. Not only were the prostitutes now subject to an extra tax they shouldn't have to pay in the first place, as they could not vote, but they were also the only ones to be taxed and examined—clients did not pay such a fee nor did they have to pass any health check to patronize the bawdy houses. This was an outrageous double standard that did more to enrich the male physicians and police officers involved than it did to improve public health.

In the *Woman's Journal* on July 26, 1873, Lucy Stone wrote a scathing article entitled, "The Shame of St. Louis," in which she criticized the law for not helping the city as its proponents claimed it would. As proof, she cited Alderman John E. Haggerty's report: "On examining the book of the Board of Health, I find the yearly expenses attending the Social Evil Law, for officers and help, to be $26,981.82, of which sum one physician gets $3600, and four examiners $10,000 per annum. . . . The salaries alone are about one-half of the whole amount collected. [The ordinance] is more of a benefit to those employed under its provisions than it is to the community at large."[102]

Stone also writes of "a number of ladies [who] met, talked the matter over, and proposed to petition the legislature to repeal this law. One thousand ladies, mostly mothers of St. Louis, signed that petition . . . [that they] were entitled to a respectful hearing. But the petition was referred to the committee of which Mr. Currie [the author of the law] was chairman." He proclaimed it "inexpedient to repeal the law," and the petition was tabled.[103]

While it is unknown whether Virginia was one of the women who signed this petition, she certainly would have agreed with it. She was already an ardent supporter of Unitarian minister William Greenleaf Eliot, who had been campaigning against the social evil ordinance since it was passed.[104] In October 1873, she was one of the founding members and a secretary of an interstate "association to promote the moral, intellectual, and physical well-being of women." The founding of this organization was reported in the *Detroit Free Press*, the *Levenworth Times*, and the *Daily Kansas Tribune*. Other founding members and officers included President Mary Livermore of Boston and Secretaries Rev. Eliza T. Wilkes of Colorado and Mrs. E. S. Tupper of Iowa. Their first meeting was held at the Union League Hall in New York.[105]

On March 4, 1874, Anna Dickinson, a famous suffragist and speaker, spoke against the social evil law at the Mercantile Library in St. Louis. She was one of a rare few who would broach the subject in public, as most people considered it taboo; but Dickinson felt "women are the best people to speak of it, especially when ministers will not."[106] She went on to blame drunkenness for the broken families that led to girls as young as ten being punished in the country's most notorious prisons for working the streets, though their circumstances had forced them into it. Instead of this, they should "be given the chance to make a living if they desire and that being trapped in marriage should not be their only choice."[107] Rallied by her words, four thousand women signed a petition to end the Social Evil Ordinance.[108] This petition was among hundreds destroyed in a fire at the Capitol in 1919, so it will never be known for sure whether Virginia signed it, but it seems likely, given that its intent was in keeping with her personal and public philosophies.

Later that month, Missouri lieutenant governor Charles P. Johnson, a well-known St. Louis criminal lawyer, along with two state senators from St. Louis, and seventy-two St. Louis attorneys—Francis was likely among them, given his influence in St. Louis and Virginia's organizing against the social evil law—petitioned the Missouri state legislature to repeal the ordinance, which they said was "trampling underfoot rights of personal liberty and personal security guaranteed to each and every citizen however humble or degraded"[109] by allowing the police to do whatever they wanted, "to enter any house without a warrant . . . force women to undergo gynecological examinations against their will, and incarcerate them for indefinite periods without due process . . . .in direct violation of the Bill of Rights."[110]

By the end of the month, the mounting pressure proved too much for the Missouri government. The state senate gathered the two-thirds majority of votes needed to repeal the ordinance and the House agreed, voting to end it 90–1.[111]

Five years later, the idea of reinstating the ordinance was put on the general ballot, but it was defeated in a landslide.[112]

OTHER SUFFRAGE WORK 1874–1882

When she wasn't involved in matters of taxation or public health, Virginia filled her days with suffrage work, just as she had done before taking her voting rights case to the courts. Lest anyone question her devotion to the movement, Virginia trained her parrot to remind her daily of her cause. "Whenever it sees Mrs. [Minor] putting on her bonnet to go out, it sets its head on one side, winks at Mr. [Minor], and asks, 'Will you vote today, Mrs. [Minor]?' then laughs heartily at its own joke."[113]

The parrot must have gotten tired of saying that after a while, for Virginia was always on the move. On May 21, 1875, during the Missouri Constitutional Convention, Virginia, Couzins, and two other women from St. Louis appeared before the Committee on Elections in Jefferson City to discuss adding language to the new state constitution that would allow women to vote.[114]

According to newspaper reports, when the chairman told the committee that a group of women were present to share their views, "everybody leaned forward in their seats in breathless awe as Mrs. Minor, an aged and matronly looking lady appeared in front of the reporters' desk with a roll of manuscript in her hand." She reminded the gentlemen present that although women could not vote, they still were taxed. Then, in what one reporter described as a "shrill and harsh tone of voice"[115] but was likely the commanding, steady, oration for which she was known, Virginia cried out,

> All that we now ask at your hands is that you shall use but one weight and one measure and make your laws apply equally to all citizens alike. . . . In making this demand we do not by it ask you to disenfranchise any citizen who now has the ballot. You will see the full force of our attainder, as under the law we have no representative in the convention, though taxed for its support. We are not admitted to plead our own cause before the very men who must decide our fate. Gentlemen, remove from us this badge of servitude, or if you refuse our prayer, then in the name of justice and manhood exempt our property from taxation, and do not compel us to support a government which thus degrades us.[116]

Her speech was said to have moved several men to tears.[117]

The following year, Virginia and Couzins represented the NWSA at the Democratic National Convention in St. Louis.[118] For the next four years, Virginia focused her attention on tax reform, until the NWSA annual convention in St. Louis on May 7–9, 1879, drew her back into the thick of the public fight for suffrage. Virginia, as vice president of the NWSA for Missouri, had the honor of calling the meeting to order and reminding the delegates why they had gathered in St. George's Hall at Seventh and Locust Streets that morning. Anthony took roll call and joked, "I wish the men to feel that they have an equal right here with us . . . except that they can't hold any of the offices or handle the money."[119]

Her statement not only elicited laughter from attendees of both sexes but alluded to the strong intention that this convention would be "the most important meeting of the Association ever held . . . a true 'ecumenical council' of the advocates of women suffrage. Delegates were expected from the South and in abundance from the great northwest,"[120] so opinions on important topics within the realm of women's suffrage, such as the inclusion of Black women, were sure to be passionately voiced.

The success of the convention led to the formation of a local branch of the NWSA at the direction of Anthony on May 13. The St. Louis Suffrage Association's birth was a reunion of sorts, as the new organization included many women who had fallen away from the WSAM when it allied with the AWSA in 1871. This included Virginia, who was named its first president. Other officers included Mrs. Eliza Patrick, Mrs. Mary C. Todd, and Couzins as vice presidents.[121]

Over the next several years, Virginia spoke at suffrage conventions across the country, and Francis accompanied her when he could. In 1878, she was quoted by a Portland, Oregon, paper as speaking out against women who opposed the suffrage movement, proclaiming, "Thousands of women all over the land, while ignorantly sneering at 'woman's rights' women, are filling their mouths with bread provided by their hands. They struck off the shackles of caste, and opened to them occupations remunerative and honorable, and though the shafts of ridicule and calumny may fall around them now, generations yet unborn will pay the just tribute to their work."[122]

Even while she traveled, Virginia kept an eye on the NWSA proceedings. The NWSA annual convention in January 1878 in Washington had been an absolute disaster. Anthony had been unable to attend due to a conflicting engagement, and without her acting as mother/principal of the group, religious zealots among the members seized control and held a prayer meeting one morning that quickly got out of hand. The NWSA generally had avoided mixing religion and politics, so Anthony was justifiably upset that she couldn't trust the membership to govern themselves in her absence. Virginia, too, was concerned for what the negative publicity could do to the respectability the movement had worked so hard to gain. She wrote to Anthony with no small amount of frustration: "Can not [sic] you and Mrs. Stanton, before another convention, manage in some way to civilize our platform and keep off that element which is doing us so much harm? I think the ship never floated that had so many barnacles attached as has ours. . . . I have a compliment for you, my dear. Wendell Phillips has just told a reporter of the St. Louis Post that, 'of all the advocates of the woman's movement, Miss Anthony stands at the head.'"[123]

Whether Virginia did anything to help Anthony and Stanton rescue the reputation of the NWSA, or just goaded them to do so, is unclear.

Virginia frequently spoke in and around St. Louis and continued to send petitions and memorials to both Jefferson City and Washington, DC. In June 1878, the Missouri State Convention of Prohibitionists took place in St. Louis. Francis, a former president of the local chapter,[124] accompanied Virginia, who attended as a member of the platform committee. However, no suffrage plank was added, despite Virginia's resolution that "in this Prohibition Party there shall be no distinction made between the citizens of Missouri and the ballot box on account of sex" coming up for a vote three times. The loss, which came after the chair broke two sequential ties, upset Francis so much that he said he "was out of the movement now," and his role as a member of the State Central Committee was immediately replaced. It is unclear whether Francis eventually returned to the organization or the group didn't take his resignation seriously, because his name was included on the Prohibition Ticket for the election of April 5, 1881, as a candidate for the City Council.[125]

Virginia also filled her time hosting NWSA leaders when they passed through town, organizing gatherings of women's suffrage advocates, and educating citizens and lawmakers about important matters and events related to suffrage.[126] In this, Francis was her helpmeet and constant support, as he continued to write and publish widely circulated essays and pamphlets as well as a regular column in *Forum Magazine* and occasional pieces in other women's suffrage journals. After his death, *Woman's Tribune* called these writings "a sacred legacy from Mr. Minor, who devoted his life and talents to the establishing of the rights of women."[127]

But their lives were not all work. Their home on Olive Street was the base of the Liberal Literary Club from at least 1880.[128] The club was "made up of intelligent people who have been led to feel that they don't know everything, and who meet once a week to learn more by means of intellectual entertainment provided generally by their own members."[129] In addition to readings from papers and books, speeches, and discussion, members also performed piano solos and vocal duets and solos.[130] Said to have a large following, its regular membership included local judges and attorneys, businessmen, and members of St. Louis's elite. Guest musicians and singers also made appearances.[131]

By 1880, Virginia had taken on the role of vice president representing Missouri in the NWSA.[132] At that time, her influence was such that her mere presence at the National Union Greenback Convention in St. Louis in March 1880 led to suspicions "of a design to have the female suffrage question brought up in some shape before the convention."[133] The Greenbackers were right to be on their guard, as that was exactly why Virginia was one of only eight women in attendance representing the NWSA.[134] Women's suffrage was the cause of frequent infighting among members; many of them supported it, but those who did not raised their voices loudly. She aimed to persuade the majority to overrule them and add a woman's suffrage plank to their platform for the 1880 election.[135] While no transcript of her speech at the convention remains, newspapers said that she "addressed the meeting, thanking the convention for the equal suffrage plank in the platform adopted yesterday, and congratulated the Greenback Party on being the first to grant equal rights to women."[136]

On November 2, Election Day, Virginia awoke to a shock: her name was listed on the Neal Dow Prohibition Ticket ballot without her consent, showing her as running for governor.[137] The ballot also included the names of several other prominent women: Phoebe Couzins, for attorney general; Mrs. E. J. Polk, for supreme judge; Lizzie Jackson, for sheriff; Mary Dodds, for coroner; Lizzie Spore and Lizzie French, for constables. In addition, Wong Lung was listed on the ballot for justice of the peace, as was George Hollingbery, for elector.[138] None of them had any intentions of running for office nor any idea their names would appear on any ballot.

After some investigation, the parties listed determined this ballot was the work of Frank Bemis of the Women's Christian Temperance Union, who was a known troublemaker and perhaps suffering from some sort of mental illness. The *St. Louis Post-Dispatch* reported that the morning after the election, "Frank Bemis, the temperance bee, was on hand early at the City Hall, but he was informed that never a lady upon his ticket had received anything like a plurality vote. Not at all downcast at this result, he proceeded to work for the cause by distributing his tickets among the crowd and showed them how they ought to have voted. . . . It is not known what secure position Mr. Bemis expected from the Prohibition party as a reward for his efforts, but he probably aspired to be the governor's chief bottle-smasher."[139]

Perhaps coincidentally, around that time Virginia began to speak publicly more often on the issue of temperance. In December 1881, she and Francis attended a meeting of the Knights and Ladies of the Father Matthew Debating Club. The subject that night was, "Is the woman's rights movement to be encouraged?" Members Patrick Long, Daniel O'Connell Tracy, and Richard D. Kerwen spoke as supporters, and several gentlemen and two ladies gave the opposing view. At some point, Virginia was acknowledged by the debaters as being in the audience, to which the other attendees responded with applause and calls for her to enter the debate. She did so, showing, according to Anthony and Stanton, "that the best temperance weapon in the hands of woman is the ballot."[140]

She continued her temperance tour of St. Louis with two speaking engagements in February 1882—first at the parlor hall of the Anchor Lodge, in Missouri,[141] and then two days later at Garfield Hall—both to the International Organization of Good Templars, a branch of the temperance movement, during which she "depicted the ruin effected in this country by intoxicating liquors."[142]

On September 20, the first meeting of the local Women's Christian Temperance Union "since last May" was held. Virginia was quoted as reminding the members how closely their two causes were aligned, if not intertwined:

> When Prohibitionists in Missouri or St. Louis get ready to recognize the suffrage workers it will be in order for the later to express an opinion, but not before. The part which stands by women will find them in earnest. Prohibition is the only thing which will secure temperance, and the wave will go unchecked through every State in the Union to carry out its prohibition measure the Republican party of Kansas will need a permanent party behind it which cannot be swayed by politics, and for that reason women will be given suffrage. [I will] not vote for Prohibition unless allowed to cast a perfect ballot.[143]

After this, temperance leaders asked whether their organization should affiliate with the local women's suffrage organization because of their shared interest in Prohibition. The ayes carried the motion, and "The W.C.T.U. was then practically dissolved and its few remaining members decided to unite with the Institutional Mission."[144]

If any question remained regarding Virginia's influence and power in the Missouri suffrage movement, the *St. Louis Post-Dispatch* put it to rest on March 12, 1880, with this observation: "Having incurred the displeasure of the Woman Suffragists we shall expect the speedy annihilation of the Bar Association. Mrs. Virginia Minor is up and in arms [*sic*] over the ungallant reception of the memorial recently sent to the association, and the legal lights who compose that body might as well prepare themselves for a terrible extinguishment."[145]

During the final decade of her life, Virginia would continue using the respect and authority she had built up to fight for rights of the women of Missouri, but she would also go on to adopt the state of Nebraska as a kind of third home, where she would advocate for women's enfranchisement alongside Anthony and seal her place in the upper echelons of women's suffrage history.

Chapter Fourteen

Never Stop Fighting

At the age of fifty-eight, most nineteenth-century women were well into their golden years, having long surpassed the average life expectancy of forty-six years,[1] grateful every day for their grandchildren and great-grandchildren and the blessings of long life.

Not Virginia Minor. At the same age, she was praying not in thanksgiving but in supplication that she would live through that very moment, as a wagon teamed by skittish mules carried her and Susan B. Anthony across the plains of Nebraska, a tornado on their heels.[2] Overhead, the sky was black, lightning flashed constantly, and "the wind was like a cyclone." Thankfully, there was no thunder; the driver had told them that the mules considered its loud boom "a personal insult" and would buck, bray, and race about wildly if they heard it.

But God was with the women, and they made it to the place they were staying unscathed. Just as they "reached the house it began to rain in torrents." Virginia put her foot out to step down, but fell "flat on [her] back on the ground and very near the heels of those peculiarly constituted mules."

By the time she, Anthony, and the driver got inside, they were soaking wet. The house contained only one stove, and it didn't put off enough heat to dry her clothes. They were still damp the following morning. Anthony, used to the hardships of travel in the western wilderness, shrugged it off, and Virginia was determined to do the same, "accept[ing] this as one of the inevitable things and went on [her] way damp, but enthusiastic." It was just one of the many adventures they would face together on their mission to bring the vote to the women of Nebraska.

STUMPING FOR SUFFRAGE OUT WEST

Official petitions for women's suffrage in Nebraska date back to 1856, when Amelia Bloomer—the same woman whose breeches were later made famous and bear her surname to this day—gave a stirring ninety-minute speech before the Nebraska Territorial Legislature on women's rights.[3] Following this, Rep. James Hoover proposed an act to bestow the right of suffrage upon the area's women. House File No. 79[4] wended its way through the legislature, passing the House 14 to 11, but the council was too busy squabbling over county boundaries to give it their full attention, and so it failed to achieve a third and final reading before the session was adjourned.[5]

One by one, Nebraska, which became a state in 1867, watched its neighboring territories to the west do what its own government would not. Wyoming gave suffrage to its women in 1869, becoming the first in the country to do so; Utah did the same within a year. Washington and Montana followed suit in 1883 and 1887, respectively.[6]

In 1871, it appeared female suffrage in Nebraska might once again have a chance when Lydia Butler, the wife of Governor David Butler, publicly declared her support; the legislature passed an "Act respecting the rights of married women,"[7] and the issue was put to the popular vote. It was roundly defeated, 12,494 to 3,502, with the all-male votership citing suffrage's connection to temperance as their main argument, followed by women not wanting the right;[8] the *Omaha Weekly Herald* claimed on July 19, just over two months before the special election that decided the issue, "ninety-nine out of every 100 women spurn the idea."[9]

The loss effectively ended any hope for women's suffrage in Nebraska until 1881, save for occasional speeches by Stanton and Anthony and regular newspaper and magazine articles by Canadian transplant Erasmus Correll.[10] The turning point came when the women of Lincoln formed a suffrage association on January 22, 1881, and the Nebraska Woman Suffrage Association was formed on January 27.[11] Support spread quickly. By spring, the state had 39 women's suffrage associations, and by the time Anthony, Couzins, and Virginia arrived in September, the state boasted more than 175 active associations[12] spread across its vast seventy-seven thousand miles.

Virginia, Couzins, and Elizabeth L. Saxon of New Orleans, a prominent suffragist who had been staying in the Minors' home,[13] left St. Louis on September 25[14] for the NWSA convention at Boyd's Opera House in Omaha, where all three were scheduled to speak.[15] Despite traveling more than 430 miles by rail,[16] they arrived in time to take the stage the following evening for the opening of the conference, where Stanton gave a rousing address.[17]

On the first day of the convention, both Virginia and Couzins declared themselves "ardent admirers" of presidential candidate Sen. Benjamin Butler, whom they called "one of the warmest friends of the cause" of female suffrage.[18]

The following day, delegates from each state reported on suffrage activity in their state. Virginia "said the question in [Missouri] had been resisted strongly by both men and women, and especially southern women, who were afraid of their husbands. She said that the ministers who formerly denounced the movement are coming to their aid, and the [sic] Chancellor Elliott of the Washington University had been converted and ably espouses their cause."[19]

That night, Virginia "urged the men of Nebraska to stand before the world and prove they had been educated up the point [sic] where willing to give women an equal political status with themselves and not assign her a position to that enjoyed by the Chinese coolie."[20] "Coolie" was the word used by the newspaper when describing, not directly quoting, Virginia's remarks. It referred to the Chinese coolie labor system and was not used as a pejorative in this case. She also unequivocally stated that "any temperance organization that did not put the woman suffrage plank in its platform was false to its own interests."[21]

Virginia and Anthony didn't waste any time; they began campaigning for suffrage in earnest on September 29, the day after the convention ended.[22] In a later interview with the *St. Louis Post-Dispatch*, Virginia revealed she had been assigned to canvas Fillmore County, which she did for several weeks, at least through October 12.[23] On October 1,

Virginia and several other women spoke at Red Ribbon Hall in Lincoln. Couzins was supposed to be the headline speaker, but she had contracted a cold, so Virginia substituted for her, kicking off the event. She began by recounting:

> [I heard a conversation yesterday] in which one lady expressed astonishment that the ladies of the convention would remain from home so long. We have left our families in the best of hands. Many of the women here have the noblest husbands in the world. And then we think the importance of the cause should outweigh all other considerations.... You say that women do not want to vote. That makes no difference. It is your duty to vote, whether you want to or not, just the same as it is to sweep your house.... The denial of the right of suffrage will be destructive of our government.... I want you women in Nebraska to claim it as your right. Don't beg for it, but demand it as your right.... The martyred [president] Lincoln said that no state could exist half free and half slave. And yet this is the fact in Nebraska where men are free and women are slaves.[24]

Women showed up to these speeches in the large cities in droves. Anthony later estimated attending at least forty of these events, and Virginia's number was probably only a little less.[25] In a private letter, Virginia confided, "The movement here I hope will succeed. The audiences have been magnificent. At one meeting in Lincoln 500 women came forward and pledged themselves to go out and work for the cause."[26]

At some point in October, Virginia was given the choice of staying in Omaha or "going out to the precincts.... [She] chose the latter because ... [she] wanted to see the people in their homes and learn by personal acquaintance what they thought of vital subjects."[27] She expressed a similar sentiment in a private letter obtained by the *St. Louis Post-Dispatch*: "I am very anxious to go into the 'dug-out' district[28] if possible, though some of them want me for parlor work in Omaha. I don't believe in parlor business, as you know."[29] Virginia wanted to experience the reality of life on the prairie and she may have gotten more than she bargained for. She did, indeed, get to see a sod house when her driver, Mrs. Yates of Geneva, mistakenly took her to the wrong location. Their transportation was often a two-horse buggy forced to travel through mud that Virginia described as "black paste, and nearly a foot deep."[30] Many times she arrived at her destination sopping wet from riding through the rain in uncovered wagons. One of her speaking venues was undergoing construction on its foundation and had been propped up on pylons, so she had to literally crawl inside to access the interior. She also faced off with a large population of German immigrants—54 percent of the foreign-born population and 36 percent of the total population.[31] Just as in St. Louis, they were very much against female suffrage, seeing it as a way for outsiders to destroy their culture and convert their people to temperance.[32] It was because of conditions such as these that she confided to a friend, "I find the work immense . . . and things are by no means sure. The organization is too confident of success to succeed."

In addition, news was slow to spread, so Virginia and Anthony often arrived before townspeople, or even their hosts, were aware they were coming, despite their transportation making only fourteen to eighteen miles a day in Virginia's estimation. One evening at the end of a fourteen-mile journey through the rain, they arrived at the farmstead that was supposed to house them. The owner said he didn't know anything about such arrangements, but they were welcome to stay the night. Pulling Virginia aside, "he added that he didn't believe his wife approved of suffrage and anyway [they] would better not discuss the topic in her hearing."

Being the persistent advocate that she was, Virginia could not bring herself to heed his advice. "I told [the hostess] that as all women had not such kind husbands as her's [sic] was she should assist in their enfranchisement, though she herself cared nothing for it, and I think from her manner she is a promising convert."

Travel delays and lack of both advertisement and timely information notwithstanding, in every location, between twenty and thirty people showed up to hear the women speak. Schoolhouses were their most common venues across the state. They "are all built on the same plan, comfortable and always a mile and a half from the nearest house. . . . I am convinced that distances in that state have been measured by rubber strings," Virginia later recounted. They were not fancy structures, and many locations had only a single "dingy lamp" to illuminate them. "It was equal to lecturing in the dark. I couldn't tell whether my hearers were negroes or white people, and even those nearest me looked like spectres [sic] in the prevailing gloom. It is an odd sensation to be talking to people who hear you and yet whose faces you can not distinguish. However, I did the best possible under such peculiar circumstances."

In another location, after Virginia had spoken only a few minutes, the weather turned threatening. This was the tornado that chased them back to the shelter of their accommodations in the opening of this chapter. Virginia recalled: "A black cloud spread over the sky . . . it became evident that a storm was brewing which everybody dreaded. We decided to adjourn and there was a rush for the door. If it hadn't been for the vivid lightning, I shouldn't have known where the wagon was. We sat down close in the straw because our host said we probably would be blown off the seats if we insisted on occupying them. The wind was like a cyclone . . . I never saw so much brilliant and rapid lightning."

Virginia and Anthony survived this harrowing ordeal only to be thrust into one of the most bizarre incidents of their careers: speaking at an insane asylum three miles outside of Lincoln. They had been invited by the superintendent of the asylum, Dr. Mattison, to dinner[33] with no inkling of what would later be asked of them.

Virginia painted a rather rosy picture of the place, so unlike the gritty, dark institutions exposed by her contemporary suffragist Nellie Bly and others. Perhaps that was what she was expecting because she recalled being shocked at the beauty of the surrounding prairie landscape and the cleanliness of accommodations, with polished mirrors, thick mattresses, and soft bedding, which she called "superior to our own in many things."

She was also surprised by the affection with which the patients greeted the doctor's wife: "It did my heart good to see the smile with which the wife of the superintendent was greeted, to see these poor insane creatures come and put their arms around her, as though she were their mother and they children—she a refined and highly-cultured woman and they rough and homely, many of them daughters of toil, and bearing on their faces the scars of life. I fear I should have shrunk from the kisses, but I bowed in reverence to the woman who smilingly accepted them."

Surely Virginia was aware that not all women committed to asylums at the time actually had mental health issues. Over the previous three decades, many women had been institutionalized for behaving in ways men found unacceptable—sins that Virginia committed every day—such as having progressive opinions, behaving in unruly ways, and not allowing themselves to be controlled by men.[34] "By the middle of the [nineteenth] century, women outnumbered men in asylums," writes scholar Madaline Reeder Walter. "[This was] for several reasons: middle-class norms were extremely important in defining the sane and insane, women had few rights when it came to confinement laws, women were rarely allowed to testify in court, and women's reproductive organs were seen as a cause of insanity."[35]

Wealthy married women were particularly vulnerable because, before the passage of the Married Women's Property Act of 1882, all of a woman's assets passed automatically to her husband if she were institutionalized,[36] giving many men reason to lock away their troublesome wives. Women in those situations faced a terrible choice: allow themselves to be wrongfully incarcerated or file for divorce, which was not easy or accepted by society.[37] In most states, adultery was the only valid reason a woman could file for divorce, though many also included failure to provide, and some allowed it in cases of abuse or impotency. "By filing suit for divorce for their husbands' faults, wives opened themselves to the same accusations," which, if they were found guilty, could mean losing their children and/or property to the very men who had had them committed.[38]

As part of the day's entertainment, the "inmates," as Virginia called them, gathered to sing in the chapel, accompanied by an organist. The guests then dined with the doctor and his wife, after which they were asked to speak to the patients. According to Stanton's recollections, Anthony responded by saying, "Bless me! It is as much as I can do to talk to the sane! What could I say to an audience of lunatics?"

To which Virginia replied, "This is a golden moment for you, the first opportunity you have ever had, according to the constitutions, to talk to your 'peers,' for is not the right of suffrage denied to 'idiots, criminals, lunatics, and women'?"[39]

Virginia volunteered to speak first. "I took the floor and did my very best, and if you will believe it, when I got on the topic of suffrage, they absolutely laughed and some of the girls giggled just as naturally as those outside would have." After she was finished, Anthony rose, "declared she had not a thing to say," but ended up regaling them with a story. As they did at the end of every one of their engagements, Virginia and Anthony asked the audience if they thought women should be allowed to vote. Most said aye, but some abstained; not a single woman voted no.

When they asked the women if they had anything to share, one stood tall and confident and declared, "I always did believe women should vote. If you will look over there at that building [the Penitentiary] you will see one of the best arguments for woman suffrage. There are 200 men in the institution and only one woman." The implication was, of course, that women on the whole were less violent and dangerous than men, so they should have a say in how the government is run.

Though she had originally intended to stay in Nebraska through Election Day, in late October, Virginia returned to St. Louis. The *St. Louis Post-Dispatch* reported she "has been requested to return and reenter the lecture field, but declines to do so on account of her health."[40] She complained of lingering pain in her leg after her fall from the wagon during the severe storm. Coupled with the effects of much travel, poor accommodations, and frequently being wet and cold, it is little surprise her health failed her.

However, Virginia wasn't down for long. By mid-November, she was hosting Anthony, who had just returned from Nebraska,[41] disappointed but not disheartened at the defeat of the suffrage measure at the polls. Together, the two women rejoiced that they raised support for female voting from one in three people to two in three. Anthony vowed "to remain until the fight was won" and work harder than ever to urge Congress to pass the Sixteenth Amendment, because the results in Nebraska proved to her that such a measure would never pass if left to the popular vote.[42]

She was correct, though neither woman lived to see it. Nebraska gave women limited suffrage rights in 1917, but women didn't gain full suffrage until the Nineteenth Amendment became law in 1920, making it "one of the last states west of the Mississippi to grant the ballot to women."[43]

SUFFRAGE AND LIFE: 1882–1884

In February 1882 at the NWSA conference in Washington, DC, Virginia presented a paper titled "The Effect of the Disenfranchisement of Taxation,"[44] proving she was still very much involved in the tax revolt movement.

Later that year, on November 2, 1882, Virginia and Francis moved into a two-story, seven-room brick home at 3311 Lucas Avenue, in St. Louis.[45] It was a popular place for social events and became the new monthly meeting place of the St. Louis branch of the NSWA.[46] Virginia and Francis both lived in this home until their deaths.

In 1884, the *St. Louis Post-Dispatch* published a lengthy list of "tax-payers in the old limits assessed over $5,000." Francis is not included, but that may have to do with the trusts he created when he and Virginia were first married and he turned his property over to her. Virginia was assessed at $17,590, which is approximately $453,700 today,[47] some of which came from rental and investment properties. For a decade,[48] the Minors had owned five lots in Aubert Place, today called Fountain Park. Their property was directly across from the south side of the park, between Lay and Bayard Streets, but they never developed it in any way.[49]

The block was originally intended for a hotel, so it is possible Francis bought the lots intending to profit when it was built. Unfortunately, that never came to pass.[50] Why the Minors still failed to act when it became clear the hotel wasn't going to materialize is a mystery that may never be solved. The area was very desirable, and one would think they would want to live there or at least build property to rent or sell. Aubert Place was an exclusive neighborhood designed to be a "pastoral retreat from congested urban areas . . . [giving residents the] ideal balance of the country and the city—offering healthy bucolic open space domesticated with civilization's amenities."[51] Known as the "lungs" of St. Louis, it boasted wide avenues, a tree-filled park, and was under the protection of "deed restrictions prohibiting the erection of slaughter houses, chemical works and various offensive factories [that] further protected Aubert Place lot owners from the blight and pollution of industry that increasingly plagued urban neighborhoods."[52] In spite of its potential, the Minors never so much as installed sewers or sidewalks, nor did they have the streets graded or paved.[53] It appears to have been purely an investment in land.

They also rented out their previous residence at 2652 Olive for fifty dollars a month.[54] Sometime in 1884, Virginia wrote a letter to her nephew in New York, the famous landscape artist and illustrator John Douglas Woodward, son of her sister, Mary Mildred. In it, she complains about the renters of this property:

> You can't think what a sunbeam your letter was in this dark home. It was a snowy melting, freezing [sic] raining day. I had just come in wet cold nasty [sic] and miserable, from welcoming out a tenant who has been the thorn in my flesh for four years.
>
> From the first day they moved in they demanded that I should have the windows washed or they would move out. I advised them to move immediately. Once a month regularly was the threat made and same advice given. Finally the water inspection got them out, and I am out $300 in repairs of their wreckage.[55]

Tenants aside, Virginia was still focused on suffrage. She spoke at both the 1885[56] and 1886 NWSA Conventions in Washington, DC.[57] The following day, February 20, she addressed the House Judiciary Committee, which had granted the suffragists a hearing while they were in town.[58] Virginia used her own court case and *United States v. Kellar* to show how the court had repeatedly ruled that nonwhite people and children of immigrants were considered citizens under the law, yet women were not. Concerned with the rights of working-class and poor women from the inception of the WSAM, she put the classism of the movement to shame, saying, "I do not stand here to represent rich women but poor women. Should you give me the right to vote and deny it to my sister I should spurn the gift. Without the ballot no class is so helpless as the working women."[59]

THE MORMON QUESTION

More and more, Virginia's attention was being drawn to Utah, where suffrage was becoming an increasingly hot topic, and it looked as though women might lose the right to vote granted to them in 1870, when Utah was still a territory. The controversy came from the female vote being tangled up with Mormonism and, by association, polygamy. Both those for and against polygamy were in favor of female suffrage but for very different reasons. Opponents of the taboo practice believed suffrage empowered women to vote to end the tradition, while supporters, mostly men, believed it showed that polygamy did not oppress women.[60]

However, a bill pending in Congress, the Edmunds-Tucker Anti-Polygamy Act,[61] would require Mormon women to swear an oath against polygamy, forcing them to choose between their faith and their rights as a citizen. This was an unconscionable ultimatum in a country supposedly founded on freedom of religion.

While the AWSA, which was firmly against polygamy, refused to engage with the issue, the bolder NWSA confronted it head-on, welcoming Mormon women regardless of their marital practices, beginning in 1869.[62] "These are the principles I want to maintain," Anthony declared, "that our platform may be kept as broad as the universe, that upon it may stand the representatives of all creeds and of no creeds—Jew and Christian, Protestant and Catholic, Gentile and Mormon, believer and atheist."[63]

Stanton and Anthony spoke openly with Brigham Young at the Mormon Tabernacle in 1870 and with the women of Salt Lake City, to understand their views and practices.[64] In 1879, they invited two Mormon women to their national convention,[65] where they passed a resolution "that it should forbear to exercise federal power to disfranchise the women of Utah, who have had a more just and liberal spirit shown them by Mormon men than Gentile women in the States have yet perceived in their rulers."[66]

By the 1880s, members of the NWSA were unabashedly defending the rights of their Mormon sisters in the papers and at the podiums. In 1882, Couzins explained why she was determined to defend the rights of Utah's women: "Suffrage for women in Utah has accomplished great good. I spent one week there in close observation. Outside of their religious convictions, the women are emphatic in condemnation of wrong."[67] And in 1884, presidential candidate Belva Lockwood called the Edmunds-Tucker Bill "unjust and revolutionary in the extreme."[68]

This overt support of Mormon women put the NWSA in the cross-hairs of the rest of the country, which was virulently anti-polygamist. "The majority of Americans saw them as living in bondage to polygamy,"[69] writes historian Joan Iversen. Debates occurred frequently in Washington, DC,[70] with Waite's Supreme Court taking away the Mormons' ability to claim polygamy was protected under the First Amendment as a form of self-expression,[71] and several presidents, including Rutherford B. Hayes, James Garfield, Chester A. Arthur, and Grover Cleveland, taking public stands against it.[72] In the Deep South, violence against Mormon missionaries was common, as people wrongly believed they were "scheming sexual predator[s] who seduced young women and lured them away to [their] polygamous harem[s] in the West."[73] They believed polygamy was dangerous to Christian society and the institution of marriage in particular.[74] This attitude, though not the violence, spread as far north as St. Louis through anti-Mormon newspaper articles, pamphlets, speeches, and sermons written and given by mostly white Protestants,[75] though lecturer Kate Field was also well known for her passionate speeches against the "Mormon Monster."[76]

By supporting Mormon women's right to vote, suffragists were seen as also supporting polygamy, even though most did not. In fact, many spoke out publicly against the practice, condemning it and supporting Christian monogamy in one breath while defending their Mormon sisters' rights in the next.[77] Anthony even went so far as to point out that "[i]f [Mormon] George Q. Cannon can sit in the Congress of the United States without compromising that body on the question of Polygamy, I should think Mormon women might sit on our platform without making us responsible for their religious faith."[78]

But that didn't stop the media from spinning their words to support the idea they liked most: that both suffragists and Mormon women were immoral. Virginia was intentionally misquoted by the *St. Louis Post-Dispatch* as saying, among other things, that "in voting solid for polygamy [Mormon women] have simply done what women always have done and always will do—[obey] their husbands" as well as asking, "Why should those bad, polygamous husbands, those wicked violators of every law, human and divine, be provided by law with harems full of mere 'voting cattle' who, in obedience to a comment from even the tenth part of a polygamous husband, will go to the polls and vote for the degradation of their own womanhood?"—none of which she ever actually said.[79]

When this false article was reprinted in the *Leavenworth Times* in Kansas,[80] Virginia wasted no time in defending herself, calling it "a perversion of the truth."[81] She lit into the editor who allowed it to be published, vehemently declaring, "You will see that I have made no such statement, but on the contrary particularly state that suffrage women oppose and will continue to oppose the Edmunds[-Tucker] Bill, because it disenfranchises the polygamous wife only, and leaves the ballot in the hands of far more guilty polygamist husbands, and I may here add what my astute critic has overlooked, the fact that the Mormon wife has only one husband."[82]

The bill the suffragists so despised proved to be too powerful for even their great numbers, loud voices, and welcoming hearts. On March 3, 1887, the Edmunds-Tucker Anti-Polygamy Act passed, taking away the right to vote for all Utah women, Mormon and non-Mormon alike.[83] It would be nine more years before it was returned to them permanently.

POLITICS AND PRESENTATIONS: 1888–1892

On January 22, 1888, the Senate Committee on Woman Suffrage agreed to hear arguments from eight members of the NWSA—Elizabeth Cady Stanton, Isabella Beecher Hooker, Abigail Scott Duniway, Laura M. Johns, Rev. Olympia Brown, Rev. Anna Howard Shaw, Alice Stone Blackwell, and Virginia Minor. Each presented arguments for the submission of a Sixteenth Amendment enfranchising women, but from different perspectives.[84] Stanton took a direct shot at those who upheld the *Minor v. Happersett* ruling, saying, "The Constitution of the United States as it is protects me. I do not come to you to petition for . . . any more amendments to the Constitution, because I think they are unnecessary, but because you say there is not in the Constitution enough to protect me."[85]

The following month, Virginia, Couzins, Hazard, and two other women were elected as delegates to the International Council of Women in Washington, DC.[86] There they were honored during the Conference of the Pioneers[87] for "the services rendered" in various cities for fighting against the evil of prostitution.[88] While the convention was taking place, Virginia was also honored as one of eleven "Woman of Note" by the *Washington Evening Star*. The reporter summarized her life to date and described her as "a quiet little lady with a thoughtful face . . . dressed demurely in black who looks quite meek and no one would ever imagine she has carried out an aggressive battle for what she claims to be her rights under the Constitution."[89]

In May, Francis was the one in the spotlight with his "Address to Republicans." The full text of the document is not available, but some of its content can be discerned from newspaper coverage. In it, he gives his advice for the future success of the party—how to avoid defeat—which he believed hinged on universal female suffrage. He was taken to task by the media for having the audacity to suggest Black women should vote. The *Chicago Tribune* roundly dismissed him, writing that the "negresses would be greatly outnumbered and outvoted by the Democratic white women North and South."[90]

But perhaps the most damning was the way the *St. Louis Post-Dispatch* portrayed Francis's words. Without the text of the address, the veracity of their ideas is difficult to refute, but given Francis's other writings, this is likely a deliberate and racist interpretation of his call for suffrage for all women.

> *In his opinion, the Republican party has little chance so long as negress suffrage is denied in the South and ten or twelve States are played like loaded dice by the Democracy in every Presidential campaign. . . . While the negro men have been driven away from the polls or been defrauded by false counting, it is predicted by this Minor that the negress will organize an amazonian [sic] march that will sweep the cotton States and overcome alike the ballot-box stuffers and the remnants of the Ku-Klux and the White League, reinforced by two or three millions of white female voters. . . . But Mr. Minor forgets that a constitutional amendment conferring suffrage on women of one race alone could never be adopted, but that the franchise if extended to any must be to all.*[91]

Francis also praised the Republican party for "ma[king] a splendid record" and making progress for the country, saying "agricultural industry is everywhere flourishing and extending."[92] To this the *Post-Dispatch* insinuated he was out of touch, writing that "farmers are getting half prices for their products and are paying a price and a half for their goods and implements, and are as a consequence up to their eyes in mortgage debt."[93]

By this stage in life, both Francis and Virginia had learned not to let the media or any of their critics get to them. When Virginia asked for ten minutes to speak at the Republican National Convention in Sedalia, Missouri, which was held about a month after Francis's controversial remarks, she was unceremoniously "hissed and howled out of the hall,"[94] as if the delegates were upset that a woman would dare try to address them.[95] A Kansas newspaper colorfully (and intolerantly) reported the overzealous reaction of the German delegates who "yelled and jeered at the top of their beery voices. 'No! No!' hoarsely screamed the German Republicans. 'No vomans [*sic*] here Ve vants no vomans mid us—no voman's rights mid us!' [*sic*] Not an American gentlemen in that convention (if there was one) rebuked those vulgar Germans for their insults to a woman whose fore fathers fought for the freedom of the country, and Mrs. Minor retired from the hall amid the hootings of the German personal liberty men of the Republican party."[96]

In contrast, the Democratic convention was relatively sedate. Virginia and Elizabeth Meriwether caused "a lively diversion" when they requested to be allowed to address the convention on behalf of the International Council of Women, though from contemporary accounts, it doesn't appear the men were intent on taking the two speakers very seriously. "There was a rustle of interest when the Secretary announced the character of the communication, and the first sentence was greeted with laughter and a ripple of applause. The pledge that the speakers would limit themselves to ten minutes only was greeted with loud applause and laughter."[97]

Unsurprisingly, neither major party adopted a women's suffrage plank for the presidential election, but the subject was well represented by Belva

Lockwood, who was making her second bid for the presidency on the Equal Rights Party Ticket.[98]

Once the election was over, Virginia and Francis happily settled in for the holidays, even having Anthony as their Thanksgiving guest,[99] and taking a bit of time for relaxation before gearing up to fight for the vote again in the new year.

Just over a year after her last appearance before the US Senate Committee on Woman Suffrage, Virginia stood before them once more on January 24, 1889. Her address that day included remarks penned by Francis, as well as her own words, and is one of her only full speeches still on record, and one of the most powerful. She said in part:

> Gentlemen, in 1884 the chairman of your committee (Mr. Cockrell) declared "that suffrage belonged entirely to the States so long as no class of citizens were disfranchised." I hold that women are a class of citizens in the different States who are disfranchised. But I am happy to say the Senator must have changed his opinion on that subject, because I notice that he has voted in Congress to take away suffrage in one of the Territories. He has gone far beyond the Constitution in taking away suffrage from the women of the Territory of Utah.
>
> You are again in session for the purpose of renewing your appeal to Congress to propose an amendment to the Constitution which shall forbid the denial of your right to vote on account of sex. Twenty-one years have elapsed since you first made application for this purpose, and yet success seems as distant as ever. For this reason some members of the association are considering the propriety of bringing the matter before the Supreme Court with the view of securing, if possible, a reversal of the decision in the case of Minor vs. Happersett. . . . An appeal to the Supreme Court, properly brought, would be based upon the ground that the right of suffrage is already established in the Federal Constitution, and is an essential privilege of all American citizens. It is not conferred in terms upon any person or class of persons but inheres in and attaches to a status or condition of being, which is expressed in the single word, citizenship. Admittance to national

citizenship, either by birth or naturalization, endues the person with the right of suffrage; its exercise is regulated by law. . . .

The first century of our national life under the Constitution is about to close. To women it has been a century of injustice, since no wrong can compare with that of disfranchisement, and while we are singing pæans in honor of the great instrument it is well to remember that women had a share in the work. . . .

I wish to ask the gentlemen of this committee, who are now acting for us in Congress, to leave to their children an inheritance they will not have to blush for. We want you to show that your prevision has been sufficient to look down the vista of the future and see what must inevitably occur. Fifty years ago a member of the Senate declared that the very mention of the subject of emancipation would never be admitted in the Congress of the United States. It was a woman's prophetic voice that then replied: "You can build out the winds and hedge out the stars, but you can never keep this question out of Congress."[100]

Tired of running up against political roadblocks and seeing ridiculous topics come up for legislation while women's suffrage was ignored, in 1889, Virginia asked Missouri state senator James McGrath to "introduce a bill establishing a legislative commission of three, one of whom shall be a woman, at a salary of $3,000 a year each, whose duty it shall be to suggest to the legislature proper and necessary subjects for legislation."[101] If this bill was ever introduced, there is no record and it certainly did not succeed, given the number of ludicrous bills still being negotiated by Missouri lawmakers more than 130 years later.

A pivotal moment in suffrage history occurred in 1890 when the NWSA and the AWSA finally put aside their differences and ended their twenty-one-year rift by becoming the National American Woman Suffrage Association (NAWSA). When the two organizations merged, Virginia was elected president of the Missouri branch, a role she held until age, poor health, and Francis's death forced her to step down two years later.[102] As such, she was the leader of hundreds, if not thousands, of midwestern suffragists; the St. Louis chapter alone consisted of two hundred to three hundred women.[103]

Virginia attended the first convention of the NAWSA in February 1890 in Washington, DC.[104] When it was her turn to speak, she urged the attendees thereafter to refer to her case not by its legal name of *Minor v. Happersett* or "the *Minor* case," but as "the woman case," as it belonged to all of them, in spite of its technically bearing her surname.[105] As the *Evening Star* explained, "It was anything but pleasing to her to have such notoriety, especially as the case was not so much that of an individual as it was of her whole sex or of the cause in general."[106]

This statement could sum up the whole of Virginia's career and even her life. Though a public figure not afraid to voice her opinions loudly, she was at heart a humble woman who did not desire notoriety for herself but rather for the cause to which she had dedicated her life. And as she grew older, she was aware that what she had begun no longer belonged to her, if it ever had; it belonged to all the women of the United States. She was determined to use her final remaining years, and the posts that she held—such as being named honorary president of the Interstate Woman Suffrage Convention in 1892[107]—to make sure all women understood the awesome responsibility and tradition they were carrying on.

CHAPTER FIFTEEN
Death Shall Not Silence Me

FEBRUARY 19, 1892, AN OTHERWISE ORDINARY FRIDAY, QUICKLY
turned heartbreaking around 11:00 a.m.[1] It began with a single cough
that rapidly progressed into wheezing and shortness of breath. Francis,
now seventy-two, took to his bed, and Virginia called the doctor, but
there was nothing to be done. By six o'clock[2] that evening, Francis was
dead. The official cause of death was "congestion of the lungs,"[3] and one
newspaper called it a "congestive chill."[4] Virginia had lost the man with
whom she had "been, in every sense of the word, united . . . in loving
bonds for so many years."[5]

After Francis's body was washed by a layer-out of the dead,[6] it is
likely that the traditional three-day wake was held in the Minors' home
in the days between his death and the funeral on February 22, as newspapers record many friends and family expressing surprise and grief at
his sudden death.[7] Virginia would have been dressed in full mourning,
with a heavy black dress and veil of crepe, which she would wear for the
next year and a day as the first step in her three-year mourning period.[8] A
male relative, likely Francis's nephew Minor Meriwether, who would have
been mourning his beloved "Uncle Frank,"[9] was present to help tend her
needs, greet guests when she could not, and handle her financial affairs
once Francis's will was proved, since she had no living father or brother
to do so.[10] If any religious service was held before or after the funeral, it
would have occurred at the Church of the Holy Communion, located at
Washington and Leffingwell, where the Minors were congregants.[11]

At 2:00 p.m. on Monday, February 22, Francis's funeral took place in his home.[12] A crepe ribbon adorned the door, and black cloth covered the casket.[13] Undoubtedly, the familiar traditions brought to Virginia's mind memories of their son's untimely death nearly twenty-six years before. Once the prayers were said and the six pallbearers[14] loaded the coffin onto the black-draped hearse, the parade of mourners, including six carriages,[15] began the three-mile journey to Bellefontaine Cemetery, where Francis was laid to rest next to his son, as specified in his will.[16]

A Movement in Mourning

This ritual marked not only the end of a life and a nearly fifty-year marriage but also a great loss to the suffrage movement. "No man has contributed to the woman suffrage movement so much valuable constitutional argument and proof as Mr. Minor,"[17] Anthony wrote. "We have lost, *this side*, a friend at all times and in all places; we should be grateful that he lived—lived so well and did so much."[18] The *Women's Tribune*, the publication in which Francis called for women to be allowed to vote for members of Congress,[19] memorialized him on March 5, 1892, calling his writing "state documents for the woman suffrage movement" and naming him a "champion . . . who devoted his life and talents to the establishing of the rights of women."[20]

Fulfilling one of Francis's lifelong dreams, Wyoming Republican Clarence Clark presented a federal suffrage bill in the US House of Representatives on April 25. It had been authored by Francis.[21] The bill, titled "An Act to Protect the Right of Citizens of the United States to Register and to Vote for Members of the House of Representatives," asked Congress to certify "that at all elections hereafter held in the several States of this Union for members of the House of Representatives, the right of citizens of the United States, of either sex, above the age of twenty-one years, to register and to vote for such Representatives shall not be denied or abridged by the United States, or by any State, on account of sex."[22] The bill was referred to the House Judiciary Committee,[23] where it eventually died of neglect.

In May, Isabella Beecher Hooker came up with the idea "to have a new national organization called the Francis Minor Federal Suffrage Association, and [she] . . . determined to come [to Chicago] . . . and propose its organization as a tribute to [his wife]."[24] The Federal Suffrage Association, founded that very weekend by Olympia Brown,[25] was inspired by Francis's article "Citizenship and Suffrage" that appeared in the *Arena*. The new organization's goal was "to obtain such legislation that will secure to every citizen of the United States the exercise of the right of suffrage and also to advocate uniformity in the election of national officers."[26]

The NASWA also honored Francis at their convention on January 14–19, 1893, in Washington, DC. At the event, Hon. A. G. Riddle declared, "As suffragists we esteem and honor men for the services rendered by them in the cause we are convened to advance, and we recognize Francis Minor, late of Missouri, as holding a high place with the ablest and most valued men and women who have advocated it."[27] Riddle also admitted Francis was "a braver man than I" for arguing his case before the Supreme Court.[28]

The attendees also passed an official resolution to be placed in the minutes: "That the members of this convention individually have heard of the passing away of Francis Minor with pain and profound regret; that this convention fully appreciates his eminent services in the cause to advance which it is convened. It deplores his loss from its ranks of advocates; it personally sympathizes with his widow and the circle of mourning friends and with all who deplore the loss of a good man."[29]

Out of all the speeches and memorials in Francis's honor, his nephew Minor Meriwether summed up Francis's life best: "The wish to see Woman Suffrage firmly established was the most earnest of his life—all else was secondary."[30] While Francis did not live to see women get the right to vote, his determination lived on in spirit as "suffragists continued to cite the Minors' arguments for women's constitutional right to the franchise up to the 1920 adoption of the Nineteenth Amendment."[31]

LIFE AS A WIDOW

There can be no doubt that for months, Virginia was inconsolable, but there were things that had to be done. While mourning etiquette required that she not leave her house unless absolutely necessary,[32] she did not shirk her duty as executor of Francis's will. In order to manage this loathsome task, she resigned from her position as vice president of the NASWA representing Missouri.[33] It had to have been difficult for her to see Mrs. Virginia Hedges of Warrensburg elected as her successor, the first time the office of president was held by someone outside of St. Louis.[34]

Francis's will was admitted to probate on February 28, 1892.[35] He left his entire estate to Virginia, minus $100 she was to pay to Bellefontaine Cemetery Association for the upkeep of Lot 1623, the location of his and Francis Gilmer's graves.[36] The value of his real estate is not listed in the appraisal, but his personal property, including a gold watch, was appraised at $167.50[37] and his household goods at $177.50,[38] a total of approximately $9,800 in today's currency.

Virginia appears to have spent her first year of mourning as society expected, in total seclusion, as no records of her activities exist. The next public mention of her is at the March 1893 NASWA convention in Washington, DC.[39] This makes sense because it falls just after the customary year and a day waiting period before a widow could emerge back into society. She still had to dress in black, but she was allowed to meet with friends.[40]

Virginia treated her return to the world more liberally than some women, who preferred to only begin having tea with friends and accepting callers at this time.[41] Instead of sticking close to home, she traveled from the convention in Washington, DC, to Old Point Comfort in Virginia, perhaps to visit family, and then to New Orleans[42] and Florida,[43] likely to speak on the issue of suffrage. Virginia was gone for about a month, returning home at the beginning of April.[44] Then in July, she was off again, headed for "the Eastern resorts"[45] before spending a fortnight in Chicago with Mr. and Mrs. Minor Meriwether, where they attended the World's Fair.[46]

Virginia was also an active member of the St. Louis Chart Club,[47] founded in St. Louis by historian, author, and suffragist Maria I. Johnson to study ancient and modern history and literature.[48] The club met every Saturday morning during the winter.[49]

By May 1894, Virginia was in her third and final year of mourning. She was allowed to wear colors like mauve, lavender, and gray and could resume her place in society. She hosted Anthony in her house once again, as Anthony was in town to speak on women's suffrage before heading to Kansas, where suffragists were again preparing for their cause to be on the ballot.[50]

This may well have been the final meeting of the two suffrage leaders. Virginia was felled sometime in June with a "serious spell of illness" but was said to be recovering by the beginning of July.[51] However, she must have suffered a relapse. By the end of the month, it was clear her illness was very grave, and she made the decision to give up her home so she could move into Baptist Sanitarium at Nineteenth and Carr Streets.[52] Though generally considered a religious woman, "she refused to attend church there because she believed that clergy had been hostile to the women's movement."[53]

THE END OF AN ERA

Virginia's stay at the Baptist Sanitarium was not a long one. She died on Tuesday, August 14, 1894,[54] at 12:15 p.m.[55] at the age of seventy from an abscess of the liver.[56] Given her age and recent illness, her death was not unexpected. One obituary recounts her final days: "A certain grace and refinement of manner made her personally attractive to the end. She was fully aware of her approaching end, which she regarded with calmness and resignation. Though without near relatives, she received devoted attention during her last hours, and the thought that she will be seen no more in her familiar haunts is a source of deep regret to the many who loved her."[57]

Virginia's death was called "an irreparable loss to the cause of woman suffrage."[58] She was mourned by suffragists and ordinary women alike across the country. No wake was held, and the public was asked not to send flowers. Her funeral began at 9:00 a.m. the following morning in her home.[59] Before the funeral procession to Bellefontaine Cemetery, a quartet sang her favorite hymns, such as "It Is Well with My Soul," "Rock of Ages," and "Nearer My God to Thee."[60] After a time of prayer, the pallbearers—"three gentlemen from the Meriwether family, and Messrs. Gaienine and Barnett, Huston T. Force"[61]—removed the coffin, and the mourners traced the same route they had followed two years earlier, when Francis passed away.

Because Virginia believed religious leaders were against equal rights for women, her funeral was held without the presence of any clergy members, a final thumb of her nose at the patriarchy. While no words of her own survive on the subject, she undoubtedly agreed with (and perhaps was) the anonymous author of a letter addressed to Mrs. Beverly Allen at the WSAM meeting on January 18, 1869: "We all know there is no priest or preacher, be he Catholic or Protestant, who does not feel it his duty to invade this divine authority to proselyte [*sic*] the wife of any husband who does not accept his [the priest/pastor and St. Paul] standards of orthodoxy. It is simply impossible for any intelligent woman to bring herself to any such subjugation, and to ask any man, be he husband or pastor, what she may believe, and Christ does not require of us impossibilities."[62]

Virginia was laid to rest next to her husband, who had been her beloved partner in life and would now lie at her right hand throughout eternity and only a few feet away from their beloved son, Francis Gilmer. Her grave, like those of the other Minors, is marked by a small headstone bearing only her name.

In a twist of fate nearly too incredible to be believed, Virginia's adversary, Reese Happersett, is buried literally across the street from her in a currently unmarked grave beneath a large pine tree.[63] Only a small, one-lane cemetery path called Willow and about forty to fifty feet separate them. According to cemetery employees, Happersett's grave may never have been marked or if it was, the monument may have succumbed to time and not been replaced.[64]

Getting the Last Word

For most people, their funeral is the end of the story; but Virginia was an extraordinary woman who was determined to have her fight for female independence and suffrage continue even after she had taken her final breath. It was customary to keep a person's will private, but Virginia's was published in the newspapers—which she likely anticipated—because it contained two very unusual bequests. The first was, "I direct that my property of every description be sold and converted into money. That $500 (five hundred dollars) to be given to each of my two single nieces, daughters of my deceased sister, Lucy Ellen Swann, of Atlanta, Ga., Should one die or marry her $500 goes to the one living or remaining single."

Virginia's requirement that her two nieces remain single in order to retain their inheritance was unheard of and set tongues wagging. Given her own experiences and her vehement hatred of the system of coverture, what Virginia was likely doing was enabling these two women to live independent lives without the need for husbands. The provision that if one married, the other was to receive her $500 was clearly done to avoid it becoming the property of the new husband, as all his wife's assets would revert to him. The *St. Louis Post-Dispatch* showed how well they had come to know Virginia over the years, noting that "the will and codicil are characteristic of the woman herself and show her to have her own ideas concerning affairs generally."[65] The second bequest stated: "I give $1000 (one thousand dollars) to Susan B. Anthony, of Rochester, N.Y. in gratitude for the many thousands she has expended for woman. Should she die before I do the money is then to be divided between the two nieces, as above with the $500."

With this endowment, Virginia could express her appreciation to her dear friend Anthony, attempt to repay her for her kindness, and ensure the movement continued on long after she was gone.

The rest of Virginia's will was ordinary, with her remaining assets being divided among Francis's nieces and her nephew. Minor Meriwether was appointed her executor. In addition, eight codicils to her will parsed out her worldly belongings to friends and relatives. Notable among them is one that "gives to her servant maid Bettie Ruken Lindahl her gold watch, plus any wages due to her at the time of Virginia's death without delay, plus one month's additional wages, $15."[66] Once again she proved her concern for working women through this affectionate act.

Virginia's estate was valued at just over $7,500 or approximately $453,345 today,[67] not including income from real estate, which included:

- The five Aubert Place lots, which were eventually sold to G. W. Davis Realty Co. for $15,000[68]
- 3311 Lucas Ave. which had to be significantly repaired before it was sold[69]

- The Minors' rental home at 2652 Olive, which also needed repairs
- 816 N. Third, a four-story brick building previously sold and currently under lease by the new owners, likely included because of conflicting accounts of who really owned it[70]
- The plot at Bellefontaine Cemetery

It took Minor Meriwether five years to fully execute Virginia's will, fitting for a complex and busy woman who had many irons in the fire throughout her life.

The Missouri Equal Suffrage Association, the new name of Virginia's WSAM, paid tribute to their founder at the first meeting following her death. On May 4, 1895, Anthony and Reverend Shaw were in attendance, as were nearly all the delegates of the Women's Christian Temperance Union Congress of Women, who stayed in the city overnight after their own conference to pay tribute to Virginia,[71] their friend and advocate.

In eulogizing Virginia, Anthony made it clear the Minors were people of outstanding significance in the suffrage movement, whose accomplishments should not be forgotten. She reminded them that "the first resolution in favor of woman suffrage ever devised was written by Mr. and Mrs. Minor in May, 1869, in St. Louis."[72] Without Virginia and Francis, none present would have been gathered together that morning to carry on the work they had begun.

EPILOGUE

Twenty-First-Century Revival

IN THE YEARS FOLLOWING THE RATIFICATION OF THE NINETEENTH Amendment on August 26, 1920, former suffragists and new female voters turned their minds to honoring those who made their newly won right possible.

In 1929, in the midst of the Great Depression, when many local chapters were struggling,[1] the National League of Women Voters took a bold step with their newest project: a National Roll of Honor to recognize pioneers of the women's suffrage movement. It was meant to mark the ten-year anniversary of women's suffrage the following year and raise money for the organization to continue.[2]

Each state organization was asked to nominate women who were integral to the enfranchisement of women in their area. According to the St. Louis League of Women Voters records, the qualifications for enrollment were "outstanding personal work for suffrage in Missouri or as a Missourian between the years 1867–1914."[3] Forty women from St. Louis were nominated, along with hundreds of others from across the country.[4]

On May 1, 1930, at the national convention in Louisville, Kentucky, the seventy-one national honorees were announced. Their names were inscribed on a bronze tablet housed in the League of Women Voters national headquarters in Washington, DC.[5] Although Virginia was not among those from Missouri—that honor went to Emily Newell Blair of Joplin, Edna Gellhorn of St. Louis, and Luella St. Clair Moss of Columbia[6]—she was part of the State Roll of Honor for Missouri. This framed vellum tablet bears the inscription, "This Tablet Is a Tribute to Those Women in Missouri Whose Courageous Work Opened the

Opportunities of Complete Citizenship to All Women in the State," and it displays the names of the twenty-eight other women whose names were accepted.[7] It, along with the other state tablets, hangs near the national honor roll.

On January 21, 1931,[8] the Missouri League of Women Voters unveiled a Woman Suffrage Pioneers Memorial Tablet dedicated to fifty-five women, including Virginia Minor, who helped make female suffrage possible in the state. The tablet, which still hangs in the Capitol Building in Jefferson City, bears the inscription, "A tribute to these women in Missouri whose courageous work opened the opportunities of complete citizenship to all women in the state."[9] It was created as part of a series of events marking the tenth anniversary of female suffrage.[10]

THE HALL OF FAMOUS MISSOURIANS

Over the next eighty years, Virginia's memory faded until she was nearly forgotten. But as history unfolded, the story of how she came roaring back to take her place in the Hall of Famous Missourians in the Capitol Building in Jefferson City is one rife with irony that she would have appreciated. Just as in life, her legacy and her supporters faced down a man with outdated, anti-female attitudes and his supporters, who were determined to see her fail. But she won lasting recognition instead.

The origins of the Hall of Famous Missourians are a bit murky, but Bob Priddy, a trustee of the State Historical Society of Missouri and early backer of the project, recalls on his blog that it began in the early 1980s, when the wives of some of the Missouri lawmakers decided they wanted to raise money for new art for the capitol.[11] They raised enough funds to commission four bronze busts of famous Missourians: author Samuel Clemens (a.k.a. Mark Twain), installed in 1982; educator Susan Elizabeth Blow, in 1983; scientist George Washington Carver, also in 1983; and artist Thomas Hart Benton, in 1985.[12]

After this initial installation, the funds were depleted and for several years, the project was forgotten. Then in 1991, Speaker of the House Bob Griffin revived it, beginning the tradition of Speakers raising money through a golf tournament to commission new busts. Over time, the area in which they were housed—part of the Missouri Capitol between the

House and Senate chambers—became known as the Hall of Famous Missourians. One or two new, noteworthy Missouri citizens were named by the Speaker annually, except for in 1998, 2001, 2002, 2005, and 2011, when no inductions took place.

Priddy noted, "The unofficial rules were that the selection of members of the hall would not be a matter of partisan politics and that no living politician would be inducted"[13]—that is, until 2012, when the rules were thrown out the window when Speaker Steven Tilley selected Rush Limbaugh, a conservative radio host and author, as his latest pick. Limbaugh, while not a politician, was clearly the mouthpiece of conservative Republicans. This made his nomination a matter of partisan politics. Democrats responded by sending letters opposing the installation,[14] and they proposed new criteria requiring bipartisan approval of all selections by three of the four top legislative leaders and allowing no more than two inductions for every two-year term.[15]

Limbaugh was a controversial choice because he had recently called Georgetown University law student Sandra Fluke a "slut" and a "prostitute" on his nationally syndicated radio show after Republicans blocked her from testifying on why contraception was needed under Obamacare.[16] Had this been a one-time occurrence, it might have been overlooked, but Limbaugh had a history of making pejorative comments about women, Black people, and Native Americans. According to journalist Eliza Relman, Limbaugh "[was] an outspoken opponent of feminism, which he said 'was established so as to allow unattractive women easier access to the mainstream of society.' He's made too many racist comments to count, including lamenting that professional football 'looks like a game between the Bloods and the Crips without any weapons' and that 'if any race of people should not have guilt about slavery, it's Caucasians.'"[17]

Given this, it's not surprising that the news that his bust would be placed alongside the likes of Scott Joplin, Laura Ingalls Wilder, and St. Rose Philippine Duchesne, while notable Missourians like T. S. Eliot, Kate Chopin, Langston Hughes, and Joseph Pulitzer awaited recognition, enraged many citizens. Over 3,500 people signed a petition against the selection of Limbaugh,[18] hundreds demonstrated in front of the Capitol,[19] students from nearby Missouri State University protested,[20] and members of the Missouri chapter of the National Organization for Women (NOW) delivered five hundred rolls of toilet paper to the Speaker's office, urging him to "flush Rush."[21]

Despite the outcry, the bust of Limbaugh was installed on May 14, 2012,[22] in a ceremony that was kept secret until less than an hour before it took place, amid fears that Limbaugh, or his likeness, might be in danger from protesters. Less than two weeks later, the statue was put under twenty-four-hour camera surveillance that reportedly cost Missouri taxpayers $1,000.[23]

As a result of the clamor around the 2012 pick, newly elected Speaker Tim Jones announced he would let the Missouri people vote for two of the next three people to be inducted into the Hall of Famous Missourians. He specifically said he was seeking the names of those who had previously been overlooked. "Is there someone in our past that was maybe great back in their time, in the 1800s (or) early 1900s, who has been forgotten, who was truly great and should be an outstanding Missourian in the Hall?" he asked.[24]

Shirley Breeze, president of the Missouri Women's Network—which includes the state chapters of NOW, American Association of University Women (AAUW), Women's Political Caucus, and the League of Women Voters—and Mary Mosley, legislative director at the time, immediately answered "yes!" They gathered a group of women from those organizations to brainstorm names. Since at the time, only seven out of the thirty-eight inductees were women,[25] they felt their nominee had to be female. According to Mosley, they decided on Virginia Minor "because people don't know about her and also for the importance of the court case."[26]

They nominated her and asked all the women's organizations in the state to vote for her. Only they were far from alone. Thousands of people submitted hundreds of names, which were whittled down to a final list of ten.[27] In the end, the female vote was split, because other women were nominated—including beloved former state Representative Sue Shear. Virginia only received three thousand votes;[28] the male candidates each had at least a thousand more,[29] the most popular gathering 38 percent of the more than thirty-four thousand total votes.[30]

The only reason Virginia made it into the class of 2013 was that the Speaker realized how important it was to the people of Missouri that a woman be included in the inductees. "It became obvious to me it was time to make a Speaker's Pick and recognize this incredible woman for her immense contributions to the suffrage movement, not only in our state, but in the entire country," Jones said in his remarks at the induction ceremony. The others chosen alongside Virginia were author Robert Heinlein, osteopathic medicine founder Andrew Taylor Still, and former US representative Mel Hancock.

Breaking with previous tradition, Speaker Jones decided not to raise funds for the busts but instead to have them all privately funded.[31] By February 2013, donors had come forward to fund the busts of the men, but no one was willing to pay for Virginia's.[32] So Mosley and Breeze decided to raise the $10,000 themselves. Realizing most people don't have a lot of money to give, they came up with the idea that if one thousand people gave only $10, they could meet their funding goal. "[We wanted] women [to] feel like they were invested in it and it was their sculpture," Mosley said.[33] They called the campaign "1,000 Strong." And it took nearly that many—the entire Missouri Women's Network pitched in, some giving as little as a dollar or two—for them to achieve their goal.

Now all they had to do was wait for the bust to be created. The Speaker was the one who picked the sculptor, so the ladies had no idea who would be chosen or how that person would portray Virginia. What they were unaware of was that a sculptor named Cynthia Hitschler had asked to be considered for the position because she had long desired to create art for the Capitol.[34] As it turned out, the fact that she was the only female sculptor to apply[35] and was from the Speaker's own district in Eureka, won him over.[36]

Having nominated Virginia, Mosley and Breeze were the ones who worked with Hitschler and approved the final product. This was the sculptor's first public commission for the State of Missouri, so everyone involved was nervous. Hitschler originally tried to work off the more famous engraving of Virginia in the Library of Congress, thinking it was the only extant image, but she found she just couldn't envision Mrs. Minor in 3D. "I was searching for anatomical landmarks like cheekbones, skeletal structure, there weren't any. The engraver had left them out," she explained.[37] A little internet sleuthing uncovered an actual portrait of Virginia,[38] and Hitschler had her muse. In order to try to understand the woman she was portraying, Hitschler read everything she could on Virginia. Still, she said she could have learned everything she needed to know from the single photograph. "[You can] see the determination in the photo. She looks very strong, very determined, you can tell that she had gone through a hefty amount of suffering. You can see it in her face, and the fact that really nothing was going to destroy her. It came through loud and clear, just in her photograph. I really wanted to capture that."[39]

Using an oil-based non-pottery clay that never dries out,[40] Hitschler set about bringing Virginia to life. When she was ready, the nominating committee visited her in her studio to approve the clay model before it was cast in bronze[41]—an emotional and exciting day for all involved. Once all agreed, Hitschler personally drove her vulnerable model over 550 miles of potholed highway in the sweltering heat of summer[42] to Atlanta-based studio The Inferno[43] to be cast.

But the struggle wasn't over quite yet. In a project where everything that could have gone wrong seemed to, another obstacle remained, as though the patriarchy was really trying to keep this statue from being erected. The women had been unaware that the $10,000 they were quoted was only for the statue itself; the base was an additional expense because it had to look just like all the others in the Hall.[44] So they suddenly needed to raise another $5,000.[45] But luckily, money was still coming in from their 1,000 Strong campaign, and with a little publicity and networking to encourage donations, they ended up having enough to pay for the base as well.[46]

Virginia was inducted into the Hall of Famous Missourians on September 10, 2013. While that date has no particular significance to Virginia's life, it was chosen because many people, women especially, were expected in Jefferson City that day for a veto session that included an override veto on an abortion bill.[47] Holding the event that day would expose as many people as possible to Virginia's story and enable them to witness her long-denied recognition.

During her opening prayer, Rev. Rebecca Turner said, "Although she only gave birth to one child, we now claim Virginia Minor as mother to all of us who work for justice. And for her legacy we are forever indebted."[48] While Anthony and Stanton rightfully are considered the mothers of the entire suffrage movement, in that moment, Virginia was finally publicly acknowledged as the mother of suffrage in Missouri, a woman who intellectually, spiritually, and emotionally influenced generations of suffragists after her and who deserved to take her place among the greatest in the state.

In his remarks, Speaker Jones praised Virginia "for her perseverance, above all, her indomitable will and desire to give women the right to vote and place women on a level playing field with their male counterparts. Her desire to achieve this equality was unwavering and even as she suffered setbacks, all the legal challenges that you've heard about, her spirit—that spirit that you see in so many Missourians—was undaunted."[49]

Hitschler was on hand for the event and beamed with pride as the bust was unveiled. "It represents my devotion to the Hall of Famous Missourians, to my state, and to the progress women have had," she said.[50]

FIRST NATIONAL RECOGNITION

In 2020, women across the United States celebrated the centennial of the Nineteenth Amendment, giving women the right to vote. Because of the prevalence of suffrage in the national consciousness, Virginia attracted more national media attention in 2020 than since she was alive. Articles connecting her to the centennial in ways large and small appeared in the *Washington Post, National Geographic, New York Times, St. Louis Post-Dispatch*, the US Courts official website,[51] and dozens of local newspapers across the country.

Each year, the National Women's History Alliance (NWHA) honors women both living and dead who fought for women in some way that is in alignment with the theme of the year. Because 2020 marked the centennial, their theme was "Valiant Women of the Vote."

On December 11, 2019, Virginia was announced as one of thirteen women who would be honored during the centennial year, finally allowing her to take her rightful place among more than 340 women who had been recognized over the last forty years.[52] The event was originally supposed to take place on Saturday, March 28, 2020.[53] However, it was postponed to August 29 because the COVID-19 pandemic made travel and large gatherings impossible.

When the pandemic continued, this event was canceled and rescheduled for August 2021. Because the centennial didn't officially end until August 26, 2021, the NWHA modified the 2021 theme to "Valiant Women of the Vote: Refusing to be Silenced," and all honorees were officially part of the 2020–2021 cohort.[54]

After more than a year of waiting, Virginia's first national honor finally took place on August 21, 2021, at the Hamilton, in Washington, DC, with both in-person and virtual attendees. During a ceremony, Virginia was publicly acknowledged for the first time on the national level for creating the New Departure, her landmark 1875 Supreme Court case, and being a woman "who exemplifie[d] the courage and drive that helped women move ahead in the United States."[55]

LOCAL EFFORTS INTRODUCE VIRGINIA TO A NEW GENERATION OF ST. LOUISANS

Even amid a global pandemic, the city of St. Louis was determined not to let its hometown suffragist go unheralded, especially during the centennial of the Nineteenth Amendment. In 2020, the Missouri History Museum, State Historical Society of Missouri, and the Missouri and St. Louis chapters of the League of Women Voters and of the AAUW held several special events honoring Virginia and other local suffragists.

One of the biggest events was a nineteen-month exhibition called "Beyond the Ballot," located at the Missouri History Museum. According to the exhibit's website, "Through an engaging mix of artifacts, images, media, and interactives, Beyond the Ballot explores women's unique roles in St. Louis history. One major element of the exhibit traces the long history of the fight for woman's suffrage in St. Louis and the events leading up to the passage of the Nineteenth Amendment in 1920."[56] Virginia was featured in a large panel depicting her life and career and was one of only a handful of women chosen to have her own section in the exhibit. She was also one of fifty women included in the companion guidebook[57] and on the exhibit website.

On August 15, 2020, the AAUW held a wreath-laying ceremony at Virginia's grave at Bellefontaine Cemetery. The event included an introduction to Virginia's life; a performance by historical reenactor Anne Williams, who gave a rousing portrayal of Virginia's January 24, 1889, speech to the US Senate Committee on Woman Suffrage; and the wreath laying. It closed with a grave blessing by Mayor Rev. Ella Jones of Ferguson, Missouri, a suburb of St. Louis, who was specially chosen because her community experienced the very type of racial strife that Virginia and Francis so vehemently opposed.

On Election Day, November 3, 2020, an unseasonably warm, sunny day, Bellefontaine Cemetery encouraged local voters to come visit the Minors and leave their "I Voted" stickers on a poster board that was part of a special temporary memorial erected at Virginia's grave. They were also invited to leave personalized notes on the poster board, many of which expressed their thanks for her efforts that led to them being able to cast a vote. Visitors also learned about Virginia's life from a special sign next to her grave and literature available nearby.

While Susan B. Anthony's grave site regularly draws thousands of visitors who leave their "I Voted" stickers, the inaugural event in St. Louis attracted about fifty participants,[58] which organizers consider good for their first year—especially during a pandemic, when people were less likely to leave home. They are hoping to grow participation with every election.

The St. Louis chapter of the League of Women Voters is currently working to raise money for a new memorial to Virginia Minor at her grave in Bellefontaine Cemetery. It will be a new marker; it will not replace the original headstone but rather serve as a memorial and educational opportunity for all who visit the cemetery.[59]

In addition, Cynthia Holmes and Pat Shores, Missouri's state coordinators for the National Votes for Women Trail, worked with the William G. Pomeroy Foundation to award a historic marker to Virginia Minor at 2652 Olive,[60] the site of her home from 1871 to 1882. The marker was installed on October 15, 2022, the 150th anniversary of Virginia's landmark attempt at registering as a voter.[61]

❧

Virginia and Francis Minor are examples of how history, which is not nearly as immutable as modern people like to believe, sometimes forgets even those who were well known during their lifetimes. For more than a century, the Minors have been overshadowed by names like Anthony, Stanton, and even Carrie Chapman Catt and Alice Paul. The Minors' court case, or at least its outcome, has been misrepresented, and their unique contribution of the New Departure has been credited to others, women of more note who used it after learning it from its source.

Even in their home state, *Minor v. Happersett* is not part of the regular history, social studies, or government curriculum for elementary or high school students, despite study of other famous cases being mandatory. It is also not listed in the nineteen units of Missouri history[62] recommended by the Missouri Department of Elementary and Secondary Education, even in their unit on "Women Change Their Roles," which features Stanton, Anthony, and the Women's Suffrage Movement.[63]

But this can and will change. One of the blessings of the twenty-first century is that Americans, as a people, are awakening to the need to tell the "hidden" stories of the forgotten, ostracized, and oppressed. They are beginning to realize that history wasn't made by a few marquee names but by thousands of ordinary people whose stories have so far gone undocumented. As these stories are told and our history books are rewritten to include them, the cultural worldview and perspective on the past will change with it; people who didn't previously think they had role models will have someone to look up to, and those who felt alone will finally see themselves represented.

While the Minors are currently primarily remembered for their Supreme Court case, they have so much else to teach. They are examples of how people raised in intolerant cultures can live lives of openness and acceptance; how ordinary citizens can influence government; how men can be allies in the female fight for equal rights; how like minds can bring about systemic change; how couples can lovingly support one another in the achievement of their dreams; how women—and others—can stand up to systems that seek to oppress them; and perhaps most of all, how perseverance in dedication to justice can and does ultimately succeed, even if it is after death.

It behooves our nation to remember the Minors and the thousands of others like them whose lifelong commitment to righting the injustices in our American democracy enable citizens to live the lives of freedom they enjoy today. Society still has a long way to go before the United States is the utopian "city on a hill" the founders intended, but each generation gets a little closer. By honoring those who have gone before, this generation not only gains strength and inspiration for their own fight but also adds to the collective historical power that propels them forward.

As Speaker Jones said at Virginia Minor's induction to the Hall of Famous Missourians, "We are today a stronger and a greater nation because of her unrelenting drive and determination. Truly, Virginia Minor changed our nation. . . . [I] hope that her name will never be forgotten and she will be discovered by a whole new generation of ladies and men . . . [and] that her life will continue to serve as a shining example for future generations."

A NOTE FROM THE AUTHOR

IF IT IS GOING TO BE READABLE, NO BIOGRAPHY CAN CONTAIN *ALL* OF THE information about a subject. That is why I created the Virginia Minor Memorial Institute at https://virginiaminor.com, a website dedicated to housing valuable information about Virginia and Francis that didn't make it into this book, as well as updates on events related to preserving their memories.

Additional information that may be found there includes a full bibliography for this book, a genealogy of the Minor family dating back to the 1600s, information on how the location of the Minors' home, Minoria, was uncovered, photos related to their lives, my research, and much more. It is my hope that this website will be seen as a companion learning resource for this book and will be of use to anyone seeking additional information on this suffrage couple and their family.

A Note from the Author

ACKNOWLEDGMENTS

WRITING A BIOGRAPHY IS NOT SOMETHING THAT CAN OR SHOULD BE done alone. In preparing to write this "chapter," I feel like an actress giving her Oscar acceptance speech, praying she doesn't miss someone. To anyone I may have forgotten: please accept my sincere apologies.

First, I would like to thank my agent, Amy Collins, at Talcott Notch, and my editor, Sarah Parke, at Globe Pequot, for taking a chance on a book about two unknown people and helping me shape my research into the best book it can be. Your confidence and trust are why I have the courage to continue to tell these types of stories. Thanks as well to the whole Globe Pequot team who helped get this book into readers' hands.

I started researching Virginia and Francis Minor in July 2017, not certain if there would be enough information available on them to write a biography. When I completed it in late 2020, we were in a global pandemic and enduring lockdowns, which meant many libraries and archives were closed. I am so grateful to the many people and institutions who helped me gather information and access resources, both in person and virtually. Thank you to:

- Bellefontaine Cemetery, especially Dan Fuller, who helped me procure Virginia's and Francis's burial certificates and answered a million questions about them. You are truly a gem.
- A. J. Medlock, at the St. Louis Research Center of the State Historical Society of Missouri, for hosting me for more days than I can count as a guest researcher for this book and others. I am so glad to have met you and that I can now call you a friend.

- Peter McCarthy and Kevin George, of the State Historical Society of Missouri Research Center in Columbia, Missouri, for making materials on the Minor trial available to me.

- Regina Rush, Anne Causey, Penny White, and all at the Albert and Shirley Small Special Collections Library at the University of Virginia for hosting me as a guest researcher for two days in June 2019. You made my first out-of-town archival experience a joy.

- Dennis Northcott and all at the Missouri Historical Society Library and Research Center, for the many hours you hosted me as a guest on-site and answered my questions related to the Minors, the Civil War in Missouri, the Great Fire, and the cholera epidemic of 1849. Also, thank you to Magdalene Linck and Katie Moon, for answering online questions.

- Michael Everman and Pat Barge for being my guides (literally) through the Missouri State Archives, especially as it related to Francis Minor's cases and career. I couldn't have written that chapter without your expertise.

- Patricia Lukas of the Albemarle Charlottesville Historical Society for direction regarding Edgehill, Charlottesville Female Academy, and Warner Washington Minor and his time at the University of Virginia.

- Amanda Ferrara and April C. Armstrong, from the Seeley G. Mudd Manuscript Library at Princeton University, for access to Francis's Princeton University records.

- Matthew Guillen and others at the Missouri State Archives, for their generous sharing of copies of documents related to *Minor v. Happersett* and Virginia's letter to Charles Henry Hardin.

- John McClure at the Virginia Museum of History and Culture, for help in researching the many Dabney Minors on the Minor family tree and their relation to slavery.

- Paul Anderson, at Christ Church Cathedral, and Susan G. Rehkopf, at the Episcopal Diocese of Missouri in St. Louis, for help in researching the Minors' religious affiliation and congregation in

St. Louis. Also, thank you to Marcy Hooker at Christ Episcopal
Church in Charlottesville, Virginia, for information on the Minor
family's history with your church.

- Lisa Caprino, at the Huntington Library for copies of the 1874
letters from Francis and Virginia, as well as Francis's university
examination.
- Washington University in St. Louis, for providing access to the
thesis "Woman Suffrage in Missouri, 1868–1880" by Loretta Mae
Walter, as well as use of the journal and microfilm databases.
- Kelly Kerney, at the Valentine Museum in Richmond, Virginia,
for access to the Woodward Collection, which contained the rare
letter from Virginia to her nephew, Douglas.
- Cecilia Brown, at University of Virginia Law Library, for access to
Francis's student records.
- Katherine Driggs, at Preservation Virginia, for her information on
and direction toward resources relating to Edgehill School.
- LeeAnn Whites, whose pioneering research into the legal maneu-
verings of Francis Minor was a huge source of information and
inspiration, as well as for her advice to look into Francis's career.
- Amanda Phillips, at the Woodlawn & Pope-Leighey House, for
direction on the possible location of Francis's home of Woodlawn.
- Jim Moore, of the Marshall County Historical Museum, for information on the Minors' time in Holly Springs, Mississippi.
- Donna McCague, from Central Rappahannock Heritage Center,
and Wayne Brooks, at the Caroline County Historical Society, for
genealogical information on the Minor family.
- Richard Buthod and Kat Bowen, from the Archives Department of
the St. Louis City Recorder of Deeds Office, and Tom Gronski and
Michael Stoecklin, from the Campbell House, for information that
helped me pinpoint the exact location of Minoria in St. Louis.
- Sarah Waitz, at the Center for Legislative Archives, National
Archives and Records Administration, for help in determining

whether or not the Minors signed the Universal Suffrage petition and other documents.

- Jan Scott, Shirley Breeze, Cynthia Hitschler, and Mary Mosley, for information on how the bust of Virginia Minor came to be at the Missouri State Capitol.

- Susan Wadsworth-Booth, of Kent State University Press, Paula R. Dempsey, at the University of Illinois, Chicago, and Accessible Archives, for access to back issues of the *Woman's Journal*, the full library of Susan B. Anthony's *Revolution*, and other periodicals.

Finally, thank you to everyone who reads this book. I hope you come to know and admire Virginia and Francis as I have over the last several years. It has been a joy and an honor to reconstruct their lives and help them take their rightful place in suffrage history.

ENDNOTES

INTRODUCTION

1. "Virginia L. Minor Buried," *St. Louis Republic*, August 16, 1894, 7.
2. Marshall D. Hier, "Virginia Minor's Struggle to Vote," *St. Louis Bar Journal*, Winter 1992, 39.
3. Donna M. Monnig, "Anything but Minor: The Suffrage, Equality, and Women's Rights Activism of Virginia L. Minor, 1867–1894" (master's thesis, University of Central Missouri, August 2018), 45.
4. Quoted in Elizabeth Cady Stanton, Susan B. Anthony, and Matilda Joslyn Gage, *History of Woman Suffrage*, vol. 4 (Rochester, NY: Charles Mann, 1887), 78, https://guten berg.org/files/29870/29870-h/29870-h.htm.
5. *Merriam-Webster*, s.v. "suffrage (*n.*)," accessed April 2, 2020, https://www.merriam -webster.com/dictionary/suffrage.
6. *Merriam-Webster*, s.v. "suffrage (*n.*)."
7. Online Etymology Dictionary, s.v. "enfranchise (*v.*)," accessed April 2, 2020, https://www.etymonline.com/search?q=enfranchisement.
8. Jane Henderson, "Women Wanted It—and Got It—100 Years Ago, but the Right to Vote Didn't Come Easy," *St. Louis Post-Dispatch*, July 30, 2020.
9. Jordan Lewis Reed, "American Jacobins: Revolutionary Radicalism in the Civil War Era" (PhD diss., University of Massachusetts–Amherst, February 2014), 58, https://scholarworks.umass.edu/cgi/viewcontent.cgi?article=1060&context=dissertations_1.
10. Sandra Weber, *The Woman Suffrage Statue: A History of Adelaide Johnson's Portrait Monument to Lucretia Mott, Elizabeth Cady Stanton and Susan B. Anthony at the United States Capitol* (Jefferson, NC: McFarland, 2016), viii.

PROLOGUE

1. "A Sad and Melancholy Event," *St. Louis Dispatch*, May 17, 1866, 4.
2. "Sad and Melancholy Event," 4.
3. "Sad and Melancholy Event," 4.
4. James M. Volo and Dorothy Denneen Volo, *Family Life in 19th-Century America* (Westport, CT: Greenwood Press, 2007), 29.
5. Suzanne Lebsock and Kym S. Rice. "A Share of Honour," in *Virginia Women 1600–1945* (Richmond, VA: The Virginia Women's Cultural History Project, 1984), 44.
6. Volo and Volo, *Family Life in 19th-Century America*, 29.

7. "Died," *St. Louis Post-Dispatch*, May 16, 1865, 1.

8. Friends of Oak Grove Cemetery, "Victorian Funeral Customs and Superstitions," accessed October 28, 2019, https://friendsofoakgrovecemetery.org/victorian-funeral-customs-fears-and-superstitions.

9. Mourning Society of St. Louis, "Consolations of Memory at Bellefontaine Cemetery," Bellefontaine Cemetery, St. Louis, MO, October 5, 2019.

10. "House of Mourning—Victorian Mourning & Funeral Customs in the 1890s," *Victoriana*, accessed February 12, 2019, http://www.victoriana.com/VictorianPeriod/mourning.htm.

11. Mourning Society, "Consolations."

12. Tanya D. Marsh, "A New Lease on Death," *Real Property, Trust and Estate Law Journal* 49, no. 3 (Winter 2015), 425, https://www.jstor.org/stable/24571002.

13. Mourning Society of St. Louis, "Campbell House by Candlelight," Campbell House Museum, St. Louis, MO, October 25, 2019.

14. "Died," 1.

15. Mourning Society, "Consolations."

16. "Died," 1.

17. Bernadette Loeffel-Atkins, *Widow's Weeds and Weeping Veils: Mourning Rituals in 19th Century America* (Gettysburg, PA: Gettysburg Publishing, 2012), 9; and Friends of Oak Grove Cemetery, "Victorian Funeral Customs and Superstitions."

18. Mourning Society, "Consolations."

19. Amy Weisser, "Virginia Minor: St. Louis Suffragist," in *Virginia Minor: A Woman in the Hall of Famous Missourians*, ed. Margot McMillen (Missouri Women's Network, 2015), 8.

20. Mourning Society, "Consolations."

CHAPTER 1

1. "Editor's Table," *Godey's Lady's Book* 60, 1860, 79.

2. Amy Weisser, "Virginia Minor: St. Louis Suffragist," in *Virginia Minor: A Woman in the Hall of Famous Missourians*, ed. Margot McMillen (Missouri Women's Network, 2015).

3. T. H. Breen, *Tobacco Culture: The Mentality of the Great Tidewater Planters on the Eve of Revolution* (Princeton, NJ: Princeton University Press, 1985), 82.

4. Breen, *Tobacco Culture*, 32.

5. Breen, *Tobacco Culture*, 107.

6. Breen, *Tobacco Culture*, 36–37.

7. Suzanne Lebsock and Kym S. Rice, "A Share of Honour," in *Virginia Women 1600–1945* (Richmond, VA: Virginia Women's Cultural History Project, 1984), 43.

8. Breen, *Tobacco Culture*, 87–88.

9. Lebsock and Rice, "A Share of Honour," 85.

10. Breen, *Tobacco Culture*, 35–36.

11. Breen, *Tobacco Culture*, 24. Text in brackets is my addition.

12. Breen, *Tobacco Culture*, 36.

13. Breen, *Tobacco Culture*, 91.

14. Breen, *Tobacco Culture*, 16.

15. Breen, *Tobacco Culture*, 48.
16. Breen, *Tobacco Culture*, 45.
17. Breen, *Tobacco Culture*, 55–56.
18. Breen, *Tobacco Culture*, 57.
19. Breen, *Tobacco Culture*, 177.
20. Breen, *Tobacco Culture*, 180–81.
21. Brooke Hunter, "Wheat, War, and the American Economy during the Age of Revolution," *William and Mary Quarterly* 62, no. 3, 508, https://www.jstor.org/stable/3491533.
22. Breen, *Tobacco Culture*, 200.
23. John Hammond Moore, *Albemarle: Jefferson's County, 1727–1976* (Charlottesville: University Press of Virginia, 1976), 88–89.
24. Hunter, "Wheat, War, and the American Economy," 509, 516.
25. Hunter, "Wheat, War, and the American Economy," 514.
26. Hunter, "Wheat, War, and the American Economy," 506.
27. Breen, *Tobacco Culture*, 204–5.
28. Lyon G. Tyler, ed., "Minor Family," *William and Mary College Quarterly Historical Magazine* 8 (1889–1900): 197–98.
29. "Fairfax County," in "County Militia Records," *Virginia's Colonial Soldiers*, Ancestry, 13–14.
30. Marshall Wingfield, *A History of Caroline County Virginia* (Richmond, VA: Press of Trevvet Christian & Co. 1924), 450.
31. "The Minor Family," in *Genealogies of Virginia Families* (Baltimore, MD: Genealogical Publishing Co., 1982), 3:705.
32. "The Minor Family," 3:706.
33. Minor Meriwether, *Lineage of the Meriwethers and the Minors from Colonial Times* (St. Louis: Nixon-Jones Printing Co., 1895), 128.
34. Jasper Burns, *Gale Hill: The Story of an Old Virginia House* (Waynesboro, VA: Pietas Publications, 2017), location 168, Kindle.
35. Sir William Gooch, Land Grant to John Minor 1735 August 19, University of Virginia Special Collections; Philip Alexander Bruce, Lyon Gardiner Tyler, and Richard Lee Morton, *History of Virginia*, vol. 5 (Chicago: American Historical Society, 1924), 43.
36. Burns, *Gale Hill*, location 188.
37. Burns, *Gale Hill*, caption and map location 164.
38. Burns, *Gale Hill*, location 192.
39. Burns, *Gale Hill*, location 184.
40. Burns, *Gale Hill*, location 1760.
41. Burns, *Gale Hill*, 233.
42. "Land for Sale in Albemarle," *Virginia Argus*, October 9, 1805, 3.
43. Dabney Minor II, various letters, University of Virginia, Albert and Shirley Jump Small Special Collections Library.
44. Minor family Bible.
45. Dabney Minor, "Last Will and Testament," *Orange County Will Book 6*, 2, University of Virginia. Special Collections.

46. Carol Barron, "Orange Co. VA, Chancery—Harris," in *Chancery—Orange County Order Bk*, 83, 84, 25, August 1803, http://files.usgwarchives.net/va/orange/court/h620 t1ch.txt.

47. Netti Schreiner-Yantis, *A Supplement to the 1810 Census of Virginia* (Springfield, VA: Netti Schreiner-Yantis, 1971), O-3.

48. Dabney Minor II, "Last Will and Testament"; Ruth L. Sparacio and Sam Sparacio, *Will Abstracts of Orange County Virginia (1778–1821)*, Will Books 3–5, 55.

49. CPI Inflation Calculator, https://www.officialdata.org/us/inflation/1798?amount =3498.

50. "Died," *Enquirer*, March 5, 1822, 3.

51. Minor family Bible.

52. "Died," *Enquirer*, 3.

53. Minor II, "Last Will and Testament," 52.

54. Minor II, "Last Will and Testament," 52.

55. *The Star*, October 3, 1894, 6.

56. Justin Glenn, *The Washingtons: A Family History: Volume 4 (Part One): Generation 8 of the Presidential Branch* (El Dorado Hills, CA: Savas Beatie, 2014); *New York Tribune*, August 25, 1894, 6; "Women of Note," *Evening Star Washington*, March 31, 1888, 3; Barry Christopher Noonan, "Descendants of Catherine Washington (1724–1750) and Col. Fielding Lewis (1725–1803)," June 23, 2008, https://www.angelfire.com/realm3 /ruvignyplus/039.html; "Descendants of Edward III: A Continuation of the Marquis de Ruvigny's The Plantagenet Roll of the Blood Royal," https://www.angelfire.com/realm3 /ruvignyplus/039.html.

57. *The Star*, October 3, 1894, 6.

58. *The Star*, October 3, 1894, 6.

59. Bruce, Tyler, and Morton, *History of Virginia*, 5:43.

60. *Virginia Militia in the War of 1812*, vol. II: "Muster Rolls," Ancestry, 170.

61. Merrow Egerton Sorley, comp., *Lewis of Warner Hall: The History of a Family* (Baltimore, MD: Genealogical Publishing, 1935), 132.

62. Moore, *Albemarle*, 107.

63. US Census Bureau, *1820 US Census*, Census Place: Hanover, Virginia, p. 63; NARA Roll: M33_138, Image: 78.

64. US Census Bureau. *1820 US Census*, Census Place: Spotsylvania, Virginia; Series: M19, Roll: 195, p. 91; Family History Library Film: 0029674.

65. Marie Frank, "It Took an Academical Village: Jefferson's Hotels at the University of Virginia," *Magazine of Albemarle County History* 59 (2001): 39.

66. Moore, *Albemarle*, 107.

67. Helen R. Pinkney, "Minor, Virginia Louisa," in *Notable American Women, 1607–1950: A Biographical Dictionary*, ed. Janet Wilson James, Paul S. Boyer, and Edward T. James (Cambridge, MA: Belknap Press of Harvard University Press, 1971), 550–51.

68. Frank, "It Took an Academical Village," 38.

69. Frank, "It Took an Academical Village," 32.

70. Frank, "It Took an Academical Village," 45.

71. Frank, "It Took an Academical Village," 35–36.

72. Frank, "It Took an Academical Village," 39.

73. Sandra Opdycke, "Minor, Virginia Louise," *American National Biography* (New York: 1999), 15:576–77.

74. Frank, "It Took an Academical Village," 39.

75. Frank, "It Took an Academical Village," 40.

76. Frank, "It Took an Academical Village," 40n12.

77. Marcus L. Martin, Kirt von Daacke, and Meghan S. Faulkner, *President's Commission on Slavery and the University: Report to Teresa A. Sullivan* (Charlottesville: University of Virginia, 2018), https://slavery.virginia.edu/wp-content/uploads/2021/03/PCSU -Report-FINAL_July-2018.pdf, 24–25.

78. John Hartwell Cocke Papers, Letter from W. W. Minor to Gen. John H. Cocke, October 1826, MSS640 Box 48, University of Virginia; Letter from W. W. Minor to John Hartwell Cocke, July 1828, MSS640 Box 48; Letter from W. W. Minor to Gen. John H. Cocke, October 25, 1828, MSS640 Box 56; W. W. Minor's Estimate of Expenses at U. VA., MSS640 Box 57.

79. Frank, "It Took an Academical Village," 41.

80. Frank, "It Took an Academical Village," 54.

81. Frank, "It Took an Academical Village," 54.

82. Frank, "It Took an Academical Village," 54n42.

83. John Hartwell Cocke Papers, Letter from W. W. Minor to Gen. John H. Cocke, October 25, 1828, MSS640 Box 56, University of Virginia.

84. Frank, "It Took an Academical Village," 49n33.

CHAPTER 2

1. Marcus L. Martin, Kirt von Daacke, and Meghan S. Faulkner, *President's Commission on Slavery and the University: Report to Teresa A. Sullivan* (Charlottesville: University of Virginia, 2018), https://slavery.virginia.edu/wp-content/uploads/2021/03/PCSU -Report-FINAL_July-2018.pdf, 21.

2. Marie Frank, "It Took an Academical Village: Jefferson's Hotels at the University of Virginia," *Magazine of Albemarle County History* 59 (2001): 47.

3. Martin, von Daacke, and Faulkner, *President's Commission on Slavery and the University*, 17.

4. Martin, von Daacke, and Faulkner, *President's Commission on Slavery and the University*, 18.

5. Frank, "It Took an Academical Village," 32.

6. Frank, "It Took an Academical Village," 48.

7. Frank, "It Took an Academical Village," 33, 39.

8. Frank, "It Took an Academical Village," 31–32.

9. Martin, von Daacke, and Faulkner, *President's Commission on Slavery and the University*, 16.

10. "Charlottesville: A Brief Urban History," Charlottesville Urban Design and Affordable Housing, last modified July 28, 2005, http://www2.iath.virginia.edu/schwartz/cville /cville.history.html.

11. "Charlottesville."

12. Frank, "It Took an Academical Village," 31, 44–45, 49.

13. Frank, "It Took an Academical Village," 55.

14. Range Community, "Aims of the Range Community," accessed June 19, 2019, https://student.virginia.edu/range/about.shtml.

15. Frank, "It Took an Academical Village," 47.

16. Frank, "It Took an Academical Village," 47–48n28.

17. Col. Charles. C. Wertenbaker, "Colonel Charles. C. Wertenbaker's Recollections of the University," *University of Virginia Alumni News* 2, no. 12 (February 18, 1914): 142.

18. Richard Mattson et al., *From the Monacans to Monticello and Beyond: Prehistoric and Historic Contexts for Albemarle County, Virginia* (Raleigh, NC: Garrow & Associates, Inc, 1995), https://nebula.wsimg.com/5a205c7473737250e207ca0603cda05c?AccessKeyId =D3E362E4074E454B6228&disposition=0&alloworigin=1, 63.

19. Loretta Mae Walter, "Woman Suffrage in Missouri, 1866–1880" (master's thesis, Washington University, St. Louis, Missouri, August 1963), 115, Washington University Special Collections.

20. "Elliott and Nye's Virginia Directory and Business Register—1852," Caroline County, New River Notes, accessed February 2, 2019, https://www.newrivernotes.com /topical_business_1852_elliott_nye_directory.htm.

21. William Timberlake, "William Timberlake to the Worshipful Court of Caroline County," letter, University of Virginia Special Collections.

22. Donna M. Monnig, "Anything but Minor: The Suffrage, Equality, and Women's Rights Activism of Virginia L. Minor, 1867–1894" (master's thesis, University of Central Missouri, August 2018), 14.

23. Annora Kelledy Koetting, "Four St. Louis Women: Precursors of Reform" (master's thesis, Saint Louis University, 1973), 8.

24. CPI Inflation Calculator, accessed January 23, 2019, https://www.officialdata.org /us/inflation/1849?amount=5.

25. Timberlake, "William Timberlake to the Worshipful Court of Caroline County."

26. CPI Inflation Calculator, accessed January 23, 2019, https://www.in2013dollars .com/1872-dollars-in-2016.

27. *Timberlake vs. Timberlake*, Complete Record, August 13, 1839–October 14, 1839, University of Virginia Special Collections.

28. CPI Inflation Calculator, https://www.officialdata.org/us/inflation/1839?endYear =2020&amount=1252.90.

29. Jasper Burns, *Gale Hill: The Story of an Old Virginia House* (Waynesboro, VA: Pietas Publications, 2017), location 1798, Kindle.

30. Olivia Taylor, "The Edgehill School," *Annual Report of the Monticello Association*, 1966–1967, 23, University of Virginia Special Collections; and John Hammond Moore, *Albemarle: Jefferson's County, 1727–1976* (Charlottesville: University Press of Virginia, 1976), 102.

31. Sandra Opdycke, "Minor, Virginia Louise," *American National Biography* (New York: 1999), 15:576.

32. Harold Mopsik, "A History of Private Secondary Schools in Charlottesville" (master's thesis, University of Virginia, 1936), 2, University of Virginia Special Collections.

33. Suzanne Lebsock and Kym S. Rice, "A Share of Honour," in *Virginia Women 1600–1945* (Richmond, VA: The Virginia Women's Cultural History Project, 1984), 41.
34. "From Thomas Jefferson to Martha Jefferson, 28 November 1783," Founders Online, https://founders.archives.gov/documents/Jefferson/01-06-02-0286.
35. Taylor, "Edgehill School," 21.
36. Taylor, "Edgehill School," 21.
37. Alma Turner Phelps, "Edgehill, the Old Home of the Randolphs," *Town and Country*, 1920, collected in "Edgehill," University of Virginia Special Collections, 2–3.
38. Phelps, "Edgehill, the Old Home of the Randolphs," 3.
39. Mopsik, *History of Private Secondary Schools in Charlottesville*, 24.
40. Phelps, "Edgehill, the Old Home of the Randolphs," 1.
41. Victoria LaFon Ballard, "Edgehill" (master's thesis, University of Virginia, Spring 1994), 9, University of Virginia Special Collections.
42. CPI Inflation Calculator, https://www.officialdata.org/us/inflation/1823?endYear =2020&amount=1800.
43. Phelps, "Edgehill, the Old Home of the Randolphs," 6.
44. Olivia Taylor, "Edgehill: 1735–1902," *Magazine of Albemarle History* 30 (1972): 63.
45. Taylor, "Edgehill," 63.
46. Taylor, "Edgehill," 20.
47. Bryan H. Mitchell, Virginia Historic Landmarks Commission Staff, "Edgehill," A National Register of Historic Places Inventory. June 15, 1982, 6.
48. Mopsik, *A History of Private Secondary Schools in Charlottesville*, 24.
49. Ballard, "Edgehill," 12; Taylor, "Edgehill: 1735–1902," 21.
50. Mopsik, *A History of Private Secondary Schools in Charlottesville*, 27.
51. Taylor, "Edgehill 1735–1902," 66.
52. Mopsik, *A History of Private Secondary Schools in Charlottesville*, 27.
53. Jeffery C. Weaver, *Albemarle of Old* (Arlington, VA: Jeffrey C. Weaver, 2001), 35, http://sites.rootsweb.com/~stevestevens/sprouse/albemarleofold.pdf.
54. Mopsik, *A History of Private Secondary Schools in Charlottesville*, 15–16.
55. Moore, *Albemarle*, 103.
56. Burns, *Gale Hill*, location 597.
57. Burns, *Gale Hill*, location 3182.
58. Burns, *Gale Hill*, location 1927.
59. Burns, *Gale Hill*, location 1927.
60. Mopsik, *A History of Private Secondary Schools in Charlottesville*, 25.
61. Ballard, "Edgehill," 12–13.
62. Patricia Rice, "Suffragist Heroine," *St. Louis Post-Dispatch*, February 7, 1975, 35.
63. Mopsik, *A History of Private Secondary Schools in Charlottesville*, 25–26.
64. Mopsik, *A History of Private Secondary Schools in Charlottesville*, 25.
65. Joan A. Cashin, "The Structure of Antebellum Planter Families: 'The Ties that Bound Us Was Strong,'" *Journal of Southern History* 56, no. 1 (February 1990): 62, https://www.jstor.org/stable/2210664.

66. John Farrar, *The Young Lady's Friend: A Manual of Practical Advice and Instruction to Young Females on Their Entering upon the Duties of Life after Quitting School* (London: John W. Parker, 1841), 191.

67. M. Nash, *Women's Education in the United States, 1780–1840* (New York: Palgrave Macmillan US, 2016), 8.

68. Ann Haddad, "Romance and Sweet Dreams: Mid-19th Century Courtship," *Merchant's House Museum*, February 13, 2018, 69, https://merchantshouse.org/blog/courtship.

69. "Determined to Vote," *St. Louis Times*, October 16, 1872; Missouri State Archives; Monnig, "Anything but Minor," 3.

70. Miss Marie Garesche Collins, "Marie Garesche Collins to CVR," November 1949, Missouri Historical Society.

71. Koetting, *Four St. Louis Women*, 6–7.

72. Marshall D. Hier, "Virginia Minor's Struggle to Vote," *St. Louis Bar Journal*, Winter 1992, 40.

73. Elizabeth Cady Stanton, Susan B. Anthony, and Matilda Joslyn Gage, *History of Woman Suffrage*, vol. 4 (Rochester, NY: Charles Mann, 1887), https://gutenberg.org/files/29870/29870-h/29870-h.htm.

74. "Virginia L. Minor Buried," *St. Louis Republic*, August 16, 1894, 7.

75. Ida Husted Harper, *The Life and Work of Susan B. Anthony: Including Public Addresses, Her Own Letters and Many from Her Contemporaries during Fifty Years* (Indianapolis, IN, and Kansas City, MO: Bowen-Merrill, 1899), 454. The photograph is also available online at House Divided: The Civil War Research Engine at Dickinson College, accessed January 24, 2019, https://hd.housedivided.dickinson.edu/node/23180.

76. Elizabeth Cady Stanton, Susan B. Anthony, and Matilda Joslyn Gage, *History of Woman Suffrage*, vol. 3 (Rochester, NY: Charles Mann, 1887), 260, https://gutenberg.org/files/28556/28556-h/28556-h.htm.

77. Stanton, Anthony, and Gage, *History of Woman Suffrage*, 3:260.

78. "The Sunday Promenade," *St. Louis Post-Dispatch*, March 31, 1889, 22.

79. Koetting, *Four St. Louis Women*, 42n160.

80. *The Star*, October 3, 1894, 6.

81. "Virginia Minor Buried,"

82. "Woman Suffragists," *Wheeling Sunday Register*, January 28, 1883, 2.

83. Stanton, Anthony, and Gage, *History of Woman Suffrage*, 3:257.

84. Monnig, "Anything but Minor," 57.

85. Monnig, "Anything but Minor," 3.

Chapter 3

1. "College of New Jersey Commencement," *Newark Daily Advertiser*, September 30, 1841, 2.

2. "College of New Jersey Commencement," 2.

3. "Princeton Literary Celebration," *New York Commercial Advertiser*, October 4, 1841, from the collections of the Seeley G. Mudd Manuscript Library of Princeton University.

4. Andrew Nicholson, "Byron and the 'Ariosto of the North,'" in *English Romanticism and the Celtic World*, ed. Gerald Carruthers and Alan Rawes (Cambridge: Cambridge

University Press, 2003), 130–50, https://www.cambridge.org/core/books/abs/english
-romanticism-and-the-celtic-world/byron-and-the-ariosto-of-the-north/76E0B114
DB84251BF8052CCE072DA5FB.

5. Varnum Lansing Collins, *Princeton* (New York: Oxford University Press, 1914), 196–97.

6. Collins, *Princeton*, 397–98.

7. April C. Armstrong, Seeley G. Mudd Manuscript Library, Princeton University, email to the author, June 10, 2020.

8. Henry Phillips Jr., "Obituary Notice of Peter McCall," *Proceedings of the American Philosophical Society* 19, no. 108 (January–June 1881): 213, https://www.jstor.org/stable/982242.

9. "Princeton Literary Celebration."

10. "Princeton Literary Celebration."

11. Teal Arcadi and Julia Grummitt, "Commencement Orations," Princeton & Slavery, accessed July 15, 2019, https://slavery.princeton.edu/stories/commencement.

12. Arcadi and Grummitt, "Commencement Orations."

13. Arcadi and Grummitt, "Commencement Orations."

14. "Death of Francis N. Minor," *St. Louis Post-Dispatch*, February 22, 1892.

15. "Died," *Virginia Herald*, October 20, 1824, 3.

16. "Died," *Virginia Herald*, 3.

17. Sarah Travers Lewis Anderson, *Lewises, Meriwethers and Their Kin* (Baltimore, MD: Clearfield, 2008), 289.

18. LeeAnn Whites, "A Tale of Two Minors," in *Women in Missouri History: In Search of Power and Influence*, ed. LeeAnn Whites, Mary Neth, and Gary R. Kremer (Columbia: University of Missouri Press, 2004), 106, 115.

19. The Minor family Bible, University of Virginia Special Collections, Charlottesville.

20. "Personal Property at Auction," *Richmond Enquirer*, October 26, 1832, 4.

21. John Hope Franklin and Loren Schweninger, *Runaway Slaves: Rebels on the Plantation* (New York: Oxford University Press, 1999), 255.

22. Robert Olwell, *Masters, Slaves, & Subjects: The Culture of Power in the South Carolina Low Country, 1740–1790* (Ithaca, NY: Cornell University Press, 1998), 198.

23. Marli Frances Weiner, *Mistresses and Slaves: Plantation Women in South Carolina, 1830–80* (Urbana: University of Illinois Press, 1998), 73.

24. Weiner, *Mistresses and Slaves*, 73.

25. Weiner, *Mistresses and Slaves*, 75.

26. Thavolia Glymph, *Out of the House of Bondage: The Transformation of the Plantation Household* (Cambridge: Cambridge University Press, 2008).

27. Franklin and Schweninger, *Runaway Slaves*, 252.

28. Franklin and Schweninger, *Runaway Slaves*, 252–53.

29. Franklin and Schweninger, *Runaway Slaves*, 254.

30. Glymph, *Out of the House of Bondage*.

31. Franklin and Schweninger, *Runaway Slaves*, 254.

32. Gene Carlton Clopton, *The Ancestors and Descendants of William Clopton of York County, Virginia* (Atlanta: Phoenix Printing, Inc. 1984), 249.

33. Clopton, *Ancestors and Descendants of William Clopton*, 107.

34. Peter Scales, *Slavery in Orange County Virginia*, manuscript ledger, 70 leaves, Orange County, Virginia, 1832–1835, https://www.vialibri.net/years/books/18775574/1832-slav ery-slavery-in-orange-county-virginia-a.

35. Lucy Minor, "Last Will and Testament," *Orange County Will Book 7*, 94, University of Virginia Special Collections.

36. Ann L. Miller, *Antebellum Orange: The Pre-Civil War Homes, Public Buildings and Historic Sites of Orange County, Virginia* (Orange, VA: Orange County Historical Society, 1988), 186.

37. Lucy Lane Erwin, *The Ancestry of William Clopton of York County, Virginia* (Rutland, VT: Tuttle, 1939), 171.

38. Whites, "Tale of Two Minors," 106.

39. John Goodwin Herndon, *The Herndon Family of Virginia, Vol. 2: The Herndons of the American Revolution* (Madison: University of Wisconsin Press, 1951), 114.

40. *The West Virginia Historical Magazine Quarterly* (Charleston, WV: West Virginia Historical and Antiquarian Society, 1901–1905), 243.

41. "Death of Francis N. Minor."

42. "College of New Jersey Commencement," 2.

43. "The American Whig-Cliosophic Society," Princeton University, accessed June 2, 2019, https://whigclio.princeton.edu/about/history.

44. "American Whig-Cliosophic Society."

45. "Francis Minor: Sketch of a Lawyer and Scholar St. Louis Has Lost," *St. Louis Republic*, February 21, 1892, 5.

46. April C. Armstrong of the Seeley G. Mudd Manuscript Library at Princeton University email to the author, June 10, 2020.

47. Helen R. Pinkney, "Minor, Virginia Louisa," in *Notable American Women, 1607–1950: A Biographical Dictionary*, ed. Janet Wilson James, Paul S. Boyer, and Edward T. James (Cambridge, MA: Belknap Press of Harvard University Press, 1971), 550–51.

48. *Catalogue of the Officers and Students of the University of Virginia Session 1842–1843* (Richmond, VA: Shepherd and Colin, 1843).

49. *Catalogue of the Officers and Students*, 15.

50. "Our History: Former Faculty: Tucker, Henry St. George (1841–1845)," University of Virginia School of Law, accessed August 12, 2019, https://libguides.law.virginia.edu/faculty/tucker.

51. Francis Minor, "Answers to an Examination in the University of Virginia Law School," BR Box 56 (24), Undergraduate Alumni Records, 19th Century, Series 2, Alumni Files 1800–1899, Princeton University, 1.

52. Minor, "Answers to an Examination," 2.

53. *Catalogue of the Officers and Students of the University of Virginia Session 1842–1843*, 16, 17.

54. "The Sunday Promenade," *St. Louis Post-Dispatch*, March 31, 1889.

55. "Man about Town," *St. Louis Republic*, September 8, 1889, 4.

56. "Francis Minor: Sketch of a Lawyer," 5.

57. "Temperance," *Holly Springs Gazette*, April 19, 1845, 2.
58. "Death of Francis N. Minor."
59. "The Court of Criminal Correction." *Daily Missouri Democrat*, October 20, 1869, 4.

CHAPTER 4

1. Ann Haddad, "Romance and Sweet Dreams: Mid-19th Century Courtship," *Merchant's House Museum*, February 13, 2018, 69, https://merchantshouse.org/blog /courtship.

2. LeeAnn Whites, "A Tale of Two Minors," in *Women in Missouri History: In Search of Power and Influence*, ed. LeeAnn Whites, Mary Neth, and Gary R. Kremer (Columbia: University of Missouri Press, 2004), 106; "Friend of My Heart: Courtship and Marriage in Early America," Virginia Museum of Fine Art Audio and Virtual Tours, accessed August 2, 2019, https://vmfa.museum/tours/wp-content/uploads/sites/14/2013/12 /VMFA_Courtship-and-Marriage-in-Early-America.pdf.

3. Albert H. Tilson Jr., "Gentry in Colonial Virginia," *Encyclopedia Virginia*, accessed May 18, 2019, https://encyclopediavirginia.org/entries/gentry-in-colonial-virginia/#start _entry.

4. Catherine Clinton, *The Plantation Mistress* (New York: Pantheon Books, 1982), 233; and Jane Turner Censer, *North Carolina Planters and Their Children, 1800–1860* (Baton Rouge: Louisiana State University Press, 1984), 84–88.

5. Bertram Wyatt-Brown, *Southern Honor: Ethics and Behavior in the Old South* (Oxford: Oxford University Press, 1982), 217–20.

6. Wyatt-Brown, *Southern Honor*, 219.

7. Joan A. Cashin, "The Structure of Antebellum Planter Families: 'The Ties that Bound Us Was Strong,'" *Journal of Southern History* 56, no. 1 (February 1990): 55n1.

8. Tiffany Nguyen, "Can You Marry a Second Cousin? What About a First Cousin or Half Sibling?" Tech Interactive, https://genetics.thetech.org/ask-a-geneticist/can -you-marry-cousin.

9. M. Islam, "Effects of Consanguineous Marriage on Reproductive Behaviour, Adverse Pregnancy Outcomes and Offspring Mortality in Oman," *Annals of Human Biology* 40 (2013), https://doi.org/10.3109/03014460.2012.760649; R. E. S. Tanner, "Fertility and Child Mortality in Cousin Marriages," *Eugenics Review* 49 (1958): 197–99, https://ncbi.nlm.nih.gov/pmc/articles/PMC2973226/pdf/eugenrev00040-0037.pdf; and Olubunmi et al., "A Review of the Reproductive Consequences of Consanguinity," *European Journal of Obstetrics & Gynecology and Reproductive Biology* 232 (January 1, 2019): 87–96, https://www.ejog.org/article/S0301-2115(18)31058-3/fulltext.

10. Cashin, "Structure of Antebellum Planter Families," 63–64.

11. Cashin, "Structure of Antebellum Planter Families," 66.

12. John C. Spurlock, "The Problem of Modern Married Love for Middle-Class Women," in *An Emotional History of the U.S.*, ed. Peter N. Stearns and Jan Lewis (New York: New York University Press, 1998), 319.

13. "Friend of My Heart."

14. Cassandra A. Good, *Founding Friendships: Friendships Between Men and Women in the Early Republic* (Oxford: Oxford University Press, 2015), 3–4.

15. Lisa McMahon, *Mere Equals: The Paradox of Educated Women in the Early American Republic* (Ithaca, New York: Cornell University Press, 2012), 119.

16. McMahon, *Mere Equals*, 120.

17. McMahon, *Mere Equals*, 119.

18. McMahon, *Mere Equals*, 118.

19. Cashin, "Structure of Antebellum Planter Families," 62.

20. "Friend of My Heart."

21. Jonathan Ned Katz, "The Invention of Heterosexuality," in *Sexualities and Communication in Everyday Life: A Reader*, ed. Karen E. Lovaas and Mercilee M. Jenkins (Thousand Oaks, CA: Sage Press, 2007), 27.

22. Good, *Founding Friendships*, 7.

23. Karen Lystra, *Searching the Heart: Women, Men, and Romantic Love in Nineteenth-Century America* (New York: Oxford University Press, 1989), 159.

24. Cashin, "Structure of Antebellum Planter Families," 66; Ann Haddad, "Mine and Mine Only: The Marriage Proposal and Engagement," *Merchant's House Museum*, March 20, 2018, https://merchantshouse.org/blog/engagement.

25. Haddad, "Mine and Mine Only."

26. Ann Haddad, "The Wedding 'Whirl and Vortex': Mid-19th Century Wedding Preparations," *Merchant's House Museum*, April 26, 2018, https://merchantshouse.org/blog/wedding-preparations.

27. "Friend of My Heart."

28. Haddad, "Wedding 'Whirl and Vortex.'"

29. Haddad, "Wedding 'Whirl and Vortex.'"

30. CPI Inflation Calculator. https://www.officialdata.org/us/inflation/1843?endYear=2020&amount=1000.

31. "Friend of My Heart."

32. "Friend of My Heart."

33. Haddad, "Wedding 'Whirl and Vortex.'"

34. "Virginia Births and Christenings, 1584–1917," FamilySearch database, Doodis Mynor in entry for Peter Mynor, citing reference FHL microfilm 873,777.

35. Philip Slaughter, *Memoir of the Life of the Rt. Rev. William Meade, D. D., Bishop of the Protestant Episcopal Church of the Diocese of Virginia* (Cambridge: John Wilson and Son University Press, 1885), 44, 52; *Journal of General Conventions of the Protestant Episcopal Church*, vol. 4 (New York: Daniel Dana Jr., 1847), 259.

36. Haddad, "Mine and Mine Only."

37. Mar. Reg., 1806–1868, fol. 84, Missouri Historical Society.

38. "Marriages," *Richmond Enquirer*, September 5, 1843, 3.

39. John Vogt and T. William Kethley Jr., *Albemarle County Marriages: 1780–1853*, vol. II (Athens, GA: Iberian Publishing Co., 1991), 569.

40. Helen R. Pinkney, "Minor, Virginia Louisa," in *Notable American Women, 1607–1950: A Biographical Dictionary*, ed. Janet Wilson James, Paul S. Boyer, and Edward T. James (Cambridge, MA: Belknap Press of Harvard University Press, 1971), 550.

41. "Victorian Era Weddings/Marriage Customs: Wedding Cakes, Celebrations, Dresses," Victorian Era, accessed July 3, 2019, https://victorian-era.org/victorian-era-wedding.html.

42. Haddad, "Wedding 'Whirl and Vortex.'"

43. "Victorian Era Weddings/Marriage Customs."

44. Haddad, "Wedding 'Whirl and Vortex.'"

45. Waterloo Village, "Wedding Traditions of the 19th Century," PartySpace, April 20, 2014, https://partyspace.com/newjersey/article/view/wedding-traditions-of-the-19th-century-441.

46. Ann Haddad, "'A Scene of Radiant Joy': The Wedding of Elizabeth Tredwell & Effingham Nichols," Merchant's House Museum, May 30, 2018, http://merchantshouse.org/tag/wedding.

47. Charles Wohlers, "Form of the Solemnization of Matrimony," in *The Book of Common Prayer, as Printed by John Baskerville*, accessed June 1, 2019, http://justus.anglican.org/resources/bcp/1662/marriage.pdf.

48. Haddad, "Scene of Radiant Joy."

49. Waterloo Village, "Wedding Traditions of the 19th Century."

50. Haddad, "Scene of Radiant Joy."

51. Waterloo Village, "Wedding Traditions of the 19th Century."

52. Haddad, "Scene of Radiant Joy."

53. Charles Astor Bristed, *The Upper Ten Thousand: Sketches of American Society* (New York: Stringer & Townsend, 1852), 43.

54. Minor Meriwether, *Lineage of the Meriwethers and the Minors from Colonial Times* (St. Louis: Nixon-Jones Printing Co., 1895), 133.

55. "Map Shewing the Connection of the Baltimore and Ohio-Rail-Road with Other Rail Roads Executed or in Progress throughout the United States." 1840. Library of Congress, https://loc.gov/resource/g3701p.rr003340/?r=0.112,0.536,0.203,0.102,0.

56. "History," Holly Springs Depot, accessed March 13, 2019, https://thehollyspringsdepot.blogspot.com/p/history-of-holly-springs-depot.html.

57. Dunbar Rowland, ed. "Hudsonville." *Encyclopedia of Mississippi History: Comprising Sketches of Counties, Towns, Events, Institutions*, vol. 1 (Madison, WI: Selwyn A. Brant, 1907), 892.

58. Lois Swanee, "Holly Springs Was a Planned Community," *South Reporter*, April 16, 1998, reprinted in "History of Holly Springs," accessed July 13, 2019, https://msgw.org/marshall/locales/hshist.php.

59. Annora Kelledy Koetting, "Four St. Louis Women: Precursors of Reform" (master's thesis, Saint Louis University, 1973), 6.

60. Suzanne W. Morse, *Smart Communities: How Citizens and Local Leaders Can Use Strategic Thinking to Build a Brighter Future* (John Wiley & Sons, 2009), 9.

61. Morse, *Smart Communities*, 9–11; National Park Service, "Utopias in America," last updated May 19, 2021, https://www.nps.gov/articles/utopias-in-america.htm.

62. Swanee, "Holly Springs Was a Planned Community."

63. Jim Moore, Marshall County Museum, email to the author, May 3, 2019.

64. Irene Walton, "Holly Springs, MS," Born and Raised in the South, September 29, 2008, https://ltc4940.blogspot.com/2008/09/holly-springs-ms.html.

65. John Mickle, "Former Editor Mickle Relates History of Holly Springs," *South Reporter*, November 25, 1965, reprinted in "The History of Holly Springs," accessed May 3, 2019, https://msgw.org/marshall/locales/hshist.php.

66. Cashin, "Structure of Antebellum Planter Families," 69.

67. Moore, email to the author.

68. "Treaty with the Chickasaw, 1832 (Also Known as Treaty of Pontitock Creek) October 20, 1832," Chickasaw TV Video Network, accessed July 13, 2019, https://www.chickasaw.tv/events/treaty-of-pontotoc-creek.

69. Moore, email to the author.

70. Walton, "Holly Springs, MS."

71. "Male School," *The Guard*, April 17, 1845, 4. This ad also ran on May 1, 1845, 4; May 22, 1845, 3; June 5, 1845, 5; and June 12, 1845, 5.

72. Moore, email to the author.

73. "Democratic Meeting," *Guard*, June 12, 1845, 3.

74. *Conservative, and Holly Springs Banner*, May 5, 1840, 4, for a sale of slaves.

75. "Temperance," *Holly Springs Gazette*, April 19, 1845, 2.

76. John B. Minor, *The Minor Family of Virginia* (Proffit, VA: John B. Minor, 1923), 106, 111, University of Virginia Special Collections.

Chapter 5

1. Frederick A. Hodes, *Rising on the River: St. Louis 1822–1850, Explosive Growth from Town to City* (Tooele, UT: Patrice Press, 2009), 682; Marshall D. Hier, "Virginia Minor's Struggle to Vote," *St. Louis Bar Journal*, Winter 1992, 39n6.

2. Christopher Alan Gordon, *Fire, Pestilence and Death: St. Louis, 1849* (St. Louis: Missouri Historical Society Press, 2018), 91.

3. Gordon, *Fire, Pestilence and Death*, 92.

4. Hodes, *Rising on the River*, 441.

5. Gordon, *Fire, Pestilence and Death*, 92.

6. Gordon, *Fire, Pestilence and Death*, 92.

7. Hodes, *Rising on the River*, 442–43.

8. Hodes, *Rising on the River*, 447–49.

9. Gordon, *Fire, Pestilence and Death*, 93.

10. Hodes, *Rising on the River*, 456–79.

11. Hodes, *Rising on the River*, 486.

12. Hodes, *Rising on the River*, 516–17.

13. Gordon, *Fire, Pestilence and Death*, 94.

14. Stephanie Lecci, "Curious Louis Finds Out What It's Like to Live in One Of St. Louis' Flounder Houses," St. Louis Public Radio, December 29, 2016, https://news.stlpublicradio.org/arts/2016-12-29/curious-louis-finds-out-what-its-like-to-live-in-one-of-st-louis-flounder-houses.

15. Hodes, *Rising on the River*, 502–4.

16. City of St. Louis, Deed Book, U3, September 17, 1845, 146.

17. City of St. Louis, Deed Book, U3, May 1, 1853, 147.

18. *St. Louis Directory*, 1847, 135.

19. *St. Louis Directory*, 1848, 166.

20. James. M. Kershaw, "Map and View of St. Louis, Mo.," 1848?, Library of Congress, accessed October 11, 2019, https://loc.gov/resource/g4164s.pm004380 /?r=0.448,0.401,0.349,0.175,0.

21. Valerie Battle Kienzle, *Lost St. Louis* (Charleston, SC: History Press, 2017).

22. Bonnie Stepenoff, "Disenfranchised and Degraded: Virginia L. Minor and the Constitutional Case for Women's Suffrage," in *Missouri Law and the American Conscience: Historical Rights and Wrongs*, ed. Kenneth H. Winn (Columbia: University of Missouri Press, 2016), 106.

23. "Virginia L. Minor Buried," *St. Louis Republic*, August 16, 1894, 7.

24. City of St. Louis, Deed Book, Y3, May 18, 1846, 519.

25. Charles Van Ravenswaay and Candace O'Connor, *St. Louis: An Informal History of the City and Its People, 1764-1865* (St. Louis, MO: Missouri Historical Society Press, 1991), 244.

26. Hodes, *Rising on the River*, 683.

27. Van Ravenswaay and O'Connor, *St. Louis*, 251.

28. "John Fletcher Darby Papers, 1785–1923," Missouri History Museum, accessed April 2, 2019, https://mohistory.org/collections/item/resource:102336.

29. Francis Minor, "To the Editor of the St. Louis Post-Dispatch," *St. Louis Post-Dispatch*, March 22, 1887, 6.

30. John Thomas Scharf, *History of Saint Louis City and County: From the Earliest Periods to the Present Day: Including Biographical Sketches of Representative Men* (Philadelphia: L. H. Everts, 1883), 1820.

31. Thekla Bernays, *Diplomatic Woman: An Essay. Read Before the Century Club of St. Louis, Mo* (St. Louis, MO: Nixon-Jones Printing Company, 1883).

32. "St. Louis Horticultural Society," *Daily Missouri Republican*, February 19, 1864, 3.

33. Van Ravenswaay and O'Connor, *St. Louis*, 251.

34. Hodes, *Rising on the River*, 693.

35. Van Ravenswaay and O'Connor, *St. Louis*, 253.

36. Scharf, *History of Saint Louis City and County*, 1752.

37. *Eighteenth Annual Report of the Board of Directors of St. Louis Public Schools: 1871–1872* (St. Louis, MO: Democrat Litho and Printing, 1873), 138, 140.

38. *Annual Report of the St. Louis Public School Library, 1871–72: Including a Historical Sketch of the Progress of the Institution during the Winter of 1872–73* (St. Louis, MO: Democrat Litho and Printing, 1873), 26.

39. "Death of Francis N. Minor," *St. Louis Post-Dispatch*, February 22, 1892.

40. "History," Christ Church Cathedral, accessed February 28, 2019, https://www .christchurchcathedral.us/about/history-2; Hodes, *Rising on the River*, 259.

41. Marrisanne Lewis-Thompson, "Christ Church Cathedral Celebrates 200 Years in St. Louis," St. Louis Public Radio, November 1, 2019, https://news.stlpublicradio.org /arts/2019-11-01/christ-church-cathedral-celebrates-200-years-in-st-louis#stream/0; "History," Christ Church Cathedral.

42. Hodes, *Rising on the River*, 678.

43. Nancy F. Cott, "Marriage and Women's Citizenship in the United States 1830–1934," *American Historical Review* 103, no. 5 (December 1998): 1452–53, https://www.jstor.org/stable/2649963.

44. Stepenoff, "Disenfranchised and Degraded," 106.

45. Charles K. Burdick, "Estates by the Marital Right and by the Curtesy in Missouri," *Bulletin Law Series* 2 (1914): 5–27, https://scholarship.law.missouri.edu/ls/vol2/iss1/3, 10.

46. Burdick, "Estates," 10.

47. Burdick, "Estates," 10–11.

48. Burdick, "Estates," 9.

49. Burdick, "Estates," 11.

50. Burdick, "Estates."

51. "Woman's Suffrage Association," *Daily Missouri Republican*, March 28, 1869, 3.

52. Lisa McMahon, *Mere Equals: The Paradox of Educated Women in the Early American Republic* (Ithaca, NY: Cornell University Press, 2012), 138.

53. Brenda Olsen Andrus, "Utopian Marriage in Nineteenth-Century America: Public and Private Discourse" (master's thesis, Brigham Young University, 1998), 24, https://scholarsarchive.byu.edu/etd/4484.

54. McMahon, *Mere Equals*, 122.

55. Robert L. Griswold, *Family and Divorce in California, 1850–1890: Victorian Illusions and Everyday Realities* (New York: SUNY Press, 1983), 120.

56. Cassandra A. Good, *Founding Friendships: Friendships Between Men and Women in the Early Republic* (Oxford: Oxford University Press, 2015), 7.

57. Griswold, *Family and Divorce in California*, 125.

58. Griswold, *Family and Divorce in California*, 127.

59. City of St. Louis, Deed Book N6, May 9, 1852, 539–40; Deed Book Y3, May 18, 1846, 518–19.

60. LeeAnn Whites, "A Tale of Two Minors," in *Women in Missouri History: In Search of Power and Influence*, ed. LeeAnn Whites, Mary Neth, and Gary R. Kremer (Columbia: University of Missouri Press, 2004), 107.

61. City of St. Louis, Deed Book N6, May 9, 1852, 540, emphasis added.

62. City of St. Louis, Deed Book N6, 541.

63. Loretta Mae Walter, "Woman Suffrage in Missouri, 1866–1880" (master's thesis, Washington University, St. Louis, Missouri, August 1963), 109, Washington University Special Collections.

64. City of St. Louis, Deed Book Q6, May 1, 1853, 226–27. This is equivalent to about $117,000 today.

65. City of St. Louis, Deed Book N6, May 1, 1853, 541.

66. City of St. Louis, Deed Book N6, 542.

67. Whites, "Tale of Two Minors," 106.

68. Nicole Evelina, "Minoria," Virginia and Francis Minor Memorial Institute, https://virginiaminor.com/minoria.

69. Whites, "Tale of Two Minors," 109.

70. They were created May 1, just before the transactions occurred; City of St. Louis, Deed Book N6, May 1, 1853, 539–42.

71. City of St. Louis, Deed Book Q6, May 1, 1853, 226–27.

72. Walter, "Woman Suffrage in Missouri, 1866–1880," 112–13.

73. Donna M. Monnig, "Anything but Minor: The Suffrage, Equality, and Women's Rights Activism of Virginia L. Minor, 1867–1894" (master's thesis, University of Central Missouri, August 2018), 17.

74. Monnig, "Anything but Minor," 16–17.

75. Monnig, "Anything but Minor," 18–19.

76. Whites, "Tale of Two Minors," 103; and Monnig, "Anything but Minor," 17.

77. James M. Volo and Dorothy Denneen Volo, *Family Life in 19th-Century America* (Westport, CT: Greenwood Press, 2007), 31.

78. Hodes, *Rising on the River*, 705.

79. Whites, "Tale of Two Minors," 106.

80. Gordon, *Fire, Pestilence and Death*, 13.

81. Margot McMillen, *The Golden Lane: How Missouri Women Gained the Vote and Changed History* (Charleston, SC: History Press, 2011), 26–27.

82. Gordon, *Fire, Pestilence and Death*, 25–26.

83. Gordon, *Fire, Pestilence and Death*, 26.

84. Hodes, *Rising on the River*, 553.

85. Volo and Volo, *Family Life in 19th-Century America*, 32.

86. Hodes, *Rising on the River*, 687.

87. Gordon, *Fire, Pestilence and Death*, 17–18.

88. Hodes, *Rising on the River*, 691.

89. Hodes, *Rising on the River*, 699.

90. Gordon, *Fire, Pestilence and Death*, 21.

91. Gordon, *Fire, Pestilence and Death*, 31.

92. Gordon, *Fire, Pestilence and Death*, 33.

93. Now Franklin Street.

94. Gordon, *Fire, Pestilence and Death*, 103.

95. Hodes, *Rising on the River*, 694–96.

96. Gordon, *Fire, Pestilence and Death*, 122–23.

97. Gordon, *Fire, Pestilence and Death*, 103–4.

98. Gordon, *Fire, Pestilence and Death*, 105–6.

99. Gordon, *Fire, Pestilence and Death*, 106.

100. Gordon, *Fire, Pestilence and Death*, 107.

101. Gordon, *Fire, Pestilence and Death*, 107.

102. *St. Louis Directory*, 1848, 166.

103. Warren Schmidt, "The Great St. Louis Fire of 1849," Lutheran Heritage Center & Museum, Perry County Historical Society, May 17, 2016, https://lutheranmuseum .com/2016/05/17/the-great-st-louis-fire-of-1849.

104. Hodes, *Rising on the River*, 695; Gordon, *Fire, Pestilence and Death*, 109.

105. Gordon, *Fire, Pestilence and Death*, 112.

106. Schmidt, "The Great St. Louis Fire of 1849" (map); Gordon, *Fire, Pestilence and Death*, 118.
107. Gordon, *Fire, Pestilence and Death*, 114–15.
108. Gordon, *Fire, Pestilence and Death*, 117.
109. Hodes, *Rising on the River*, 696; Gordon, *Fire, Pestilence and Death*, 118.
110. Gordon, *Fire, Pestilence and Death*, 119.
111. Hodes, *Rising on the River*, 699.
112. Gordon, *Fire, Pestilence and Death*, 37.
113. Hodes, *Rising on the River*, 700.
114. Hodes, *Rising on the River*, 37.
115. Gordon, *Fire, Pestilence and Death*, 27; and US Census Office, Seventh Census, 1850, 164.
116. Gordon, *Fire, Pestilence and Death*, 37–38.
117. Gordon, *Fire, Pestilence and Death*, 38.
118. Gordon, *Fire, Pestilence and Death*, 56.
119. Hodes, *Rising on the River*, 700.
120. Gordon, *Fire, Pestilence and Death*, 56.
121. Hodes, *Rising on the River*, 699.
122. Hodes, *Rising on the River*, 700.
123. Hodes, *Rising on the River*, 701.
124. Gordon, *Fire, Pestilence and Death*, 44.
125. Mourning Society of St. Louis, "Consolations of Memory at Bellefontaine Cemetery," Bellefontaine Cemetery, St. Louis, MO, October 5, 2019.
126. Hodes, *Rising on the River*, 702.
127. Gordon, *Fire, Pestilence and Death*, 36.
128. Gordon, *Fire, Pestilence and Death*, 53–54.
129. Gordon, *Fire, Pestilence and Death*, 14.
130. Hodes, *Rising on the River*, 702.
131. Hodes, *Rising on the River*, 705.

CHAPTER 6

1. Frederick A. Hodes, *A Divided City: A History of St. Louis 1851–1876* (St. Louis, MO: Bluebird Publishing, 2015), 10; William C. Winter, *The Civil War in St. Louis: A Guided Tour* (St. Louis, MO: Missouri Historical Society Press, 1994), 3.
2. Hodes, *Divided City*, 17.
3. "Immigrant Experience Research Guide," State Historical Society of Missouri, accessed July 2, 2019, https://shsmo.org/research/guides/immigrant.
4. "A Preservation Plan for St. Louis Part I: Historic Contexts," StLouis-Mo, accessed September 19, 2019, https://www.stlouis-mo.gov/government/departments/planning/cultural-resources/preservation-plan/Part-I-Peopling-St-Louis.cfm.
5. Milton D. Rafferty, *Ozarks: Land and Life* (Fayetteville: University of Arkansas Press, 2001), 62.
6. "Political Decline and Westward Migration," Virginia Museum of History and Culture, accessed May 5, 2019, https://virginiahistory.org/learn/story-of-virginia/chapter/political-decline-and-westward-migration.

7. Frederick A. Hodes, *Rising on the River: St. Louis 1822–1850, Explosive Growth from Town to City* (Tooele, UT: Patrice Press, 2009), 485–86, 689.

8. Winter, *Civil War in St. Louis*, 3.

9. Hodes, *Rising on the River*, 484–85.

10. Hodes, *Divided City*, 43.

11. Winter, *Civil War in St. Louis*, 3.

12. Hodes, *Divided City*, 27–28.

13. Steve Rowan, *Germans for a Free Missouri: Translations from the St. Louis Radical Press, 1857–1862* (Columbia: University of Missouri Press, 1983), 87.

14. Rowan, *Germans for a Free Missouri*, 90.

15. Record books accessed at the Missouri State Archives, St. Louis, April 19, 2019.

16. Record books accessed at the Missouri State Archives, St. Louis, April 19, 2019.

17. "Private Instruction," *Daily Missouri Republican*, January 21, 1848, 3.

18. *St. Louis Directory*, 1848, 166.

19. "Bounty Land Warrants," *Weekly Reveille*, July 5, 1847, 8.

20. A. J. D. Stewart, *The History of the Bench and Bar of Missouri: With Reminiscences of the Prominent Lawyers of the Past, and a Record of the Law's Leaders of the Present* (St. Louis, MO: Legal Publishing Company, 1898), 192.

21. Revolutionary War, the War of 1812, the Mexican War, and Indian wars between 1775 and 1855; "Bounty-Land Warrants for Military Service, 1775–1855," National Archives and Records Administration, https://www.archives.gov/files/research/military/bounty-land-1775-1855.pdf.

22. "About the Revolutionary War Bounty Warrants," Library of Virginia, last revised February 2021, https://lva-virginia.libguides.com/bounty-claims.

23. L. U. Reavis, *Saint Louis: The Future Great City of the World* (St. Louis, MO: St. Louis, by order of the St. Louis County Court, 1871), 514.

24. *St. Louis Directory*, 1852, 177.

25. *Report of the Commissioner of the General Land Office* (Washington, DC: US Government Printing Office, 1852), 152.

26. "Resignation," *Weekly Missouri Republican*, January 7, 1853, 5.

27. "Francis Minor," *St. Louis Globe-Democrat*, January 9, 1854, 3.

28. "Correspondence of the *Richmond Whig*," *Richmond Whig*, June 25, 1858, 1.

29. *Kennedy's St. Louis Directory*, 1857, 156.

30. "Minor & Sherrard," *Richmond Enquirer*, January 20, 1857, 3.

31. "Western Lands," *Richmond Enquirer*, February 20, 1857, 2.

32. "For Sale," *Daily Missouri Republican*, March 5, 1857, 3.

33. *Report of the Commissioner of the General Land Office*, 144–57.

34. *Report of the Commissioner of the General Land Office to the Secretary of the Interior for the Year Ended: 1857–1858* (Washington, DC: US Government Printing Office, 1902), 277; *Message from the President of the United States to the Two Houses of Congress at the Commencement of the . . . Session of the . . . Congress, with Reports of the Heads of Departments and Selections from Accompanying Documents*. Washington, DC: US Government Printing Office, 1858.

35. "Western Lands," 2.

36. Patricia Rice, "Suffragist Heroine," *St. Louis Post-Dispatch*, February 7, 1975, 35.

37. Supreme Court Case Files 1856, Respondent Land Records 1777–1969, Missouri Supreme Court Historical Database, Box 366, Folder 11, https://s1.sos.mo.gov/Records /Archives/ArchivesDb/supremecourt/Detail.aspx?id=4977.

38. "Died," *Daily Missouri Republican,* June 18, 1858, 2.

39. "Notice," *Daily Missouri Republican,* June 1, 1857, 3.

40. "Land and Lots for Sale Cheap," *Daily Missouri Republican,* June 26, 1857, 1.

41. "Notice," *Richmond Enquirer,* July 28, 1857, 2.

42. "Removals," *Daily Missouri Republican,* August 28, 1857, 2.

43. "Valuable Florissant Valley Land for Sale," *Daily Missouri Republican,* January 22, 1858, 2.

44. *Michael S. Mephaim et al. v. John Nevison,* Record 28: 1858 to 1859, Washington University Library, December 13, 1858, 274, http://repository.wustl.edu/concern/texts /vm40xw180.

45. "Dissolution of Law Partnership," *Daily Missouri Republican,* November 14, 1859, 4.

46. "Splendid Farm in St. Louis County," *Daily Missouri Republican,* May 21, 1859, 4.

47. "Law Notice of Edward Bates," *Daily Missouri Democrat,* November 23, 1860, 1.

48. Onward Bates, *Bates et al. of Virginia and Missouri: Onward Bates His Book. Printed for Private Distribution* (Chicago: Press of P. F. Pettibone, 1914), 77; Thomas Maitland Marshall, ed., *The Life and Papers of Frederick Bates* (St. Louis: Missouri Historical Society, 1926), 3.

49. Edward Bates, *The Diary of Edward Bates, 1859–1866* (New York: Da Capo Press, 1971), 49.

50. "Wm. N. White & Co," *St. Louis Globe-Democrat,* January 6, 1859, 3.

51. "In the Matter of Henry S. Gee and Peter R. Black," Record 29: 1859 to 1860, St. Louis Circuit Court, 168, Washington University Library, http://repository.wustl.edu /concern/texts/79408056h.

52. Christopher Alan Gordon, *Fire, Pestilence and Death: St. Louis, 1849* (St. Louis: Missouri Historical Society Press, 2018), 155.

53. Gordon, *Fire, Pestilence and Death,* 157.

54. Ebony Jenkins, "Freedom Licenses in St. Louis City and County 1835–1865," National Park Service, accessed November 20, 2019, https://www.nps.gov/jeff/learn /historyculture/upload/Freedom%20License%20Report.pdf.

55. Bob Moore and Ebony Jenkins, "Freedom Licenses," Gateway Arch, National Park Missouri, accessed May 11, 2020, https://www.nps.gov/jeff/learn/historyculture/freedom -licenses.htm.

56. Jenkins, "Freedom Licenses in St. Louis City and County," 7.

57. Adam Arenson, "Freedom through Bondage," *New York Times,* September 22, 2011, https://archive.nytimes.com/opinionator.blogs.nytimes.com/2011/09/22/free dom-through-bondage.

58. Jenkins, "Freedom Licenses in St. Louis City and County," 8.

59. Gordon, *Fire, Pestilence and Death,* 158.

60. Jenkins, "Freedom Licenses in St. Louis City and County," 3.

61. Gordon, *Fire, Pestilence and Death,* 158.

62. Arenson, "Freedom through Bondage."

63. Arenson, "Freedom through Bondage."

64. Arenson, "Freedom through Bondage."

65. US Supreme Court, Roger Brooke Taney, John H. Van Evrie, and Samuel A. Cartwright, *The Dred Scott Decision: Opinion of Chief Justice Taney* (New York: Van Evrie, Horton & Co., 1860), https://loc.gov/item/17001543.

66. Arenson, "Freedom through Bondage."

67. Jenkins, "Freedom Licenses in St. Louis City and County," 3.

68. Arenson, "Freedom through Bondage."

69. "Free Negro Bond for John Carter Brown," filed April 26, 1861, S. W. Eager Jr., secretary, Washington University Libraries, Freedom Bonds, Identifier: coll: fnb, fre1015.1861.000, mhs_A1643_B63f3i1015, http://repository.wustl.edu/concern/texts /v692t770r.

70. "Free Negro Bond for William Gaseway," filed & approved May 27, 1861, S. W. Eager Jr., secretary, Washington University Libraries, Freedom Bonds, Identifier: mhs _A1643_B63f4i1067, fre1067.1861.000, coll: fnb, http://repository.wustl.edu/concern /texts/np193b68m.

71. "Freedom Suits," National Park Service, accessed May 11, 2020, https://www.nps .gov/jeff/learn/historyculture/freedom-suits.htm.

72. Freedom Suit database index obtained from the Missouri Historical Society, May 11, 2020.

73. Missouri State Archives Case File 709, 1861, Term of Court 2., Box 15, Folder 40, ID 140269.

74. Donna M. Monnig, "Anything but Minor: The Suffrage, Equality, and Women's Rights Activism of Virginia L. Minor, 1867–1894" (master's thesis, University of Central Missouri, August 2018), 22.

75. Missouri State Archives Case File 712, 1861, Term of Court 2., Box 15, Folder 42, ID 140799.

76. Missouri State Archives Case File 51, 1865, Term of Court 2., Box 67, Folder 50, ID 143142; "The Courts," *Daily Missouri Democrat*, December 25, 1866, 4.

77. "Special Order No. 233," *Daily Missouri Democrat*, April 4, 1862.

78. "Judges of Election," *Daily Missouri Democrat*, October 13, 1865, 4.

79. Richard Franklin Bensel, *The American Ballot Box in the Mid Nineteenth Century* (Cambridge: Cambridge University Press, 2004), 18, 22, https://assets.cambridge.org /97805218/31017/sample/9780521831017ws.pdf.

80. Bensel, *American Ballot Box*, 18.

81. "Vigilance Committees," *Daily Missouri Democrat*, April 2, 1864, 1.

82. "We Are Authorized to Announce," *Daily Missouri Democrat*, October 31, 1863.

83. "Francis Minor, Esq.," *Missouri Daily Democrat*, October 31, 1863, 1.

84. William Hyde and Howard Louis Conard, eds., *Encyclopedia of the History of St. Louis: A Compendium of History*, vol. 4 (New York; Louisville, KY; St. Louis, MO: Southern History Company, 1901).

85. Walter Barlow Stevens, "Edgar R. Rombauer," *Centennial History of Missouri (the Center State): One Hundred Years in the Union, 1820–1921* (St. Louis, MO: S. J. Clarke, 1921), 587.

86. "Land Court," *Tri-Weekly Missouri Democrat*, March 18, 1856, 2.

87. Howard Louis Conard, *Encyclopedia of the History of Missouri: A Compendium of History and Biography for Ready Reference* (New York, and Louisville, KY: Southern History Company, Haldeman, Conard & Company, proprietors, 1901), 454.

88. *Journal of the Senate of the State of Missouri* (1863), 408.

89. *The Revised Ordinance City of St. Louis, No. 17188, Approved April 7, 1893* (St. Louis, MO: Nixon-Jones Printing Company, 1895), 1219S.

90. The original documentation for this and the following four paragraphs can be found in Missouri State Archives Case File, No. 1178, 9-1861, State v. Romyn, Circuit Court of St. Louis.

91. "Office of Public Administrator," *Daily Missouri Democrat*, February 4, 1862, 3.

92. "Office of Public Administrator," 3.

93. "Office of Public Administrator," 3.

94. "Provisional Judge of the Court of Criminal Correction," *Daily Missouri Democrat*, March 18, 1870, 2.

95. "Court of Criminal," *Missouri Republican*.

96. "Judge Minor," *Daily Missouri Democrat*, March 3, 1870, 4.

97. George B. Mangold, "Social Reform in Missouri: 1820–1920," *Missouri Historical Review* (1920): 193.

98. "Provisional Judge of the Court of Criminal Correction," *Daily Missouri Democrat*, March 8, 1870, 4.

99. "Wife with Whom He Lived 69 Years, He Dies of Grief," *St. Louis Post-Dispatch*, October 14, 1908, 9.

100. "A Curious Writ of Error," *Daily Missouri Democrat*, May 6, 1870, 5.

101. "The Court of Criminal Correction," *Daily Missouri Democrat*, October 20, 1869, 4.

102. "Provisional Judge of the Court of Criminal Correction," March 18.

103. "Provisional Judge of the Court of Criminal Correction."

104. *Daily Missouri Republican*, November 16, 1866, 3.

105. "The Courts," 4.

106. "Additional Returns of All Incomes Over $1,000," *Tri-Weekly Missouri Democrat*, September 14, 1866, 4.

107. *Edwards' St. Louis Business Directory*, 1867, 1065.

108. James Cox, *Old and New St. Louis: A Concise History of the Metropolis of the West and Southwest, with a Review of Its Present Greatness and Immediate Prospects* (St. Louis, MO: Central Biographical Publishing Company, 1894), 295.

109. "An Appeal to the Public," *Daily Missouri Democrat*, September 23, 1869, 4.

110. "Case No. 764: In the District Court of the United States," *Daily Missouri Democrat*, October 8, 1869, 4.

111. "Benj. L. Hickman," *Daily Missouri Republican*, May 9, 1869, 2.

112. Marshall D. Hier, "Virginia Minor's Struggle to Vote," *St. Louis Bar Journal*, Winter 1992, 39.

113. "Francis Minor: Sketch of a Lawyer and Scholar St. Louis Has Lost," *St. Louis Republic*, February 21, 1892, 5.

114. Michael Everman, Missouri State Archives, email to the author, May 3, 2019.

115. "Records of the Supreme Court," *Daily Missouri Democrat*, January 24, 1871, 4.

116. "Sixteenth Amendment," *Daily Missouri Republican*, December 7, 1876, 8.

117. H. Charles Ulman, *Trow's Legal Directory and Lawyers' Record of the United States: Containing a Convenient and Comprehensive Digest of the Laws of the Several States Touching Subjects of Commercial Law, Laws Relating to Estates of Decedents and Descent of Property, and the Insolvent Laws of the Several States, Blank Legal Forms and Instructions for Taking Depositions: Together with the Rules of the Supreme Court of the United States, Judiciary, Jurisdiction, and Terms of the United States Courts, with Counties Composing U.S. Districts: and a Complete Directory of All Practicing Lawyers throughout the United States* (New York: John F. Trow, 1875), 492.

118. Hier, "Virginia Minor's Struggle to Vote," 39.

119. *Charter, Constitution, By-Laws, Rules, Officers, Committees, and Members of the Bar Association of St. Louis* (St. Louis, MO: Hughes & Company, 1902), 6. It took another month for the paperwork to be filed and finalized.

120. "BAMSL History," Bar Association of Metropolitan St. Louis, accessed August 20, 2019, https://www.bamsl.org/index.cfm?pg=History.

121. "BAMSL History."

122. Hier, "Virginia Minor's Struggle to Vote," 38.

123. "Francis Minor: Sketch of a Lawyer," 5.

124. Missouri State Archives, Case File No. 51819.

125. "Francis Minor: Sketch of a Lawyer," 5.

Chapter 7

1. Lewis S. Gerteis, *The Civil War in Missouri: A Military History* (Columbia: University of Missouri Press, 2012), 4.

2. Abraham Lincoln, *Abraham Lincoln's Speeches* (New York: Dodd, Mead, 1923), 252.

3. Frederick A. Hodes, *A Divided City: A History of St. Louis 1851–1876* (St. Louis, MO: Bluebird Publishing, 2015), 331.

4. James Denny and John Bradbury, *The Civil War's First Blood: Missouri 1854–1861* (Boonville, MO: MissouriLife, 2007), 2.

5. Hodes, *Divided City*, 335.

6. "Record Group 005: Office of the Secretary of State: Special Collections, Constitutions and Constitutional Conventions, 1845–1875; arranged chronologically," Guide to Civil War Resources at the Missouri State Archives, accessed June 2, 2019. https://www.sos.mo.gov/archives/resources/civilwar/3.

7. Denny and Bradbury, *Civil War's First Blood*, 4.

8. Regina Donlon, *German and Irish Immigrants in the Midwestern United States, 1850–1900* (Cham, Switzerland: Palgrave Macmillan, 2018), 187.

9. "Record Group 005."

10. Harriet C. Frazier, *Runaway and Freed Missouri Slaves and Those Who Helped Them, 1763–1865* (Jefferson, NC: McFarland, 2004), 23.

11. "African-American Life in St. Louis, 1804–1865," National Park Service, last revised April 22, 2021, https://www.nps.gov/jeff/learn/historyculture/african-american-life-in-saint-louis-1804-through-1865.htm.

12. "Missouri Constitution of 1820," Local History Website of the SMSU Department of History, accessed April 12, 2019, https://images.procon.org/wp-content/uploads/sites /48/1820_mo_constitution.pdf.

13. William C. Winter, *The Civil War in St. Louis: A Guided Tour* (St. Louis, MO: Missouri Historical Society Press, 1994), 2.

14. Winter, *The Civil War in St. Louis*.

15. Denny and Bradbury, *Civil War's First Blood*, 3.

16. Winter, *Civil War in St. Louis*, 3.

17. Winter, *Civil War in St. Louis*, 21.

18. Hodes, *Divided City*, 17.

19. Winter, *Civil War in St. Louis*, 3.

20. "Slave Sales," National Park Service, accessed July 2, 2019, https://www.nps.gov/jeff /learn/historyculture/slave-sales.htm.

21. Dawn Dupler and Cher Petrovic, *St. Louis in the Civil War* (Charleston, SC: Arcadia Publishing, 2014), 15.

22. Denny and Bradbury, *Civil War's First Blood*, 4.

23. Dupler and Petrovic, *St. Louis in the Civil War*, 136; "Slave Sales."

24. "Missouri's Dred Scott Case, 1846–1857," Missouri State Archives, accessed December 18, 2018, https://www.sos.mo.gov/archives/resources/africanamerican /scott/scott.asp.

25. "Missouri's Dred Scott Case, 1846–1857."

26. "Missouri's Dred Scott Case, 1846–1857."

27. Sharon Cromwell, *Dred Scott v. Sandford: A Slave's Case for Freedom and Citizenship* (Mankato, MN: Compass Point Books, 2009), 10.

28. "Missouri's Dred Scott Case, 1846–1857."

29. Dupler and Petrovic, *St. Louis in the Civil War*, 9; Winter, *Civil War in St. Louis*, 27.

30. Dupler and Petrovic, *St. Louis in the Civil War*, 11.

31. "Record Group 0005."

32. LeeAnn Whites, "A Tale of Two Minors," in *Women in Missouri History: In Search of Power and Influence*, ed. LeeAnn Whites, Mary Neth, and Gary R. Kremer (Columbia: University of Missouri Press, 2004), 105.

33. Galusha Anderson, *The Story of a Border City during the Civil War* (Boston: Little, Brown, 1908), 9.

34. "Union Emancipation Central Committee," *Daily Missouri Republican*, March 24, 1863, 1.

35. "Union Emancipation Mass Meetings," *Daily Missouri Republican*, October 31, 1862, 2.

36. "Judicial Candidates at the Jacobin Convention," *Daily Missouri Republican*, September 4, 1863, 2.

37. For a full discussion of the evolution of Jacobian and abolitionist thought in the United States, see Jordan Lewis Reed, "American Jacobins: Revolutionary Radicalism in the Civil War Era" (PhD diss., University of Massachusetts–Amherst, February 2014), https://scholarworks.umass.edu/cgi/viewcontent.cgi?article=1060&context =dissertations_1.

38. Reed, "American Jacobins," v.
39. Reed, "American Jacobins," 181.
40. Reed, "American Jacobins," 1, 149.
41. Reed, "American Jacobins," 294.
42. Reed, "American Jacobins," 209.
43. Reed, "American Jacobins," 220.
44. "The Union Ticket," *Daily Missouri Republican*, September 12, 1863, 2.
45. "The Union Ticket," *Daily Missouri Republican*, September 7, 1863, 2.
46. "Judicial Candidates at the Jacobin Convention."
47. "The Union Ticket," September 7, 1863.
48. "The Union Ticket," *Daily Missouri Republican*, October 27, 1863, 2.
49. "Our History: Former Faculty: Tucker, Henry St. George (1841–1845)," University of Virginia School of Law, accessed August 12, 2019, https://libguides.law.virginia.edu/faculty/tucker; "Judge John Debos Sharp Dryen," Missouri Courts: Judicial Branch of Government, 2017, accessed August 12, 2019, https://www.courts.mo.gov/page.jsp?id=120116; "Judge William Van Ness Bay," Missouri Courts: Judicial Branch of Government, 2017, accessed August 12, 2019, https://www.courts.mo.gov/page.jsp?id=120132; Megan Vancil, "Judge Barton Bates," Missouri Courts: Judicial Branch of Government, 2018, accessed August 12, 2019, https://www.courts.mo.gov/page.jsp?id=130873; Eugene Morrow Violette, *A History of Missouri* (Boston: D. C. Heath & Company, 1918), 412–13.
50. Dupler and Petrovic, *St. Louis in the Civil War*, 11.
51. John Hammond Moore, *Albemarle: Jefferson's County, 1727–1976* (Charlottesville: University Press of Virginia, 1976), 124.
52. Louisa H. A. Minor, Personal Diary, 1855–1866, in Records of the Ante-Bellum Southern Plantations from the Revolution through the Civil War, series E, part 2, reel 26 (Frederick, MD: University Publications of America).
53. Marcia Pointon, "Slavery and the Possibilities of Portraiture," in *Slave Portraiture in the Atlantic World*, ed. Agnes Lugo-Ortiz and Angela Rosenthal (New York: Cambridge University Press, 2013), 48.
54. Moore, *Albemarle*, 124.
55. "Notice," *Conservative, and Holly Springs Banner*, May 5, 1840, 4.
56. "Also," *Conservative, and Holly Springs Banner*, May 5, 1840, 4.
57. Eric Foner, *Gateway to Freedom* (New York: W. W. Norton, 2015), 197–98.
58. Foner, *Gateway to Freedom*, 198–99.
59. T. Felder Dorn, *Challenges on the Emmaus Road: Episcopal Bishops Confront Slavery, Civil War, and Emancipation* (Columbia: University of South Carolina Press, 2013), 158–59, 238–39.
60. J. Johns, *A Memoir of the Life of the Right Rev. William Meade, D.D.* (Baltimore, MD: Innes & Company, 1867), 77, 476, https://archive.org/details/memoiroflifeofri00john/page/n9; "African-American Life in St. Louis, 1804–1865," 222.
61. Dorn, *Challenges on the Emmaus Road*, 39.
62. Hodes, *Divided City*, 23; William E. Colai, Lawrence O. Christensen, and Brad D. Lookingbill, *Missouri: The Heart of the Nation* (Hoboken, NJ: John Wiley and Sons, 2020), 124.

63. Winter, *Civil War in St. Louis*, 3.

64. Dupler and Petrovic, *St. Louis in the Civil War*, location 96, Kindle.

65. Cyprian Clamorgan, *The Colored Aristocracy of St. Louis* (Columbia: University of Missouri Press, 1999), 14–15.

66. "African-American Life in St. Louis, 1804–1865."

67. Clamorgan, *Colored Aristocracy of St. Louis*, 16.

68. "Thomas Jefferson to Edward Coles, August 25, 1814," Library of Congress, https://loc.gov/resource/mtj1.047_0731_0734.

69. Hodes, *Divided City*, 24.

70. Clamorgan, *Colored Aristocracy of St. Louis*, 7–8.

71. Jasper Burns, *Gale Hill: The Story of an Old Virginia House* (Waynesboro, VA: Pietas Publications, 2017), location 716, Kindle.

72. John B. Minor, *The Minor Family of Virginia* (Proffit, VA: John B. Minor, 1923), 106, University of Virginia Special Collections.

73. Minor Meriwether, *Lineage of the Meriwethers and the Minors from Colonial Times* (St. Louis: Nixon-Jones Printing Co., 1895), 133.

74. David L. Bright and National Archivists, "Biography of Minor Meriwether," accessed January 5, 2019, https://www.csa-railroads.com/Essays/Biography_of_Minor_Meriwether.htm.

75. Elizabeth Avery Meriwether, *Recollections of 92 Years, 1824–1916* (Nashville: Tennessee Historical Commission, 1958), 54, 63.

76. Maddie McGrady, "Battling Memory from Memphis: Elizabeth Avery Meriwether as Guardian of the Lost Cause" (paper, 2015 Rhodes Institute for Regional Studies), 18–19n62. https://www.rhodes.edu/sites/default/files/McGrady_RIRS_2015.pdf.

77. Meriwether, *Recollections of 92 Years*, 150.

78. Meriwether, *Recollections of 92 Years*, 204.

79. Burns, *Gale Hill*, location 763.

80. Lucy Lane Erwin, *The Ancestry of William Clopton of York County, Virginia* (Rutland, VT: Tuttle, 1939), 171.

81. "Monticello and the Civil War," Thomas Jefferson Encyclopedia, accessed June 23, 2019, https://www.monticello.org/research-education/thomas-jefferson-encyclopedia/monticello-and-civil-war.

82. Brendan Wolfe, "A Civil Occupation," *Virginia Magazine*, Spring 2015, https://uvamagazine.org/articles/a_civil_occupation.

83. Wolfe, "A Civil Occupation."

84. Louisa H. A. Minor, Personal Diary, 1855–1866, June 1862 entries.

85. "The Civil War on Civilians," History Engine, accessed June 18, 2019, https://historyengine.richmond.edu/episodes/view/2561.

86. Louisa, H. A. Minor, Personal Diary, 1855–1866, March 5, 1865.

87. Minor, Personal Diary, March 6, 1865.

88. Dupler and Petrovic, *St. Louis in the Civil War*, 7.

89. Denny and Bradbury, *Civil War's First Blood*, 13.

90. Denny and Bradbury, *Civil War's First Blood*, 13.

91. Denny and Bradbury, *Civil War's First Blood*, 4.

92. Denny and Bradbury, *Civil War's First Blood*, 5.

93. Hodes, *Divided City*, 340.

94. CPI Inflation Calculator, accessed January 23, 2019, https://www.in2013dollars
.com/1872-dollars-in-2016.

95. Dupler and Petrovic, *St. Louis in the Civil War*, 20.

96. Dupler and Petrovic, *St. Louis in the Civil War*, 26.

97. Dupler and Petrovic, *St. Louis in the Civil War*, 20.

98. Dupler and Petrovic, *St. Louis in the Civil War*, 25.

99. Dupler and Petrovic, *St. Louis in the Civil War*, 7.

100. Winter, *Civil War in St. Louis*, 38–39.

101. Dupler and Petrovic, *St. Louis in the Civil War*, 7.

102. Dupler and Petrovic, *St. Louis in the Civil War*, 19.

103. Dupler and Petrovic, *St. Louis in the Civil War*, 20.

104. Winter, *Civil War in St. Louis*, 39.

105. Anderson, *Story of a Border City during the Civil War*, 76.

106. Denny and Bradbury, *Civil War's First Blood*, 19.

107. Denny and Bradbury, *Civil War's First Blood*, 20.

108. Hodes, *Divided City*, 336.

109. Anderson, *Story of a Border City during the Civil War*, 85.

110. Anderson, *Story of a Border City during the Civil War*, 78.

111. Anderson, *Story of a Border City during the Civil War*, 78; Winter, *Civil War in St. Louis*, 50.

112. Anderson, *Story of a Border City during the Civil War*, 97.

113. Winter, *Civil War in St. Louis*, 50.

114. Anderson, *Story of a Border City during the Civil War*, 97.

115. Winter, *Civil War in St. Louis*, 52.

116. Hodes, *Divided City*, 352.

117. Winter, *Civil War in St. Louis*, 53.

118. Dupler and Petrovic, *St. Louis in the Civil War*, 7.

119. Anderson, *Story of a Border City during the Civil War*, 101.

120. Hodes, *Divided City*, 353.

121. Winter, *Civil War in St. Louis*, 62.

122. Tim O'Neil, "Oct. 12: The USS St. Louis, a Civil War Gunboat, Is Launched," *St. Louis Post-Dispatch* (St. Louis, MO), October 12, 2016, https://www.stltoday.com/news/archives/oct-the-uss-st-louis-a-civil-war-gunboat-is/article_42fced90-510a-57a5-a1ba-0d778a2a2750.html.

123. Denny and Bradbury, *Civil War's First Blood*, 34–44.

124. Mark A. Van Es, "Peculiar History of Women's Suffrage in Jasper County, Missouri" (master's thesis, Pittsburg State University, 2014), Electronic Thesis Collection 119, 23. https://digitalcommons.pittstate.edu/etd/119.

125. "Wilson's Creek: Oak Hills," American Battlefield Trust, accessed June 13, 2019. https://www.battlefields.org/learn/civil-war/battles/wilsons-creek.

126. William E. Parrish, Lawrence O. Christensen, and Brad D. Lookingbill, *Missouri: The Heart of the Nation* (Hoboken, NJ: John Wiley and Sons, 2020), 18.

127. Denny and Bradbury, *Civil War's First Blood*, 51.

128. "Wilson's Creek: Oak Hills."

129. Dupler and Petrovic, *St. Louis in the Civil War*, 35.

130. "Wilson's Creek: Oak Hills."

131. Earl. J. Hess, *Civil War Logistics: A Study of Military Transportation* (Baton Rouge: Louisiana State University Press, 2017), 151.

132. John S. Haller, *Battlefield Medicine: A History of the Military Ambulance from the Napoleonic Wars through World War I* (Carbondale: Southern Illinois University Press, 1992), 52.

133. Denny and Bradbury, *Civil War's First Blood*, 53.

134. "Railroads of the Confederacy," American Battlefield Trust, accessed March 2, 2019, https://www.battlefields.org/learn/articles/railroads-confederacy.

135. Parrish, Christenson, and Lookingbill, *Missouri*, 18.

136. Dupler and Petrovic, *St. Louis in the Civil War*, 96.

137. Parrish, Christenson, and Lookingbill, *Missouri*, 18.

138. Dupler and Petrovic, *St. Louis in the Civil War*, 96.

139. Roland G. Union, "A Bibliography of Sanitary Work in St. Louis During the Civil War," in *Missouri Historical Society Collections*, vol. 4: 1912–1913 (St. Louis: Missouri Historical Society, 1912), 75.

140. William E. Parrish, "The Western Sanitary Commission," *Civil War History* 36, no. 1 (1990): 20.

141. Linus Pierpont Brockett and Mary C, Vaughan, *Woman's Work in the Civil War: A Record of Heroism, Patriotism and Patience* (Philadelphia: Zeigler, McCurdy & Co., 1868), 630.

142. Anderson, *Story of a Border City during the Civil War*, 293.

143. Kathryn Elizabeth Bloomberg, "Charitable Women: Volunteerism in the St. Louis Ladies Union Aid Society" (master's thesis, University of Missouri–Rolla, 2009), 1, https://irl.umsl.edu/thesis/167.

144. John DePriest, *American Crusades: The Rise and Fulfillment of the Protestant Establishment* (Lanham, MD: Lexington Books, 2019), 40.

145. Garrett Ward Sheldon and Daniel L. Dreisbach, *Religion and Political Culture in Jefferson's Virginia* (Lanham, MD: Rowman & Littlefield, 2000), 13.

146. Eric Sandweiss, ed., *St. Louis in the Century of Henry Shaw: A View beyond the Garden Wall* (Columbia: University of Missouri Press, 2003), 29–31.

147. Bloomberg, "Charitable Women," 10–11.

148. Elizabeth Robertson, "The Union's 'Other Army': The Women of the United States Sanitary Commission," accessed April 10, 2019, https://www.gilderlehrman.org/sites/default/files/inline-pdfs/Elizabeth%20Robertson_0.pdf, 7.

149. G. K. Eggleston, "The Work of Relief Societies during the Civil War," *Journal of Negro History* 14, no. 3 (July 1929), 272, https://www.jstor.org/stable/2713854.

150. Brockett and Vaughn, *Woman's Work in the Civil War*, 44, 630.

151. Bernard Rostker, "The Civil War," in *Providing for the Casualties of War: The American Experience through World War II* (RAND Corporation, 2013), 78n13, https://www.jstor.org/stable/10.7249/j.ctt2tt90p.

152. Katharine T. Corbett, *In Her Place: A Guide to St. Louis Women's History* (St. Louis: Missouri Historical Society Press, 1999), 85–86.

153. Anderson, *Story of a Border City during the Civil War*, 293.

154. Winter, *Civil War in St. Louis*, 91.

155. Paula Coalier, "Beyond Sympathy: The St. Louis Ladies' Union Aid Society and the Civil War," *Gateway Heritage* 11, no. 1 (Summer 1990): 41–42.

156. Coalier, "Beyond Sympathy," 42, 44.

157. Hodes, *Divided City*, 418, and Sharon Romeo, "Vagrancy and Women's Rights in Reconstruction-Era St. Louis," *Sporting Woman* (Fall 2004): 24.

158. Bloomberg, "Charitable Women," 63.

159. Parrish, "Western Sanitary Commission," 20.

160. Brockett and Vaughn, *Woman's Work in the Civil War*, 638.

161. Parrish, Christensen, and Lookingbill, *Missouri*, 176.

162. Coalier, "Beyond Sympathy," 44.

163. Katie Moon, "The Ladies' Union Aid Society. Missouri Historical Society," Missouri Historical Society, August 2, 2019, https://mohistory.org/blog/the-ladies-union-aid-society.

164. Bloomberg, "Charitable Women," 68.

165. Bloomberg, "Charitable Women," 26–27.

166. Parrish, "Western Sanitary Commission," 18–19.

167. Helen R. Pinkney, "Minor, Virginia Louisa," in *Notable American Women, 1607–1950: A Biographical Dictionary*, ed. Janet Wilson James, Paul S. Boyer, and Edward T. James (Cambridge, MA: Belknap Press of Harvard University Press, 1971), 550–51.

168. Winter, *Civil War in St. Louis*, 16.

169. Parrish, "Western Sanitary Commission," 20.

170. Dupler and Petrovic, *St. Louis in the Civil War*, 97.

171. "Hamilton Rowan Gamble, 1861–1864," Missouri Digital Heritage, accessed January 15, 2019, https://www.sos.mo.gov/archives/mdh_splash/default?coll=hrgamble.

172. Winter, *Civil War in St. Louis*, 158.

173. Christopher Phillips, *The Rivers Ran Backward: The Civil War and the Remaking of the American Middle Border* (New York: Oxford University Press, 2016), 143.

174. "Hamilton Rowan Gamble, 1861–1864."

175. Phillips, *Rivers Ran Backward*, 143.

176. Winter, *Civil War in St. Louis*, 159.

177. Anderson, *Story of a Border City during the Civil War*, 291.

178. Anderson, *Story of a Border City during the Civil War*, 291.

179. Thomas Sweeney, "Civil War Era Medicine," Community and Conflict: Impact of the Civil War on the Ozarks, accessed March 2, 2019, https://ozarkscivilwar.org/themes/medicine.

180. Brockett and Vaughn, *Woman's Work in the Civil War*, 631.

181. Coalier, "Beyond Sympathy," 43.

182. Coalier, "Beyond Sympathy," 43; Gary Laderman, *The Sacred Remains: American Attitudes toward Death, 1799–1883* (New Haven, CT: Yale University Press, 1996), 97.

183. Rostker, "Civil War," 91.

184. Sweeney, "Civil War Era Medicine."

185. Parrish, "Western Sanitary Commission," 19–20.

186. Van Es, "Peculiar History of Women's Suffrage in Jasper County, Missouri," 25.

187. Coalier, "Beyond Sympathy," 44.

188. John I. Knight, "Horse Power," *Mechanics Magazine* 39 (July 1–December 30, 1843); Ann Norton Greene, *Horses at Work: Harnessing Power in Industrial America* (Cambridge, MA: Harvard University Press, 2008), 178.

189. "Couzins Collection," clipping, Missouri Historical Society.

190. Frederick A. Hodes, *Rising on the River: St. Louis 1822–1850, Explosive Growth from Town to City* (Tooele, UT: Patrice Press, 2009), 373, 409.

191. Bruce Nichols, *Guerrilla Warfare in Civil War Missouri, Volume III, January–August 1864* (Jefferson, NC: McFarland, 2014), 183.

192. Winter, *Civil War in St. Louis*, 159.

193. Winter, *Civil War in St. Louis*, 159.

194. US Record and Pension Office, *Missouri Troops in Service during the Civil War: Letter from the Secretary of War* (Washington, DC: Government Printing Office, 1902), 187–88.

195. Bloomberg, "Charitable Women," 63.

196. Sandra Opdycke, "Minor, Virginia Louise," *American National Biography* (New York: 1999), 15:576–77.

197. Margot McMillen, *The Golden Lane: How Missouri Women Gained the Vote and Changed History* (Charleston, SC: History Press, 2011), 17.

198. Virginia Minor, "Virginia Minor to unknown recipient, April 12, 1864," letter, Missouri Historical Society Library; and Francis Minor, *Record Books of Civil War Claims*, vol. 6, *Western Sanitary Commission*, Missouri History Museum Archives, St. Louis.

199. Bloomberg, "Charitable Women," 80.

200. Bloomberg, "Charitable Women," 80.

201. Fifth Street Hospital. "Acknowledgement." *Daily Missouri Democrat*, January 21, 1862.

202. Corbett, *In Her Place*, 133.

203. Annora Kelledy Koetting, "Four St. Louis Women: Precursors of Reform" (master's thesis, Saint Louis University, 1973), 8.

204. Amy Weisser, "Virginia Minor: St. Louis Suffragist," in *Virginia Minor: A Woman in the Hall of Famous Missourians*, ed. Margot McMillen (Missouri Women's Network, 2015), 6.

205. Winter, *Civil War in St. Louis*, 74.

206. Koetting, *Four St. Louis Women*, 7.

207. Koetting, *Four St. Louis Women*.

208. Dupler and Petrovic, *St. Louis in the Civil War*, 95.

209. Bloomberg, "Charitable Women," 63.

210. Bloomberg, "Charitable Women," 78; Brockett and Vaughn, *Woman's Work in the Civil War*, 631.

211. Bloomberg, "Charitable Women," 73.

212. Bloomberg, "Charitable Women," 67.

213. Bloomberg, "Charitable Women," 79.

214. Bloomberg, "Charitable Women," 80.

215. Brockett and Vaughn, *Woman's Work in the Civil War*, 640.

216. Bloomberg, "Charitable Women," 84.

217. Bloomberg, "Charitable Women," 84.

218. Bloomberg, "Charitable Women," 84.

219. Bloomberg, "Charitable Women," 79.

220. Dupler and Petrovic, *St. Louis in the Civil War*, 106.

221. Winter, *Civil War in St. Louis*, 74.

222. Winter, *Civil War in St. Louis*, 74.

223. McMillen, *Golden Lane*, 17.

224. Bloomberg, "Charitable Women," 79.

225. "Ladies Loyal League Meeting," *Daily Missouri Republican*, May 3, 1863, 3.

226. Editors of Encyclopedia Britannica, "Women's National Loyal League," *Encyclopedia Britannica*, accessed March 22, 2018. https://www.britannica.com/topic/Womens-National-Loyal-League.

227. Ellen Carol Dubois, *Suffrage: Women's Long Battle for the Vote* (New York: Simon & Schuster, 2020), 49.

228. At the time of this writing, the Center for Legislative Archives National Archives and Records Administration was closed due to the COVID-19 pandemic, so they could not verify whether Virginia was among the signatories. However, they do have her signature on other petitions.

229. "Universal Suffrage," Center for Legislative Archives, last updated July 25, 2019, https://www.archives.gov/legislative/features/suffrage.

230. Marvin A. Kriedberg and Merton G. Henry, *History of the Military Mobilization of the United States Army: 1775–1946* (Washington, DC: 1955), 99.

231. Lincoln Riddle, "The Drafts—Building the Armies of the American Civil War," War History Online, accessed April 3, 2019, https://www.warhistoryonline.com/american-civil-war/drafts-building-the-armies-civil-war.html.

232. Riddle, "The Drafts."

233. Michael T. Meier, "Civil War Draft Records: Exemptions and Enrollments." *Prologue Magazine* 26, no. 4 (Winter 1994), genealogy notes, https://www.archives.gov/publications/prologue/1994/winter/civil-war-draft-records.html.

234. Riddle, "The Drafts."

235. Meier, "Civil War Draft Records."

236. *Missouri Troops (Union and Confederate) in Service during the Civil War* (Washington, DC: Government Printing Office, 1902), 49.

237. "Militia Enrollment," *Daily Missouri Democrat*, July 28, 1862, 3.

238. "Missouri Troops in Service during the Civil War: Letter from the Secretary of War, in Response to the Senate Resolution Passed on June 14, 1902, Transmitting a Paper Prepared by the Chief of Record and Pension Office of the War Department, Showing Various Classes of Missouri Volunteers, Militia, and Home Guards in Service during the Civil War, and the Laws, Etc. under which They Were Raised; Also What Classes of Such Are Recognized by the War Department as Being in the Military Service of the United

States and What Classes Are Not So Recognized," June 18, 1902, Laid on the Table and Ordered to be Printed (Washington, DC: US Government Printing Office, 1902), 48.

239. "Missouri Troops in Service during the Civil War."

240. Office of Adjutant General, "Historical and Biographical Notes," 2.

241. "Instructions to Enrolling Officers from the Missouri Sixth District Board of Enrollment," July 30, 1863, Comingo, A[bram], Finley, R. W., and F. Cooley, Lexington, Missouri, to John D. McKown, McKown, John D., Papers, 1851–1897, C2335, f. 5, item 3, State Historical Society of Missouri–Columbia.

242. Whites, "Tale of Two Minors," 116.

243. Albert Sigel, "State Militia Bounty," *Daily Missouri Democrat*, July 18, 1868, 1.

244. Dupler and Petrovic, *St. Louis in the Civil War*, 7.

245. Dupler and Petrovic, *St. Louis in the Civil War*, 8.

246. Office of the Adjutant General, "Civil War Claims Commissions," Missouri State Archives, finding aid 133.10, accessed December 14, 2018, https://www.sos.mo.gov /CMSImages/Archives/resources/findingaids/RG133.10.pdf.

247. Kyle L. Sinisi, *Sacred Debts: State Civil War Claims and American Federalism 1861–1880* (New York: Fordham University Press, 2003), 34.

248. Claire Kluskens, "Union Civil War Pensions," National Archives Virtual Genealogy Fair, September 4, 2013, accessed January 23, 2019, https://www.archives.gov/files /calendar/genealogy-fair/2013/presentations/Wed12pm-Kluskens_Presenation-Union CivilWarPensions.pdf.

249. Donald R. Schaffer, "I Do Not Suppose That Uncle Sam Looks at the Skin," in *The Civil War Veteran: A Historical Reader*, ed. Larry M. Logue and Michael Barton (New York: New York University Press, 2007), 206.

250. Peter David Blanck and Michael Millender, "Before Disability Civil Rights: Civil War Pensions and the Politics of Disability in America," *Alabama Law Review* 42, no. 1 (Fall 2000): 31, https://law.ua.edu/pubs/lrarticles/Volume%2052/Issue%201/Blanck.pdf.

251. Schaffer, Donald R. "I Do Not Suppose That Uncle Sam Looks at the Skin," 203.

252. Sinisi, *Sacred Debts*, 45.

253. "War Claims Free of Charge," *Daily Missouri Democrat*, June 8, 1865, 3.

254. Blanck and Millender, "Before Disability Civil Rights," 31.

255. "Oath: Francis Minor," October 26, 1863, Missouri State Archives–St. Louis.

256. Letter, Francis Minor to the secretary of the Missouri Historical Society, November 12, 1866, in Minor, *Record Books of Civil War Claims, Vol. 1*, Missouri History Museum Archives–St. Louis.

257. Sigel, "State Militia Bounty," 1.

258. Sigel, "State Militia Bounty," 1.

259. Minor, *Record Books of Civil War Claims, Vol. 1*.

260. Minor, *Record Books of Civil War Claims, Vol. 4*.

261. Business cards in Minor, *Record Books of Civil War Claims, Vols. 2–7*, plus index.

262. G. C. Bingham, *Report of the Adjutant General of Missouri: Upon the Certificates Issued by the Missouri War Claims Commission of 1874* (Jefferson City, MO: Hugh Stephens Printing Company, 1907), 10.

263. Bingham, *Report of the Adjutant General of Missouri*, 11.

264. Bingham, *Report of the Adjutant General of Missouri*, 12.

265. Bingham, *Report of the Adjutant General of Missouri*, 11.

266. Rostker, "The Civil War," 103.

267. Bingham, *Report of the Adjutant General of Missouri*, 12.

268. Fifth Street Hospital, "Acknowledgement."

269. Weisser, "Virginia Minor," 7.

270. Elizabeth Cady Stanton, *The Collected Works: The Woman's Bible; The History of Women's Suffrage from 1848 to 1885; Eighty Years and More: Reminiscences 1815–1897* (Musaicum Books, 2018), https://www.google.com/books/edition/The_Collected_Works/Nx FkDwAAQBAJ?hl=en&gbpv=0.

271. Minor, *Record Books of Civil War Claims, 1864–1877, Vol. 6, Western Sanitary Commission*. Copy of this letter is included in the front papers.

272. Minor, *Record Books of Civil War Claims*.

273. Sandra E. VanBurkleo, "Virginia Minor: Women's Fight for Suffrage," in *100 Americans Making Constitutional History*, ed. Melvin I. Urofsky (Washington, DC: CQ Press, 2004), 137.

CHAPTER 8

1. Kathryn Elizabeth Bloomberg, "Charitable Women: Volunteerism in the St. Louis Ladies Union Aid Society" (master's thesis, University of Missouri–Rolla, 2009), 87, https://irl.umsl.edu/thesis/167.

2. Bloomberg, "Charitable Women."

3. Ellen Carol Dubois, *Suffrage: Women's Long Battle for the Vote* (New York: Simon & Schuster, 2020), 60.

4. Dubois, *Suffrage*, 61.

5. Dubois, *Suffrage*, 55.

6. Dubois, *Suffrage*, 55.

7. Dubois, *Suffrage*, 59.

8. Tom Rea, "Right Choice, Wrong Reasons: Wyoming Women Win the Right to Vote," Tom Rea, accessed May 5, 2020, http://tomrea.net/Right%20Choice%20 Wrong%20Reasons.html.

9. Rea, "Right Choice, Wrong Reasons."

10. Dubois, *Suffrage*, 62.

11. Dubois, *Suffrage*, 67.

12. Dubois, *Suffrage*, 67–68.

13. Helen R. Pinkney, "Minor, Virginia Louisa," in *Notable American Women, 1607–1950: A Biographical Dictionary*, ed. Janet Wilson James, Paul S. Boyer, and Edward T. James (Cambridge, MA: Belknap Press of Harvard University Press, 1971), 550–51.

14. Bonnie Stepenoff, "Disenfranchised and Degraded: Virginia L. Minor and the Constitutional Case for Women's Suffrage," in *Missouri Law and the American Conscience: Historical Rights and Wrongs*, ed. Kenneth H. Winn (Columbia: University of Missouri Press, 2016), 108.

15. DuBois, *Suffrage*, 55–56.

16. Dubois, *Suffrage*, 57.

17. Elizabeth Beaumont, *The Civic Constitution* (New York: Oxford University Press, 2014), 174.

18. Sandra L. Myres, *Westering Women and the Frontier Experience, 1800–1915* (Albuquerque: University of New Mexico Press, 1982), 217.

19. Myres, *Westering Women*, 217–18.

20. Donna M. Monnig, "Anything but Minor: The Suffrage, Equality, and Women's Rights Activism of Virginia L. Minor, 1867–1894" (master's thesis, University of Central Missouri, August 2018), 28; Loretta Mae Walter, "Woman Suffrage in Missouri, 1866–1880" (master's thesis, Washington University, St. Louis, Missouri, August 1963), 2, Washington University Special Collections.

21. Walter, "Woman Suffrage in Missouri, 1866–1880," 2.

22. Elizabeth Cady Stanton, Susan B. Anthony, and Matilda Joslyn Gage, *History of Woman Suffrage*, vol. 2 (Rochester, NY: Charles Mann, 1887), 140, https://gutenberg.org/files/28039/28039-h/28039-h.htm#FNanchor_107_107.

23. Stanton, Anthony, and Gage, *History of Woman Suffrage*, 2:141.

24. Stanton, Anthony, and Gage, *History of Woman Suffrage*, 2:142–43.

25. Stanton, Anthony, and Gage, *History of Woman Suffrage*, 2:142–43.

26. Stanton, Anthony, and Gage, *History of Woman Suffrage*, 2:143.

27. Stanton, Anthony, and Gage, *History of Woman Suffrage*, 2:143–44.

28. Beaumont, *Civic Constitution*, 174–75.

29. Carole Pateman, *1883–1993 [i.e. 193–1993]: Three Questions about Womanhood Suffrage* (Los Angeles: C. Pateman, 1993).

30. Adam Winkler, "A Revolution Too Soon: Woman Suffragists and the Living Constitution." *New York University Law Review* 79 (2001): 1521.

31. Monnig, "Anything but Minor," 27.

32. Frederick A. Hodes, *A Divided City: A History of St. Louis 1851–1876* (St. Louis, MO: Bluebird Publishing, 2015), 468.

33. Monnig, "Anything but Minor," 4.

34. Stanton, Anthony, and Gage, *History of Woman Suffrage*, 2:136–37.

35. Walter, "Woman Suffrage in Missouri, 1866–1880," 5.

36. Walter, "Woman Suffrage in Missouri," 42; Elizabeth Cady Stanton, Susan B. Anthony, and Matilda Joslyn Gage, *History of Woman Suffrage*, vol. 3 (Rochester, NY: Charles Mann, 1887), 599.

37. Amy Weisser, "Virginia Minor: St. Louis Suffragist," in *Virginia Minor: A Woman in the Hall of Famous Missourians*, ed. Margot McMillen (Missouri Women's Network, 2015), 7.

38. Stanton, Anthony, and Gage, *History of Woman Suffrage*, 3:599.

39. Monnig, "Anything but Minor," 29.

40. Quoted in Katharine T. Corbett, *In Her Place: A Guide to St. Louis Women's History* (St. Louis: Missouri Historical Society Press, 1999), 130.

41. "Want to Vote," *Daily Missouri Democrat*, March 11, 1867, 4.

42. Sandra Opdycke, "Minor, Virginia Louise," *American National Biography* (New York: 1999), 15:576–77.

43. Pinkney, "Minor, Virginia Louisa," 550–51.

44. *St. Louis Directory*, 1867, 579, 965, 973.

45. "Virginia Minor and Women's Right to Vote," National Park Service, January 16, 2018, https://www.nps.gov/jeff/learn/historyculture/the-virginia-minor-case.htm.

46. Christine Orrick Fordyce, "Early Beginnings," in "History of the Woman Suffrage Movement in Missouri," edited by Mary Semple Scott, *Missouri Historical Review* XIV, nos. 3–4 (April–July 1920): 289; Sandra E. VanBurkleo, "Virginia Minor: Women's Fight for Suffrage," in *100 Americans Making Constitutional History*, ed. Melvin I. Urofsky (Washington, DC: CQ Press, 2004), 137.

47. Linda K. Kerber, *No Constitutional Right to Be Ladies: Women and the Obligations of Citizenship*. New York: Hill and Wang, 1998, 102.

48. "Female Suffrage—Movement Organized for Missouri," *Daily Missouri Republican*, May 19, 1867.

49. Stanton, Anthony, and Gage, *History of Woman Suffrage*, 3:604.

50. Walter, "Woman Suffrage in Missouri, 1866–1880," 42.

51. Carol Ferring Shepley, "Virginia Minor," in *Movers and Shakers, Scalawags and Suffragettes: Tales from Bellefontaine Cemetery* (St. Louis: Missouri History Museum Press, 2008), 113.

52. "Woman's Suffrage: Meeting of the Association Saturday," *Daily Missouri Democrat*, January 18, 1869.

53. Katharine T. Corbett, *In Her Place: A Guide to St. Louis Women's History* (St. Louis: Missouri Historical Society Press, 1999), 130; Philip Foner, "Women and the American Labor Movement: A Historical Perspective," in *Working Women: Past, Present and Future*, ed. Karen Shallcross Koziara, Michael H. Moskow, and Lucretia Dewey Tanner (Washington, DC: Bureau of National Affairs, 1987), 160.

54. "Working Women's Meeting," *Daily Missouri Republican*, April 16, 1869, 3.

55. Walter, "Woman Suffrage in Missouri, 1866–1880," 68.

56. Mark A. Van Es, "Peculiar History of Women's Suffrage in Jasper County, Missouri" (master's thesis, Pittsburg State University, 2014), Electronic Thesis Collection 119, 25, https://digitalcommons.pittstate.edu/etd/119.

57. Kerber, *No Constitutional Right*, 102.

58. Linda Schelbitzki Pickle, "German Speaking Women in Nineteenth-Century Missouri," in *Women in Missouri History: In Search of Power and Influence* (Columbia: University of Missouri Press, 2004), 48.

59. Elyssa Ford, "Women's Suffrage in the Midwest," National Park Service, accessed October 16, 2018, https://www.nps.gov/articles/woman-suffrage-in-the-midwest.htm.

60. Linda Harris Dobkins, "Politics, Economic Provisioning, and Suffrage in St. Louis: What Women Said, What Men Heard," *American Journal of Economics and Sociology* 71, no. 1 (January 2012): 69, https://www.jstor.org/stable/23245178.

61. Dobkins, "Politics, Economic Provisioning, and Suffrage in St. Louis," 60.

62. Elizabeth Cady Stanton, Susan B. Anthony, and Matilda Joslyn Gage, *History of Woman Suffrage*, vol. 4 (Rochester, NY: Charles Mann, 1887), 791.

63. Monnig, "Anything but Minor," 29.

64. Francis Minor, "Mr. Minor to *The Revolution*," January 22, 1868.

65. Stanton, Anthony, and Gage, *History of Woman Suffrage*, 3:600.

66. Laura Staley, "Suffrage Movement in St. Louis during the 1870s," *Gateway Heritage* 3, no. 4 (Spring 1983): 38.

67. Vice president, Mrs. Beverly Allen; corresponding secretary, Mrs. Wm. T. Hazard; recording secretary, Mrs. Geo. D. Hall; treasurer, Mrs. N. Stevens, St. Louis, Missouri.

68. Stanton, Anthony, and Gage, *History of Woman Suffrage*, 3:599–600.

69. Stanton, Anthony, and Gage, *History of Woman Suffrage*, 3:599–600.

70. Corbett, *In Her Place*, 130.

71. "Woman Suffrage," *Daily Missouri Republican*, January 4, 1869, 3.

72. Elizabeth Cady Stanton, Susan B. Anthony, and Matilda Joslyn Gage, *History of Woman Suffrage*, vol. 2 (Rochester, NY: Charles Mann, 1887, 107), https://gutenberg.org/files/28039/28039-h/28039-h.htm#FNanchor_107_107.

73. "Woman's Suffrage," *Daily Missouri Democrat*, January 18, 1869, 4.

74. Kerber, *No Constitutional Right*, 103.

75. "Woman's Suffrage: Meeting of the Association Saturday," 4.

76. "Woman's Suffrage," *Daily Missouri Democrat*, 4; Shepley, "Virginia Minor," 113.

77. "Women's Suffrage Association," *Daily Missouri Republican*, November 13, 1870, 4.

78. "Woman's Suffrage," *Daily Missouri Democrat*, 4.

79. "Woman's Suffrage: Meeting," 4.

80. Stanton, Anthony, and Gage, *History of Woman Suffrage*, 3:601; William E. Parrish, Lawrence O. Christensen, and Brad D. Lookingbill, *Missouri: The Heart of the Nation* (Hoboken, NJ: John Wiley and Sons, 2020), 212.

81. Mona Cook Morris, "The History of Woman Suffrage in Missouri, 1867–1901," *Missouri Historical Review* 25, no. 1 (October 1930): 70.

82. "Woman's Rights Meeting," *Daily Missouri Republican*, February 14, 1869, 2.

83. "Woman's Rights Meeting."

84. "Woman's Suffrage," *Daily Missouri Democrat*, 4.

85. "Woman's Rights Meeting."

86. Stanton, Anthony, and Gage, *History of Woman Suffrage*, 3:601.

87. Parrish, Christenson, and Lookingbill, *Missouri*, 212.

88. Morris, "History of Woman Suffrage in Missouri, 1867–1901," 70.

89. "Woman's Rights Meeting."

90. "Woman's Rights Meeting."

91. Parrish, Christenson, and Lookingbill, *Missouri*, 212.

92. Stanton, Anthony, and Gage, *History of Woman Suffrage*, 3: 601.

CHAPTER 9

1. ERA, "ERA History," https://www.equalrightsamendment.org/history.

2. A. E. Meriwether, "Meriwether Denounces the Louisville Woman Resolution," *St. Louis Post-Dispatch*, May 21, 1893, 32.

3. "All Privileges and Immunities of Citizens in the Several States," Legal Information Institute, Cornell Law School, accessed May 23, 2019, https://www.law.cornell.edu/constitution-conan/article-4/section-2/clause-1/all-privileges-and-immunities-of-citizens-in-the-several-states.

4. Elizabeth Cady Stanton, Susan B. Anthony, and Matilda Joslyn Gage, *History of Woman Suffrage*, vol. 2 (Rochester, NY: Charles Mann, 1887), 450–56, 662–65, https://

gutenberg.org/files/28039/28039-h/28039-h.htm#FNanchor_107_107, for a detailed account of these arguments. For a shorter version, see Ellen Carol Dubois, *Woman Suffrage and Women's Rights* (New York: New York University Press, 1998), 98–99, 117–18.

5. Adam Winkler, "A Revolution Too Soon: Woman Suffragists and the Living Constitution." *New York University Law Review* 79 (2001): 1459, 1469.

6. Winkler, "Revolution Too Soon," 1468–69.

7. Winkler, "Revolution Too Soon," 1470–71.

8. Angela G. Ray and Cindy Koenig Richards, "Inventing Citizens Imagining Gender Justice: The Suffrage Rhetoric of Virginia and Francis Minor," *Quarterly Journal of Speech* 93, no. 4 (November 2007): 375.

9. Ellen Carol Dubois, *Suffrage: Women's Long Battle for the Vote* (New York: Simon & Schuster, 2020), 73.

10. Dubois, *Suffrage*, 72–73.

11. Dubois, *Suffrage*, 75.

12. Dubois, *Suffrage*, 75.

13. Frederick Douglass, Letter, Frederick Douglass to Josephine Griffing, September 27, 1868, Ms. Griffing Papers, Columbia University.

14. Ida Husted Harper, *The Life and Work of Susan B. Anthony: Including Public Addresses, Her Own Letters and Many from Her Contemporaries during Fifty Years* (Indianapolis, IN, and Kansas City, MO: Bowen-Merrill, 1899), 324.

15. Stanton, Anthony, and Gage, *History of Woman Suffrage*, 2:383–84.

16. Dubois, *Suffrage*, 79–81.

17. Dubois, *Suffrage*, 80–81.

18. Dubois, *Suffrage*, 81.

19. Elizabeth Cady Stanton, Susan B. Anthony, and Matilda Joslyn Gage, *History of Woman Suffrage*, vol. 3 (Rochester, NY: Charles Mann, 1887), 603–4.

20. Dubois, *Suffrage*, 75.

21. Stanton, Anthony, and Gage, *History of Woman Suffrage*, 2:370.

22. Joe Holleman, "Spotlight: Cobblestone, Brick Streets Cling Tight to Hang On in St. Louis," *St. Louis Post-Dispatch*, November 11, 2017, https://www.stltoday.com/news /local/columns/joe-holleman/spotlight-cobblestone-brick-streets-cling-tight-to-hang -on-in-st-louis/article_4e1d88a3-cc00-5714-99c4-545be32189e5.html.

23. "Woman Suffrage, Convention at Mercantile Library Hall Yesterday," *Missouri Republican*, October 7, 1869, extra sheet.

24. "Convention of Publishers and Editors," *Daily Missouri Democrat*, May 20, 1869, 2.

25. Vadim Rossman, *Capital Cities: Varieties and Patterns of Development and Relocation* (London: Taylor & Francis, 2018), foreword.

26. Dan Thurber, "St. Louis, Missouri: Capital of the United States?" Untapped New York, April 19, 2016, https://untappedcities.com/2016/04/19/st-louis-missouri-capital -of-the-united-states.

27. Joseph Medill, "Removal of the Capital," *Chicago Daily Tribune*, July 5, 1869, 2.

28. Frederick A. Hodes, *A Divided City: A History of St. Louis 1851–1876* (St. Louis, MO: Bluebird Publishing, 2015), 504–5.

29. Thurber, "St. Louis, Missouri."

30. Ray and Richards, "Inventing Citizens Imagining Gender Justice," 378.

31. Elizabeth Cady Stanton, *The Collected Works: The Woman's Bible; The History of Women's Suffrage from 1848 to 1885; Eighty Years and More: Reminiscences 1815–1897* (Musaicum Books, 2018), https://www.google.com/books/edition/The_Collected_Works/NxFkDwAAQBAJ?hl=en&gbpv=0.

32. Stanton, Anthony, and Gage, *History of Woman Suffrage*, 2:410.

33. Stanton, *Collected Works*.

34. Linda Kerber, "'Ourselves and Our Daughters Forever': Women and the Constitution: 1787–1876," in *One Woman, One Vote*, ed. Marjorie Spruill Wheeler (Troutdale, OR: NewSage Press, 1995), 34.

35. Quoted in Henry Campbell Black, *Handbook on the Construction and Interpretation of the Laws* (St. Paul, MN: West Publishing Company, 1911), 22.

36. Robert P. J. Cooney, *Winning the Vote: The Triumph of the American Woman Suffrage Movement* (Santa Cruz, CA: American Graphic Press, 2005), 33.

37. Elizabeth Cady Stanton, Susan B. Anthony, and Matilda Joslyn Gage, *History of Woman Suffrage*, vol. 4 (Rochester, NY: Charles Mann, 1887), 3.

38. Laura Staley, "Suffrage Movement in St. Louis during the 1870s," *Gateway Heritage* 3, no. 4 (Spring 1983): 38.

39. Stanton, Anthony, and Gage, *History of Woman Suffrage*, 2:408.

40. "7 Suffragist Men and the Importance of Allies," Turning Point Suffragist Memorial, July 7, 2020, https://suffragistmemorial.org/7-suffragist-men-and-the-importance-of-allies.

41. Joan Hoff, *Law, Gender and Injustice, A Legal History of U.S. Women* (New York: New York University Press, 1991), 170–77; LeeAnn Whites, "A Tale of Two Minors," in *Women in Missouri History: In Search of Power and Influence*, ed. LeeAnn Whites, Mary Neth, and Gary R. Kremer (Columbia: University of Missouri Press, 2004), 104n5.

42. These will be discussed at length at the end of chapter 10.

43. Winkler, "Revolution Too Soon," 1458.

44. Winkler, "Revolution Too Soon," 1456.

45. *Missouri v. Holland*, 252 US 416 (1920).

46. Ray and Richards, "Inventing Citizens Imagining Gender Justice," 377.

47. Winkler, "Revolution Too Soon," 1463.

48. Jan Lewis, "'Of Every Age Sex & Condition': The Representation of Women in the Constitution," *Journal of the Early Republic* 15, no. 3, special issue on "Gender in the Early Republic" (Autumn 1995): 359, accessed November 28, 2018, https://www.jstor.org/stable/3124115.

49. Ray and Richards, "Inventing Citizens Imagining Gender Justice," 380.

50. Lewis, "'Of Every Age Sex & Condition,'" 359.

51. David M. Dismore, "Live-Blogging Women's History: March 29, 1875," *Ms. Magazine*, March 29, 2011, https://msmagazine.com/2011/03/29/live-blogging-womens-history-march-29-1875.

52. Ray and Richards, "Inventing Citizens Imagining Gender Justice," 380.

53. Stanton, Anthony, and Gage, *History of Woman Suffrage*, 3:602–3.

54. Donna M. Monnig, "Anything but Minor: The Suffrage, Equality, and Women's Rights Activism of Virginia L. Minor, 1867–1894" (master's thesis, University of Central Missouri, August 2018), 33.

55. Ray and Richards, "Inventing Citizens Imagining Gender Justice," 377.

56. Anna D. Gordon, *The Selected Papers of Elizabeth Cady Stanton and Susan B. Anthony, Volume II* (New Brunswick, NJ: Rutgers University Press, 2000), xxiv.

57. Gordon, *Selected Papers*, II:348.

58. Theodore Tilton, The Golden Age *Tracts, No. 2. The Constitution: A Title-Deed to Woman's Franchise: A Letter to Charles Sumner* (New York: Office of the *Golden Age*, 1871), 3, https://loc.gov/resource/rbnawsa.n3452/?sp=1.

59. Tilton, The Golden Age *Tracts, No. 2*, 4.

60. Tilton, The Golden Age *Tracts, No. 2*, 10.

61. Mary Gabriel, *Notorious Victoria: The Life of Victoria Woodhull, Uncensored* (New York: Algonquin Books, 1998), 54.

62. Gabriel, *Notorious Victoria*, 73.

63. Victoria Claflin Woodhull, *The Victoria Woodhull Reader*, ed. Madeleine B. Stern (Weston, MA: M & S Press, 1974), 95.

64. Jill Lepore, "Rock, Paper, Scissors: How We Used to Vote," *New Yorker*, October 6, 2008, https://www.newyorker.com/magazine/2008/10/13/rock-paper-scissors.

65. Richard Franklin Bensel, *The American Ballot Box in the Mid-Nineteenth Century* (Cambridge: Cambridge University Press, 2004), 11, 13, https://assets.cambridge.org/97805218/31017/sample/9780521831017ws.pdf.

66. Bensel, *American Ballot Box*, 14.

67. Bensel, *American Ballot Box*, 11, 13.

68. Bensel, *American Ballot Box*, 56.

69. Lepore, "How We Used to Vote."

70. Bensel, *American Ballot Box*, 56.

71. Angela Ray, "The Rhetorical Ritual of Citizenship: Women's Voting as Public Performance, 1868–1875," *Quarterly Journal of Speech* 93, no. 1 (February 2017): 1; Bensel, *American Ballot Box*, 9.

72. Bensel, *American Ballot Box*, 20–22.

73. Ray, "Rhetorical Ritual of Citizenship," 2.

74. Lepore, "How We Used to Vote," 240.

75. Ray, "Rhetorical Ritual of Citizenship," 3.

76. Ray, "Rhetorical Ritual of Citizenship," 5.

77. Kathi Kern and Linda Levstik, "Teaching the New Departure: The United States vs. Susan B. Anthony," *Journal of the Civil War Era* 2, no. 1 (March 2012): 127.

78. Cooney, *Winning the Vote*, 33.

79. Ray, "Rhetorical Ritual of Citizenship," 16.

80. Leslie Friedman Goldstein, *The Constitutional Rights of Women: Cases in Law and Social Change* (New York: Oxford University Press, 2007), 73.

81. Ray, "Rhetorical Ritual of Citizenship," 7.

82. Ray, "Rhetorical Ritual of Citizenship," 15.

83. Ray, "Rhetorical Ritual of Citizenship," 25n68.

84. Winkler, "Revolution Too Soon," 1492–93.

85. Winkler, "Revolution Too Soon," 1492–93.

86. "Tributes to Mrs. Minor," *St. Louis Post-Dispatch*, May 4, 1895.

87. Ray, "Rhetorical Ritual of Citizenship," 9.

88. Ray, "Rhetorical Ritual of Citizenship," 6.
89. Ray, "Rhetorical Ritual of Citizenship," 6.
90. Ray, "Rhetorical Ritual of Citizenship," 8.
91. Quoted in Ray, "Rhetorical Ritual of Citizenship," 16.
92. Ray, "Rhetorical Ritual of Citizenship," 6.
93. Lois Beachy Underhill, *The Woman Who Ran for President* (New York: Penguin Books, 1995), 176–77.
94. Ray, "Rhetorical Ritual of Citizenship," 6.
95. Ray, "Rhetorical Ritual of Citizenship," 10.
96. Ray, "Rhetorical Ritual of Citizenship," 4.
97. Rosalyn Terborg-Penn, *African American Women in the Struggle for the Vote: 1850–1920* (Bloomington: Indiana University Press, 1998), 40.
98. Terborg-Penn, *African American Women in the Struggle for the Vote*, 40.
99. Ray, "Rhetorical Ritual of Citizenship," 13.
100. Quoted in "Mount Vernon Women Again," *Revolution*, October 15, 1868, 237.
101. Special Correspondent to the *Enquirer*, "Prohibition President-Making: National Convention of the Temperance Party," *Cincinnati Daily Enquirer*, February 26, 1872, 1.
102. Ray, "Rhetorical Ritual of Citizenship," 13.
103. Ray, "Rhetorical Ritual of Citizenship," 13.
104. Staley, "Suffrage Movement in St. Louis during the 1870s," 38–39.
105. Parker Pillsbury, "The Mortality of Nations: An Address Delivered before the American Equal Rights Association in New York, Thursday Evening, May 9, 1867," https://tile.loc.gov/storage-services/service/rbc/rbnawsa/n8620/n8620.pdf.
106. Monnig, "Anything but Minor."
107. Barbara Welter, "The Cult of True Womanhood: 1820–1860," *American Quarterly* 18, no. 2, part 1 (Summer 1966): 173, https://www.jstor.org/stable/2711179.
108. Welter, "Cult of True Womanhood," 152.
109. Welter, "Cult of True Womanhood," 172.
110. Sharon Estes and Elizabeth Witherell, "From the Periodical Archives: Susan Warner's 'How May an American Woman Best Show Her Patriotism?'" *American Periodicals* 19, no. 2 (2009): 228, https://www.jstor.org/stable/23025161.
111. Donald L. Ackerman and Jonathan H. Mann, *That's the Ticket! A Century of American Political Ballots* (New York: Rail Splitter Press, 2012), 96.

Chapter 10

1. John M. Krum and Francis Minor, "Interesting Suffrage Case," *Missouri Republican*, November 11, 1872, 6.
2. Amy Weisser, "Virginia Minor: St. Louis Suffragist," in *Virginia Minor: A Woman in the Hall of Famous Missourians*, ed. Margot McMillen (Missouri Women's Network, 2015), 10.
3. Joan Hoff, *Law, Gender and Injustice, A Legal History of U.S. Women* (New York: New York University Press, 1991), 171.
4. Elizabeth Cady Stanton, Susan B. Anthony, and Matilda Joslyn Gage, *History of Woman Suffrage*, vol. 3 (Rochester, NY: Charles Mann, 1887), 606.

5. Carol Ferring Shepley, "Virginia Minor," in *Movers and Shakers, Scalawags and Suffragettes: Tales from Bellefontaine Cemetery* (St. Louis: Missouri History Museum Press, 2008), 113.

6. Kathi Kern and Linda Levstik, "Teaching the New Departure: The United States vs. Susan B. Anthony," *Journal of the Civil War Era* 2, no. 1 (March 2012): 131–32.

7. Donna M. Monnig, "Anything but Minor: The Suffrage, Equality, and Women's Rights Activism of Virginia L. Minor, 1867–1894" (master's thesis, University of Central Missouri, August 2018), 36.

8. Bonnie Stepenoff, "Disenfranchised and Degraded: Virginia L. Minor and the Constitutional Case for Women's Suffrage," in *Missouri Law and the American Conscience: Historical Rights and Wrongs*, ed. Kenneth H. Winn (Columbia: University of Missouri Press, 2016), 113.

9. Stepenoff, "Disenfranchised and Degraded," 113.

10. Monnig, "Anything but Minor," 24.

11. LeeAnn Whites, "A Tale of Two Minors," in *Women in Missouri History: In Search of Power and Influence*, ed. LeeAnn Whites, Mary Neth, and Gary R. Kremer (Columbia: University of Missouri Press, 2004), 105.

12. Whites, "Tale of Two Minors."

13. Angela Ray, "The Rhetorical Ritual of Citizenship: Women's Voting as Public Performance, 1868–1875," *Quarterly Journal of Speech* 93, no. 1 (February 2017): 398.

14. Loretta Mae Walter, "Woman Suffrage in Missouri, 1866–1880" (master's thesis, Washington University, St. Louis, Missouri, August 1963), 104, Washington University Special Collections.

15. Angela G. Ray and Cindy Koenig Richards, "Inventing Citizens Imagining Gender Justice: The Suffrage Rhetoric of Virginia and Francis Minor," *Quarterly Journal of Speech* 93, no. 4 (November 2007): 381.

16. Stanton, Anthony, and Gage, *History of Woman Suffrage*, 3:606.

17. Ray and Richards, "Inventing Citizens Imagining Gender Justice," 382.

18. John M. Krum, Francis Minor, and John B. Henderson, "Argument and Brief," Missouri Supreme Court Archives; Jane Henderson, "Women Wanted It—and Got It—100 Years Ago, but the Right to Vote Didn't Come Easy," *St. Louis Post-Dispatch*, July 30, 2020, 8.

19. Evelyn Glenn, "Citizenship and Inequality: Historical and Global Perspectives." *Social Problems* 47, no. 1 (February 2000): 5, https://www.jstor.org/stable/3097149.

20. Ray and Richards, "Inventing Citizens Imagining Gender Justice," 382.

21. David M. Dismore, "Live-Blogging Women's History: March 29, 1875," *Ms. Magazine*, March 29, 2011, https://msmagazine.com/2011/03/29/live-blogging-womens-history-march-29-1875.

22. William E. Nelson, "Reason and Compromise in the Establishment of the Federal Constitution, 1787–1801," *William and Mary Quarterly* 44, no. 3, *The Constitution of the United States* (July 1987): 470–71, https://www.jstor.org/stable/1939766.

23. Quoted in Nelson, "Reason and Compromise in the Establishment of the Federal Constitution."

24. Quoted in Nelson, "Reason and Compromise in the Establishment of the Federal Constitution."

25. Quoted in Nelson, "Reason and Compromise in the Establishment of the Federal Constitution."

26. Quoted in Nelson, "Reason and Compromise in the Establishment of the Federal Constitution."

27. Nelson, "Reason and Compromise in the Establishment of the Federal Constitution."

28. Nancy F. Cott, "Marriage and Women's Citizenship in the United States 1830–1934," *American Historical Review* 103, no. 5 (December 1998): 1445, https://www.jstor.org/stable/2649963.

29. Francis Minor, "Citizenship and Suffrage; The Yarbrough Decision," *The Arena* 5 (December 1891): 69.

30. Ellen Carol Dubois, "Taking the Law into Our Own Hands: *Bradwell, Minor*, and Suffrage Militance in the 1870s," in *Visible Women: New Essays on American Activism*, ed. Nancy A. Hewitt and Suzanne Lebsock (Urbana: University of Illinois Press, 1993), 29; Adam Winkler, "A Revolution Too Soon: Woman Suffragists and the Living Constitution," *New York University Law Review* 79 (2001): 1515.

31. "The Enforcement Acts of 1870 and 1871," US Senate, accessed September 15, 2019, https://www.senate.gov/artandhistory/history/common/generic/Enforcement Acts.htm.

32. Weisser, "Virginia Minor," 11.

33. Catherine Allgor, "'Remember . . . I'm Your Man': Masculinity, Marriage, and Gender in Hamilton," in *Historians on Hamilton*, ed. Renee C. Romano and Claire Bond Potter (New Brunswick, NJ: Rutgers University Press, 2018), 104–6.

34. Walter, "Woman Suffrage in Missouri, 1866–1880," 106.

35. Smith P. Galt, "Toast: 'The Street Railway in the Courts' Responded to by Mr. Smith P. Galt," Verbatim Report of the Fifth Annual Meeting of the American Street-Railway Association: 1896–1897 (Chicago: Pettibone, Sawtell and Co., 1896), 178.

36. Smith P. Galt, "Brief of the Defendant in Error," Missouri State Supreme Court Archives.

37. Smith P. Galt, "Demurrer to Petition," St. Louis Circuit Court Archives.

38. Ray, "Rhetorical Ritual of Citizenship," 11.

39. Walter, "Woman Suffrage in Missouri, 1866–1880," 106.

40. Director of Education, "The Significance of the Virginia Minor Trial," *Virginia Minor Trial Packet*, 2006, appendix, Jefferson National Expansion Memorial, https://www.gatewayarch.com/wp-content/uploads/2018/07/A-Trial-for-the-Right-to-Vote-4-12-Grade.pdf.

41. Laura Staley, "Suffrage Movement in St. Louis during the 1870s," *Gateway Heritage* 3, no. 4 (Spring 1983): 38.

42. Marshall D. Hier, "Virginia Minor's Struggle to Vote," *St. Louis Bar Journal*, Winter 1992, 40.

43. Monnig, "Anything but Minor," 21–24.

44. Christine Orrick Fordyce, "Early Beginnings," in "History of the Woman Suffrage Movement in Missouri," edited by Mary Semple Scott, *Missouri Historical Review* XIV, nos. 3–4 (April–July 1920): 291.

45. Krum, Minor, and Henderson, "Argument and Brief," 12–13.

46. Fordyce, "Early Beginnings."

47. Walter, "Woman Suffrage in Missouri, 1866–1880," 110.

48. Staley, "Suffrage Movement in St. Louis during the 1870s," 39.

49. John Lewis, "Judgement Affirmed," State of Missouri County of St. Louis, Records of the Missouri State Archives, Virginia L. Minor and Francis Minor her husband PE vs. Reese Happersett DE, March Term 1873, no. 122, Box 727, no. 15, 5.

50. Krum and Minor, "Interesting Suffrage Case."

51. "Mrs. Minor Not Allowed to Vote," *Missouri Republican*, November 10, 1872, 6.

52. Emphasis in the original.

53. Emphasis and capitalization in the original.

54. Monnig, "Anything but Minor," 42.

55. *Buffalo Morning Express and Illustrated Buffalo Express*, November 13, 1872, 2.

56. "Determined to Vote," *St. Louis Times*, October 16, 1872, np, Missouri State Archives.

57. "Supreme Court Clerk," *Missouri Republican*, May 1, 1873, 8; "Virginia Minor and Women's Right to Vote," National Park Service, January 16, 2018, https://www.nps.gov /jeff/learn/historyculture/the-virginia-minor-case.htm.

58. "Virginia Minor and Women's Right to Vote."

59. "Virginia Minor and Women's Right to Vote."

60. Claude Peter Magrath, *Morrison R. Waite: The Triumph of Character* (New York: Macmillan and Company, 1963), 119.

61. All information and quotes in this paragraph come from *Bradwell v. The State*, Legal Information Institute, Cornell Law School, accessed May 24, 2019, https://www .law.cornell.edu/supremecourt/text/83/130.

62. Staley, "Suffrage Movement in St. Louis during the 1870s," 39.

63. H. M. Vories, "Virginia L. Minor et al. vs. Reese Happersett Respondent: Opinion per Vories," Missouri Supreme Court Case Files, 53 Mo., 58, 1873, 4.

64. Vories, "Virginia L. Minor et al. vs. Reese Happersett Respondent," 5.

65. Truman A. Post, *Reports of Cases Argued and Determined in the Supreme Court of the State of Missouri*, vol. LIII (St. Louis, MO: W. J. Gilbert, 1878), 58.

CHAPTER 11

1. Loretta Mae Walter, "Woman Suffrage in Missouri, 1866–1880" (master's thesis, Washington University, St. Louis, Missouri, August 1963), 111, Washington University Special Collections.

2. "The Court and Its Traditions," US Supreme Court, accessed March 2, 2020, https://www.supremecourt.gov/about/traditions.aspx.

3. Walter, "Woman Suffrage in Missouri, 1866–1880," 111.

4. Bonnie Stepenoff, "Disenfranchised and Degraded: Virginia L. Minor and the Constitutional Case for Women's Suffrage," in *Missouri Law and the American Conscience:*

Historical Rights and Wrongs, ed. Kenneth H. Winn (Columbia: University of Missouri Press, 2016), 115.

5. *Minor v. Happersett,* Legal Information Institute, Cornell Law School, https://www.law.cornell.edu/supremecourt/text/88/162#writing-USSC_CR_0088_0162_ZS.

6. Paul Kens, *The Supreme Court under Morrison R. Waite, 1874–1888* (Columbia: University of South Carolina Press, 2010), 2.

7. Kens, *Supreme Court under Morrison R. Waite,* 2.

8. Clerk of the Court, "Guide for Counsel in Cases to be Argued before the United States Supreme Court," October Term 2015, Supreme Court of the United States, 2015, accessed April 12, 2019, https://www.supremecourt.gov/casehand/guidefor counsel.pdf.

9. *Minor v. Happersett;* Virginia Minor, "Statement before the U.S. Senate Committee on Woman Suffrage—Jan. 24, 1889," Iowa State University, https://awpc.cattcenter.ia state.edu/2019/12/16/statement-before-the-u-s-senate-committee-on-woman-suffrage -jan-24-1889.

10. Minor, "Statement before the U.S. Senate Committee."

11. George Washington Julian, "Suffrage in the District of Columbia," January 16, 1866, in *Speeches on Political Questions [1850–1868]* (New York: Hurd and Houghton, 1872), 291–95.

12. Eric Foner, *The Second Founding: How the Civil War and Reconstruction Remade the Constitution* (New York: W. W. Norton, 2019), 44–45.

13. Elizabeth Cady Stanton, Susan B. Anthony, and Matilda Joslyn Gage, *History of Woman Suffrage,* vol. 2 (Rochester, NY: Charles Mann, 1887), 730, https://gutenberg .org/files/28039/28039-h/28039-h.htm#FNanchor_107_107.

14. John M. Krum, Francis Minor, and John B. Henderson, "Argument and Brief," Missouri Supreme Court Archives; Elizabeth Cady Stanton, Susan B. Anthony, and Matilda Joslyn Gage, *History of Woman Suffrage,* vol. 2 (Rochester, NY: Charles Mann, 1887), 730, https://gutenberg.org/files/28039/28039-h/28039-h.htm#FNanchor_107_107.

15. Angela G. Ray and Cindy Koenig Richards, "Inventing Citizens Imagining Gender Justice: The Suffrage Rhetoric of Virginia and Francis Minor," *Quarterly Journal of Speech* 93, no. 4 (November 2007): 388.

16. Foner, *Second Founding,* 3.

17. Evelyn Glenn, "Citizenship and Inequality: Historical and Global Perspectives," *Social Problems* 47, no. 1 (February 2000): 4, https://www.jstor.org/stable/3097149.

18. Glenn, "Citizenship and Inequality," 2.

19. Teresa Anne Murphy, *Citizenship and the Origins of Women's History in the United States* (Philadelphia: University of Pennsylvania Press, 2013), 3.

20. Murphy, *Citizenship and the Origins of Women's History,* 103–4, 123.

21. Lydia Maria Child and Carolyn L. Karcher, *A Lydia Maria Child Reader* (Durham, NC: Duke University Press, 1997), 406.

22. Child and Karcher, *Lydia Maria Child Reader,* 411.

23. Child and Karcher, *Lydia Maria Child Reader,* 411.

24. Foner, *Second Founding,* 5–7.

25. Murphy, *Citizenship and the Origins of Women's History,* 9.

26. Emphasis in the original. Susan Zaeske, *Signatures of Citizenship: Petitioning, Antislavery, & Women's Political Identity* (Chapel Hill: University of North Carolina Press, 2003), 121.

27. Foner, *Second Founding*, 94.

28. Stanton, Address to the Legislature of New York, 4.

29. Murphy, *Citizenship and the Origins of Women's History*, 1.

30. Murphy, *Citizenship and the Origins of Women's History*, 8.

31. Judith A. Baer, *Equality under the Constitution: Reclaiming the Fourteenth Amendment* (Ithaca, NY: Cornell University Press, 1983), 73, https://www.jstor.org/stable/10.7591/j.ctt207g5jg.

32. Quoted in Foner, *Second Founding*, 68.

33. Foner, *Second Founding*, 75.

34. Foner, *Second Founding*.

35. Foner, *Second Founding*, xxv, 68.

36. Martha Jones, Susan Goodier, Kate Clarke Lemay, and Lisa Tetrault, *Votes for Women: A Portrait of Persistence* (Princeton, NJ: Princeton University Press, 2019), 118; "Cable Act of 1922," Immigration History, University of Texas at Austin, accessed April 3, 2020, https://immigrationhistory.org/item/cable-act.

37. Quoted in Foner, *Second Founding*, 115.

38. Nancy F. Cott, *Public Vows* (Cambridge, MA: Harvard University Press, 2009), 96. In this, he agreed with Senator Lyman Trumble.

39. Rogers M. Smith, *Civic Ideals: Conflicting Visions of Citizenship in U.S. History* (London: Yale University Press, 1999), 306.

40. Quoted in Cott, *Public Vows*, 96.

41. Stepenoff, "Disenfranchised and Degraded," 115–16.

42. *New York Times*, February 10, 1875.

43. Stepenoff, "Disenfranchised and Degraded," 116.

44. Foner, *Second Founding*, 113.

45. Quoted in Foner, *Second Founding*.

46. Adam Winkler, "A Revolution Too Soon: Woman Suffragists and the Living Constitution," *New York University Law Review* 79 (2001): 1466.

47. Stanton, Anthony, and Gage, *History of Woman Suffrage*, 2:720.

48. Jonathan Elliot and James Madison, *The Debates in the Several State Conventions on the Adoption of the Federal Constitution as Recommended by the General Convention at Philadelphia in 1787: Together with the Journal of the Federal Convention, Luther Martin's Letter, Yates's Minutes, Congressional Opinions, Virginia and Kentucky Resolutions of '98–'99, and Other Illustrations of the Constitution* (Philadelphia: Lippincott, 1901), 352.

49. Elliot and Madison, *Debates in the Several State Conventions*, 351–52.

50. Stanton, Anthony, and Gage, *History of Woman Suffrage*, 2:722.

51. Emphasis mine.

52. Judith Apter Klinghoffer and Lois Elkis, "'The Petticoat Electors': Women's Suffrage in New Jersey, 1776–1807," *Journal of the Early Republic* 12, no. 2 (Summer 1992): 164–65. https://www.jstor.org/stable/3124150.

53. Klinghoffer and Elkis, "Petticoat Electors," 164–65.

54. Klinghoffer and Elkis, "Petticoat Electors," 159.

55. Klinghoffer and Elkis, "Petticoat Electors," 160.

56. Klinghoffer and Elkis, "Petticoat Electors," 162–63.

57. Klinghoffer and Elkis, "Petticoat Electors," 162–63.

58. Klinghoffer and Elkis, "Petticoat Electors," 168.

59. Klinghoffer and Elkis, "Petticoat Electors," 177.

60. Marylynn Salmon, "The Limits of Independence," in *No Small Courage: A History of Women in the United States*, ed. Nancy F. Cott (New York: Oxford University Press, 2004), 159.

61. Klinghoffer and Elkis, "Petticoat Electors," 175, 177–78.

62. Klinghoffer and Elkis, "Petticoat Electors," 186.

63. Klinghoffer and Elkis, "Petticoat Electors," 188.

64. Klinghoffer and Elkis, "Petticoat Electors," 189.

65. "Woman's Suffrage Centennial," New Jersey State League of Municipalities, accessed April 2, 2019, https://njlm.org/1080/Womans-Suffrage-Centennial.

66. Stanton, Anthony, and Gage, *History of Woman Suffrage*, 2:722–25.

67. Stanton, Anthony, and Gage, *History of Woman Suffrage*, 2:722–32.

68. Stanton, Anthony, and Gage, *History of Woman Suffrage*, 2:733.

69. Walter, "Woman Suffrage in Missouri, 1866–1880," 113.

70. Walter, "Woman Suffrage in Missouri, 1866–1880," 113.

71. "Female Suffrage," *The Clarion-Ledger*, January 28, 1874, 1.

72. Formally known as *Bradwell v. Illinois*.

73. Formally referred to as *US v. Susan B. Anthony*.

74. Lisa Tetrault, *The Myth of Seneca Falls: Memory and the Women's Suffrage Movement, 1848–1898* (Chapel Hill: University of North Carolina Press, 2014), 73.

75. Kens, *Supreme Court under Morrison R. Waite*, 4.

76. Winkler, "Revolution Too Soon," 1505.

77. Ellen Carol Dubois, "Taking the Law into Our Own Hands: *Bradwell, Minor,* and Suffrage Militance in the 1870s," in *Visible Women: New Essays on American Activism*, ed. Nancy A. Hewitt and Suzanne Lebsock (Urbana: University of Illinois Press, 1993), 33.

78. Herbert A. Johnson, "Series Editor's Preface," in Kens, *Supreme Court under Morrison R. Waite*; Kens, *Supreme Court under Morrison R. Waite*, xi.

79. Kens, *Supreme Court under Morrison R. Waite*, 151.

80. Kens, *Supreme Court under Morrison R. Waite*, 7.

81. Johnson, "Series Editor's Preface," xii.

82. Kens, *Supreme Court under Morrison R. Waite*, 15–16.

83. Kens, *Supreme Court under Morrison R. Waite*, 15–16.

84. Kens, *Supreme Court under Morrison R. Waite*, 17.

85. Quoted in Kens, *Supreme Court under Morrison R. Waite*, 151.

86. Claude Peter Magrath, *Morrison R. Waite: The Triumph of Character* (New York: Macmillan and Company, 1963), 119.

87. C. J. Waite, *Minor v. Happersett*, Legal Information Institute, Cornell Law School, https://www.law.cornell.edu/supremecourt/text/88/162.

88. Jennifer K. Brown, "The Nineteenth Amendment and Women's Equality," *Yale Law Journal* 102, no. 8 (1993): 2180.

89. Waite, *Minor v. Happersett.*

90. Norma Basch, "Reconstructing Female Citizenship: Minor v. Happersett," in *The Constitution, Law, and American Life: Critical Aspects of the Nineteenth-Century Experience*, ed. Donald G. Nieman (Athens: University of Georgia Press, 1992), 61.

91. Waite, *Minor v. Happersett.*

92. Joan Hoff, *Law, Gender and Injustice, A Legal History of U.S. Women* (New York: New York University Press, 1991), 173.

93. Waite, *Minor v. Happersett.*

94. Donna M. Monnig, "Anything but Minor: The Suffrage, Equality, and Women's Rights Activism of Virginia L. Minor, 1867–1894" (master's thesis, University of Central Missouri, August 2018), 46.

95. Waite, *Minor v. Happersett.*

96. Linda Kerber, "'Ourselves and Our Daughters Forever': Women and the Constitution: 1787–1876," in *One Woman, One Vote*, ed. Marjorie Spruill Wheeler (Troutdale, OR: NewSage Press, 1995), 34.

97. Waite, *Minor v. Happersett.*

98. Waite, *Minor v. Happersett.*

99. Kerber, "Ourselves and Our Daughters Forever," 35.

100. "Matilda Joslyn Gage's Argument against the Supreme Court Decision in *Minor v. Happersett* at the 1875 NWSA Convention," in *The Women's Suffrage Movement*, ed. Sally Roesch Wagner (New York: Penguin Books, 2019), 275–76.

101. "The Ku Klux Cases," 110 US 651, 65. 12, 1884, FindLaw, https://caselaw.findlaw .com/us-supreme-court/110/651.html.

102. Samuel F. Miller, "'The Ku-Klux Cases.' Ex Parte Yarbrough and Others," Legal Information Institute, Cornell Law School, https://www.law.cornell.edu/supremecourt /text/110/651.

103. Joan Hoff, *Law, Gender and Injustice, A Legal History of U.S. Women* (New York: New York University Press, 1991), 182–83.

104. Francis Minor, "Citizenship and Suffrage; The Yarbrough Decision," *The Arena* 5 (December 1891): 72.

CHAPTER 12

1. Marisa Iati, "This Woman Sought the Right to Vote from the Supreme Court. The Nine Men Denied Her," *Washington Post*, August 6, 2020, https://www.washingtonpost .com/graphics/2020/local/history/suffrage-supreme-court-virginia-minor-vote.

2. Quoted in Jennifer K. Brown, "The Nineteenth Amendment and Women's Equality," *Yale Law Journal* 102, no. 8 (1993): 2180n25.

3. Bonnie Stepenoff, "Disenfranchised and Degraded: Virginia L. Minor and the Constitutional Case for Women's Suffrage," in *Missouri Law and the American Conscience: Historical Rights and Wrongs*, ed. Kenneth H. Winn (Columbia: University of Missouri Press, 2016), 105.

4. Lisa Tetrault, *The Myth of Seneca Falls: Memory and the Women's Suffrage Movement, 1848–1898* (Chapel Hill: University of North Carolina Press, 2014), 74.

5. Judith A. Baer, *Equality under the Constitution: Reclaiming the Fourteenth Amendment* (Ithaca, NY: Cornell University Press, 1983), 106, https://www.jstor.org/stable/10.7591/j.ctt207g5jg.

6. Stepenoff, "Disenfranchised and Degraded," 117.

7. C. J. Waite, *United States v. Reese et al.*, 92 US 214 23 L.Ed. 563, October Term, 1875, Legal Information Institute, Cornell Law School, https://www.law.cornell.edu/supremecourt/text/92/214.

8. Waite, *United States v. Reese et al.*

9. Waite, *United States v. Reese et al.*

10. Andrew Kirshenbaum, "The Injustice of the Poll Tax and Why It Took a Constitutional Amendment to Stop It," Fair Vote: The Center for Voting and Democracy, May 1, 2003, https://archive3.fairvote.org/articles/the-injustice-of-the-poll-tax-and-why-it-took-a-constitutional-amendment-to-stop-it.

11. "Virginia Minor and Women's Right to Vote," National Park Service, January 16, 2018, https://www.nps.gov/jeff/learn/historyculture/the-virginia-minor-case.htm.

12. Stanley J. Folmsbee, "The Origin of the First 'Jim Crow' Law," *Journal of Southern History* 15, no. 2 (1949): 244–45. https://doi.org/10.2307/2197999.

13. Henry Billings Brown, *Plessy v. Ferguson*, Legal Information Institute, Cornell Law School, accessed May 1, 2019, https://www.law.cornell.edu/supremecourt/text/163/537.

14. Brown, *Plessy v. Ferguson.*

15. History.com Editors, *Plessy v. Ferguson*, History.com, accessed February 21, 2020, https://history.com/topics/black-history/plessy-v-ferguson.

16. Donna M. Monnig, "Anything but Minor: The Suffrage, Equality, and Women's Rights Activism of Virginia L. Minor, 1867–1894" (master's thesis, University of Central Missouri, August 2018), 47; Aileen S. Kraditor, *The Ideas of the Woman Suffrage Movement: 1890–1920* (New York: W. W. Norton and Company, 1981), 174–77.

17. Garth E. Pauley, "W. E. B. Du Bois and the Crisis of Women's Suffrage," in *Protest and Propaganda: W. E. B. Du Bois, the Crisis, and American History*, ed. Amy Helene Kirschke and Phillip Luke Sinitiere (Columbia: University of Missouri Press, 2019), 141.

18. Rosalyn Terborg-Penn, *African American Women in the Struggle for the Vote: 1850–1920* (Bloomington: Indiana University Press, 1998), 111.

19. Brent Staples, "When the Suffrage Movement Sold Out to White Supremacy," *New York Times*, February 2, 2019.

20. "Voting Rights for Native Americans," Library of Congress, accessed December 3, 2019, https://www.loc.gov/classroom-materials/elections/right-to-vote/voting-rights-for-native-americans.

21. Patty Ferguson-Bohnee, "How the Native American Vote Continues to Be Suppressed," American Bar Association, February 9, 2020, https://www.americanbar.org/groups/crsj/publications/human_rights_magazine_home/voting-rights/how-the-native-american-vote-continues-to-be-suppressed.

22. "History of Federal Voting Rights Laws," US Department of Justice, accessed February 18, 2020, https://www.justice.gov/crt/history-federal-voting-rights-laws.

23. Henry Billings Brown, "Opinion of the Court, SAMUEL DOWNES, Doing Business under the Firm Name of S. B. Downes & Company, Plff. in Err., v. GEORGE R. BIDWELL," Legal Information Institute, Cornell Law School.

24. Monnig, "Anything but Minor," 131.

25. "Puerto Rico and the 19th Amendment," National Park Service, August 23, 2019, https://www.nps.gov/articles/puerto-rico-women-s-history.htm.

26. Emilio Del Toro, *Morales v. Board of Registration, 33 P.R. 76 (1924)*, April 25, 1924, Supreme Court of Puerto Rico, nos. 219 and 220, Caselaw Access Project, https://cite .case.law/pr/33/76/#p83.

27. Monnig, "Anything but Minor," 48.

28. Alicia Ault, "How Women Got the Vote Is a Far More Complex Story Than the History Textbooks Reveal," *Smithsonian*, April 9, 2019.

29. Richard Briffault, "The Contested Right to Vote," *Michigan Law Review* 100, no. 2002, 1521–22, https://repository.law.umich.edu/mlr/vol100/iss6/16.

30. *Literacy Tests and Voter Requirements in Federal and State Elections: Hearings before the Subcommittee on Constitutional Rights of the Committee on the Judiciary, United States Senate, Eighty-Seventh Congress, Second Session, on S. 480, S. 2750, and 2979: Bills Relating to Literacy Tests and Voter Requirements in Federal and State Elections, March 27, 28; April 5, 6, 10, 11, and 12, 1962* (Washington, DC: US Government Printing Office, 1962), 376, 560, 577, 605, 608.

31. "History of Federal Voting Rights Laws."

32. *Annie E. Harper et al., Appellants, v. Virginia State Board of Elections et al. Evelyn Butts, Appellant, v. Albertis Harrison, Governor, et al.*, Legal Information Institute, Cornell Law School, accessed September 12, 2019, https://www.law.cornell.edu/supreme court/text/383/663.

33. Monnig, "Anything but Minor," 48.

34. Joel William Friedman, *Champion of Civil Rights: Judge John Minor Wisdom* (Baton Rouge: Louisiana State University Press, 2009), 284.

35. *Amendments to the Voting Rights Acts of 1965: Hearings, Ninety-First Congress, First and Second Sessions* (Washington, DC: US Government Printing Office, 1970), 417, 643.

36. Baer, *Equality under the Constitution*, 283.

37. Briffault, "Contested Right to Vote," 1542.

38. "LWVUS to U.S. House: Restore the Voting Rights Act," League of Women Voters, August 18, 2019, https://www.lwv.org/fighting-voter-suppression/lwvus-us-house -restore-voting-rights-act.

39. American Civil Liberties Union, "Oppose Voter ID Legislation–Fact Sheet," last updated May 2017, https://www.aclu.org/fact-sheet/oppose-voter-id-legislation-fact -sheet.

40. American Civil Liberties Union, "Oppose Voter ID Legislation."

41. Briffault, "Contested Right to Vote," 1525.

42. "Fighting Voter Suppression," League of Women Voters, accessed March 29, 2020, https://www.lwv.org/voting-rights/fighting-voter-suppression.

43. American Civil Liberties Union, *League of Women Voters v. Brian D. Newby and the United States Election Assistance Commission*, last updated December 16, 2016, https:// www.aclu.org/cases/league-women-voters-v-brian-d-newby-and-united-states-election -assistance-commission.

44. "H.R. 4: Voting Rights Advancement Act of 2019," Congress.gov., accessed May 21, 2020. https://www.congress.gov/bill/116th-congress/house-bill/4.

45. John Nichols, "Time for a 'Right to Vote' Constitutional Amendment," *The Nation*, March 5, 2013, https://www.thenation.com/article/archive/time-right-vote-constitutional-amendment.

46. John William Burgess, *Political Science and Comparative Constitutional Law* (Boston: Ginn, 1890), 42.

47. Garrett Epps, "What Does the Constitution Actually Say about Voting Rights?" *The Atlantic*, August 13, 2013, https://www.theatlantic.com/national/archive/2013/08/what-does-the-constitution-actually-say-about-voting-rights/278782.

48. Johnathan Soros, "The Missing Right: A Constitutional Right to Vote," *Democracy: A Journal of Ideas*, no. 28 (Spring 2013), https://democracyjournal.org/magazine/28/the-missing-right-a-constitutional-right-to-vote.

49. "ERA History," ERA, accessed December 9, 2019, https://www.equalrightsamendment.org/history. As of March 2022, thirty-eight states have ratified the ERA, but it is still not law. Many reasons for this quandary exist, including that the deadline for ratification passed in 1982, and now some states are threatening to rescind their ratifications.

50. "Why We Need the Equal Rights Amendment," ERA, accessed December 9, 2019, https://www.equalrightsamendment.org/why.

51. "Frequently Asked Questions," ERA, accessed December 9, 2019, https://www.equalrightsamendment.org/faq.

52. "Next Steps on Women's Rights as 19th Amendment Centennial Nears," American Bar Association, November 2019, https://www.americanbar.org/news/abanews/publications/youraba/2019/november-2019/19th-amendment-panel-looks-at-what-still-needs-to-be-done-on-vot.

53. Ruth Bader Ginsburg, "Sexual Equality under the Fourteenth and Equal Rights Amendments," *Washington University Law Quarterly* 1979, no. 1 (1979), https://openscholarship.wustl.edu/law_lawreview/vol1979/iss1/19.

54. "Why We Need the Equal Rights Amendment."

55. Baer, *Equality under the Constitution*, 118–19.

56. Julie C. Suk, *We the Women: The Unstoppable Mothers of the Equal Rights Amendment* (New York: Skyhorse, 2020), 137.

57. Baer, *Equality under the Constitution*, 123.

58. Nina Totenberg, "Justice Ruth Bader Ginsburg, Champion of Gender Equality, Dies at 87," NPR, September 18, 2020, https://www.npr.org/2020/09/18/100306972/justice-ruth-bader-ginsburg-champion-of-gender-equality-dies-at-87.

59. Totenberg, "Justice Ruth Bader Ginsburg."

60. Catharine A. MacKinnon and Kimberlé W. Crenshaw, "Reconstituting the Future: An Equality Amendment," *Yale Law Journal Forum*, December 26, 2019, 347, https://www.yalelawjournal.org/forum/reconstituting-the-future-the-equality-amendment.

61. MacKinnon and Crenshaw, "Reconstituting the Future," 349.

62. "Frequently Asked Questions."

63. "Why We Need the Equal Rights Amendment."

64. Ginsburg, "Sexual Equality under the Fourteenth and Equal Rights Amendments," 174.

65. Ginsburg, "Sexual Equality under the Fourteenth and Equal Rights Amendments," 162. See note 6 for the *Minor v. Happersett* notation, as well as 163n11.

66. Ginsburg, "Sexual Equality under the Fourteenth and Equal Rights Amendments," 175.

67. MacKinnon and Crenshaw, "Reconstituting the Future," 358–62.

68. MacKinnon and Crenshaw, "Reconstituting the Future," 358.

69. MacKinnon and Crenshaw, "Reconstituting the Future," 359–60.

70. MacKinnon and Crenshaw, "Reconstituting the Future," 361–62.

71. MacKinnon and Crenshaw, "Reconstituting the Future," 362.

72. Elizabeth Cady Stanton, Susan B. Anthony, and Matilda Joslyn Gage, *History of Woman Suffrage*, vol. 2 (Rochester, NY: Charles Mann, 1887), 755, https://gutenberg.org/files/28039/28039-h/28039-h.htm#FNanchor_107_107.

CHAPTER 13

1. Loretta Mae Walter, "Woman Suffrage in Missouri, 1866–1880" (master's thesis, Washington University, St. Louis, Missouri, August 1963), 113, Washington University Special Collections.

2. "Tributes to Mrs. Minor," *St. Louis Post-Dispatch*, May 4, 1895.

3. Donna M. Monnig, "Anything but Minor: The Suffrage, Equality, and Women's Rights Activism of Virginia L. Minor, 1867–1894" (master's thesis, University of Central Missouri, August 2018), 44–45.

4. Jennifer K. Brown, "The Nineteenth Amendment and Women's Equality," *Yale Law Journal* 102, no. 8 (1993): 2181.

5. Norma Basch, "Reconstructing Female Citizenship: Minor v. Happersett," in *The Constitution, Law, and American Life: Critical Aspects of the Nineteenth-Century Experience*, ed. Donald G. Nieman (Athens: University of Georgia Press, 1992), 56.

6. Allison Sneider, "Women Suffrage in Congress," in *Votes for Women: The Struggle for Suffrage Revisited*, ed. Jean H. Baker (Oxford: Oxford University Press, 2002), 79.

7. Angela G. Ray and Cindy Koenig Richards, "Inventing Citizens Imagining Gender Justice: The Suffrage Rhetoric of Virginia and Francis Minor," *Quarterly Journal of Speech* 93, no. 4 (November 2007): 394.

8. "The Hallenscheids," *St. Louis Globe-Democrat*, December 10, 1875, 1.

9. "The End of a Tragedy," *The Advertiser-Courier*, November 12, 1875, 4.

10. David V. Baker, *Women and Capital Punishment in the United States: An Analytical History* (Jefferson, NC: McFarland, 2015), 308.

11. Harriet C. Frazier, *Death Sentences in Missouri, 1803–2005: A History and Comprehensive Registry of Legal Executions, Pardons, and Commutations* (Jefferson, NC: McFarland, 2006), 63.

12. Baker, *Women and Capital Punishment*, 308.

13. "The End of a Tragedy," *Advertiser-Courier*, November 12, 1875, 4.

14. "The End of a Tragedy."

15. Baker, *Women and Capital Punishment*, 308.

16. Virginia Minor, Letter from Mrs. Francis Minor to Charles Henry Hardin, December 12, 1875, Papers of Charles Henry Hardin, Box 6, Folder 14, Missouri State Archives—Jefferson City.

17. "Treatment of Female Prisoners," *Daily Missouri Democrat*, June 8, 1869, 4.

18. Minor, Letter from Mrs. Francis Minor to Charles Henry Hardin.

19. Minor, Letter from Mrs. Francis Minor to Charles Henry Hardin.

20. Monnig, "Anything but Minor," 63.

21. *Office of the Governor: Charles Henry Hardin*, Missouri State Archives Finding Aid 3.22, accessed June 2, 2019, 270, https://s1.sos.mo.gov/CMSImages/Archives/rg003-22 .pdf.

22. "Henry Hallenscheid's End," *Advertiser-Courier*, December 17, 1875, 4.

23. *Advertiser-Courier*, December 24, 1875, 5.

24. "Henry Hallenscheid's End," 4.

25. Elizabeth Cady Stanton, Susan B. Anthony, and Matilda Joslyn Gage, *History of Woman Suffrage*, vol. 2 (Rochester, NY: Charles Mann, 1887), 842, https://gutenberg .org/files/28039/28039-h/28039-h.htm#FNanchor_107_107.

26. Stanton, Anthony, and Gage, *History of Woman Suffrage*, 2:842.

27. Stanton, Anthony, and Gage, *History of Woman Suffrage*, 2:829–30.

28. Elizabeth Cady Stanton, Susan B. Anthony, and Matilda Joslyn Gage, *History of Woman Suffrage*, vol. 3 (Rochester, NY: Charles Mann, 1887), 28.

29. Stanton, Anthony, and Gage, *History of Woman Suffrage*, 3:28.

30. David M. Dismore, "Live-Blogging Women's History: March 29, 1875," *Ms. Magazine*, March 29, 2011, https://msmagazine.com/2011/03/29/live-blogging-womens-his tory-march-29-1875.

31. Robert P. J. Cooney, *Winning the Vote: The Triumph of the American Woman Suffrage Movement* (Santa Cruz, CA: American Graphic Press, 2005), 42–43.

32. National Woman Suffrage Association, "Declaration and Protest of the Women of the United States by the National Woman Suffrage Association," Philadelphia, July 4, 1876, https://loc.gov/item/rbpe.16000300.

33. National Woman Suffrage Association, "Declaration and Protest."

34. Stanton, Anthony, and Gage, *History of Woman Suffrage*, 3:30.

35. Stanton, Anthony, and Gage, *History of Woman Suffrage*, 3:29.

36. Dismore, "Live-Blogging Women's History."

37. Cooney, *Winning the Vote*, 42–43; Stanton, Anthony, and Gage, *History of Woman Suffrage*, 3:30–31.

38. Stanton, Anthony, and Gage, *History of Woman Suffrage*, 3:30–31.

39. National Woman Suffrage Association, "Declaration and Protest."

40. National Woman Suffrage Association, "Declaration and Protest."

41. Marisa Iati, "This Woman Sought the Right to Vote from the Supreme Court. The Nine Men Denied Her," *Washington Post*, August 6, 2020, https://www.washingtonpost .com/graphics/2020/local/history/suffrage-supreme-court-virginia-minor-vote.

42. Monnig, "Anything but Minor," 60.

43. Virginia Minor, "An Open Letter to the Board of Freeholders," *St. Louis Democrat*, June 8, 1876.

44. Elizabeth Cady Stanton, Susan B. Anthony, and Matilda Joslyn Gage, *History of Woman Suffrage*, vol. 1 (Rochester, NY: Charles Mann, 1887), 259, https://gutenberg .org/files/28020/28020-h/28020-h.htm.

45. Stanton, Anthony, and Gage, *History of Woman Suffrage*, 1:259–60.

46. Stanton, Anthony, and Gage, *History of Woman Suffrage*, 1:565.

47. Stanton, Anthony, and Gage, *History of Woman Suffrage*, 1:849.

48. *The Proceedings of the Woman's Rights Convention, Held at Syracuse, September 8th, 9th, & 10th, 1852* (Syracuse, NY: J. E. Masters, 1852), 34–35.

49. Juliana Tutt, "'No Taxation without Representation' in the American Woman Suffrage Movement," *Stanford Law Review* 62, no. 5 (May 2010): 1478, https://www.jstor.org/stable/25681867.

50. Caroline C. Jones, "Dollars and Selves: Women's Tax Criticism and Resistance in the 1870s," *University of Illinois Law Review*, no. 2 (1994): 275.

51. Jones, "Dollars and Selves," 269.

52. Tutt, "'No Taxation without Representation,'" 1485–86.

53. "Women's Rights," *Greensboro Patriot*, October 29, 1863, 3.

54. Jones, "Dollars and Selves," 265–69.

55. Tutt, "'No Taxation without Representation,'" 1474.

56. Stanton, Anthony, and Gage, *History of Woman Suffrage*, 2:410.

57. Stepenoff, Bonnie. "Disenfranchised and Degraded," 108.

58. Stanton, Anthony, and Gage, *History of Woman Suffrage*, 3:600–601.

59. CPI Inflation Calculator, https://www.officialdata.org/us/inflation/1869?endYear=2020&amount=14490199.

60. Frederick A. Hodes, *Rising on the River: St. Louis 1822–1850, Explosive Growth from Town to City* (Tooele, UT: Patrice Press, 2009), 468; and Frederick A. Hodes, *A Divided City: A History of St. Louis 1851–1876* (St. Louis, MO: Bluebird Publishing, 2015), 488.

61. "Tax Rate, State," *Encyclopedia of the History of Missouri: A Compendium of History and Biography for Ready Reference*, ed. William Hyde and Howard Louis Conard (New York, and Louisville, KY: Southern History Company, 1901), 158.

62. CPI Inflation Calculator, https://www.officialdata.org/us/inflation/1869?endYear=2020&amount=75000.

63. Emphasis in the original; Stanton, Anthony, and Gage, *History of Woman Suffrage*, 3:600–601.

64. Jones, "Dollars and Selves," 275.

65. Angela Ray, "The Rhetorical Ritual of Citizenship: Women's Voting as Public Performance, 1868–1875," *Quarterly Journal of Speech* 93, no. 1 (February 2017): 10–11.

66. Jones, "Dollars and Selves," 301–2.

67. Tutt, "'No Taxation without Representation,'" 1478.

68. "Anti-Tax League," *St. Louis Post-Dispatch*, May 1, 1897, 3.

69. "The Anti-Tax League," *Boston Globe*, December 15, 1879, 1.

70. "The Anti-Tax Convention: What Good Has It Done?" *Pittsburgh Daily Post*, March 22, 1860, 2.

71. "They Say They Won't," *Kansas City Times*, December 21, 1873, 3.

72. "Morning Telegrams Condensed," *St. Louis Post-Dispatch*, February 14, 1878, 2.

73. *Andrew County Republican*, March 6, 1874, 4.

74. "Taxation without Representation," *New York Herald*, October 15, 1873, 6.

75. Monnig, "Anything but Minor," 53.

76. Monnig, "Anything but Minor," 54.

77. Monnig, "Anything but Minor," 52.

78. *New Northwest*, September 18, 1878, 2.

79. *Cincinnati Daily Star*, September 1, 1879, 4.

80. *New Northwest*, September 18, 1878, 2.

81. *Richmond Democrat*, September 11, 1879, 1.

82. Tutt, "'No Taxation without Representation,'" 1489–90.

83. Lisa Tetrault, *The Myth of Seneca Falls: Memory and the Women's Suffrage Movement, 1848–1898* (Chapel Hill: University of North Carolina Press, 2014), 220n67.

84. Tutt, "'No Taxation without Representation,'" 1480.

85. Tutt, "'No Taxation without Representation,'" 1483n53.

86. Sharon Romeo, "Vagrancy and Women's Rights in Reconstruction-Era St. Louis," *Sporting Woman* (Fall 2004): 24.

87. Romeo, "Vagrancy and Women's Rights," 24.

88. *St. Louis Daily Globe*, January 10, 1874, 4.

89. Romeo, "Vagrancy and Women's Rights," 29.

90. Romeo, "Vagrancy and Women's Rights," 29.

91. Harper Barnes, "The Madame Years," *St. Louis Magazine*, June 23, 2009, https://www.stlmag.com/The-Madame-Years.

92. Everett Wilson Pattison, "Houses of Ill Fame," *The Revised Ordinance of the City of St. Louis . . .* (St. Louis, MO: The City, 1871), 439.

93. James Wunsch, "The Social Evil Ordinance," *American Heritage* 33, no. 2 (February/March 1982), 1–2, https://www.americanheritage.com/social-evil-ordinance.

94. Wunsch, "Social Evil Ordinance," 1–2.

95. Lucy Stone, "The Shame of St. Louis," *Woman's Journal* 4, no. 30 (July 26, 1873), seq. 246, https://iiif.lib.harvard.edu/manifests/view/drs:48856485$246i.

96. Wunsch, "Social Evil Ordinance," 2.

97. Wunsch, "Social Evil Ordinance," 2.

98. Wunsch, "Social Evil Ordinance," 2.

99. Hodes, *Divided City*, 558.

100. Hodes, *Divided City*, 558.

101. Wunsch, "Social Evil Ordinance," 3.

102. Stone, "Shame of St. Louis," 246.

103. Text in brackets added by the author for clarification; Stone, "Shame of St. Louis," 246.

104. Hodes, *Divided City*, 559.

105. "Association to Promote the Well-Being of Women," *Daily Kansas Tribune*, October 16, 1873, 1.

106. "The Fallen Ones," *Daily Missouri Democrat*, March 8, 1874, 4.

107. "The Fallen Ones."

108. Wunsch, "Social Evil Ordinance," 4.

109. Quoted in Wunsch, "Social Evil Ordinance," 3.

110. Wunsch, "Social Evil Ordinance," 3–4.

111. Wunsch, "Social Evil Ordinance," 4.

112. Wunsch, "Social Evil Ordinance," 4.

113. H. D. Pittman, "Wit and Wisdom of Pretty Polly," *Harpers Round Table* 9, January 24, 1888, 220, and February 28, 1888, 311.

114. "Current Topics," *Highland Weekly News*, January 3, 1875, 1.

115. "Jefferson City," *Sedalia Daily Democrat*, May 22, 1875, 1.

116. "Women's Wrongs," *Daily Missouri Republican*, May 24, 1875, 2.

117. "Jefferson City."

118. Stanton, Anthony, and Gage, *History of Woman Suffrage*, 3:27.

119. "National Woman Suffrage Association," *National Citizen and Ballot Box*, June 1879, 1.

120. Walter, "Woman Suffrage in Missouri, 1866–1880," 148.

121. Margot McMillen, *The Golden Lane: How Missouri Women Gained the Vote and Changed History* (Charleston, SC: History Press, 2011), 33.

122. *New Northwest*, September 26, 1878, 2.

123. Ida Husted Harper, *The Life and Work of Susan B. Anthony: Including Public Addresses, Her Own Letters and Many from Her Contemporaries during Fifty Years* (Indianapolis, IN, and Kansas City, MO: Bowen-Merrill, 1899).

124. "The Prohibitionists," *Daily Missouri Republican*, October 20, 1876, 5.

125. "Neither Wine nor Women," *St. Louis Globe-Democrat*, June 7, 1878, 8, and "The Prohibition Ticket," *St. Louis Post-Dispatch*, April 2, 1881, 1.

126. Monnig, "Anything but Minor," 61.

127. "Francis Minor," *Woman's Tribune*, March 5, 1892, 68, in Nineteenth Century Collections Online, http://tinyurl.galegroup.com/tinyurl/9ZDsS7.

128. "About Town," *St. Louis Post-Dispatch*, February 22, 1881, 4.

129. *Literary World* 13, no. 3 (February 11, 1882): 39.

130. Harvard University, Class of 1837, *Memorials of the Class of 1837 of Harvard University* (Boston: Geo. H. Ellis, 1887), 104; "Bowman, Dr. A. G.," *St. Louis Globe Democrat*, December 1, 1880, last modified April 9, 2020, https://stlgs.org/research-2/publications/newspapers/news-items-from-the-st-louis-globe-democrat-1880; *Literary World* 13, no. 3 (February 11, 1882), 39.

131. Rattler, "St. Louis," *Music Trade*, March 11, 1882; "Bowman, Dr. A. G."

132. Lillie Devereux Blake Papers, Missouri Historical Society Library, St. Louis, Missouri.

133. "Union Greenbackers," *St. Louis Post-Dispatch*, March 4, 1880, 4.

134. Ernest Joseph Phillipp, "The Presidential Election of 1880" (PhD diss., University of Wisconsin–Madison, 1917), 50.

135. Ruth Augusta Gallaher, *Legal and Political Status of Women in Iowa: An Historical Account of the Rights of Women in Iowa from 1838 to 1918* (Iowa City: State Historical Society of Iowa, 1918), 268.

136. "The Greenbackers," *Chicago Tribune*, March 6, 1880, 2.

137. "St. Louis," *Cincinnati Enquirer*, November 3, 1880, 1.

138. "Bad Luck of the Dow Ticket," *St. Louis Post-Dispatch*, November 4, 1880, 4.

139. "Bad Luck," 4.

140. Stanton, Anthony, and Gage, *History of Woman Suffrage*, 3: 607.

141. "About Town," *St. Louis Post-Dispatch*, February 2, 1882, 2.

142. "City News," *St. Louis Post-Dispatch*, February 4, 1882, 5.

143. "Ladies' Logic: Prohibition Discussed by the Fair Sex," *St. Louis Post-Dispatch*, September 21, 1882, 8.

144. "Ladies' Logic," 8.

145. *St. Louis Post-Dispatch*, March 12, 1880, 4.

Chapter 14

1. J. David Hacker, "Decennial Life Tables for the White Population of the United States, 1790–1900," *Historical Methods* 43, no. 2 (2010): 45–79. https://ncbi.nlm.nih .gov/pmc/articles/PMC2885717.

2. Unless otherwise noted, information for this section comes from Virginia's own retelling as written in "Mrs. Minor's Mission: Interesting Chat Concerning the Woman Suffrage Canvass in Nebraska," *St. Louis Post-Dispatch*, October 24, 1882, 8.

3. Stevens, Betty. *A Dangerous Class: A History of Suffrage in Nebraska and the League of Women Voters of Nebraska* (League of Women Voters of Nebraska Education Fund, 1995), 2.

4. Stevens, *Dangerous Class*, 2–3.

5. Ann L Wiegman Wilhite, "Sixty-Five Years Till Victory: A History of Woman Suffrage in Nebraska," *Nebraska History* 49 (1968): 150, https://history.nebraska.gov /sites/history.nebraska.gov/files/doc/publications/NH1968Sixty-Five.pdf.

6. "Map: States Grant Women the Right to Vote," Centuries of Citizenship: A Constitutional Timeline, National Constitution Center, accessed May 2, 2019, https:// constitutioncenter.org/timeline/html/cw08_12159.html.

7. Stevens, *Dangerous Class*, 4.

8. Stevens, *Dangerous Class*, 4.

9. Stevens, *Dangerous Class*, 4–6.

10. Stevens, *Dangerous Class*, 5–6.

11. Stevens, *Dangerous Class*, 7.

12. David L. Bristow, ed., *Votes for Women: The 19th Amendment in Nebraska*, special edition of *Nebraska History Magazine*. Lincoln: History Nebraska, 2019, 38.

13. "Southern Women," *St. Louis Post-Dispatch*, September 25, 1882, 4.

14. "The Woman Suffragists," *St. Louis Post-Dispatch*, September 23, 1882, 8.

15. "National Woman Suffrage Association," *Omaha Daily Herald*, September 16, 1882, 8.

16. "Addressing Lunatics: The Women Suffrage Campaign in Nebraska," *St. Louis Post-Dispatch*, October 9, 1882, 4.

17. "The Suffering Sisters," *Omaha Daily Bee*, September 27, 1882, 9.

18. "The Last Say: Final Sessions and Reception of the National Woman Suffragists," *Omaha Daily Herald*, September 29, 1882, 8.

19. "The Suffragists," *Omaha Daily Bee*, September 29, 1882, 9.

20. "Woman Suffrage: A Letter from Mrs. Francis Minor," *Daily Missouri Democrat*, January 17, 1874, 4.

21. "The Last Say."

22. "Woman Suffragists."

23. "Women's Suffrage Meetings," *Omaha Daily Herald*, October 11, 1882, 2, and "Campaign Work," *Nebraska State Journal*, October 7, 1882, 3.
24. "Suffrage: Seeking the Ballot," *Nebraska State Journal*, October 1, 1882, 3.
25. "Some Tall Lying," *Omaha Daily Bee*, November 25, 1882, 2.
26. "Mrs. Virginia Minor," *St. Louis Post-Dispatch*, October 6, 1882, 2.
27. "Mrs. Minor's Mission," 8.
28. "Mrs. Minor's Mission," 8.
29. "Addressing Lunatics."
30. Unless otherwise noted, quotes and information for this section all come from "Mrs. Minor's Mission."
31. Laura McKee Hickman, "Thou Shalt Not Vote: Anti-Suffrage in Nebraska, 1914–1920," *Nebraska History* 80 (1999): 55–56, https://history.nebraska.gov/sites/history.nebraska.gov/files/doc/publications/NH1999Anti-Suffrage.pdf.
32. Hickman, "Thou Shalt Not Vote," 55–57.
33. Unless otherwise noted, details and quotes for this section come from "Addressing Lunatics," 4.
34. Katherine Pouba and Ashley Tianen, "Lunacy in the 19th Century: Women's Admission to Asylums in United States of America," *Oshkosh Scholar* I (April 2006): 95, 102; J. R. Thorpe, "Women Who Defied Gender Roles Were Once Imprisoned in Asylums," *Bustle*, May 10, 2017, https://www.bustle.com/p/women-who-defied-gender-roles-were-once-imprisoned-in-asylums-55320; and Hendrik Hartog, "Mrs. Packard on Dependency," *Yale Journal of Law & the Humanities* 1 (1989): 81n7, https://openyls.law.yale.edu/handle/20.500.13051/7240.
35. Madaline Reeder Walter, "Insanity, Rhetoric and Women: Nineteenth Century Women's Asylum Narratives" (PhD diss., University of Kansas, 2011), 7, https://mospace.umsystem.edu/xmlui.
36. Naomi Chan, "Faithless Wives and Lazy Husbands: Gender Norms in Nineteenth Century Divorce Law," *University of Illinois Law Review* 651 (2002), 8; and Hartog, "Mrs. Packard on Dependency," 85–86, 88.
37. Hartog, "Mrs. Packard on Dependency," 85; Chan, "Faithless Wives and Lazy Husbands," 24–26, 39.
38. Chan, "Faithless Wives and Lazy Husbands," 21.
39. Elizabeth Cady Stanton, *Eighty Years and More: Reminiscences 1815–1897* (New York: European Publishing, 1898), in Nineteenth Century Collections Online, http://tinyurl.galegroup.com/tinyurl/9ZFLz7.
40. *St. Louis Post-Dispatch*, October 25, 1882, 7.
41. "Some Tall Lying," 2.
42. "Some Tall Lying," 2.
43. Hickman, "Thou Shalt Not Vote," 55.
44. "Woman Suffragists."
45. Virginia Minor Probate File, No. 20,726, 18. Missouri State Archives, copy in author's possession.
46. "Woman's Suffrage Advocates," *St. Louis Globe-Democrat*, January 31, 1884, 12.
47. "The B.T. List," *St. Louis Post-Dispatch*, March 10, 1884, 2.

48. Virginia Minor Probate File, 18.

49. Virginia Minor Probate File, 36–37.

50. National Register of Historic Places, Aubert Place/Fountain Park Historic District, St. Louis, St. Louis (Independent City), Missouri, National Register #82004730, 12–14, 24.

51. National Register of Historic Places, Aubert Place/Fountain Park Historic District, 12.

52. National Register of Historic Places, Aubert Place/Fountain Park Historic District, 13.

53. Virginia Minor Probate File, 36–37.

54. Virginia Minor Probate File, 18–19.

55. "Virginia Minor to Her Nephew John Douglas Woodward," letter, Valentine Museum, Richmond, Virginia.

56. "About Women," *Morning Oregonian*, January 25, 1885, 3.

57. "The Women Suffragists," *Memphis Daily Appeal*, February 19, 1886, 1.

58. Virginia Minor, "Address to the House Judiciary Committee," February 20, 1886, in Elizabeth Cady Stanton, Susan B. Anthony, and Matilda Joslyn Gage, *History of Woman Suffrage*, vol. 4 (Rochester, NY: Charles Mann, 1887), 78.

59. Stanton, Anthony, and Gage, *History of Woman Suffrage*, 4:78–79.

60. "Utah and the 19th Amendment," National Park Service, last updated November 23, 2019, https://www.nps.gov/articles/utah-women-s-history.htm.

61. Alan Barnett, "Remembering the Edmunds-Tucker Act," Utah Division of Archives and Records Service, accessed March 14, 2019, https://archivesnews.utah.gov/2019/03/14/remembering-the-edmunds-tucker-act.

62. Susan Ware, "Sister-Wives and Suffragists: Mormonism and the Women's Suffrage Movement," Women's Vote Centennial, accessed August 1, 2020, https://cybercemetery.unt.edu/archive/womensvote100/20201214204149/https://www.womensvote100.org.

63. Stanton, Anthony, and Gage, *History of Woman Suffrage*, 4:169.

64. Joan Iversen, "The Mormon-Suffrage Relationship: Personal and Political Quandaries," *Frontiers: A Journal of Women Studies* 11, nos. 2–3 (1990): 9, https://www.jstor.org/stable/3346814.

65. Iversen, "Mormon-Suffrage Relationship," 8.

66. Elizabeth Cady Stanton, Susan B. Anthony, and Matilda Joslyn Gage, *History of Woman Suffrage*, vol. 3 (Rochester, NY: Charles Mann, 1887), 128–29.

67. Stanton, Anthony, and Gage, *History of Woman Suffrage*, 3:24.

68. "Belva A. Lockwood and 'Mormon' Mothers," *Woman's Exponent*, March 1, 1886, 6.

69. Iversen, "Mormon-Suffrage Relationship," 9.

70. Patrick Q. Mason, "Opposition to Polygamy in the Postbellum South," *Journal of Southern History* 76, no. 3 (August 2010): 543, https://www.jstor.org/stable/25700140.

71. Mason, "Opposition to Polygamy," 547.

72. Mason, "Opposition to Polygamy," 547–49.

73. Mason, "Opposition to Polygamy," 543.

74. Mason, "Opposition to Polygamy," 545, 549.

75. Mason, "Opposition to Polygamy," 543–44.

76. Sarah Barringer Gordon, "The Liberty of Self-Degradation: Polygamy, Woman Suffrage, and Consent in Nineteenth-Century America," *Journal of American History* 83, no. 3 (December 1996): 815, https://www.jstor.org/stable/2945641.

77. Stanton, Anthony, and Gage, *History of Woman Suffrage*, 3:24.

78. "The National Woman Suffrage Association and Fringe Marriage Ideology Suffragists," *Ezra's Archives* 9, no. 1 (Spring 2019): 68, https://ecommons.cornell.edu/handle/1813/69946.

79. *St. Louis Post-Dispatch*, January 21, 1886, 4.

80. "Obeyed Their Husbands," *Leavenworth Times*, January 23, 1886, 2.

81. "The Edmund's Bill," *Leavenworth Times*, April 23, 1886, 2.

82. "Edmund's Bill."

83. "Utah and the 19th Amendment."

84. Stanton, Anthony, and Gage, *History of Woman Suffrage*, 4:156.

85. Reva B. Siegel, "She the People: The Nineteenth Amendment, Sex Equality, Federalism, and the Family," *Harvard Law Review* 115, no. 4 (February 2002): 975n77, https://law.yale.edu/sites/default/files/documents/pdf/Faculty/Siegel_SheThePeople.pdf.

86. "A Preacher of Female Suffrage," *St. Louis Post-Dispatch*, February 19, 1888, 19.

87. International Council of Women, and National Woman Suffrage Association (US), *Report of the International Council of Women: Assembled by the National Woman Suffrage Association, Washington, D.C., U.S. of America, March 25 to April 1, 1888* ([Washington, DC?]: National Woman Suffrage Association, 1888), 17.

88. International Council of Women, *Report of the International Council of Women*, 255–56.

89. "Women of Note," *Evening Star Washington*, March 31, 1888, 3.

90. "An Amazonian March Proposed," *Chicago Tribune*, May 15, 1888, 4.

91. *St. Louis Post-Dispatch*, May 20, 1888, 4.

92. "Amazonian March Proposed," 4.

93. "Amazonian March Proposed," 4.

94. *Petaluma Courier*, July 4, 1888, 2.

95. "Mrs. Merriwether and the Democracy," *Belle Plaine News*, July 14, 4.

96. "Mrs. Merriwether and the Democracy," 4.

97. "Latest Edition, with Wild Cheers," *St. Louis Post-Dispatch*, June 6, 1888, 2.

98. Julia Hull Winner and Belva A. Lockwood, "Belva A. Lockwood—That Extraordinary Woman," *New York History* 39, no. 4 (1958): 321, https://www.jstor.org/stable/23154072.

99. "Susan B. Anthony Talks," *St. Louis Post-Dispatch*, November 29, 1888, 5.

100. Virginia Minor, "Statement before the U.S. Senate Committee on Woman Suffrage—Jan. 24, 1889."

101. *St. Louis Post-Dispatch*, April 6, 1889, 1.

102. Helen R. Pinkney, "Minor, Virginia Louisa," in *Notable American Women, 1607–1950: A Biographical Dictionary*, ed. Janet Wilson James, Paul S. Boyer, and Edward T. James (Cambridge, MA: Belknap Press of Harvard University Press, 1971), 550–51.

103. "Woman Suffrage Entertainment," *St. Louis Globe-Democrat*, February 1, 1890, 7.

104. "Woman Suffrage Entertainment."

105. "No Filibustering Here," *Evening Star*, February 20, 1890, 2.

106. "No Filibustering Here."

107. "Women in Council," *Greenwood County Republican*, February 24, 1892, 3.

CHAPTER 15

1. Minor Meriwether, *Lineage of the Meriwethers and the Minors from Colonial Times* (St. Louis: Nixon-Jones Printing Co., 1895), 133.

2. Francis Minor Necrology File, Missouri Historical Society Library, St. Louis, Missouri, 59.

3. Francis Minor, burial certificate, February 19, 1892, file no. 1487, Bellefontaine Cemetery, copy in author's possession.

4. "Death of Francis N. Minor," *St. Louis Post-Dispatch*, February 22, 1892.

5. "Francis Minor," *Woman's Tribune*, March 5, 1892, 68. Nineteenth Century Collections Online, accessed March 23, 2019, http://tinyurl.galegroup.com/tinyurl/9ZDsS7.

6. Francis Minor Probate File, no. 18,823, 32, Missouri State Archives, copy in author's possession.

7. "Francis Minor: Sketch of a Lawyer and Scholar St. Louis Has Lost," *St. Louis Republic*, February 21, 1892, 5.

8. Mourning Society of St. Louis, "Consolations of Memory at Bellefontaine Cemetery," Bellefontaine Cemetery, St. Louis, MO, October 5, 2019.

9. Meriwether, *Lineage of the Meriwethers and the Minors*, 133.

10. Mourning Society, "Consolations."

11. Susan G. Rehkopf, Archivist and Registrar, Diocese of Missouri, email, September 2, 2019; email from Paul Anderson, volunteer archivist Christ Church.

12. Francis Minor Necrology File, 59.

13. Francis Minor Probate File, 32.

14. Francis Minor Probate File, 32.

15. Francis Minor Probate File, 32.

16. Francis Minor Probate File, 4.

17. Anna D. Gordon, *The Selected Papers of Elizabeth Cady Stanton and Susan B. Anthony, Volume V* (New Brunswick, NJ: Rutgers University Press, 2000), 275n1.

18. Emphasis in the original; "In Memoriam," *Woman's Journal*, March 5, 1892, 79, http://tinyurl.galegroup.com/tinyurl/8tYtdX.

19. Francis Minor, "The Right of Women to Vote at Congressional Elections," *Women's Tribune*, January 28, 1888, 1.

20. "Francis Minor," *Women's Tribune*, March 5, 1892, 68, in Nineteenth Century Collections Online, http://tinyurl.galegroup.com/tinyurl/9ZDsS7.

21. Elizabeth Cady Stanton, Susan B. Anthony, and Matilda Joslyn Gage, *History of Woman Suffrage*, vol. 4 (Rochester, NY: Charles Mann, 1887), 7–8.

22. Stanton, Anthony, and Gage, *History of Woman Suffrage*, 4:7–8.

23. Clara Berwick Colby, "Report of Federal Suffrage Committee," *Woman's Tribune*, February 11, 1893, 1.

24. *Chicago Tribune*, May 9, 1892, 5.

25. Janet Wilson James, Edward T. James, and Paul S. Boyer, *Notable American Women, 1607–1950: A Biographical Dictionary* (Cambridge, MA: Belknap Press of Harvard University Press, 1971), 258, 356.

26. *Chicago Tribune*, May 9, 1892, 5.

27. Harriet Taylor Upton, ed., *Proceedings of the Twenty-Fifth Annual Convention of the National American Woman Suffrage Association Held in Washington D.C. January 16, 17, 18, 19, 1893* (Washington, DC: Stormont & Jackson Printers, 1893), 26–27.

28. Upton, *Proceedings of the Twenty-Fifth Annual Convention*, 28.

29. Upton, *Proceedings of the Twenty-Fifth Annual Convention*, 26–27.

30. Meriwether, *Lineage of the Meriwethers and the Minors*, 134.

31. Angela G. Ray and Cindy Koenig Richards, "Inventing Citizens Imagining Gender Justice: The Suffrage Rhetoric of Virginia and Francis Minor," *Quarterly Journal of Speech* 93, no. 4 (November 2007): 394–95.

32. Mourning Society, "Consolations."

33. Loretta Mae Walter, "Woman Suffrage in Missouri, 1866–1880" (master's thesis, Washington University, St. Louis, Missouri, August 1963), 117, Washington University Special Collections.

34. Mona Cook Morris, "The History of Woman Suffrage in Missouri, 1867–1901," *Missouri Historical Review* 25, no. 1 (October 1930): 76.

35. "In the Probate Court," *St. Louis Republic*, March 1, 1892, 8.

36. Francis Minor Probate File, 3, 30.

37. Francis Minor Probate File, 12.

38. Francis Minor Probate File, 9.

39. Donna M. Monnig, "Anything but Minor: The Suffrage, Equality, and Women's Rights Activism of Virginia L. Minor, 1867–1894" (master's thesis, University of Central Missouri, August 2018), 84.

40. Mourning Society, "Consolations."

41. Mourning Society, "Consolations."

42. "Gossip," *St. Louis Post-Dispatch*, March 19, 1893, 26.

43. "Departures," *St. Louis Post-Dispatch*, April 9, 1893, 26.

44. "Returns," *St. Louis Post-Dispatch*, April 6, 1893, 3.

45. "Departures," 26.

46. "Returns," *St. Louis Post-Dispatch*, July 23, 1893. 2.

47. "Society," *St. Louis Globe Democrat*, October 15, 1893, 30.

48. Mrs. Chas P. Johnson, *Notable Women of St. Louis* (Published by the author, 1914), 121, https://archive.org/stream/notablewomenofst00john/notablewomenofst00john_djvu.txt.

49. Johnson, *Notable Women*, 126–27.

50. "Woman's Champion."

51. "Society," *St. Louis Globe Democrat*, July 1, 1894, 28.

52. Walter, "Woman Suffrage in Missouri, 1866–1880," 34.

53. Walter, "Woman Suffrage in Missouri, 1866–1880," 34.

54. Virginia Minor Necrology File, Missouri Historical Society Library, St. Louis, Missouri.

55. "Virginia L. Minor Dead," *St. Louis Post-Dispatch*, August 15, 1894, 7.

56. Virginia L. Minor, burial certificate, August 14, 1894, file no. 5610, City of St. Louis Health Department, Bellefontaine Cemetery & Arboretum, copy in author's possession.

57. "Virginia L. Minor Buried," *St. Louis Republic*, August 16, 1894, 7.

58. Stanton, Anthony, and Gage, *History of Woman Suffrage*, 4: 791.

59. Virginia Minor Necrology File.

60. "Virginia L. Minor Dead."

61. "Virginia L. Minor Dead."

62. "Woman's Suffrage: Meeting of the Association Saturday," *Daily Missouri Democrat*, January 18, 1869, 4.

63. Find a Grave, database and images (https://www.findagrave.com/memorial /6164862/reece-grier-happersett, accessed April 8, 2022), memorial page for Reece Grier Happersett (October 16, 1837–March 30, 1876), Find a Grave Memorial ID 6164862, citing Bellefontaine Cemetery, Saint Louis, St. Louis City, Missouri, USA; maintained by Find a Grave.

64. Dan Fuller, Bellefontaine Cemetery, email message to author, January 3, 2021.

65. "Must Not Marry: Conditions under Which Mrs. Minor's Nieces Become Heirs," *St. Louis Post-Dispatch*, August 17, 1894, 5.

66. Virginia Minor Necrology File.

67. Virginia Minor Probate File, 25.

68. Virginia Minor Probate File, 36–37.

69. Virginia Minor Probate File, 40–41.

70. Virginia Minor Probate File, 19.

71. "Equal Suffrage Association," *St. Louis Globe-Democrat*, May 3, 1895, 12.

72. "Tributes to Mrs. Minor," *St. Louis Post-Dispatch*, May 4, 1895.

EPILOGUE

1. Avis Carlson, *The League of Women Voters of St. Louis: The First Forty Years, 1919–1959* (St. Louis, MO: League of Women Voters, 1959), 40.

2. Winnifred Mallon, "Honors 71 Workers in Suffrage Cause," *New York Times*, May 2, 1930, 11.

3. League of Women Voters of Missouri Records (S0530) F. 277 Memorial Fund, 1929–1931, State Historical Society of Missouri Archives, University of Missouri at St. Louis.

4. Mallon, "Honors 71 Workers in Suffrage Cause," 11.

5. "National Roll of Honor of Leaders in the Suffrage Movement," Announced May 1, 1930, 1929–1930, Box 1, Folder 14, S0232 League of Women Voters of Missouri, Papers, 1911–1976, State Historical Society of Missouri, Mercantile Library, St. Louis, Missouri.

6. Mallon, "Honors 71 Workers in Suffrage Cause," 11.

7. "National Roll of Honor of Leaders in the Suffrage Movement."

8. "League of Women Voters to Unveil Tablet Wednesday," *St. Louis Democrat*, January 19, 1931.

9. "Biographical Data Sheets for State Honor Roll, 1931," Box 1, Folder 15, League of Women Voters of Missouri, Papers, 1911–1976, State Historical Society of Missouri, Mercantile Library, St. Louis, Missouri.

10. "League of Women Voters to Unveil Tablet Wednesday."

11. Bob Priddy, "The Hall of Famous Missourians," *Missourinet Blog*, March 2, 2012, https://blog.missourinet.com/2012/03/06/the-hall-of-famous-missourians.

12. "Hall of Famous Missourians," Missouri House of Representatives, accessed March 28, 2020, https://house.mo.gov/famous.aspx.

13. Priddy, "Hall of Famous Missourians."

14. "Mo. House Dems: Don't Allow Installation of Limbaugh Bust in State Capitol," St. Louis Public Radio, March 7, 2012, https://news.stlpublicradio.org/government-politics-issues/2012-03-07/mo-house-dems-dont-allow-installation-of-limbaugh-bust-in-state-capitol.

15. "Mo. House Dems Propose Rules for Induction into Hall of Famous Missourians," St. Louis Public Radio, March 15, 2012, https://news.stlpublicradio.org/government-politics-issues/2012-03-15/mo-house-dems-propose-rules-for-induction-into-hall-of-famous-missourians.

16. Mark Memmott, "Student Is Outraged by Rush Limbaugh Calling Her a 'Slut' and 'Prostitute,'" St. Louis Public Radio, March 2, 2012, https://www.npr.org/sections/the-two-way/2012/03/02/147809138/student-is-outraged-by-rush-limbaugh-calling-her-a-slut-and-prostitute.

17. Eliza Relman, "Trump Just Gave Rush Limbaugh the Country's Highest Civilian Honor. Here Are Some of the Racist, Misogynist, and All-Around Awful Things He's Said," *Insider*, February 5, 2020, https://www.businessinsider.com/presidential-medal-awardee-rush-limbaughs-racist-and-sexist-comments-2020-2.

18. Tim Mak, "Mount Rush-More It's Not," *Politico*, May 14, 2012, https://www.politico.com/story/2012/05/mt-rush-more-its-not-076288.

19. Marshall Griffin, "Rally at Mo. Capitol Opposes Limbaugh Induction into Hall of Famous Missourians," St. Louis Public Radio, March 28, 2012, https://news.stlpublicradio.org/politics-issues/2012-03-28/rally-at-mo-capitol-opposes-limbaugh-induction-into-hall-of-famous-missourians.

20. Megan Rice, "Students Protest Limbaugh's Bust in Hall of Famous Missourians," KOMU, March 8, 2012, https://www.komu.com/students-protest-limbaughs-bust-in-hall-of-famous-missourians/article_1b23d96e-179c-52b6-b3e9-68371db3746e.html.

21. Wes Duplantier, "Group Drops Toilet Paper in Capitol to Protest Limbaugh Bust," *The Missourian*, March 20, 2012, https://www.columbiamissourian.com/news/group-drops-toilet-paper-in-capitol-to-protest-limbaugh-bust/article_1aed6d7f-12f1-5cce-ae39-48b09610ce30.html.

22. Marshall Griffin, "Rush Limbaugh Inducted into Hall of Famous Missourians," St. Louis Public Radio, May 14, 2012, https://news.stlpublicradio.org/politics-issues/2012-05-14/rush-limbaugh-inducted-into-hall-of-famous-missourians; Marshall Griffin, "Dred Scott Inducted to Hall of Famous Missourians," St. Louis Public Radio, May 9, 2012, https://news.stlpublicradio.org/government-politics-issues/2012-05-09/dred-scott-inducted-to-hall-of-famous-missourians.

23. Mackenzie Weinger, "Limbaugh Bust Gets 24-Hour Security," *Politico*, May 24, 2012, https://www.politico.com/story/2012/05/limbaugh-bust-gets-24-hour-security -076737.

24. Marshall Griffin, "Public Input Sought for Nominees to Hall of Famous Missourians," St. Louis Public Radio, August 21, 2013, https://news.stlpublicradio.org/politics -issues/2013-08-21/public-input-sought-for-nominees-to-hall-of-famous-missourians.

25. Gretta Russell, "Hall of Famous Missourians," Missouri Women, December 10, 2012, https://missouriwomen.org/2010/12/07/hall-of-famous-missourians.

26. Margot McMillen, *Virginia Minor: A Woman in the Hall of Famous Missourians* (Missouri Women's Network, 2015), 26.

27. "MO House Speaker Tim Jones Inducts Virginia Minor into the Hall of Famous Missourians," September 11, 2014, https://www.youtube.com/watch?v=U5KNj4FrWl4.

28. McMillen, *Virginia Minor*, 27.

29. Mary Mosley, email to the author, September 9, 2020.

30. Chris Blank, "Doctor Honored through Hall of Famous Missourians Induction," *The Missourian*, April 16, 2014, https://www.columbiamissourian.com/news/state_news /doctor-honored-through-hall-of-famous-missourians-induction/article_b456cabc -d6d5-5d03-a3f1-bc891d616633.html.

31. McMillen, *Virginia Minor*, 28.

32. McMillen, *Virginia Minor*, 28.

33. McMillen, *Virginia Minor*, 34.

34. McMillen, *Virginia Minor*, 36–37.

35. Mosley, email to the author.

36. McMillen, *Virginia Minor*, 31.

37. McMillen, *Virginia Minor*, 38.

38. Jan Scott, email to the author, August 29, 2020.

39. McMillen, *Virginia Minor*, 39.

40. McMillen, *Virginia Minor*, 39.

41. McMillen, *Virginia Minor*, 31.

42. McMillen, *Virginia Minor*, 40.

43. McMillen, *Virginia Minor*, 39.

44. McMillen, *Virginia Minor*, 32.

45. "Suffragette Pioneer Virginia Minor Inducted into Hall of Famous Missourians," KCUR 98.3, September 14, 2014, https://www.kcur.org/politics-elections-and-govern ment/2014-09-13/suffragette-pioneer-virginia-minor-inducted-into-hall-of-famous -missourians.

46. Mosley, email.

47. McMillen, *Virginia Minor*, 33.

48. "Prayer in the MO House," September 11, 2014, https://www.youtube.com /watch?v=bbUU0d-gO6c.

49. "MO House Speaker Tim Jones Inducts Virginia Minor."

50. McMillen, *Virginia Minor*, 36.

51. Nicole Evelina, "News Roundup about Virginia Minor," August 11, 2020, https:// nicoleevelina.com/2020/08/11/news-roundup-about-virginia-minor.

52. "NWHP Honorees of Past 40 Years," National Women's History Alliance, accessed May 2, 2020, https://nationalwomenshistoryalliance.org/nwhp-honorees-of-past-40-years.

53. "2020 Honorees," National Women's History Alliance, accessed February 3, 2020, https://nationalwomenshistoryalliance.org/2020-2021-honorees.

54. Robert Cooney, National Women's History Alliance, email to author, September 14, 2020.

55. National Women's History Alliance, 2021 National Women's History Honorees, "Valiant Women of the Vote: Refusing to Be Silenced," event program, the Hamilton, Washington, DC, August 21, 2021, 6.

56. "Beyond the Ballot: St. Louis and Suffrage," Missouri History Museum, accessed August 1, 2020, https://mohistory.org/exhibits/beyond-the-ballot.

57. Katie Moon, *Groundbreakers, Rule-Breakers and Rebels: 50 Unstoppable St. Louis Women* (St. Louis: Missouri Historical Society Press, 2000), 23.

58. Dan Fuller, Bellefontaine Cemetery, email message to author, January 3, 2021.

59. The author is chairing the committee.

60. Cynthia Holmes, email message to author, March 15, 2021.

61. Cynthia Holmes, email message to author, October 3, 2022.

62. "Missouri Heritage Project," Missouri Department of Elementary and Secondary Education, accessed June 4 2020, https://dese.mo.gov/missouri-heritage/finding-missouri-our-history-heritage.

63. "Women Change Their Roles," Unit 12: Changing Places, Missouri Department of Elementary and Secondary Education, accessed April 12, 2020, https://dese.mo.gov/missouri-heritage-project/finding-mo-our-history-heritage/unit-12-changing-places.

INDEX

AAUW. *See* American Association of
   University Women
abolition, 108–9, 111, 161, 280n37
ACLU. *See* American Civil Liberties Union
activism
   by Anthony, 193–94
   antislavery, 72
   in Civil War, 27, 110–11
   by Minor, F., 116–20, 131–32, 145–47,
      208, 226–27
   by Minor, V., 187, 194–96, 199–202,
      211–20
   by Minor family, 175–85
   in Minoria, 56–61
   in Missouri, 92–99
   in New Departure, 2, 134–42
   in St. Louis, 53–56
   by St. Louis Ladies Union Aid Society,
      92–99, 107
   against slavery, 110–11
   Woman Suffrage Association of
      Missouri, 2, 54
   women and, 9–10, 52, 113–20, 141
   for women's suffrage, 80
   by WSAM, 114–20
Adams, Washington, 154
AERA. *See* American Equal Rights
   Association
Alband, Christian, 189–90
Alband, Wilhelmina, 189–90
Alcock, Joseph, 13
Alexander, Augustus W., 70
Allan, Penelope, 114
Allgor, Catherine, 148–49

American Association of University Women
   (AAUW), 242, 246–47
American Civil Liberties Union (ACLU),
   181
American Dictionary of the English Language
   (Webster), 160
American Equal Rights Association
   (AERA), 108, 124–25
American Woman Suffrage Association
   (AWSA), 125–26, 187–88, 191–92,
   197, 208, 223, 229–30
ancestry, 10–17, 20, 40
Anderson, Galusha, 95
Anderson, Sarah Elizabeth, 34
Annals of Human Biology, 40
Anne (queen), 165
Anthony, Susan B.
   activism by, 193–94
   for AERA, 108
   Foster and, 124–25
   Hazard and, 114–15
   in leadership, 207–8
   Minor, V., and, 142, 167–68, 187,
      215–20, 234–35, 237–38
   on Minor, F., 232
   Minor family and, 1, 130–31
   on *Minor v. Happersett*, 185
   in Nebraska, 213–14
   reputation of, 178
   scholarship on, 28
   at Seneca Falls Convention, 110
   Stanton and, 2, 27, 55, 99, 109, 116, 124,
      127, 245, 248
   Stone and, 111

ABOUT THE AUTHOR

Nicole Evelina is a *USA Today* best-selling author and biographer who writes historical fiction, nonfiction, and women's fiction. Her writing tells the stories of strong women from history and today, with a focus on little-known figures of women's history and literature. When she's not writing, she can be found reading, fighting for women's rights, enjoying theater, dance, and music, and dreaming of living in downtown Chicago.